# Love on a Plate

## Recipes for Serving Love

by

Sandra Sage

*AuthorHouse™*
*1663 Liberty Drive, Suite 200*
*Bloomington, IN 47403*
*www.authorhouse.com*
*Phone: 1-800-839-8640*

*©2008 Sandra Sage. All rights reserved.*

*No part of this book may be reproduced, stored in a retrieval system, or transmitted by any means without the written permission of the author.*

*First published by AuthorHouse 1/30/2008*

*ISBN: 978-1-4343-4703-9 (sc)*

*Library of Congress Control Number: 2007908246*

*Printed in the United States of America*
*Bloomington, Indiana*

*This book is printed on acid-free paper.*

*Cover Artist - Carolyn Feddema*
*Editor - Anna Harris*

*For the love of memories this book is dedicated to the loves of my life: Kellie, Korrie and Kate; the family I needed to grow my heart.*

*To the children who will keep this love of food alive: Nicole, Alec, Mackenzie, Karlee and Kamille.*

*To Helen, the inspiration behind everything I create.*

*And to Grandma Stella, my Nana for teaching me the gift of giving the old-fashioned way. Her love saved me.*

*Food is more than what we set on the table. The pleasures of the table are what we share together that are as nourishing to body and mind as the food itself.*

*In a cooks mind you will find a place of poetry where the experience of taste, smells and touch compose the meal. She captures the brilliance of color, engages senses of taste, uses the opulence of presenting and composes the gift of spirit that comes out of food: a graciousness that adds layers, depth, dimension and a gratitude that family can taste.*

*Eating places you in the moment and becomes the yoke that binds us together for life. Giving to one another are the rights of passage that heal us from hurts and show continued commitment. It is time to give family its due.*

# Dream: Exalting Influence

In my dream, I was in a sacred room of purple and red with a table in the middle. The light looked brilliant from the candles sitting in the center. There were many places set at the table, and I felt stillness in the room, until a priest in a white robe quietly entered.

He came close to me and stood in silence. Then he began to walk peacefully around the table. He stopped at each place setting, looking as though he were feeling who would be seated in each place. He called me to his side and asked me to walk with him. I did. I felt the presence of every soul I had ever prepared food for come up to me from the table. I felt their joy, their gladness in sitting at this table. I now felt the spirit of who had passed and all who were to come to me in the future. I began to breathe in magic from them that seemed to lift my spirit and soul above the table, and I gazed upon the miraculous scene from above.

I was standing again next to the priest, whose presence was love of a very different kind. He took my hand in his, still looking towards the table, and spoke: "You have done your job well. Now I must tell you there is going to be a change in the setting of this table." He walked to the end of the table, picked up a place setting, and walked slowly around the table, musing. He put the place setting at another spot at the sacred table and walked over to me and stood silently for a moment. "There is going to be a change. With every change, you will know what to do. There are not always answers, but there are choices. I mean choices of love. Now go and nourish those you love."

I awoke to red and purple, which are colors of passion and spirit. It was a dream of my spiritual passion. I knew at that moment I would continue to serve by writing about food, the food of the soul. I allowed the tumble of emotions and images to flow from my subconscious mind into awareness without filtering them.

I began to write this book.

# Passing the Peach

*Her kitchen is a museum
of old spices, family recipes,
and secrets; hidden by olive
green cupboards, holding
the desserts of my childhood.*

*I flip through an unlocked metal
treasure chest containing hand written
sweets to be, and point with
sticky finger to my favorite.*

*My grandmother sits and cradles
a bowl of peeled peaches that I have
picked for her famous cobbler, crust of
biscuit dough and graham crackers.*

*She kneads with both hands
pinching thumbs to index fingers
in opposite direction of the same
uneven circle. And I know she
is passing me a slice of her
southern way.*

*She mixes cinnamon, sugar and melted
churned butter that spreads like missing
skin over sun soaked fruit. Pie flesh patiently
waiting for its homemade soul.*

*Before sealing every corner of
doughy fat, she forks
me a bite of dripping fruit
glistening in yellow stove light and
waits for the bulge of my eyes,
the blossom of my taste buds, offering
her my sugared praise.*

*I watch her pinch and dash, dusting
freckles on it's lumpy face before an
oven's gentle burn. She closes her
sleepy eyes while genuflecting
a safe journey to our empty tummies.*

*Somehow, in the perspiration of
late afternoon and steaming peaches,
I can feel the Texas sun burning my
grandma's family recipes into the palm
of my floured hand.*

*~ Lindsey Holmes*

# Table of Contents

Acknowledgments ..................................................................................... XII

Introduction ............................................................................................. XIII

Chapter 1
   "Family" ................................................................................................ 1

Chapter 2
   Joyful Celebrations ............................................................................. 26

Chapter 3
   Tradition ............................................................................................. 48

Chapter 4
   Among FriendsThere is Spirited Kinship ........................................... 62

Chapter 5
   Five Roses Catering ............................................................................ 85

Chapter 6
   Simply Sandarella's ........................................................................... 118

Chapter 7
   Covered In Grace .............................................................................. 125

Chapter 8
   Soup Comforts ................................................................................. 151

Chapter 9
   Sensational Starters .......................................................................... 169

Chapter 10
   Delightful Salads .............................................................................. 192

Chapter 11
   Casseroles from Scratch ................................................................... 211

Chapter 12
   Farmer's Harvest .............................................................................. 222

Chapter 13
   Best Sunday Family Dinners ............................................................ 238

Chapter 14
   Soufflé Fluff ...................................................................................... 255

Chapter 15
   Beloved Veggie Meals ...................................................................... 262

CHAPTER 16
　　Brunch Celebrations ..................................................................................... 289
CHAPTER 17
　　Breads We Love ............................................................................................. 322
CHAPTER 18
　　Ideal Fish Recipes .......................................................................................... 332
CHAPTER 19
　　Italian Dinning .............................................................................................. 339
CHAPTER 20
　　Sassy Sauces and Zesty Dressings ................................................................ 360
CHAPTER 21
　　Favorite Chicken Recipes .............................................................................. 378
CHAPTER 22
　　South of the Border Cha-Cha-Cha ............................................................... 388
CHAPTER 23
　　Caterer's Pride Gets Its Due ......................................................................... 415
CHAPTER 24
　　Simply Sandarella's Formulas ...................................................................... 449
CHAPTER 25
　　Take a Gander at Our Thanksgiving Feast .................................................. 474
CHAPTER 26
　　Christmas Spice ............................................................................................ 491
CHAPTER 27
　　Simply Handmade Giving ............................................................................. 516
CHAPTER 28
　　Sweet Retreat ................................................................................................ 543
CHAPTER 29
　　Treasure Trove of Menus .............................................................................. 569

# Acknowledgments

I am deeply appreciative for the inspiration of my best friend Diana Stein who has always been my greatest cheerleader in my life. She has believed in the meaning of this book from the start and has been a motivation that has moved me to write. Diana believed the message.

There are no words to thank Helen Gropen for what she taught me so long ago. She too believed in me and set standards for me to rise to and I believe I have. She is my teacher, my friend and my mom.

I asked for help and Anna Harris showed up to edit this book. Her belief and steadfast desire behind the meaning of this book is unwavering in its development. I could not have done it without you Anna.

A special thanks to Yvette Streeter who navigated and steered the book to completion and into a manuscript. In the end she is what I needed and she showed up with enthusiasm and grit! What a celebration day; complete with champagne and food…I will never forget!

This book would not be what it is without the spiritual vision of Carolyn Feddema my artist. Together and alone she heard what my heart sang and interpreted the prophecy into visions of magical art. Her work alone tells a story; thank you Carolyn for your gift. Your talent is eloquent.

And to my children: you are my life in the book. Thank you for believing in me.

Thank you to everyone who has waited and listened to me share about this book and remained my cheerleaders.

# Introduction

Some time ago I began thinking about writing a cookbook. The thinking became a knowing, I call it, just one of those things I know I will do. The knowing phase never leaves me; sometimes… it haunts me.

The more I planned this book; the more it became a project between God and myself. These are always my favorite projects. I know that when God is involved it's His idea so He will be doing the creating through me. The only problem has been the time.

Finding or taking the time to stop and listen has been a struggle. Finally, time has turned into some years and friends and family are still asking when the book is going to be finished.

For the past twelve days, I have watched the sun set at my favorite home away from home, Laguna Beach, in Southern California. I have allowed time to be my friend. In exchange I have opened my heart and listened. The divine inspiration that has come through me is written in the pages of this book.

The love of people and food and the passion for shared experience has driven me to write this book. This is not an ordinary cookbook. It is rather an experience within each recipe. The deepest, most meaningful times in my life have all been focused around food and I have shared them with you… I have shared pieces of my heart.

I have been burdened for quite some time about the business of our families and the lack of togetherness shared within them. I have been wife, mother and businesswoman. I have gone from being a stay-at-home mother to a struggling single parent. I am not alone in the quest for balancing our womanhood and our families. How do we shift gears? How do we get back to the desire to nourish our children, as we desired when they were at our breast? How do we produce children that feel full emotionally instead of empty? How can we find the time or take time to feed our family's spirit?

I have come to realize that it was the little things that were done for me as a child that made me feel special. It is that *SPECIAL* feeling that I clung to in the deepest times of despair in my life. It is that special experience that I grabbed a hold of as a little girl. I tucked it deep inside my heart until the day I had my first child. Little by little, year after year, I have reached down and scooped up more magic. The magic has turned into a lifetime of memories. One of the blessings has been sharing this magic with adults. I watch what this does for them and I realize we are all the same; we are all in grown up bodies with childlike hearts, hearts that now appreciate and cling to the richness of togetherness.

When I started my catering business, I gifted it with all the passion I had inside of me. I built a reputation of producing food with impeccable taste. The presentation had an extravaganza of elegant style. When I added love, it began to grow. When I gave more than what I was asked of, it came back to me. At the end of a wedding a bride handed me a note as she left for her honeymoon. The words read, "Thank you for making my dream come true. Love, Lynda"… I got it.

During the years of my restaurant, Simply Sandarella's, I served my customers with the same kind of love. Each day the elementary school teachers would come in for a quick bowl of soup, and we called them our "Soup dragons." One cold and rainy day as I cleaned up, I found an envelope left on the table. After the doors were closed and I sat down and sipped a cup of tea, I opened the envelope. One of the teachers was expressing her gratitude for my restaurant and the food I served. At the end of the note she wrote, "Your food feels like it is served with *love*." It was one of those moments you had to be alone. If you were not, you would feel like you were. It was one of those spontaneous moments that suddenly interrupted and, in my case, grabbed me. In the stillness of the room, it was memorable. It was… serendipity. As I wiped away my tears, I didn't realize then that it was the magic I had used.

The serendipity would come back again until I realized what to do with it. Six years later on the Island of Molokai in Hawaii I found the answer. I prepared a beautiful dinner for a Hawaiian family I met on the island.

The next day before leaving the island I drove to a remote spot and climbed to the top of a cliff overlooking the ocean. In my journal I wrote these words, "I found myself on an island in my element preparing food for my Hawaiian guests, serving; "*Love on a Plate*." As the trade winds blew against my face, I closed my eyes and slowly took in the gift I had just received. God once again was blessing me. He had just handed me the title of my cookbook. I said thank you.

I have shared stories in a wide range of experiences in these chapters of my life. They are the memories and perspectives dear to my heart. I invite you to laugh and cry with me. I hope this book will bring encouragement and bless you. I hope most of all that you will feel loved and share your love with your family.

*Cooking began in my imagination,*
 *now in my memory.*
*Cooking is about love.*
*It is not labor, it's desire.*
*It's not separate…it is …me.*
*Cooking is about*
*dreaming it up,*
*preparing and making mistakes*
*and starting over.*
*It's about intrinsic beauty…*
*the spirit, the backbone,*
*the blood that runs in our family.*
*Cooking is about serving*
*and receiving.*
*It is about giving love*
*and getting it back.*
*Cooking is life.*

Sandarella

*Chapter 1*

*"Family"*

*"Everything now is so fast-paced, and people
don't sit down together anymore for dinner.
People need to remember what is important.
It's families sharing what they have: their work,
their food, their good times and bad, no matter how hard things get."*
*- Vern Berry*

# FAMILY

I ask every senior I meet the question, "What memory do you have of your family's mealtime?" Most of them answer without hesitation, "Oh, Mother rang that bell outside our door on the farm and all us kids came running into the house for one of Mother's homemade meals. We took off our hats, washed our hands, and all sat down together. It was just what we did back then. That's where we talked and shared and learned about one another. Working on your land and running a farm was hard work for everyone. By the end of the day, you were tired and dragged yourself in knowing you still had chores to finish after supper. But we stopped and sat down together as a family."

Some elders answer the question by pausing and going deep inside and back in time. I can see them reliving a part of their childhood just by studying their eyes. At this point, they become very sentimental and focused on a certain experience pertaining to the family table. One senior remembers the best apricot jam he has ever tasted on the breakfast table every morning. He recalls how it was his job to pick the fallen fruit from the ground and keep it separate from the fruit on the tree. "Mother would then put up dozens of jars of that golden fruit and sell it to the grocer man at the country store. I knew how many hours it took her, and she counted on this money to help buy our shoes, but always kept a jar for our breakfast table. It made me feel so good." Each story tells of a special dish or tradition that took place at their family table and made them feel special.

Every old friend who has shared with me remembers how their grandparents shared their lives (and some of the greatest stories ever told) around the Sunday dinner table. "On that Sunday table sat fried chicken, squirrel, and possum. From mustard greens to turnips to anything that grew in the garden, Mother found a way to feed us," Alice recalls. "Most of all, there was a lot of love sitting on the table and all around it."

This family connection of long ago was a part of the molding and shaping of children. It was a time when values were insisted upon. It was a time when the focus was tending to the family. In our parents' and grandparents' time, money was thought of more for survival than pleasure. Today we have more money than our parents had and less time for pleasure. If you ask an old person what they value most of their childhood, nearly every time you will get the same answer. They remember their favorite toy or Christmas, but they value the time spent together as a family most of all.

I have paid attention to people talking about food and recipes. Frequently, when they are sharing the ingredients, they move their attention to the memory connected to the serving of the special dish. It's like glancing at an old photograph or smelling a familiar perfume—it evokes feelings that are attached to the heart. They are recollections of love shared around the table, some of the richest times of your life. That is why you keep making the same favorite recipes your family loves year after year. It is one of the ways we love our families.

*"Try to put in the hearts of your children a love for home. Make them long to be with their families. So much sin could be avoided if our people really loved their homes".*
*- Mother Teresa*

*"There is no Limit, because God is love
And love is God. And so you are really
In love with God, and God's love is infinite.
That's why it's not how much you do, but
How much love you put into the action."*
- Mother Teresa

# LOVE IS IN THE DETAILS

There are some people who rest deep inside of me. My grandmother Stella is one of these people. To me, she was Nana.

Nana was born in 1892. Raised with her brother and sisters on a farm in Illinois, she was a typical farm child who learned her chores along with the value of hard work. By the time I met her, she had survived World War I, the Great Depression, and World War II. Nana watched as history and technology made their marks. She watched as the old buggy that carried their family to town and church was replaced with the automobile. From the first air flight to dishwashers to the man on the moon, Nana's mind had surveyed it all. She was like a timepiece of history—through it all; she still had hands that were never still and a heart that never stopped giving.

When I met Nana in 1950, she was fifty-eight years old. From the day I was born to the day she died, she always told me I was the most beautiful baby she had ever seen. She always reminded me of my rosebud lips and the most perfect little ears any baby ever had. After my children were born, she would put her hand under my chin and lift my face up just to take a little look at me. Then she would whisper, "You know, Sandy, you just get more beautiful the older you get." My Nana had a way about her that always made me feel like the most special girl in the world. When I was a child, there was no one who loved me like Nana.

After I was born, Nana moved to Los Angeles. She lived in a very large apartment building owned by actress and dancer Mitzie Gaynor's father. (She would remind me of that every time I came to visit her.) When we went to visit her, I was off to the old elevator that would take me to Nana's third-floor apartment before my mother could get the car parked. As I tried hard to push back the steel bar from the elevator, my mother warned me not to run. "They don't allow children to run here," she would remind me. So I had to walk as fast as my little legs could to try and make it to her door before my brother Rick did. I always wanted to be the first to enter the enchanted world of Nana's studio apartment.

Rick and I fought over who would push the buzzer next to her door. Rick always won because he was taller. I can still hear her high-pitched voice, "Come in!" Before she was finished, I was turning the knob and running to her arms that hugged me like no one ever could. I can still smell the cream on her face and detect a hint of whatever she was nibbling.

I was always quickly out of her arms, because I wanted to be the first to see what surprises she was preparing for us in her tiny kitchen that felt like love.

I would follow the wonderful smells around the corner to the stove. In the winter, there was always a pot of soup on the stove and a wonderful pie on the counter. In the summer, I would find a fresh cobbler still warm from the oven. Nana would have a small plate at each place setting with lettuce arranged like a bouquet. A slice of pear and a scoop of cottage cheese sat on top of the greens. On the side of the plate, wrapped up in wax paper, perched a slice of her banana nut bread, the most wonderful sweet bread I have ever tasted. It was my favorite, and I knew there was always more than just that slice waiting for me somewhere.

The table was always set in style: lots of detail and a dollop of elegance. I would study the just-polished silverware, the perfectly ironed napkins, and the linen cloth with the lace cover over it, the sparkling glass flutes from the top shelf, and the old china that had been brought in barrels on the train from Chicago. Fresh flowers sat in the center of the table. This little old mahogany table that sat next to the window with white Priscilla curtains looked like it was waiting for a celebration.

As a child, I didn't stop to think how many hours it took Nana to compose such a delight of food and flair for our Sunday visits. To me she was just Nana, a big-hearted grandma who made me feel so special.

There is always a time in childhood when the door opens and our future walks in. For me, it was every visit to Nana's home.

*"What a child doesn't receive, he can seldom later give."*
*-P.D. James*

Grandma Stella's Sunday Spice Cake can be found in Best Sunday Dinners Chapter.

# A Slice of Love

*Often the deepest relationships can be developed during the simplest activities.*
*~ Gary Smalley ~*

My brother, Rick, and I would fight over who would go first and stay with our Nana during the summer months. Sometimes we would flip a quarter. If Rick won, I would beg and plead for him to let me go, or threaten to tattle on him if I did not get the first month with our grandmother. If none of my tactics worked, I would usually just pout all the way to Los Angles.

Rick's biggest reason for wanting to visit Nana was the great trip to Dodger Stadium. It was a rule in my mother's house that if you were not a Republican and a Dodger fan, you did not live there. This rule turned into a family obsession over Dodger baseball. Nana and my mother were Cub fans when they left Chicago. In 1958, when the Brooklyn Dodgers moved to Los Angles and became the Dodgers I think they brought some of Chicago with them; because both of them turned in their Cub hats for blue ones.

As much attention I paid those Dodgers at that age, they were not the only reason I loved to stay a month at Nana's. My interest was in the kitchen, in cooking, and in Nana's old-fashioned dressing room.

At night, I would pull aside the old, printed fabric that hung in place of a door to her dressing room. It was just like something in an old movie I had watched with my mother. There were two milk glass lamps with shades made of dotted Swiss sitting on the vanity. The skirt attached to the table was made of the same fabric as the hanging panel. Beautiful cut-glass crystal perfume bottles stood on a china tray etched in tiny pink flowers. At night Nana laid her rings there. Next to the tray were all of her grandchildren's pictures. There we were: Judy, Janet, Joan, Rick, and Sandy. Hatboxes lined the shelves, and a couple of fur coats hung in the closet next to all of her dresses. I thought this was a room made for real ladies, like those in the movies.

I would sit down in front of the dressing table. As quiet as a mouse, I would put on her clip earrings, drape a beautiful strand of pearls around my neck, and start painting on my lips with the reddest of her lipsticks.

Once in a while Nana would give a holler, "what are ya doin'?" "Oh, just looking," I would answer. Pretty soon I would walk out of my celebrity dressing room and surprise my grandmother with my renditions of a silver screen actress. "Oh, my! Aren't you looking stunning tonight?" was always her reply. She would always act surprised, as if she had had no idea what I was up to. That made the fashion show I was about to present to her even more special.

She would wait patiently as I tripped back and forth on her high heels. After about an hour or so, she would tell me I'd have to end the show and clean things up. "We have a big day tomorrow." I knew that meant shopping downtown and riding the bus.

I quickly cleaned up the dressing room because getting ready for bed was always my favorite at Nana's. It involved finding the secret bed and having dessert. While I put on my pajamas, Nana would dish up something wonderful, like bread pudding, custard, or my favorite, ginger pound cake. I didn't even know what ginger was, but I loved what it tasted like in her cake.

When I arrived at the table, waiting next to the stunning glass cake pedestal was my slice of ginger cake. Next to it was half a cup of hot chocolate. I acted as though I didn't know it was mostly milk. There we chatted and sipped from our real teacups of cocoa.

Now there was one more fun thing to do before we went to sleep. As Nana pulled the hidden bed from the wall, she would ask me what I thought was hiding in the bed. It was her game, and she laughed as I lifted the covers to make sure nothing had gotten in there from behind the walls. I reminded her each visit about the very first time I came to visit her. "Remember, Nana, how you fooled me?" When I had explored every inch of her old apartment, I finally asked her where her bed was. Nana kept telling me there was a bed in this room; I would just have to find it. How did a four year old know about a Murphy bed?

Now our bed was ready. Nana always had fresh sheets and puffy feather pillows. My tummy was full of ginger, I used to tell her, and I couldn't wait for tomorrow. "Go to sleep, Sandy, tomorrow is a big day" was the last thing I heard before drifting off to sleep.

*Getting things accomplished*
*Isn't nearly as important as*
*taking time for love.*

_~ Janette Oke~

The Ginger Pound Cake recipe is found in Sweet Retreat Chapter.

*"Family faces are like magic mirrors. Looking at people who*
*Belong to us; we see the past, present, and future."*
*~ Gail Lumet Buckley ~*

# Why Do We Cook It?

More than four decades ago, I remember learning to cook at the hands of my grandmother and mother in that old kitchen on Beacon Street. I was mostly underfoot and in the way. I did a lot of watching and handing of spoons or rags.

I pestered them with questions. "What is this?" I would often ask. Most of the time Stella and Beatrice were so busy chatting about old family tales and friends and their own stories of cooking that they hardly knew I was there.

I will never forget my mother and grandmother sharing the love of ingredients that made a perfect Italian sauce. Sometimes I was able to pull the kitchen chair over to the stove and stir the sauce with the big metal spoon while trying not to fall in the pot. The smell of perfumed garlic, oregano, and olive oil always reminds me of the spaghetti sauce they were so proud of. Each time they prepared the sauce together, I think they added something different. It was just fun for them to get together and cook. As the day wore on and the sauce simmered, they would do some tasting and agree or disagree about what needed to be added. I remember my mother always thinking it needed a little more cooking wine and my grandmother remarking, "The sugar is the most important ingredient."

Today we have grocery stores filled with shelves of tried and tested pasta sauces, some good and some not so good. To some, it seems like a waste of time to make the very thing you can buy pre made.

Why did previous generations of my family make their spaghetti sauce from scratch? I believe it was to them a way of sharing a skill they were proud of. Their time in the kitchen was a time of sharing their talents, cleverness, and expertise. If they had paid attention, they would have seen that I was gifted with the same knack.

I am blessed with daughters and a granddaughter that love mixing and making it up in the kitchen just like Stella and Beatrice did. My mother and grandmother did more for me than help me find my place in the kitchen. They planted seeds of tradition, each one sweet, fragrant, and embedded deeply into my memory.

*There is work and there is love. That is what life is.*
*Make sure you have the time and energy for both.*
*~ Sigmund Freud ~*

# WHIP IT! WHIP IT GOOD!

I can still hear the sound of the old potato masher clanging against my mother's favorite aluminum pot. "Whip it good," my mother would repeat over and over again to my father, whose job it was to mash the potatoes every Sunday afternoon.

Every Sunday, we enjoyed my mother's fried chicken, peas, a green salad, and my father's mashed potatoes. She was proud of this dinner and of the perfect potatoes, even though it was my father's labor that went into them.

When I was old enough to help in the kitchen, I could not understand why I could not use an electric mixer to prepare the mashed delight. Wouldn't it make my job easier? The mere question would raise my mother's eyebrow and serve as a lead-in for her cooking lectures. Having lived through the Depression, she was careful, efficient, and old fashioned. I always thought she was just stubborn, but by the time her drill was over, I had created light and fluffy potatoes—the best I had ever tasted.

I bought a Bosch kitchen machine in 1977. I still own the same machine and make our family's mashed potatoes in it. Maybe the Bosch Company invented the potato masher because it whips a potato into the same perfect texture as my mother's famous whipped potatoes.

Some years ago, I took the advice of my friend Diana, who recommended adding cream cheese to the potatoes along with a spice called Nature's Seasoning. Wow, what an addition! (If I am baking something and have the oven on, I will roast some garlic and then add this to the potatoes. The cream cheese and garlic are a great combination.)

I think because my mother raised me with the same mindset with which her mother raised her, I don't think twice about putting "a little effort into it," as my mother used to say. My girls think there is no other mashed potato on the face of the planet like these. Since the girls have been on their own, they often say to me, "Mom, I miss your mashed potatoes, no one makes them like you do."

My eighteen-year-old daughter, Katie, just produced her first batch of "Mom's real mashed potatoes." She never once complained about following my instructions using a potato masher. She did complain that there were not enough potatoes for leftovers! I decided her efforts were worth a hand mixer and bought her one.

Now that I think of it, when I gave Katie the instructions over the phone, she asked me what to do to make them like mine. I gave her one of my mother's famous last word: "Don't be afraid of it, and whip it good!"

I have a sneaking suspicion that those mashed potatoes my family claims are the best in the world are so good because they are whipped with love—and it doesn't matter what kind of beater you use.

*I am beginning to learn that it is the sweet, simple things of life, which are the real ones after all.*
*~ Laura Ingalls Wilder ~*

# Fabulous Baseball Fudge

In 1958 the Brooklyn Dodgers moved to Los Angeles California and became the L.A. Dodgers. That is when I started my love affair with baseball.

I lived in Anaheim California, about one hour or so away from the Dodgers. I was the only girl in my neighborhood and every once in a while the boys would let me play catch with them. Only thing is I didn't have a mitt, so I would have to use my brothers when he was doing his chores.

My brother was left-handed and being right handed made it difficult to catch with his glove. I was determined to show those boys that I was just as good as they were. I had to work hard not to throw like a girl and not act like one either. It paid off. I would sit on the curb and stare at them for hours and finally they would feel sorry for me and make my brother give me his glove and I was in the game!

My mother was from Chicago Ill., the home of baseballs Chicago Cubs. When she came to California she brought her stories of watching baseball from out her apartment window onto the field. Somehow she became a Dodger fan. And that's where it all started was in our living room when the game was on.

There were two rules in my mother's home; you were a republican and a Dodger fan. And when the game was on if you valued your life, you would never walk in front of the black and white television because you may never see a game again. If the Dodgers were on during the dinner hour the old metal T.V. trays went up. Sometimes it was just a T.V. dinner we were served. If the Dodgers were playing the Giants, we were lucky to get dinner. What I loved the most was when she made her fabulous fudge. There has never been anything like it. It was such a rich flavor and pure sweet to the taste. When the innings became tense she brought out the fudge. I would help make the candy the day before the game was scheduled on the T.V. It seemed like it took too long to cook and too long to set up, until you took one bite of it.

Sandy Kofax, Don Drysdale, Morry Wills were household names in our house. After I was supposed to be asleep I listened to the game on my radio next to the bed. I can still hear the voices of the Los Angeles radio announcers Jerry Dogen and Vince Scully calling out a play; there has never been any one like those two guys in baseball announcing, nor will there ever be any fudge like my mothers or the memory that goes with it.

After I moved to Northern California I attended Dodger-Giant games in San Francisco. I brought my kids, my good luck, Dodger blue jackets and my mitt. It is one of our favorite family memories; in our living room in black and white.

*"One feels great Comfort
in good dinners."*
  *~ Zora Neale Hurston ~*

# MY SECOND FAMILY

February 15, 1965 I met my new family I had to come to live with. It was a strange day for me in that everything was very different. It wasn't wrong or bad; it was just different from the life I had been living.

The family circle was there to greet me. Grandma and Grandpa Petty, Aunt Maggie and Uncle Chuck, Uncle Tom and Aunt Cherie, all came to welcome me to the Hart and Petty family. The Hart family consisted of Lee, Teri, Debi, Chuck and Tommy. All of the excitement made me feel like I was floating for a while and then soon life began.

It didn't take any time at all for me to become one with everyone in this family. I became apart of the daily rushing around to get to school, the chores, family outings, and sister arguing. Soon after I arrived, Debi realized she was no longer the big girl on the block, beings that I was five years older. We had our scraps and screaming matches everyday for about a week, until Mom set us down for a serious talk, which would have been easier than if Dad got a hold of us (that's what Terry told us). So we listened and Deb pouted for a while and then we just kind of grew into one another like we had never known life without one another.

We grew all right! We grew to a different kind of trouble, not arguing with one another anymore, oh no… all the trouble we got into was agreed upon. Most of the time we were bored and too big to play with dolls so we made up stuff; like secretly planning to change bedrooms with the boy's room when they were away with Mom. Spying on the cute guy Larry across the street and all of his guy friends and then calling them and holding the phone up to the record player that played, "Little Red Riding Hood," and hanging up. Or still spying and catching a robber breaking into a car in front of Larry's house, we were really proud of that one. But then there was the time we un-wrapped every one of our Christmas gifts under the tree and thought we were so cool until the next morning when we un-wrapped them again and I slipped and now Terry was on to us. The next year she numbered all of the gifts!!! It seemed like we were always on restriction (they called it). I remember so many times we knew we were busted and would turn out the light in our bedroom and pretend we were asleep when Lee came into lecture us. Finally one night he said, "All right girls, I know you are not asleep and we need to have a talk!" Oh those were the days!

And then there was Teri's cooking, so different than what I was used to, yet so good. Teri was born in Shreveport Louisiana. Her father we called Papa Petty was from Louisiana also and her mother who was known as Memaw Petty was a Puckett from Texas. Teri gleaned her southern style from her roots and a lot of it showed up in her cooking. The Hart family lived on a small income and Teri had to stretch a dollar to feed us. Maybe there's something about being raised in the south that teaches you to cook on a budget and cook something up when it looks like there isn't going to be a meal. I remember every Friday was payday and that meant Thursday night's dinner was going to be a meager meal. Well it was sparse in the fact that Teri fixed what was left over from the week and if there wasn't anything we had biscuits and gravy. I love this memory for two reasons. Teri used her resourcefulness and her creativity. On Thursdays she put her apron on and rolled out the biscuit dough and then put the Crisco in the black iron skillet and began the gravy. Now this is what amazed me; some weeks it would be country sausage gravy and other weeks she served up tomato gravy and there was hamburger gravy or hardboiled egg gravy. She served it with a slice of Papa Petty's homegrown tomatoes or a vegetable. There was always plenty of the gravy to keep you filled up and someone was forever grabbing the last biscuit and spreading some jelly on it. As poor as Thursday nights were, we sat around a table rich in love in those days.

Biscuits and gravy was not the only favorite food Teri cooked. There were the tacos that no one but Teri made. She added oatmeal as a filler to her hamburger meat to stretch the amount and then added some taco seasoning. She fried up her shells and added the meat and some cheese inside and then fried them again with the filling inside for just a few minutes. We had tacos the traditional way, and then complained that we would have rather she made them her special way. The goulash and tamale pie, which I had never eaten stand out in my mind, but then there was the homemade pizza like none I've ever had before. I don't remember ever sitting down to a meal in the Hart home that I wasn't satisfied with. I cannot say enough about a woman who worked with what she had in her cupboards and molded it into a family spread every night.

Those days have long gone but the memories are some of my greatest in my heart. Not long ago Debe e-mailed me and at the end of her message she wrote:

"Boy we had so many good times didn't we! But the best times were when you would teach me how to put on make up and do my hair, I just loved having a big sister who would take the time to show me these girlie things, and the long, long nights we would sit up and talk about what ever."

Deb and Sandy are not related by blood, rather sisters of experience in the heart.

*You can find the following recipes in The Casserole and South of the Border Chapters: Goulash and Teri's Tacos*

*"The Real moment of success is not the moment apparent to the crowd."*
*George Bernard Shaw*

# Rarebit Flame

I swept into action that school day in 1968. I was in a hurry to get the flame on under the metal saucepan in my eleventh-grade home economics class.

I really wanted an A in Mrs. Clark's home economics class. After all, I had studied harder that year than any other before. It was so nice to sit through a class I understood and enjoyed, unlike of the drudgery of math, which seemed so difficult. Cooking came easily to me, and it was refreshing.

There would be no sitting that day. It was our class final, and it seemed like a cooking contest. The assignment was to break up into small groups and prepare a meal. Part of the task was to set the table as creatively as we could, clean up our kitchen area, and be sitting down at our table before the buzzer on Mrs. Clark's desk rang. Each group would be graded on presentation, timing, and taste. If we added any extras, then that represented extra points.

We were off! Some of us brought crystal glasses, flowers, candles, and our mothers' table linens. My group worked smoothly as a team. As soon as the table was set, we began making the rue for the main course, Welsh rarebit. I remembered that it was important to cook the flour, or we would taste it in the sauce. My grandmother had made this old-fashioned sauce over toast for me once. I was the only one in the group who trusted our selection, one of simple preparation and elegant display.

Two of the girls prepared a green salad on a separate salad plate. Someone lit the candles on our table and poured Seven Up into our goblets. I poured the sauce over a piece of toast and laid the almost-limp piece of broccoli next to it. We took our aprons off and sat at our places that had been assigned by place cards. The rest of the groups were scrambling around like chickens.

Someone noticed we were sitting down and announced it to the class. The announcement soon sent a wave of silence and disappointment through the room. "They're done, and the buzzer hasn't even gone off," one of the girls announced. A lot of mumbling followed, and then Mrs. Clark announced she would be joining us, the winning group.

I had wondered why she had told us to prepare enough food for six instead of four. Then came the best part. Mrs. Clark told each group to prepare two extra plates of their creations and bring them to the winning table as part of our reward. Some of our plates were presented with frowns, but our group did not care. We felt a little like royalty for the remainder of the class period.

Our group received an A for food and table presentation, a B+ for taste, and an A overall. I was proud of the grade and the hustle our group put into our task. Little did I know that down the road I would use that ability to work quickly and calmly in the kitchen again and again in my home and work life.

# Music for My Soul along the California Coast

Being lost …is worth the coming home…la…la…la…la …la…la…stones…

The music coming from the eight-track player rang in my ears, but the words pierced through my soul as my blue Datsun pickup turned the curves of the California Malibu coast. I was bound for Santa Barbara, where I was spending a week camping at Refugio State beach.

It was 1974: flower power, drugs, and a self-indulgent "me generation," the children of the Baby Boom. We were all searching for what our parents didn't find, and to complete what they didn't finish, even if we did it our own way. The voice of Neil Diamond sang out as loud as my speakers could go, floating into the cab of the truck, into the minds of my two small children. The music of this superstar rang into their minds on this sunny beach-trip day; they did not realize that years later they would be affected by the sounds of his guitar and the magic of his lyrics.

*Crackling Rosie…you make me smile*
*We got all night*
*To set the world right!*

How many times did I nearly scream these words out the window, secretly hoping someone would hear me… until I realized the song was about a guitar? Rosie was a musical instrument that lit the creative flame in the heart!

There I was, twenty-four and the mother of two beautiful daughters. My friends were in college seeking life's opportunities, and I was part Suzy homemaker and part soul searcher. My way I found entrance into my core was through music. In the sixties, Roy Orbison and the Beatles helped me interpret my feelings, and now it was Neil.

*Reach my hand and I will never stray.* It seemed like I was talking to God as I sang out loud. I was reaching for God, for my identity, and into the hearts of my children. The words Neil sang to me in my little pickup conveyed more than I was ready to comprehend, yet I was moved to a place of both stirring and peace. It was his words that rang deeply enough that I wept as I drove. It was those tears that my children didn't see that healed my heart.

We drove, we sang, we reached our hearts out into that blue ocean in front of us while we drove on along the Pacific Coast Hwy.

*Song sung blue*
*Everybody knows one.*
*Song sung blue,*
*Every garden grows one.*
*Me and you are subject to the blues… now and then*
*When you take the blues and make a song,*
*You sing them out again.*

Our week camping at the ocean was celebrated with yummy food I brought in our ice chest. I remember the red and white checked tablecloth I put on the picnic table. We sat there eating, playing cards, and listening to the same tunes from my portable eight-track player.

As Neil Diamond wrote songs of his youth in Brooklyn in the seventies, I was beginning to check in and look at my own childhood. The lyrics and melodies of his music blazed into my memory, my children's memories, and the world.

It was in the eighties that I walked the beach wearing headphones and listening to Neil sing out the words of Jonathan Livingston Seagull. As I dug my toes into the wet sand, I watched the seagulls soar high, wondering which one was Jonathan. All the while it was my self who strummed differently than the rest.

My girls grew up singing songs with me, not paying attention to the artist until they got into high school. When I was ready to go to my first Neil Diamond concert, both of the girls fought over who would use the last ticket. What a memory for my oldest daughter to experience. There was the man whose music floated through our lives. Now he stood on top of a piano singing "Blue Jeans" seventeen times in a row!

I have often wondered how many other lives were affected by this performer's music, how many other tears were cried, releasing hurts and healing hearts, as the listeners began to build foundations for those they loved.

*Tears have healed my heart and tears heal the world.*
*I am… I said*
*I am… I cried…*

*Mother maintains, on the fact that the cake is made "strictly from scratch" From my earliest memories; her chocolate fudge cake has graced every birthday in our extended family. An honored tradition, it's also a rite of passage. For new members know they've been fully accepted when the cake is served on their birthday.*

*To me, it's also a symbol of family unity. Like the many different ingredients in my mother's cake, each of us has our own unique identity, with our own separate strengths. But somehow we're even stronger and better, when we're blended together, by love and time, to form a family.*

*-Rae Turnbull 2000*

# THAT TAKES THE CAKE!

My mother made the best chocolate cake I've ever tasted, rich and moist and light. She never let me forget about the sifting step: "That makes the difference; don't forget to sift." Licking the chocolate icing was my favorite part, and I always hoped that when I offered to wash the bowl that there would be some frosting left.

I marveled at how she used a butter knife to make the attractive swirls on the sides and top of the cake. I thought it looked so great. I asked her once, "How do you know how to do that?" She answered, "Oh, I just do," as she kept swirling the knife.

She made this wonderful cake on my ninth birthday. I remember how special it made me feel. I said to myself, "This is my birthday cake." To this day whenever I see a homemade chocolate frosted cake, it takes me back to the one my mother made.

Forty years later, my youngest daughter Katie's favorite cake is "your birthday cake, Mom, the one you make."

I used to think little girls' birthday parties deserved a beautiful hand-decorated cake made by an expert, which I am not. With all the other details that go into a child's party, it's so nice to just order a cake from a bakery.

On one of Katie's birthdays, I had toned down the glitter and decided just to make my mother's homemade cake for the occasion. After I finished the icing the cake, I grabbed some decorative sugar sprinkles. While the frosting was still sticky, I put them on top and all around the sides of the cake. Then I added the candles. Not bad, but definitely homemade. I thought Katie would complain. Instead, she opened her mouth wide and squealed, "Wow, Mom, that is so beautiful!"

From that day on, I knew what was number one on her birthday list. Maybe Katie feels the same power of comfort that I felt when I looked at the cake my mother made. It feels like homemade from Mom with a big red heart on top of it!

*"I think the one lesson I have learned
is that there is no substitute for paying attention."*
*~ Diane Sawyer ~*

# DELECTABLE SPUDS

I don't remember anyone ever teaching me to cook or ever taking a cooking class. I just did a lot of observing as a child. I would watch my mother nearly every meal she fixed. I must have been fascinated enough to keep watching. I think cooking was just a part of my journey to love other people with it.

One of my favorite dishes she prepared was scalloped potatoes. I think it would be an injustice if I did not duplicate the amazing potatoes just the way she did. Fortunately, the potatoes I make are just like mothers.

I would watch her slice the potatoes and put them in cold water so they did not turn brown until the rest of the ingredients were ready. I remembered all of the steps years later when I made my first batch of these yummy potatoes at age 18. Mother poured a little milk in the bottom of the glass dish. Next she put a layer of the potatoes that were waiting in the bowl of cold water until they covered the dish. Then a little more milk was poured over the top of the potatoes so that the flour she was about to sprinkle on would stick. Salt and pepper, dots of butter and a little finely chopped onion were next and topped off with grated cheddar cheese. Mother did the same thing again. She covered the casserole with foil and then baked the potatoes slowly.

As a child these potatoes always tasted like some kind of important dish. Little did I know they were just a family casserole.

My children and everyone I have ever served these potatoes to react the same way I did. It's everyone's request on Easter and Christmas; and the most asked about recipe I own!

I am glad I paid attention to cooking and grateful I have been able to love so many people through food.

*A Mother's Touch...*

# NEST EGG

When I was raising my girls, I often wondered if it was all worth it. I would have these thoughts especially on days when I had put forth extra effort. No one seemed to notice the freshly ironed tablecloth and the flowers on the dining table, or the smell of homemade bread.

I would quickly remind myself that I was building a nest for my children. Someday each of these little girls would search their hearts and remember what they cherished the most about their own childhood—a mother's touch!

Nearly every Friday, I made a homemade quiche for our breakfast on the weekends. When the girls arrived home after school, there was that wonderful breakfast meal sitting on the counter like a grand pie. Only it wasn't desert; it was breakfast.

I took pride in my knowledge of how to make such a great dish. My friend Helen Gropen passed it on to me. It was Helen who had taught me that the most important ingredient was the nutmeg. "Don't ever forget the nutmeg," she always reminded me.

There was always quiche on Christmas morning and every Easter brunch. There is something about quiche and women—they just go together. Our family is proof of that. It was a little extra effort put forth, but really nothing more than a mother's touch.

The Quiche recipe is found in the Brunch Chapter.

*"Learning stamps you with its moments.*
*Childhood's learning is made up of moments.*
*It isn't steady. It's a pulse."*
*~ Eudora Welty ~*

*"Memory is more indelible than ink."*
*~ Anita Loos ~*

# Pass the Pasta

Twenty-two years ago, my good friend Eileen gave me this pasta salad recipe. Since then, we've made this together many times. During my daughters' junior high and high school years, I was involved with their scouting and school activities. I remember that the first time I made this salad their friends went crazy. Mothers called me to ask for the recipe because it was such a big hit with their children. I continued to make it for every party or whenever the girls were supposed to bring a food dish. "Is your mom going to make her salad?" they would ask.

When I opened my restaurant, I made it as a side dish and served it with a slice of French bread. The wonderful reviews started again. When customers would order their meals, sometimes they would ask, "Did she make the spaghetti salad today?"

This has to be the easiest and fastest pasta salad ever. My oldest daughter has made this favorite on many occasions and every time someone wants the recipe. There is something about the seeds and the dressing that is a wonderful combination. The recipe calls for a spice, Salad Supreme. Since I have made this recipe for volumes of people, however, I simply made up my own spice mix. I will give you both versions.

Another pasta crowd-pleaser, the noodle casserole, hasn't vanished despite the fact it rarely appears on restaurant menus. Modern cookbooks often don't include casseroles, even though over the decades home cooks have gone on serving these easy, wonderful dishes.

Noodle casseroles can be made well in advance. They are easy to prepare and serve. They cook in their own serving dish and most often can be made from ingredients on hand. The casseroles can be made in the morning, refrigerated, and baked in the evening.

The Spaghetti Salad recipe will be found in the Delightful Salads Chapter.
Enjoy and pass the pasta!

*"Food is like a beautiful woman:
It is sometimes more dramatic and more appealing
when simply and honestly presented."*
*~ Pierre Bardiche ~*

# OPEN HEARTED COOK

Do you remember a childhood event that made you feel warm inside? Most of us have at least a few occasions that we cherish because no one can ever take them from us. They are the threads that are woven through each family's personality, creating a language all their own.

When did most of these special memories take place? Probably during the holidays, birthdays, vacations, or other special celebrations. Do your memories involve food and passing the plate at the family dinner table? After you married, did you discuss with your spouse whose home you would be visiting on your first holiday together? Do you remember secretly hoping that you could just go to *your* family's house? That is because your comfort lies there, with all of the familiar foods and shared traditions. Whatever you recall is your family's history. What is the history you are making in your home today for your family to remember? Does your family mealtime invoke the presence of love?

I remember how I felt every time I visited my grandmother. It was a mixture of love, acceptance, and welcome. There she was, greeting me with outstretched arms, ready to embrace me with her warmth, as she invited me to share with her.

We all need to feel that same love in order to share it. If we first embrace our inner hunger and love ourselves, we will be more likely to share with those around us. We must call in the love we need to nourish ourselves before we can feed anyone else. If we don't, our lives, our meals, and our togetherness become mundane.

Start by seeing the beauty in yourself and the beauty in your life. If there is pain or change in your life, embrace it. Open yourself to the desires in your heart. After you have taken a look inside, you will be more open to nurturing your family.

What if you are just not interested in the domestic life or cooking? What if you feel this way and have started a family? What if you are a single parent and strapped with the responsibility of being mother, father, and breadwinner and just feel overwhelmed? Take a look at that amazing little person you have created and know that it will be part of your journey to learn and understand how to take care of him and your self and love both of you along the way.

Cooking, like any craft, takes practice, patience, and most of all, love. Cooking does not require hours of work. When you approach it with love, you find that you put yourself into the food, and the meal becomes nourishment for your family's soul. A family meal is not about the food; it's about the connection at the table. If you have worked hard and drag yourself in the front door like I did many a night, take the burritos out of the freezer and put them into the microwave. Serve them on a plate with a vegetable, cottage cheese or some fruit. Push the mail aside, light a candle, and share a twenty-minute meal with your family. If there are two of you, or six, you are a family and you are the only one who can take these twenty minutes today to celebrate your love with your family.

When my oldest girls were growing up, I was in my element as homemaker and mother. I loved every moment of every day providing for my family. As hard as I worked, I never tired of planning and preparing meals, dinner parties, special occasions, holidays, and church events. One day my life changed, and my world seemed like it turned upside down. Now I was on the other end of managing life, time, children, and a home.

I was a single parent with two businesses. Sometimes I worked seven days a week without a day off for five or six weeks. I realized my problems were not going to just go away. I had to find a way to deal with the problems, the pain, and the change. I dug deep inside and found a reserve. I learned how to look at each obstacle as a new challenge. I decided that no matter what I was facing, life would go on and my family still looked to me as the leader.

I realized my family was more important than any problem facing me. I learned how to put the stuff on the shelf for the time it needed to be there and open my heart to those around me. When I did this, the feeling it evoked was welcome! My willingness to open up regardless of what was going on around me helped to create an even deeper level of passion in giving. And through it all, I learned lessons and found answers for every problem. At the other side of each problem, God was waiting for me.

The next time you prepare a meal for your family, say to yourself, "I think I'll go whip up some love and serve it." Then feel your heart start to grow!

*"It's what we do with our hearts that affects others most deeply."*
*~ Gerald Jampolsky ~*

# SMILEY FACES IN HEAVEN

Aunt Junie was born March 9, 1921. She was my grandmother Stella's second child, and she was one of the happiest people I ever knew.

I met her as a little girl through the letters we shared all of my childhood. Aunt Junie lived in Grand Rapids Michigan with my Uncle Jack and five cousins. Judy, Janet, Joan, Jean and James along with their parents they were considered the 7 J's.

I did not meet my aunt in person until 1974. I took the train across the United States to meet her and my cousins. I met a woman with a huge spirit; unlike any I had ever known. In all my life I don't remember ever hearing a negative word out of her mouth. I learned as a little girl that she was different than most people I knew. I found later in life that Aunt Junie was often misunderstood. Her happy spirit confused a lot of people and even her own children did not understand her completely.

Junellen possessed two gifts. First she approached life with what she could give and second she lived life from the inside out. She never veered from her heart course. And in the end of her life she had no regrets because she always sang her song. She did not die with her song inside her; rather it was and is around her even now. For me she was my gift of the heart. I am ever grateful to have known her and to have been loved by her. We were kindred spirits.

Before she died, I told her about this book I was writing and ask her to send me her favorite recipes she prepared for her family. She was in a retirement home by then and not in good health. She became so excited for the possibility of this book and sent the following recipes. I would have loved to share these meals with my cousins. Her children have said, "Mom wasn't a great cook." It doesn't take a great cook to serve love.

All my life, every faithful letter she wrote me ended with her gratitude of her life and her children, then her grand children and then her great grand children. And one more thing, there was always a little smiley face at the end of every note next to her name. Those smiley faces are on the recipe cards too. Her spirit is probably helping me write this book. I bet she teaches smiley faces in heaven just like she did here on earth. My life is rich because of knowing her.

# The Rake

The first time I came to Paradise, California, I knew it was the place I wanted to call home. All I could see were blue skies and pine trees. It was so beautiful, I thought only the lucky would be allowed to live in such a peaceful surrounding.

When Katie and I lived in the cottage, our property had about twenty-five trees. They were all beautiful, but what flourishes with beauty and shade and tenaciously tries to cling to the tree, finally falls to the ground when autumn calls. It was Katie's job to rake, and I made sure she did it. After all, the least she could do was the job I didn't want to do.

And rake she did. Every day after school or dance, she reluctantly picked up her rake and began the job. She usually was so mad at me that she said very little, even if I joined her with the blower to help. After a while, she couldn't stand not talking and broke her silence with, "Hey Mom, guess what happened today at school?" We would rake until it was dark and share our day, returning the next day when the cleared path to our house was completely covered again with those darn leaves.

One day I came home and Katie was in her room talking to her sister on the phone. She did not know I was there, and I heard her say, "Korrie, my life sucks. All I do is go to school, go to dance, and rake leaves for Mom!" I had to cover my mouth and not let her know I heard. That was such a thirteen year old voicing her opinion.

Other times we had rake wars. Katie would do anything to get out of raking. One day she walked in the house and said, "Sorry, Mom, I can't rake." Somehow I knew this was going to be a really good excuse.

"Why not?" I asked.

"The rake broke."

I took her outside and looked at it and said, "Here, hold this," while I got some tape. Yes, I really did tape the rake! Just when Katie thought this tool she hated was gone, I had no empathy and taped it back together good as new and handed it to her. She was not happy, needless to say.

Another time I came home to find her not raking. This time she told me; with just a hint of a smile on her face she didn't have a rake because her friend's mom borrowed it. I bought a new one for the family and got Katie's old rake back. And the last Christmas we lived in the cottage, our family watched Katie open her eyes Christmas morning to a brand-new rake standing near the tree with a very large bow on it.

Although Katie has had raking trauma in her life, this hard work was one of the ways she learned discipline and the two of us working as a team. For every leaf she has raked in her life, I can only imagine the power of her thoughts weaving in and out of her mind, creating new dance steps and planning her life. And after every raking in that fall season, we came into the house and shared a meal together.

The following recipe is one of Katie's favorite foods:
Cream Cheese Garlic Mashed Potatoes recipe can be found in the
Take a Look at Our Thanksgiving Feast Chapter.

*Eat soup first and eat it last,*
*And live till a hundred years be past.*
   *~ French Proverb ~*

# A Simple Thing Like Soup

Comfort is a warm bowl of soup on a cold winter night. In our family, soup evokes memories of the warmth of a childhood home and a little, simple tradition.

I don't know how it got started; I just got in the habit of baking a loaf of homemade bread and a homemade soup every Friday. There was something about the simmering of ingredients and smelling the aromas of both a pot of soup and freshly baked bread that made me feel good.

I had shopping and errands to run every Friday or the girls had their own plans for Friday night. I guess I got into the habit of throwing whatever was left over from the week into a pot and making a soup out of it or grabbing a recipe book and turning to the soup section. Soups are one of the easiest things to prepare, and I wanted an easy menu for Fridays because I had other things to do.

One of the girls' favorite Friday night soups was the Potato Chile Cheese. I started making Caesar salad and French bread to go with the soup. This was a very big hit. Most of the time they would walk through the door asking, "Is it potato soup tonight?"

I didn't always make homemade bread, and sometimes my soups were so easy that I felt like I had only taken the time to open a can of soup. Canned soup would be great, too, and crackers or toast. It is all comfort. It feels like warmth on a cold night.

Later, when my youngest daughter was about nine, she started paying attention to the soups I made. Of all the soups I prepared, her favorite was lentil. I could never figure it out. To this day if she is sick or has just visited the dentist, she will call me and ask if I will make her some lentil soup.

When she was growing up, we were on our own and she ate a lot of soup. Maybe she relates the soup to our connection or to gratitude or to the times just the two of us sat at our family table eating toast and lentil soup.

# Vegan Heaven

I love vegetarian food! Some of my favorite dishes are polenta and grilled veggies and kidney bean veggie patties.

While they were growing up, my two oldest girls' friends were nearly all vegetarians. This allowed me the opportunity to learn and create some very good meatless dishes—I was feeding the friends a lot of the time. Kellie and Korrie grew to love several of our family's favorite veggie dishes. The one they raved over the most was the mushroom patty.

I learned first hand the value of real food prepared without the use of any meat or poultry product. I also did not like the idea of using canned veggie products, unless they contained very few additives and sodium. If I was going to cook vegetarian, I didn't need artificial substitutes.

Later on, my friend Diana and I were eating at a restaurant and ordered a veggie burger. It was so outrageous, we had to get the recipe from the waiter, who had to bother the chef, who was in the middle of tomorrow's soup. He wrote the recipe down on a napkin for us and I still have it. I changed it and added to it and still think it is, by far, the best veggie burger ever.

Vegetarian cooking was a wonderful experience for me, and goes right to the heart of my children's childhoods.

All of our family's favorite veggie dishes will be found in Beloved Veggie Meals Chapter.

*Chapter 2*

# Joyful Celebrations

# Joyful Celebrations

*Hearts can inspire other hearts with their fire*

Think about the last time you felt driven to do something. What moved you? And when you were in the middle of your endeavor, working so hard that you hardly noticed the time go by, did you realize your actions were guided by another influence—inspiration?

The word "inspire" comes from the state of being "in spirit." Spirit is our essence—what a beautiful concept and fulfilling truth. If we stopped to think of every time in our life we got an idea and wanted to act on it, we would realize we are more inspired than we think.

Inspiration is the very reason you are reading this book. Something in you is drawn to learn and to create. That is what happened to me every time I fixed a meal or planned a party. We all do it: whether it's a family dinner or a birthday party, we are moved to create a celebration. Illuminating the human spirit through joyful celebrations blesses everyone.

I have wanted to celebrate every friend I have ever had; the thought of the delight that will be felt by another calls me to create an event. Remember when you were a small child and your birthday was one month, one week, one day away? Remember how much excitement filled your heart? Remember how you felt when your little friends showed up at the door with their gifts and later, when everyone sang happy birthday? Something inside of you felt special, so special that it lingered on inside of you for days. That is the *special* we give to others every time we celebrate them. In this busy world we live in, we have to find ways to keep from missing valuable opportunities to celebrate one another. Every time we celebrate, even in the smallest ways, we bring honor to our relationships.

When Oprah turned fifty and the world celebrated her, it was not just the extravaganza that touched her heart, but also the thought that was behind it. Her best friend, Gail, knocked herself out with ideas, labor, and most of all, love. Oprah felt the love in every touch that was put into her birthday celebrations, which made her feel like the most special person in the world.

My friend Diana has always said I have a way of creating magic and turning a dull event into champagne. I have thought a lot about that, and I'm ever so grateful that I have the ability to do this, but for me, the magic of the event is in the eyes of the receiver and the fullness I know is in their heart.

My children grew up in a home that did a lot of celebrating. I decorated a fall table for my daughter Korrie's bunco group about a year ago. When her friends arrived, they looked around and said to Korrie, "You really go all out!" Korrie replied, "Well, my mom taught us to celebrate everything."

*At the table with friends and family, laugh, and if you eat, then smell. The aromas are not impediments to your day. Steak on the grill, coffee beans freshly ground, cookies in the oven. And taste. Taste every ounce of friendship. Taste every ounce of life; because it is most definitely a gift.*

# Dinner for Oprah

*The greatest gifts are those we pass along.*
—*Oprah Winfrey*

My daughter Kellie called me and told me about a contest *The Oprah Winfrey Show* was holding. It was called "Welcome to My Home." They asked for a video of your home; sharing how it felt inviting. Whatever you had that was unique or special, Oprah wanted to see it. The next thing I knew, I was having girlfriends over and fixing dinner for Oprah.

While I prepared for the evening, I could not possibly imagine what I would have in my tiny cottage that Oprah's show would be interested in. But I mulled over in my mind what the possibilities were while I planned ahead. I wanted to create such an elegant evening that I would be proud to seat even Oprah at my dining table. I made a beautiful flower arrangement of pink and purple tulips, white roses, lavender, and white larkspur. The table started with antique glass soup bowls set in the middle of each plate. Crystal and silver candlesticks and gold-rimmed wine glasses captivated the eye. Each course was garnished as if for royalty and stood out on glass pedestals and in silver bowls. Truly, it was a table of elegance and Oprah would have felt special sitting here.

Still not knowing what it was I was supposed to be offering Oprah, I began to contemplate. I looked around me and decided it would be the same gifts I offered everyone who walked through my door: First, love, and then the memories they depart with. So how could I make Oprah feel loved and like one of the girls? Invite other girls and talk to Oprah on video! This is exactly what we did.

I told my wonderful friends to dress up, because they were having dinner with Oprah at my house. Wear your jewels and bring your flair—we're having a celebration! Janet and Cathy arrived first. I would have to say they were a perfect pair; with modeling careers and diamonds, they had much to talk about. Danny strolled in with her beauty and grace and listened and laughed as the other two poured the perfect wine that Cathy brought.

I told them it was their job to share on camera what they experienced when they stepped inside this abode. So they got silly before they got serious, and the laughter began. Adam, the photographer, must have thought this group was a little off their rockers and probably never knew what real women talk about or do when they are pulled together until now. We felt free to say pretty much anything we wanted because we knew Oprah would understand, or we could have Adam just cut it out. Finally Diana and my daughter Korrie arrived, and we got serious enough for a couple of them to speak into that camera.

Cathy said she was ready and walked over to the old fireplace with its mantel lined with keepsakes of my heart. She looked beautiful in the stunning pearls that lined the curves of her neck and the purple dress that she insisted all evening was her queen attire, and Cathy could easily pass as royalty. And the queen spoke: "Hello, Oprah, I have a really good friend named Sandy. You and I both know

God gives everybody special gifts early in life. You know what yours is, and I know Sandy knows what hers is. If I'm ever sad or life isn't going my way, if I just talk to her I feel better. If I come to her home, and I've come on some of the worst days of my life and I've always felt better…and I also want you to know if Sandy lived in a tent, it would look wonderful and we would all be jealous. So, Oprah, I hope you get to come visit Sandy one day because she has a lot of friends and we all love her." Everyone was quiet from the impact of Cathy's words, and then the energy shifted into gladness with delighted applause.

Now the pressure was on to compete with Cathy's words. So Janet got silly as she set herself down in a chair in front of the dining table. She tossed her silver hair here and there and asked her audience if her face was too shiny. "Do I have any shadows? I want to look good for Oprah." She was bleeding the moment and stealing the show. She quickly turned her head to the angle of the camera, just like a true model would, and said, "Hello, Oprah, I'm Janet. My friend Sandy makes every gathering in her home a celebration of life, as you can see. She's also a great cook. In fact, my husband nearly left me over her liver pâté. So here's to Sandy!"

Diana managed to shift everyone's attention into another room, explaining that she needed her own space. Cathy said, "OK, everyone, quiet on the set. We need to go to a corner and quietly be quiet."

Diana sat on the couch and started to talk before she started to cry. "Hi, Oprah, what an honor I have to stop and think of the most special thing about my bud Sandy and her cottage. When I think of her little place and how welcome you feel when you go there I think of the root word "we." Anybody that comes here leaves sparked up and definitely well fed and leaves with a memory. When you look around, everything is about family fiber, friendship, and about memories and about love." Her voice was just starting to lift as she broke into tears.

Six years later, I watch the uncut version of the tape I sent to Oprah, and I am nearly on the floor with laughter at the behind-the-scenes look at six great women. What a night, what an honor, and what an experience to look back on. I am so glad my oldest daughter, Kellie, felt this was something I should do. Now I realize it was not about winning a prize or going anywhere. Rather, it was supposed to capture what "home" feels like. It was meant to teach and show how celebrating feels in the heart. And most of all, it is the gift of love and special ness one leaves with and tucks away inside. It is the gifts of ourselves we pass on.

While watching the uncut video, my daughter Korrie suggested that I write out the menu that I was serving. I didn't pay much attention to what she was saying, but she had a point—Oprah would miss a key part of the dinner if I didn't. She would miss the food.

So Oprah, your special *Dinner for Oprah* menu can be found in the Treasure Trove of Menus file.

*We laugh – we cry, we make time fly.*
  *Best friends are we,*
   *my daughter and me*
   *~ unknown ~*

*We must be our own before we can be another's.*
  *~ Ralph Waldo Emerson ~*

# BIRTHDAY LASAGNA

My three girls grew up among big-hearted adults who tried and mostly succeeded in doing the right things. Their lives are a timeless story about being cared for and accepting that care. It was with family pride I carefully tended to every birthday as though it were a grand celebration. It was my way of once a year reminding my daughters of how special they were to me.

By the time they were approaching adulthood, I had just about run out of party themes. We had celebrated the big sixteen the year before, now the seventeenth birthday was approaching and I wanted to celebrate with an intimate party. Kellie agreed and invited a few of her friends to join us for a birthday lunch celebration after church.

My focus this year and gift to Kellie was the meal itself. Although I had made many birthday dinners, I wanted this one to be special because she was growing out of the little girl birthday parties.

I had found a Martha Stewart's recipe for lasagna in, of all places, K-Mart. I decided it sounded so elegant that I would use this as my main entree. It was different than anything I had ever made before; in fact, I was a little intimidated by the many steps and ingredients. I studied the recipe and tried to imagine the taste it would produce for my guests. After many hours of worrying over this, I decided to change a few things and give it a try.

Creating a new dish with noise and interruptions can produce a failure. I managed to find some alone time and work on the lasagna dish. It turned out to be the most beautiful Italian lasagna I had ever made. I enjoyed every minute of all the separate preparations. I felt like I was going to be serving a true cuisine dish.

Before Kellie got home the afternoon before her birthday, I had managed to set the table. This was as important as the lasagna. Setting the table is my way of creating memories for my children. This was no ordinary birthday-girl table. It was a statement of adulthood. It said, "You are splendid." It honored her beauty, her growth, her becoming a young woman. All those who would be seated next to her were those who cared for her and who had shared in her growth.

When Kellie arrived home and saw the table set for the next day, she stood for a moment and took it all in. This was the first part of her gift; the other half would arrive when the seats were filled and the sharing of food and laughter and love began. This was a gift of experience, her very first of many to come in her life.

Our lunch was perfect. The lasagna was even better than I had anticipated, and our entire table of guests agreed it was unique. We shared birthday cake, and Kellie opened her gifts. At the end, she opened all of her cards and found a message from me. She cried. She realized that I understood she was growing up and that I was honoring her. It was a beautiful day.

# Pleased as Punch to Have You for My Brunch

If you asked me what my favorite meal or event is for entertaining; I would jump at the chance to tell you its brunch. And to make it even better, I take it outside to the garden.

When you take the party outdoors, grass and trees give color and lushness, and flowers add sweet smells like gifts from nature, right there in your garden. Setting a romantic or country table in the garden can be simply fun! I start with the tables, either many tables placed together to make one long table or several oblong tables spaced intimately. I drape them with anything from a collection of quilts to shimmering organza. Mix-and-match china or all-white plates go well with mixed bouquets set in mason jars or china pitcher. I bring out the old chairs from the dining room to add to the collection I keep in storage. I always set up a beverage station and plenty of lawn chairs for a relaxed feeling. When my guests arrive late Sunday morning, they arrive to the sound of my waterfall and classical music.

My favorite brunch is on Easter morning. I add a row of wheat grass down the center of the table and line it with porcelain bunnies and jelly beans. I fill giant plastic eggs with money and candy along with a couple dozen other smaller plastic eggs and hide them for the children to find. While mom and dad are visiting, the children are having fun looking for eggs.

When it's time to eat, the guests serve themselves from an enormous buffet or pass serving dishes family style at the table. The wonderful thing about entertaining is that no two parties have to ever be the same.


To find all the brunch recipes go to Brunch Celebrations Chapter.

*"He who thanks but with the lips
Thanks but in part;
The full, the true Thanksgiving
Comes from the heart.
~J.A. Shedd ~*

# Take a Gander at Our Thanksgiving Feast

I not only inherited many of my family's recipes, but also my grandmother's talent as a host. Two of my passions are cooking and entertaining. They just seem to go together. And since Thanksgiving is everyone's favorite feast, it's my favorite time of the year to cook for those I love. I would say on everyone's favorite eating holiday, I am in my element.

I start a few days before with the preparations. Our family wants the old-fashioned menu. Each year, I add something new to my Thanksgiving repertoire. No one minds the addition, and some don't notice just as long as there is lots of it—that's the must on this day of days.

The stuffing is everyone's favorite, and it usually takes an hour or two to make. I prepare the cranberries, the Jell-O mousse, some of the casseroles, and the pies ahead of time. On Thanksgiving Day, I wake up very early and stuff the turkey and then get it in the oven. I work in the kitchen for a while trying to finish up any last preparations.

Sometime in the morning I set the table. This to me is as important as the meal. I think a beautifully set table on Thanksgiving is a statement that the meal will be bountiful. The linen napkins, china, crystal, silver, and special serving dishes somehow embellish the food to be served. It has always been my favorite time to let my family know that they are special.

As guests arrive, football is heard in one room, while lovely music comes from another, along with the sounds of laughter, gossip, and the noise of dishes going in and out of the oven. All the while, the kitchen is full of familiar aromas, and the turkey smells better and better. Someone offers to baste the turkey, and then someone else, and soon too many guest fill up my kitchen space. As I try to find jobs for my helpers, hopefully in another room. I am reminded why I do most of the preparation the day before. Finally, it is time to eat.

My girls grew up with lots of friends joining us for this celebration and lots of guests around our table. We held hands around that table and shared our gratitude and asked for God's blessing to surround us all. They have memories of games played for hours and dessert being served at least twice.

I noticed years ago that Thanksgiving doesn't go on and on like Christmas does. Everyone leaves early the next day, Christmas shopping or traveling home. Why, then, is it such an important celebration?

I am reminded of the movie *Planes, Trains, and Automobiles*. In it, Thanksgiving was around the corner, and actor Steve Martin would have done anything to get home to his family. He learned many lessons about himself in his struggle to get back. When he finally arrives and sees the faces behind the door greeting him, he understands. As he looks around the room and embraces each family member, he realizes that nothing—not his work, his ego, not even the feast everyone's waiting for—is as important as his family. He learned compassion, kindness, and humanity and brought it home along with a new friend. He grew a new heart.

If Thanksgiving were important enough to get home to, I would think it's not just the feast, but also the splendor of hearts connecting…enough to last all year.

Our families' treasured Thanksgiving recipes can be found in the
Take a Gander at Our Thanksgiving Feast Chapter.

# Sweet Potatoes ~ Cajun Style

What do Thanksgiving and crispy sweet potatoes have in common? Everything. What would a table set with your family's finest china and grandma's specialty be like without those sweet potatoes? It would be like showing up and not passing the cranberry sauce.

Whether you like 'em or not, your mother always made you taste the sweet potatoes. When you think about it, most folks just pass the sweet potatoes on to the nearest person, just like the cranberry sauce. So for years, good cooks have been trying to come up with a sweet potato recipe that would not just be passed, but really eaten!

I have seen just about every version of cooked sweet potato possible. Every year someone has found what they think is going to change the taste of those traditional spuds. I was one of those cooks, until I tasted Katie's formula.

I first tasted this sensational potato one Christmas dinner my daughter and I shared with our friends the Hadley's. I waited for awhile, not wanting to pay to much attention to what I thought was sweet potatoes, before I asked, "Who brought this dish?" Katie, who held a reputation as a distinguished cook, proudly answered it was her recipe. I had guessed as much, and before the night was over I knew I had to find out what exactly was in this masterpiece.

The following Thanksgiving was approaching. My best bud, Diana, and her husband, Jim, my daughters Korrie and Katie and Korrie's boyfriend, Brian, flew to Washington to spend this holiday with my oldest daughter, Kellie. I could not find the recipe when I was packing, and I was not going to settle for any other sweet potato on this year's festive table. I called Katie and, for the second time, she dictated the ingredients.

Our visit was days of laughter and food preparation. On the big day, as always, I had many things going all at once, and the sweet potatoes were one of them. Because they are topped with corn flakes and because I forgot them in the oven, I served what looked like crispy, brown flakes, not potatoes! I was not happy, afraid no one would even try this dish after I had spent two days convincing everyone of its worth.

When I set the dish down on the hot pad, Kellie's friend Holly looked at them and said, "Oh look, Cajun potatoes." Everyone burst into laughter! I really think the laughter drew so much attention to the dish that everyone decided they had to try them. They were glad they did.

Kellie said they were a must, and Diana called the following Thanksgiving to get the recipe because Jim asked for those potatoes.

It was amazing that even with the burnt topping, everyone loved them. I suggest you prepare the sweet potatoes the "Katie" way, but remember they will be eaten Cajun style...just in case you forget they are in the oven. Happy Thanksgiving!

The Sweet Potato Soufflé recipe can be found in the Take a Gander at Our Thanksgiving Feast Chapter.

# Warming Up the House with Homemade Pies

*Thanksgiving is the perfect time to enjoy pie as the sweet aroma that travels throughout the house grabs hold of any guest who enters; telling them pie will be served here today.*

When we moved to Paradise in 1980, we left behind our best friends, Sue and Larry, and their children, Neil and Sybil. The first Thanksgiving we celebrated in our new home brought Sue and Larry, and for the next seven years in a row, they drove five hundred miles to sit at our table.

They usually arrived the night before. I always had dinner or snacks set out along with the first pumpkin pie to start off the holiday. Larry is a big guy and can eat a pie in one setting and not blink.

Each year I made several pies, but it seemed like it was never enough. The first was eaten when they arrived, and then everyone consumed another pie before we even ate the holiday dinner. And each year, my family would complain that we didn't have enough dessert.

The third year and every year after that, I made more desserts. When our friends arrived they found that I had made fourteen pumpkin pies, a chocolate orange cheesecake, a peach cobbler, an apple cobbler, a white and dark chocolate raspberry tart, an apple pie, and an orange chiffon pie. I had so many pies that I had to lay a sheet on the living room floor and let them cool off until I could put them away in our extra refrigerator. I did get a little carried away, but I enjoyed every moment of the preparation because of the anticipation I felt. I knew I would get a reaction when everyone walked through the door! I would not know the exact words to accurately describe the expression on the faces of our friends. The best I can do is say they were very much speechless and, to use the old expression, dumbfounded. I looked up at Larry and said, "Well, do you think this might be enough dessert for you??"

I know this is hard to believe, and I don't have an answer for this either, but I remember that we came close to finishing all of the desserts—please don't tell anyone!

The dessert recipes of the infamous 1982 Thanksgiving can be found in the Sweet Treat, Thanksgiving and Christmas Spice Chapters.

*Do not put off till tomorrow what can be enjoyed today.*
*~ Josh Billings ~*

# Holiday Friendship Gathering

It seemed like such a long time since I had really spent time with my friends; we are all so busy and in the month of December time is valuable and women are careful where they use it. I really wanted to create a mini getaway as a gift and a small friendship connection, even for just a few hours. So I came up with the perfect plan!

I made a simple meal of light and yummy appetizers and a hearty leek and sweet potato soup, butter leaf lettuce salad, and a gingerbread bundt cake with pumpkin butter. I knew that in this busy season, my friends would only be able to spare a few hours in their busy schedule, so it was important that when they arrived they didn't have to wait while I was still preparing the meal. I set the stage with garland and lights lit around the front door, the banister on the porch and candles lit and sitting on the walk way. When they entered the Christmas music was playing and the tree was bursting with brilliant colors from the ornaments that reflected the glow of the lights. On my large pine coffee table sat tall silver candle sticks, the appetizers on silver trays, a small glass punch bowl, a silver ice bucket with champagne and white wine and champagne flutes. The soup was warming on the stove with a hint of cinnamon spice in the air. The girls joined right in and helped themselves to the spread waiting for them on the pine table. The laughter and conversation began when I gave them their surprise.

In my office waited two talented people, a Massage Therapist and a Reflexologist. They were ready to take turns with their treatments on all of the girls. A waterfall, soothing music and white lights made the room calm and relaxing. While one received a neck massage the other sipped champagne, closed her eyes and felt her stress leave thru her toes. The girls were so surprised and felt special just like I wanted them to feel. The evening was not long, but enough to connect during the season and stop and feel the magic.

The key was making the meal light, simple and ready when my friends arrived.

And because they liked the soup so much, you will find the recipe in the Soup Chapter under: Pumpkin-Potato-Leek and Roasted Sweet Potato Soup.

*In the years of our childhood, Mama stored the hard Arkansas Black apples that had set in her closet from December until spring. Daddy and Grandpa carried the burlap bags of apples out into our kitchen, filling the entire house with their hearty, fruity fragrance.*
*~ Jane Watson Hopping ~*

# Adam's Apple

I love apple anything, and apple pie is one of my favorite comfort foods. I also like applesauce, but prefer it to have more texture… more of a bite! Sometime ago I added sugar, nutmeg, cinnamon, and a little apple juice instead of water to my pot of cut-up apples. When they were finished cooking, I turned off the fire, left the lid on, and forgot about the mashing. Hours later, when I remembered the apples sitting on the stove, I dipped my spoon in for a taste. I can't believe I didn't eat the whole pot of goodness. It tasted just like a bite of homemade apple pie.

I decide to keep the apple's chunky texture. I served the applesauce in one of my grandmothers antique glass bowls and put it on our Thanksgiving table. It looked so old fashioned, with a sense of warmth. Sure enough, someone at the table said, "This tastes like apple pie."

This last Thanksgiving I spent with my oldest daughter and family in their farmhouse in Enumclaw, Washington and we cooked for thirty-four of us, and my chunky applesauce was part of the menu. When Nicole, my six-year-old granddaughter, ate all of the applesauce on her plate, she said, "I want some more of Grammy's applesauce." I was pleased.

Not mashing the apples and leaving the chunks in added the bite I wanted and also grabbed my heart.

*Our joy is connected to our giving; the closest thing to God's heart.*
*~ Joel Osteen ~*

# SEASONED SOULS

Sometimes it is said that Christmas is for kids, and that is mostly true. Put a room full of seniors together for a senior Christmas party, and a room full of kids show up.

On Christmas 2000, I was setting yet another table of joyous celebration. The Christmas decorations gave the house a spark of cheerfulness, one I wanted to jump out at the seniors who would be walking through the door that evening. Six of the seniors I wrote life stories for would be allowing me to spread what I was hoping was a large amount of Christmas magic upon them.

Elmer, Doris, Frank, Lucille, Ruby, and Iris arrived in the glorious splendor of old age. They were taken back to their youth when they saw the decorations, smelled the festive aroma of favorite foods, and heard the sounds of the season as Bing Crosby sang, "White Christmas." It was when they all noticed the table set in their honor with place cards that held each of their names that they began to feel the special I worked for.

We played some games, and then shared who we were before we seated ourselves to the table. As I brought out each course and set it in front of them, I heard the little sighs and aah's whisper from their lips. My joy of the evening was watching them, faces shadowed by age and lit by joy. These were the souls who fought for our country, who waited for peace, who lived through the Depression and the hardest times our country has ever faced. Each one of these beautiful seniors had lost a loved one or child and faced abandonment, loss, war, grief, and joy the old-fashioned way. And these incredible people who sat before me at my table had allowed and trusted me with the privilege of sharing their lives. This was a generation that had taught the meaning of sacrifice, and that message rang loud in my mind and reminded me of the honor we need to keep in our families and our country.

Some of the seniors shared their favorite childhood Christmas memories while the rest of us listened. We completed the evening with dessert and a gift exchange that brought out the little child in each one of us. Oh, how they spread a laughter that made the room sparkle brighter than the twinkle lights or the candles glowing on the table.

All six of my precious seniors experienced an evening in their honor. It was nothing less than magical, and the love magic was felt down to their souls. The magic made them feel special—the special I wanted to give because they had given their entire lives.

*Teach us delight in simple things...*
*~ Rudyard Kipling*

# BIRTHDAY - POTLUCK - GATHERING

It seems I have been cooking for a long time, probably most of my life. It would feel strange for me to not be planning some type of event, party, or special meal. But every now and then it is nice and so appreciated when someone else prepares a meal for me.

For the longest time, I have wanted to have a potluck lunch for my birthday. How nice it would be for all of the people who love me to make their special dishes or my favorite foods and serve me. I had requested this birthday treat before, but it seemed to get vetoed every time I brought the idea up for discussion. Soon, we were all seated at another wonderful restaurant celebrating another year to come.

Finally, this year, I just called all of my friends and family up and told them I was having a potluck birthday party. For some reason, no one tried to tell me it wasn't special enough and seemed excited about the idea and what he or she were bringing.

My birthday is in December, so the tree is always up and the house feels festive. I decorated one large Victorian tree and four other small trees, each with themes. Friends arrived with the main dish to the dessert in hand. I took a picture of each person arriving at the door entrance. I was not allowed in the kitchen while my cooking crew prepared their dishes to be displayed on the buffet table. When it was time to eat, each of the chefs served my portion on the dinner plate for me. Heather, who has helped me in catering, made a baked Alaskan cake and brought it to me with the candles lit. All the details were taken care of by everyone else.

This was a birthday I had wanted for a long, long time. I wanted to feel the birthday magic, and I did. There is something wholesome, real, and genuinely authentic about a potluck gathering. Put glistening lights, Christmas spirit, and the magic of giving hearts together, and it makes for a wholehearted zestful experience.

If you have a birthday that is near a busy time of the month or a holiday, and you know everyone is tired of shopping and short of money, ask your friends to bring his or her best dish and watch how wonderful it makes you feel!

The birthday menu can be found in the Treasure Trove of Menus Chapter.
Nancy's Minestrone Soup is found in Soup Comforts.
Heather's Baked Alaskan Cake is in the Sweet Treats Chapter.
Enjoy!

*Your life stands as a monument,*
*    Your memory as a monolith,*
*Your blessings as sunbeams along life's path…*
*Unknown ~*

# Barn Party

Have you ever loved someone so much for whom they are and for what they have given to you that you wanted to give back to them ten-fold the same love? Love in a gift. How do you figure out what that extraordinary package would contain?

The answer is easy. Ask yourself what makes this person the happiest in the world, and there you will find their passion and your gift to them.

My friend Tim was not hard to figure out, but took some planning to make the perfect gift come together. Tim is the best father I have ever met. Just to watch his two grown children, Lisa and Brian, with Tim are magical. And that is what I knew I had to create—a magical party with the three of them together. There is nothing that Tim would enjoy more than spending his birthday with his kids.

Lisa and Brian live about six hundred miles away from their father, and getting them here took some planning and secrecy on everyone's part. So the phone calls and emails started, and we were on our way. Somehow two months of planning was kept a secret, and even his extended family living in Arizona never breathed a word of it.

I had planned to have the party in my backyard; garden setting with the twinkle lights and sounds of the waterfall and beautiful music to serenade us through the night. I worked for a month in the yard getting it ready and making everything perfect for May ninth. The week of the party, I had two catering jobs. Between the jobs, I needed to clean my house, wrap gifts, prepare food, and do all the rest of the tasks on the endless list I had hidden out of Tim's sight for the last two months. The day before the party, it rained. Not just normal rain, but a powerful downpour with thunder storms. The forecast predicted rain on the ninth of May also, the day of the party. I was so tired from all the work and stress that I found it hard to figure out what to do. I had my mind set on a garden party, and I also knew it would be hard to get all the people on the guest list comfortably in my home.

On one side of my house is a very large, tall shop. I quickly decided I was going to turn that large room into a barn, and I did. Two friends, Brenda and Heather, came over, and we hung white sheets up over a rope and made it the backdrop. We stored all the junk and shop things behind the sheets. Brenda strung lights across the walls. We put old wood everywhere and bales of hay outside and all over the cement floor. In the middle I placed the large picnic table, where we would enjoy our celebration dinner. There were lanterns and anything else that looked like it belonged in a country scene, including an old claw-foot bathtub for his gifts. We decorated in the rain and made just that a memory.

I had told Tim I was taking him away, and so he met me at the house. The guests, including his beautiful children, were waiting for him in the barn. I led Tim by his hand around the side of the house with his eyes closed. He thought he was about to see one of his gifts before we left.

When I said "open," he tried to focus, but by that time, Lisa and Brian were already in his arms. This sight was magical. This was what I had anticipated. The love gift I wanted to give him was in his arms, and there was silence in the barn, and some tears. This was a gift in Tim's arms that sent a heart message to him: "You are special."

The old building will never be the same, but we will always carry the love shared there that night in our hearts. Love can be shared anywhere.

The Barn Party Menu cam be found in the Treasure Trove of Menus Chapter.

*Nothing creates a firmer belief in heredity than
having a beautiful daughter. ~Anonymous ~*

# BRIDAL LUNCHEON

I was honored to be a part of giving my daughter Korrie's bridal shower. It was all part of the dream a mother has, just like the daughter, concerning every aspect of her wedding plans. It was my delight to prepare the food for the bridal luncheon.

The shower was held at my friend Candy's beautiful home overlooking the canyon. We set up several tables outside with white linen, and Candy made exquisite flower arrangements for each table. I framed different pictures of Brian and Korrie in small gold frames with large bows. I set these on the tables next to the flower vases. I set up a long table on one side of the deck, where I displayed an array of pictures in silver and pewter frames of Korrie and Brian as children and as a couple. The beverage table was skirted with a luscious garden vintage print and topped with ivory linen. On the table was a silver punch bowl and one of the most beautiful flower arrangements I've ever seen. The florist used peach tulips; coral and white stalk, white lizianthus, lavender, larkspur, and peach and ivory roses in the arrangement, and the coral flowers matched the fabric.

The food table was a gala affair decorated in a Victorian theme. I created heights and themes all along the lengthy table. I used a Victorian rose-print fabric on top of a taupe background. The presentation gave the look of polished art at its finest. I created everything I had envisioned in my heart for my daughter.

Preparing the food called for time, creativity, and organization. I did not go to bed the entire night, and I loved every minute of it. I had waited for this day, and now it was here. The food was prepared with the same hands that first held this beautiful woman, the same hands that cared for her all her life—nothing had changed.

Brian's mother and I presented Korrie with a

piece of the past while opening her gifts. I covered pieces of cardboard with ivory satin, and on one of them was a crochet piece that Brian's great aunt had made. On the other was one of Korrie's great grandmother's hankies, the one she held in her hand as she took her wedding vows eighty years ago. I typed out the information and attached it at the bottom of each. This was an emotional moment.

The idea of giving something so wonderful to your child is formed in the heart, and the love pushes the idea into view. A mother's love never stops giving of her heart, for all of her days.

The Bridal Luncheon menu is found in the Treasure Trove of Menus Chapter.

*Where love is concerned, too much is not even enough.*
*~ Pierre-Augstin de Beaumarchairs ~*

# WEDDING DRESS FASHION SHOW LUNCHEON

My daughter Korrie flew to Seattle, Washington, to find her dream wedding dress. Korrie probably tried on every dress in the fabulous boutique while her sister Kellie critiqued each one. Korrie kept coming back to the one with the biggest skirt, which made her feel like a princess. She ordered the Vera dress, shoes, tiara, and the jewelry. It would take awhile for it to be sent to California, but there was time.

The day came when the dress arrived, and no one, not even her mother or bridesmaids, knew what the dress looked like. Korrie and I decided to make a fun afternoon out of the dress's arrival.

We invited the bridesmaids and a couple of friends for the unveiling of her wedding attire. To make it fun, I planned a luncheon at the home of one of Korrie's friends. It was March and raining, so I thought warm soup would be good start. I made copies of a picture of Korrie and Brian and placed them in petite frames next to each place setting on the table. I also placed gift bags with lotions and girlie stuff in them. I wanted each bridesmaid to feel like a special friend and a part of the celebration.

We enjoyed the lunch and gifts, and then it was time for Korrie to change into her dress and jewels and unveil herself to us. We waited and waited, and finally the hallway door was opened and the princess bride stepped out. So many sighs escaped our lips, followed by applause. She looked stunning as she paraded up and down the room just like when she was a little princess years before in dress-up clothes.

We ended the day by all driving over to the bridal shop and all of the girls trying on their dresses for the wedding. It was truly a magical day of fun and girlie-girl bliss!

The Cream of Asparagus soup served this day can be found in the Soup Comforts Chapter.

*Zest is the secret of all beauty.*
   *There is no beauty that is attractive without zest.*
*~ Christian Dior ~*

# THIRTY AND BEAUTIFUL

It was hard to believe that my daughter Korrie was about to turn thirty. It made me feel old, and when I looked at her, I could see she had grown more beautiful—from the inside out.

I asked Korrie if I could give her a sit-down, served dinner party, and she was elated at the idea. We invited twelve guests, and I planned a menu.

I set a table that glistened with the soft luster of light from about a dozen candles, the romance of pale peach roses all tightly tucked in a pewter container. There were place settings with each guest's name written on place cards in calligraphy. To the left of each serving plate sat a salad with a small mold of lemon mousse on top. I strung white lights through the trees behind the dinning room table. It was a perfect celebration setting.

Guests arrived to appetizers and drinks and soft music. I managed to get everyone seated while I watched each guest pause and take in the beauty of the table prepared for the party. Korrie's husband Brian stood to give his beautiful wife a birthday toast. I began the serving, and the guests settled as the glint of the evening began to shine in the sparkle from the candles and the inner celebrating light. This was an evening that touched not just the birthday girl, but also each guest. Everyone felt honored.

Korrie finished the evening with cake and birthday candles, gifts, and a limousine ride out on the town.

The Thirty and Beautiful birthday menu can be found in the
Treasure Trove of Menus Chapter.

*A daughter is God's sparkle of love, of light, of laughter within the heart of a family.*
  *~ Anonymous ~*

# THE TIE

    Kellie was turning fourteen and she and I worked on a theme for her party. We decided it was going to be way out there because it was so different. She was a little worried some of her junior high school friends would think it was not cool. The invitations were made with a cutout tie on the front. On the inside the instructions told each invited guest to wear a men's tie. This got all the girls going because the word got out that there would be prizes given for different facets of the ties. Kellie was surprised that her friends thought this was such a good idea. The girls quickly got busy trying to con their dads out of their best, hideous or worst tie hanging in their closets.

    When Kellie's guests arrived they walked in wearing huge smiles and outfits designed around the tie they wore. To their surprise they stepped into a restaurant in our living room. Tables were set up with cloths, napkins folded, crystal and silver flatware and flowers in the center of the tables. Waiters popped out of nowhere and held their arm out to each guests and asked them to be seated. As they seated her they handed each girl a menu that read, "Carte du Jour." When the menus were opened I heard a lot of giggles and comments because no one could figure out what in the world the selections were. Soon the waiters with their stiff white shirts and aprons tied around the waist showed up at each table asking for the guests order. The girls were laughing and asking what was a pig foot or the shoestring? Orders were complete and the chef (that was me) prepared the plates, but when they arrived in front of each setting, the faces were looks of shock, disappointment, and panic as though they were not going to get a good meal. Quickly it turned into laughter, because a plate might have a carrot slice, a pickle and a chip or three olives and a piece of broccoli. The ordering continued for about an hour and finally the waiters took pizza to each table and there was applause in the air. The birthday dinner was so much fun that everyone forgot about the ties they were wearing. The parents voted and gave prizes for the tie that looked most like it should be worn in church, the most flamboyant, most colorful, and the tie that should never be worn again!

    Fun, fun, fun, shared; another birthday memory celebrating with ties of friendship and laughter and lots of love on those plates. I recommend parties like this that makes a girl feel special.

# Dear Sandy:

This is a thank you note I received from a guest who along with many other friends shared a garden dinner in my home. I share this with you because it emanates the power and pleasure of sharing a meal together. The following is a message from my friend Marte:

*Dear Sandy,*

*It was such a delight to visit your home-what a warm and homey place it is! It was such fun poking here and there and always finding treasures.*

*The food was delicious-as we knew it would be! But it did more than fill our appetite, it filled our soul. I had forgotten what a delight it is to get together with friends and spend time just "being" together-I had forgotten how social a shared meal can be. Thanks for remembering me!*

*Though the evening was relaxing, refreshing and renewing for us I know that it took much effort on your part. I console myself with the thought that you seem actually to enjoy entertaining us all. It rests my soul to remember.*

*Once again, thank you very much for the delicious meal, but thank you also for the shared moments!*

*Fondly,*
*Marte*

*Chapter 3*

# Tradition

# A Journey to Remember

*"If you bring forth what is within you,
what you bring forth will save you."*
—*The Gospel of Thomas*

Imagine finding your way into the attic of an old house; your hand brushes back the cobwebs as you look around and see in front of you pieces of time past, someone's past. You're still standing at the top step when your eye rests on an old tattered trunk. Of all the treasures in the dusty room, you are most drawn to the mystery inside of this trunk. The old piece is made of tin and held together with strips of wood that you can hardly recognize because of the years of dust layered upon it. Kneeling next to this piece of history, your mind wonders and envisions where this old trunk has traveled. Was it transported from a ship or carried on the back of a stagecoach? How did it climb to the top of this old house? If only it could talk, what stories it would tell you. Taking hold of the dilapidated leather handle, you carefully pull to open the top.

The inside is well preserved. The hint of lavender slowly fills the air you breathe while the extravagance of Victorian lace shapes the walls of this box, holding in those artifacts of the past. You continue to search further until you find old letters bound with string, poetry books, folklore, hankies, a quilt, and faded faces in photographs. Feeling drawn to these things that tie you to some stranger's life, you try to envision what story lies behind these pieces in front of you like a large puzzle. Searching, your eye falls upon a collection of notebooks; the mystery beckons you—what lies inside these now frayed and threadbare old books? Slowly turning, you find pages and pages of sentiments, recipes, and stories of established traditions within a family. As you read through the handwritten notes, you begin to discover the beliefs, observances, formal and informal practices that were customary among the people you are reading about. Someone took the time to write down this family's favorite pastimes, some of which your own family has shared and others you find new desire to partake in, even as you sit holding their life treasure.

Traditions in families vary and can be as simple as a Fourth of July picnic in the same park every year or as formal as spiritual traditions. Every family creates its own customs along its journey. Tradition acknowledges relationships and makes a contribution to feed our souls. Some things do not change, and one of those things is the human heart. Everything we create will be remembered tomorrow. In our need to "make it" in this world, we have forgotten our families. This realization should humble us as parents and as the children of generations past who have given us the greatest example of hope and character. Why would we not want to hold onto these traditions?

I invite you to explore what the generations before you did to celebrate family and to begin to create your own *special* traditions to be remembered in your family member's hearts as the family's legacy.

I have had an old steamer trunk, just like the one I asked you to imagine discovering, for over thirty years. My kids think it is a large piece of junk. When I am old and carry very little with me, that trunk will be one of my last possessions I will leave behind. Someday, my girls and grandchildren will open it and find my heart in volumes inside. If they don't know me now or if the memories of our family have faded, they will find us there among my keepsakes. Every hope, dream, accomplishment, talent, failure, tear I've cried, family memory, and history will be left inside. Our children see us as parents, when we pass they learn who we really are—the human spirit from the inside out. The truth is…our story won't let us go.

# Generations - Passing the Hanky

*If past events have left their trace, it is likely
that future events have their roots in the present.*

My granddaughter Nicole sat in an oversized chair under an antique floor lamp. She had just enough light to examine each square piece of fabric her precious little seven-year-old fingers held up towards the lamp.

I sat in the chair across from her, in awe of what I was watching. There was a fourth generation looking at the very hanky collection I did forty-eight years ago.

The memory weaved in and out of my heart: my small fingers touching the same pieces of cloth as Nicole touched now. The Victorian box sitting on Nicole's lap held the treasures I coveted and longed for as a seven-year-old child. Inside the box were the many hankies my grandmother Stella accumulated through out her young and adult life, like the pieces of her journey.

Many years ago, I sat holding the same collection asking my grandmother if I was going to be the one to get these beautiful hankies some day. She always answered, "We'll see."

In her day, the hanky represented many things, especially a friendship token. The box held the linen hanky with the soft ivory and yellow tatting that she carried down the aisle in the 1900s. It held the silk hanky with the American flag next to the word "Sis" that her brother, a solider in World War I, had sent to Stella. There was a collection of keepsakes lying in this special box, and each could tell a story of love and friendship.

Nicole continued to take each one out and hold it up to the light as she examined it. She carefully folded each hanky back to its original square and went on to the next. Every now and then she would look over at me, and finally she said, "Grammy, who do you think is going to get these some day?" She was still looking at me while holding the box when I said, "Oh, probably you." She just smiled and continued on.

That night we made hot chocolate and sipped it out of real teacups, just like I did with my grandmother. We talked about the hankies, and I told her stories of my childhood with my grandmother. I realized this little girl already valued the same things I did. It was truly like going back into time.

Since then Nicole has gone to antique stores with her mother and bought and sent me hankies. I have sent her hankies in the mail, and she has started a collection of her own. My grandmother would send me a hankie inside a card every time she wrote to me. During my last visit with Nicole, we made a special hankie box for her collection. We collected old costume jewelry and glued the pieces over the entire box. It glistened, just like Nicole did as she looked at it.

The following is one of my grandmother's recipes that would go well with hot chocolate, hugs, and memories. Take time to create something special from your past with your grandchild. They will protect it with their heart, just like I did. A few years ago, I went through the box of Stella's hankies, and at the bottom I found all the cards and letters I had written to her as a little girl. She planned all along to give me the collection. Standing there with the cards in my hand was like having Nana hand them to me and allowed me to experience the bond between us once again. I felt so special at that moment, the biggest heart kind of special there is.

My grandmother's Banana Nut Bread recipe is found in the Brunch Chapter.

# Cell Phone:
# "Find Mom—I need help"

I get the call often. This time it is Korrie: "OK Mom, I'm in the bread aisle. How many packs of these buns do I need to buy for fifty hamburgers?"

I replied, "You didn't bring your calculator?" She didn't answer, so I just gave her the information.

She said, "Thanks, I'll call you when I get to the veggies." An hour before that call, she had called to ask what she should buy for her office's barbeque on Saturday.

All my girls call me on my cell phone constantly, to ask for a recipe, when they are grocery shopping and have a question about what to buy. I love these calls, anytime, anywhere. I don't think its' because it's so easy to answer, but that they connect us to the place of family we know so well.

We have had hours of discussions on everything—psychology, decorating, gardening, children, friends and family - but they always end back at food and parties. As a mom, I am touched that my children feel comfortable enough to call me anywhere for a recipe—not write it down, just call mom. Most of all I know that when I am no longer able to cook someday, they will still ask me for the recipes. I hope they never write them down.

Recipes and food are our legacy that will now and forever keep tradition in our family. What is your legacy? What do your children love that you love? What do you do that they love sharing with you? Share it with them now, and you will share it forever.

# I Love You As Big As....

Korrie was about four years old when I heard her voice from the back seat of the car while I was driving, "I love you, Mommy, as big as the sky."

I replied, "I love you as big as the ocean." Then it was her turn.

She said, "Now what, Mommy?"

I thought for a moment, and with a big smile, I asked, "How about, we love each other as big as the whole wide world?"

She said, "Yes, yes, Mommy, that's it!"

And so that is how it began…our little words of love that spoke our own kind of love language were spoken over and over again until Korrie grew up. When she was twelve, I painted the words on paper and added a background of a rainbow, birds, and blue sky and put it in a frame. I will never forget Korrie opening that simple, homemade gift—when her eyes fell upon the words, then looked up to find me in the room, they were filled with tears. No one but us knew what the silly little scribbling meant to the heart.

I made a story quilt for Korrie and embroidered the words on one of the squares, and she designed a scrapbook page for a memory book for me with our sentimental verse. Every mother and child creates their own kind of playfulness, laughter, and sentiment; it's their signature of love between them.

*"I love you as big as the sky.*
*I love you as big as the ocean.*
*We love each other as big as the whole wide world."*
*Mommy and Korrie*
*- 1976*

# King of the Squash: A Bowl of Tradition

When the girls were young, I always celebrated every season and holiday with zest and something to remember it by. Autumn brought glorious colors, crunchy leaves, and lots of pumpkins in a variety of sizes and colors. Just before Halloween, I would cut the top off of a very round pumpkin and clean the inside out. Then I would make some kind of fall soup or wonderful stew. When it was time to serve dinner, I put the main dish inside the pumpkin with a ladle and set it in the middle of our table. This was a way to celebrate fall. I always made homemade biscuits and orange Jell-O. Using a cookie cutter I cut the Jell-O into pumpkin shapes.

Several times, I made what is called a five-hour stew. It was everybody's favorite and one of the first recipes I made on my own, at about age 18.

After dinner, our family would carve out the Halloween pumpkins ready to light up our front porch. The meal in the pumpkin set the stage for the carving and created a fall tradition, a custom the girls will pass down to their children.

The following is one of the recipes I used for filling the fall pumpkin that sat on our table with honor.

Five Hour Stew is found in the Best Sunday Dinners Chapter.

*If success could be measured in the act of giving to others,*
 *Then you ,Madge and Lee are the stars in the galaxy of greatness.*

# BIRTHDAY DESSERT

"What do you want for dessert?" For Madge's granddaughter Lindsey, this question will always be synonymous with home. The question is almost like a riddle or a special game played between just the two of them because Madge knows the answer she is going to hear on the other end of the phone: "Grandma, I want your peach cobbler."

Lindsey grew up with her grandmother's good cooking and remembers hearing stories of her grandpa hiding Madge's mincemeat pies at Thanksgiving time so his daughter wouldn't find them before he could eat the pies himself. Any kind of chicken Grandma made, Lindsey would eat. Before their Sunday fried chicken dinners, Lindsey loved to open the container of biscuits because of the popping sound. "Grandma would always hand it to me and then run!" She remembers that on her birthday her grandma made her a birthday dinner and dessert—it was just what Madge did for her granddaughter.

Although Lindsey was almost raised in her grandmother's kitchen, one day she feared that she really didn't know how to cook. She thought to herself, "I really should be in Grandma's kitchen learning from her." What she didn't realize was that by growing up under Madge's feet, she was in cooking school all her life. Lindsey remembers that her grandmother didn't need to measure; she cooked with her heart, and that meant a pinch of this and a dash of that. "Grandma adds her own formality to cooking; she's from the South and adds her own Southern flair to it. And I love it that she tells me, 'Well, I think it needs a little bit of this and that.'"

Lindsey recalls when, during a visit to her Grandma's house about four years ago, Madge brought out old pictures of herself and Lindsey's Grandpa Lee. She spread them over the table and began to share her life. Lindsey found herself crying, overwhelmed with the simplicity and beauty of her grandparents' life. While looking at the pictures, it seemed to her that life had had more purpose in her grandmother's day. As she studied them, she wished that she could have lived in her grandparents' time.

She studied the two faces in the pictures. The love and devotion they shared years ago became profound to her now, because it is the same love they share today. She told her grandma that all she knew from this generation was divorce. Looking at those pictures gave Lindsey new insight into their lives. She realized their life has given Lindsey grounding in her own. Lindsey knows that her grandparent's mentality has been a staple for the family because of what they have brought to it. At Lindsey's young age, she has already gleaned much from the two people in the pictures on that table.

There are also memories of the garden and Grandma's roses. "I loved working and helping out in the garden. I would always pick the carrots. And Grandma would let me help trim the roses. When I was little, I used to think that the buds were dead roses—I didn't know they were going to open up. There was one rose bush that grandma had been babying because she couldn't get anything to bloom from it. Finally there was one purple bud on it, and she had been waiting and waiting for it to bloom. Well, I cut it! Poor Grandma."

Lindsey loves holidays with her family. She says regardless of tension or family problems, her family always pulls together. "I love it when the holidays are here at my Grandma's house because it feels like home to me."

Madge's Peach Cobbler recipe is found in the Sweet Retreat Chapter.

# Sacredness in the Home, Sanctuary in the Heart

For many years Kellie, Korrie, and I created a special night for God and us. Each week, we took turns planning the evening that involved togetherness, fun, food, and spirit. The rule was no TV; our activity was to be focused around the three of us in a relationship and nurturing our spirits.

We all enjoyed this immensely, and the girls never failed to contribute in creative ways. They designed their evening days before and always started the evening out with lighting candles and prayer. Somehow we began to make sacred moments before the fun began. There were discussions about our spirituality, feelings about how church and God made us feel, and mostly, how we felt connected to God and his love for us.

The evening always started off in the living room with all three of us kneeling around the coffee table. It was the consecrated place, like the altar in a church, where our hearts began the binding of relationship and spirit together. Two of us waited for the third to lead us in the ceremony. I loved watching my girls bring their sensitivity and faith of the infinite to the table in such a humble spirit for a child. It was truly beautiful, and I began to respect the passion they brought to the beginning and the sentiment it gave us at the end of the experience.

Years later, I realize how a simple little experiment turned into a powerful adventure within. The lesson cut between church and the temple within each of us. It provided a place where the girls felt safe in sharing their devotion and taught me that I need that sanctuary in my home and my heart. How perfect to call an idea and watch as it grows into a traditional blessing.

Prayer is a spiritual practice needed in our daily lives. Finding a special place in the home for prayer is refining sacred energy. It is humble and it is serious. I have created a comfortable, spiritual place I can go to each day and call upon God. When I am not home, I go to the sanctuary in my heart, and this is where all of us will truly find God.

# Keepsake Travel

I met Lucille through my personal historian business. Part of her life story is about her children, and five of them are daughters. Although Lucille is a senior, she is very active and loves to get up and go and travel with her daughters.

Each year, they all plan a short vacation somewhere together. The six of them have been doing it for so long that now it is a mother-daughter tradition. Each year, each of the girls has a different job—picking the location or the entertainment or which restaurant they will eat in. Even if they wind up in one of their homes for the weekend, they all plan it together. One of my favorite things they do is one of Lucille's daughters buys everyone the same girly PJs. They wear them and have a real slumber party. I have seen the pictures, and they are one big, delightful bunch.

I love to capitalize on a good thing. I decided my three girls, my granddaughter Nicole and I were going to start creating the same experience Lucille does. I made reservations for a week in Laguna Beach, our favorite vacation spot, at the Laguna Riviera Hotel. The four of us planned and schemed until we made it happen.

On our big day, Korrie, Katie, and I flew to Southern California and waited for Kellie and Nikki to fly in from Washington. We were all like little girls waiting for fun. When I saw Nikki and Kellie walk off the plane, the joy just spilled out of me and into their arms.

We rented a car, and beach-bound we were for seven glorious days. What fun we had over those days. We shopped and ate and talked and laughed and shopped some more, as only girls do. We found a jewel store that we bought treasures from and stayed up late into the night making bracelets. And then there were the quiet moments of listening to the waves below us, and the late evenings of deep woman discussion. And I surprised each of the girls with matching PJs and novels. They wore their PJs and lost themselves in the books.

Although I did prepare a few meals for them, and we had breakfast and coffee on our glorious beachfront every morning, we mostly ate out. It was wonderful not having to spend time cooking and cleaning and trying to fit in some visiting when you are so exhausted.

When the time came to leave, each of us on different flights, it was hard. By the end of the week, it felt as though we had gleaned years of togetherness, just like in the beginning before there were extended families. How wonderful to have all of my daughters together and to myself for one week. There were tears saying goodbye, but each of us was full inside.

I am so grateful for Lucille's idea and happy I paid attention to what brought them closer. There is nothing better for the soul than relationship connection. Now we have made it a tradition.

# Pizza, a Book, and a Movie: Love Repeats Itself

In my catering years, my youngest daughter, Katie, and I didn't have a lot of time to share. When we did, it was the same date every month. The bookstore, a slice of pizza at the mall, and a good movie with a pack of red vines was our favorite kind of fun.

Katie enjoyed dance class every day after school and spent half of her life on the phone with her friends, even from age eight to eleven. She looked forward to doing something different, just the two of us. There was not a lot of time for either of us, so we both felt comfortable with and looked forward to our usual outing. We started at the mall in the bookstore where Katie would go to her book section and I would go to cooking or self-help. After about forty-five minutes went by, Katie would show up with a couple of books in her hand, thinking she could bribe me into two instead of one. She usually did. After our purchase, we went around the corner to the food court and ordered a slice of pizza. We sat down and shared our worlds with each other. Sometimes we became so engrossed in our conversations that we would almost make ourselves late for the next stop, the movies.

We took turns choosing the movie, and I loved it when it was my choice because it was like having my best friend their watching it with me. Katie was very wise and old for her age. She has always had a fascination with actors and can remember every star and every movie they have played in. She would make a great movie critic. If I leaned over to ask her, "Who is that?" she knew the answer, but would tell me to hush! Then sometimes I would ask her what they said, and she would say, "Mom, be quiet!"

There we sat, eating popcorn and red vines. By the middle of the movie, her head was on my shoulder, not asleep, just snuggling with me.

Today when I go to the movies, I always remember this. It's funny when you don't have a lot of time how even the smallest efforts make a difference and then make a larger memory.

This week Katie called me up and said, "Mom, do you think we could take Mackenzie to the movies this week?" Mackenzie is Katie's daughter, my granddaughter. Love repeats itself.

# The Tent

August fourth every year the tent went up in the back yard. It was Katie's birthday and for eight years the tradition was a sleep over in the tent.

It started on her fifth birthday. I made the usual family favorites and invited all of her best friends from preschool for a slumber party. This year she asked me if they could sleep in the tent since they were older and not afraid. I thought how nice that would be that I might possibly get a few hours sleep and the giggles wouldn't be right next to my bedroom door. Well…it was a thought.

The party was every little girls delight with games, mom's cooking, Katie's favorite sprinkle cake design, piñata and gifts. Now the best part was to come but not for this mom. Parents kissed their darlings good-bye knowing they were in store for a quiet evening at home. The girls dragged their sleeping bags into the tent and slipped their pajamas on. The stars lit the sky and I saw a few yawns, making me think it would be quiet in about an hour. Wrong! Fitting eight girls in that small tent wasn't easy and of course all of them did not agree where they were going to sleep. After lengthy bedding down, we came to an agreement that they could talk all night as long as it was a whisper tone.

I settled down myself with the window next to my bed opened. I was about to drift off to sleep when the faint sound of voices I heard coming out of the tent. It began slowly with a few giggles that became mixed in with shrills and different tones of vocal excitement. After about thirty minutes I got up and went out side to quiet things down a bit. Half way to the tent I heard a shhhh sound echo in the back yard. By the time I stuck my head in the tent there wasn't a movement of bodies or lips. I said, "Girls, I know you are awake and I need you to be a little quieter so that you don't wake up the neighbors." No one answered. When the screen door closed behind me, I heard a burst of laughter. I said so they could hear me, "Quiet!" Not long after I went back to bed, the bathroom brigade started. Every time I was about to nod off the old screen door would slam shut. So I got up and decided that someone needed to be on duty and that was I. Stepped out side for about an hour on the patio enjoying the summer evening and they were still awake. Went inside and turned the TV on just knowing it would be any time and the gang would be in a tent of slumber. Not so. I think it was about four in the morning before this girly crew of five year olds drifted off. I opened the tent zipper and covered twisted bodies and put some heads on pillows. I smiled as I laid my head on the pillow thinking this would be over soon and we could say we did that one!

I did say that over and over for the next eight years in a row, but no was not the answer Katie wanted and good old mom gave in every August fourth. It was the same routine and I offered big themes, big ideas, but all she wanted was the same cake with the sprinkles and the tent up in the back yard. By the time she turned thirteen Katie had the same eight friends, and the same tent. Sleeping now meant their legs were hanging out of the tent. Katie made her own birthday tradition, I lost one night sleep a year and we have another wonderful memory.

# Who Has the Almond?

If your family celebrates Christmas with a special meal on Christmas Eve or the day of, try adding an almond for a flavorful memory.

When preparing your Christmas celebration dinner for your family, try adding some pudding to the menu one year. Instant, traditional, nutmeg bread pudding, or chocolate mousse served in individual dishes or glass flutes, sitting at each place setting. After the meal, ask everyone to partake in the new dessert, and when someone gets to the bottom of the dish and finds the almond you have placed there, hand him or her a special gift waiting on the table.

If your family celebrates on Christmas Eve, this is a great evening starter just before the opening of gifts. The special gift could be a video of last year's events, and everyone would enjoy watching it after the gifts are opened; or if your family consists of small children, perhaps a Christmas family video. If you start this tradition early, your children will look forward to it every year.

## Chapter 4

# *Among Friends There is Spirited Kinship*

☙

# Among Friends There is Spirited Kinship

*...It is that my friends have made my life. In a thousand ways they have turned my limitations into beautiful privileges.*
*~ Helen Keller ~*

Have you ever given thought to the why's of how a friend came into your life or the timing? When you start putting the pieces together, you realize there are no accidents in our lives. You look back at events or circumstances and you can usually see the presence of a friend there to help you through, like an angel sent on your behalf.

Girlfriends are the gifts whom wake us up when you've nearly given up on yourself and through it you end up feeling like family to your friend. Friends not only comfort us, but they ask us to come out and play. It is in a good friend we find the child within and exuberance to be lighthearted again.

Every good friend I have, I've been doubly blessed to share the love of food and cooking. In fact, a lot of my relationships were started and built around food. Some of my greatest memories have been made around the table, late into the night still connecting while the candles slowly burned. I would not trade any of these beautiful souls or the memories we share.

In an old box I have carried around forever it seems, is a worn-out collection of recipes from my friends. When I look at these recipes now, they seem priceless to me; written on old paper, note cards, the back of receipts or letters. All of them in different handwriting usually scribbled and now stained with my thumbprint. The waiter wrote one of my favorite recipes down on the back of the receipt at one of Diana's favorite restaurants and when I found it years later I also found the chewing gum I had placed there…laughing my head off and remembering that wonderful evening. Now in that old box these faded timeworn, secondhand scraps of paper looks to me like time-honored ornaments. And more than that they are the missing links I have found to my past, it is truly now a treasure box of love. I cannot seem to get rid of them.

As you read through these stories in this book, I invite you to start recalling your favorite recipes and I promise you the memory connected to the recipe will be far more important than the food. Once you start you will be flooded with memories of sharing love and find your own thumbprint.

*The heart, like the mind,
has a memory. And in it are
kept the most precious keepsakes.
~Henry Wadsworth Longfellow ~*

# Ardor-Spirits

I met Helen in 1974. This was my first introduction to a Jewish home and lifestyle and a world of intellect, knowledge, food, cooking, a mother's love and hope. I worked in the Gropen home for about two and a half years, and learned a passion for cooking and a taste of finesse.

Helen was the mother of four gifted children whom she gave to every moment she was awake. Each day once the children were driven to school, Helen would return home to give me instructions of work for the day. Some days it was laundry and ironing or changing the sheets and cleaning out the closets. And there was always cooking to be done. I thought I knew how to cook and do it well, but I would soon learn there was a way to cook for the Gropen family. The only way I would learn this fine craft was by Helen herself.

She began with Chicken soup that was made from scratch at least once a week. It was important that the children had a dose of this medicine she called it, as often as possible. Every day I learned and gleaned knowledge from Helen's kitchen, which soon became her classroom and I was the student. Upon arriving she would give me my chores and tell me to finish and meet her in the kitchen. She introduced me to a food processor, chopping, dicing sauces and brazing. I learned the flair of Pâtés, Greek food, South Western and Spanish cuisine, Rugelach, Matzoh Balls, and a world of tradition.

Something else happened in that kitchen far grander than the most panache cooking school in the world and that was the ardor-spirit; the warmth of feelings shared between us as we grew talent and confidence. I worked hard at first to gain Helen's approval and trust, always allowing her to lead. It wasn't long before we added laughter and hours of sharing of our lives and our selves. I don't know exactly when it happened, but one day Helen began to look at me with love. She grew to respect me and every day with her was an adventure in work and spirit.

Helen didn't drive the freeways and so that became my job too. Once a month the kids would pile in the station wagon and I would drive them to their orthodontist in Beverly Hills. Helen and I dropped them off and we then drove to another elegant restaurant in the area. After experiencing a new kind of cuisine, we would find time to shop at Saks Fifth Avenue or many of her favorite stores. I was just the chauffeur on these days, but she never treated me like one. The kids usually complained when we got back to pick them up because they said they were starving. I can't remember if we would stop and feed them, but I do remember I was content.

Helen became my teacher in her kitchen and one of my teachers in life. My style and confidence gave birth before her and thirty-two years later I give her the credit for helping me to develop and explore my cooking style. She will always be the inspiration behind all of my creations.

You will find the Rugelach recipe honoring Helen in the Christmas Spice Chapter.

# DESIRES ROAD

*There were many different roads to take, and I couldn't take all of them.*
*Some of them were smoothly paved. But off to the side I saw a road made of earth,*
*an overgrown footpath through a forest.*
*Overhead a cloud was giving birth to a morning sun.*
*I could feel the life in that road.*
*I could smell it's clean perfume as if it were part of my blood.*
*I walked past the sign at its entrance hardly noticing*
*the two words written in gold- Desires Road*
*John Evans ~ 1982*

"I did take this road I chose for 43 years," Cynthia would tell you. It was a good road for a while and then I knew, or should I say my soul knew where I should be. It seemed like it was not enough time here and yet it took so long to return to where the core of me wanted to be. I finally gave into the calling and left on June 4th 1992. I am not sorry, yet I miss all of you as much as you remember me.

How I miss you dear Cynthia. There are not many days that go by that even after 15 years I still call on you for comfort and advice. I can still hear you're soft like whisper, "Sandy, you are so good at what you do." If you only knew how many times I have had to recall those words that I needed so desperately in moments of self-doubt.

My beautiful little petite French friend Cynthia was golden to me. From the moment I first met her in the early 1980's until she died, she was unlike anyone I had ever known. There was something fragile about her and yet her character out weighed her delicate demur. We shared many years of laughter and acceptance. If anyone in my life ever understood and at the same time accepted me it was Cynthia.

Cynthia was diagnosed with cancer in September of 1991. She was given 6 months to live. She lived 9 more.

One of my favorite memories with Cynthia was when we made Pissaladare together. She wanted me to try this French pizza cut into squares for an appetizer for catering. She impressed upon me the importance of cooking the onions and using kalamata olives. I made it over and over and over until it was perfect according to Cynthia. The best part of the memory is that I had the hardest time pronouncing the word Pissaladare. Making this dish was like combing a French cooking and language class together.

In January of 1992 Cynthia's cancer returned for the worse as we had been told it would. We took a short trip together to a hot springs and then to her last trip to the coast.

There were times she could hardly walk to the sulfur tub in the meadow she so desperately wanted to get to but she did. We sat in silence together looking up at the stars and the full moon. I can still feel her quiet tears fall.

From January to May I helped take care of Cynthia while she was confined to a hospital bed. I cooked for her and every day I made her a different soup. There were weeks I lived in her home and stayed up nights holding her close to me. The soul intimacy and connection I shared with her in the last days was like none I have ever shared with anyone. One quiet early morning she pulled me close to her and whispered, "Sandy, I want you to speak at my funeral because you know my heart, please tell me you will do this." I said yes.

The day Cynthia passed I went home and turned on the computer. I sat in silence for a while and then began to type. I did not stop until the speech was written. I read it over once. The day of the funeral I sat in the front row of the chapel and waited to be called to the front to speak. I put the three pages on the stand and did not realize until later that I would look down at the paper for the next paragraph, but I was finishing each one with out reading it from the paper. I know in my heart that I did not know this speech and I know that there was a spirit of love that was helping me.

I have a short video of the two of us in her back yard together. She is asking me to pronounce "Pissaladier" and I'm laughing through my struggling and she is smiling at me. And today the sunlight in the video looks like golden light surrounding her.

The following are my two favorite Cynthia recipes:
Pissaladier - Sensational Starters chapter
Salde Dressing ala Tomatis - Sassy Sauces and Zesty Dressings Chapter

# You Can't Loose Me

*I suppose there is one friend in the life of each of us*
*who seems not a separate person, however dear and beloved,*
*but an expansion, an interpretation, of one's self,*
*the very meaning of one's soul.*
*~Unknown~*

What do any two friends have in common? A bond that says you can't loose me, so come and let's make memories. And that is just what we did.

I cried nearly the entire 10-hour trip to Northern California in 1980. I was leaving one life to start another and it all became real on the road north. I had lived in Southern California all of my life and now I was moving to a small community where there were blue skies, pine trees and peacefulness. A safe place to raise my children- called Paradise.

It was only a few days after I arrived in my new homeland that I met Diana. I took my girls to the skating rink the next town away and it was there that this 24-year friendship began. We skated together as though we were one of the kids on the floor. Round and round we traveled sharing who we were, what we loved and what we wanted. It was a whirlwind meeting, which took only minutes to make the heart connection it takes to know this is going to be my bud.

Through these 24 years I think we have experienced everything humanly possible two girl friends could share. We have done it all, said it all, and been it all together.

We loved each other's children, and watched them grow. We went through divorces at the same time and cried in each other's arms. I remember reading the same books at the same time and then dissecting them word for word over the phone. We had our own restaurant that we visited on Thursdays. We dreamed up recipes and then cooked them up. We shared friends, holidays and special occasions over and over that made us each other's families. We believed in one another and became each other's allies.

And then there was Laguna Beach California. It became our magical get away. I do think this is the very place, every time we got there, that the two of us shared a piece of our souls to one another that we possibly did not even know we owned. We laughed until someone needed to tell us to shut up and cried over our mistakes and failures in life. We watched the sun come up with coffee on our deck and the sun go down with a glass of wine. And each visit grew harder to leave. Our last look back at the waves hitting the shore as we carried out luggage to the rental car brought silence between us. To this day it is something we cannot explain and we never needed to for deeper than our hearts, our souls knew what words could not convey.

In 1994 Diana married Jim. It was a happy day for her and one of the saddest in my life. As I stood next to her at the Alter, I ached inside because of the loss I was experiencing. I knew this was her new life and our heart friendship would never change, but our time would. I accepted the change with a smile.

Not long after the wedding Diana and Jim moved away and then away again to Washington. I have seen her very little in the last 10 years, but nothing has ever lessened in either of our hearts. I know that some day when we are old and purple we will hold each other's hands and talk again as though one of us never left. Our friendship is rare and will never be replaced, because it is those life events that created our bond. And no matter how far or how long the distance goes on, we will always be together inside. Diana, you can't loose me.

# Heart of Gold ~ In the Mail

*Female friendship's that work
are relationships in which women help each other
belong to themselves.*
            *~ Louise Bernikow ~*

I met Terry in 1978 in Riverside California. Our Children both attended the same elementary school and we were both taking porcelain doll classes from the same teacher. The first day I met her I felt not just her warmth, but also the goodness about her.

Just after I moved to Northern California Terry moved to Fresno California. This is where our friendship developed. We became long distance friends, not over the phone, or e-mail, but through old-fashioned letters. I began to receive a letter or two a week from Terry and I answered every one of them. Some of her letters were a page and others were 10 or more pages. Sometimes I would savor them for after the kids were in bed. Nearly every letter she enclosed copies of recipes from magazines or newspapers. These recipes became my starting library that grew into folders over the years. Little did I know then, that these acts of kindness sent in the mail would be some of the first recipes I would use in my catering business?

A few years passed and we began meeting in Sacramento with Eileen and all of us spending a day near the capital. Terry and I would visit each other and spend a weekend or so with one another and our families. I would take the train to Fresno, which took about 5 hours, but I loved every moment of it because I could unwind and it made me feel like I was taking a real trip.

Every time I came to visit Terry, she had special gifts made for me, sitting in my guest room and treated me like a queen. We cooked together and sat up long after everyone went to bed and extended our friendship beyond our letters.

The first real Caesar salad I tasted was made by Terry, while her husband Dave barbequed a turkey. I can still taste those two wonderful foods when I think about them with the memory of our friendship eating at their table together.

Terry also did long distance sewing for me. Every week I received a box in the mail from her with a new doll dress or clothes made for me. I still have the pillows on my couch she made as well as the cross-stitch that hangs on the wall.

In 1997 Terry drove to the Little River Inn in Mendocino County where my first daughter's wedding took place. Once again she brought me a beautiful basket of goodies and her friendship. She helped me prepare food for the reception and brought love and acceptance and kindness to the table once again. That was the last time I saw Terry until this September. Just as long ago, there were several gifts wrapped and laying on the guest bed waiting for me. We ate appetizers out by the pool the first evening and when I got up the next morning I sat down to muffins and fruit. The second breakfast was the most amazing pancakes I had ever eaten. Every meal was given such attention to and served with friendship - love that I really felt like I was staying at a Bed and Breakfast Cottage.

I had a chance to look at Terry with new eyes. I saw a woman who has lost her husband after a long health battle, and it was amazing to me to see how Terry has made herself happy with her home and many projects and friends. I appreciate the passion she has for cooking and how she shares food as a gift of love. I now fully grasp the connections we share have been created around and through food.

Terry has another recipe friend that she met on line. It was ten years ago on a chat-cooking online board she met "Bam". People on that board would trade recipes, stories, emotions and what was going on in their lives at that time. It was a very diverse group and she and Bam just clicked. After ten years of sharing and getting to know each other through e-mail they eventually met in San Francisco. A gal from California and a gal from Illinois met on the Internet sharing recipes and found one another's cuisine passion and became dear friends.

I know that when we are old we will still be writing to one another. I look forward to her letters, because they will always be filled with joy and laughter. But for now, Terry is my favorite e-mail buddy. Once a week, just like her old letters; I receive an up-date in her life with children and friends. I love hearing what movies she has seen and the wonderful family meals she plans for the weekends. She attends a monthly dinner with the girls and they take turns making one another a gourmet meal. She tells me everything in detail and it feels like we are sitting on the couch and sipping wine and sharing. And now instead of the clipped and copied recipes sent in the mail, I receive tons of wonderful – amazing recipes from her through e-mail. When ever I have an event coming up with a special theme, I scream help and the recipes start flowing in!

There are so many recipes that are truly my favorites of Terry's that it would take up the entire book, so I am including my very favorite, the ones I can't live without recipes.

White Chocolate Cranberry Bread – Simply Handmade Giving Chapter<br>
Spinach Soufflé Stuffed Mushrooms – Take a Gander at Our Feast Chapter<br>
Apple Pecan Baked Pancakes – Brunch Celebrations Chapter<br>
Orange Oatmeal Scones – Brunch Celebrations Chapter

# Love Shared in the Kitchen

*True friends are those who really know you*
*but love you anyway.*
*~Unknown~*

I have come to believe that for every thing we go through in life it is on purpose. And there seems to always be someone right there with you, for me it's a girl friend.

Eileen is one of those good girlfriends that you never stop loving or can even begin to forget the memories you've created together.

We went to the same high school and had some of the same friends. But friendship didn't begin until we were married. Both of us were born homemakers at a very young age. While our friends were experiencing life in the late 60's we were married and reading Betty Crocker.

I have the fondest memories of Eileen, our children and myself. The girls, Kellie, Korrie and Amber would play until the sun came up if we let them. We called them the three musketeers because they were such comrades together. All the while, Eileen and I were cooking, baking or planning a party. Every Christmas, we baked for a week, and then proudly gave out our gift baskets to family and friends. It was always the planning that was the favorite part and hearing the girls jumping up and down over hot dogs and macaroni and cheese. It was truly a time of love shared in the kitchen together.

It was a time of friendship bliss for me. My life was so simple and yet to me it was a large life and Eileen and Amber were a large part of my wonderful world. I treasure every moment we had before I moved to Northern California.

The following two of my favorite memory recipes Eileen and I made together. The Butter Crunch was made at Christmas. The Clam Chowder was derived from a little restaurant around the corner from Eileen's home. We would go there and get a bowl of it just to taste it and try and figure out what the ingredients were. We never thought to ask, but it wouldn't have been so much fun!! I remember a couple of times we made our own Clam Chowder and it tasted better than the restaurant, or so we thought it did. These cooking days with Eileen will always be with me.

The following recipes are in memory of our friendship:

Cold Artichoke Salad – Delightful Salads Chapter
Spaghetti Salad – Delightful Salads Chapter
Butter Crunch – Simply Handmade Giving Chapter

# OLD FRIENDS

*The best mirror is an old friend.*
*~George Herbert~*

I met Vicky in 7th grade. Arizona Intermediate Jr. High in Riverside California. 1963, the United States had been devastated by the assassination of President Kennedy, the Beatles were about to give birth, I lip sang in my bedroom mirror to Roy Orbison and I was the new girl in school. I don't ever remember formally meeting Vicky; I just remember she was Sue's friend. I became Diane Okert's bud and some how Sue, Vicky, Diane and I became a 'click' around school. One day we were up and it seemed like we were burning the world up and the next we were down and all of us ended up in Mrs. Atkins' counseling office. Our nicknames were Pimp, Flatty, Booba and Fatty. Now this is real 7th grade thinking!

We went through the Beatles, boyfriends and the rebellious craze together. We destroyed Mr. Crawford's class with spit wads on the ceiling, stole bugs from our science class and Mr. Christensen took our 'Payton Place' novels away. My friends watched me come alive in drama as Trudy and we all knew each other's secrets. It was truly priceless camaraderie. I remember Jr. High was my haven and I loved every day, every moment of it. It is one of my best memories.

We grew up a little and Vicky and I were having babies together. Then she moved to Northern California and 3 years later I followed. Our children graduated from the same high school together and we helped each other with their weddings.

My best memory ever with Vicky was planning and giving her 50th birthday party. We did it together and enjoyed every moment of it. It was a garden party and 85 guests came. I had sent a letter and material to all of these people and asked them to make a scrapbook page for Vicky. The night of the party there was a continuous circle of guest around the 100 page completed book. It was truly a story of her life.

I have grown to realize that Vicky and I are as different as night and day, like black and white. And although there have been times we have needed our space to breath, there will always be love for one another.

The following are two recipes that remind me of Vicky: The Tortellini Caesar Salad is her favorite salad that I make and can be found in the Caterer's Pride Gets It's Due Chapter.

Chili Verdi is my favorite food she has prepared for me and is in the South of the Border Chapter.

# Harmony

*I always feel that the great high privilege,*
*relief and comfort of friendship*
*was that one had to explain nothing.*
*~Katherine Mansfield~*

My friendship with Candy has been one of smooth sailing for a long time now. She is a good example of how not to judge a book by its cover. Candy doesn't say a lot, she observes. So in watching her you might think she was reserved or somewhat standoffish. I thought this at one time and have come to realize she is truly a quiet server.

I don't know how she really showed up in my life, I just know she has always believed in me and continues to give. I think it was around the time of my restaurant years, she brought a different friend in nearly every week. She would show up there after a shopping day with a special gift for me and now she shows up on my doorstep with the same acts of kindness.

Candy has one of the most beautiful perennial flower gardens I've ever seen. She had made some amazing arrangements for my catering jobs or for one of my garden parties. We have dug deep and I have brought transplants from her garden to mine. We have shared recipes, taken long walks on the flume and spent days climbing Yosemite together. We have planned and given countless parties together and always-in ease. She is organized and we are always on the same page. There is no stress is friendship with her. I think it is so comfortable and effortless because there is complete respect and love flowing between us. Our energy is like a spiritual harmony, similar to a melody that's sounds are in agreement. I am so blessed to know her.

One of my favorite attributes I love about Candy is her willingness to look deep inside and feel who she needs to help and serve. Quite some time ago she began helping a young boy named Eric. He had been placed in foster home after foster home. She would visit him weekly and became apart of his life. He has since been moved about 4 hour away, but she still manages to visit him and is apart of the team now that helps makes decisions in his life.

Candy reminds me of a beautiful gem. The small facets among the gem are what give it its beauty just like the many ways she accomplishes, gives and loves. It is not necessarily amazing, but it is lovely. I am honored to know her.

The following recipes are some of my favorites of Candy's:
Candy's Noodles, Mac and Cheese, Poppy Seed Casserole,
Southern Potatoes, can all be found in the Casseroles from Scratch Chapter.

*"The most beautiful discovery true friends make is that they can grow separately without growing apart."*
*~Elizabeth Foley ~*

# FRIENDSHIP FORTUNE

Not too long ago, I got an e-mail that talked about people who come and go in our lives. Some are here for a short time for a reason or blessing and some are here forever. Everyone, for whatever time period is here for a purpose and I not only believe this, I know it with my soul.

Susie is one of those amazing beams of light that came and went in my life, but her light will always shine in my heart. It is her light that opened doors of self-awareness, beauty, grace, elegance, spunk and accountability. And even more than all of this was her gifted child like side, which exuded fun, fun and more fun. The kind I had forgotten the combination to. Susie helped me turn the knob and unlock the key. She helped to re-birth me. I am blessed.

Somewhere in the middle of the 1980' when big hair and shoulder pads were in, I met my new friend Susie. My hair stopped in the middle of my waist and I am sure that my hair was going to be one of Susie's first projects. It was long like a 70's surfer girl and it needed a new look badly. Susie was graceful in her tactics; she softly mentioned hair and everything that came with it. I remember our talks were not just about looks on the outside but rather the inside in such debt that I would often ponder our discussions days and days after they occurred. She was teaching me about life and fun.

Our families along with three more seemed to have come together more often than not. When I look back and feel this past, it seems we were all pulled in the same direction, towards the center of life happening. We each needed fulfillment of some kind and each was in our thirties; a real time of self-exploring and self-expression. Not like when we were teens, but on a deeper level, because we now possessed such responsibility in our family lives, yet we were growing emotionally at leaps and needed a way to express it. The guys shared hunting, fishing and as families we enjoyed camping together. The girls shared shopping, parties, kids, family dinners, school events and their hearts and the most laughter I have ever been connected to in my life.

To this day my girls talk about the vacations we shared and the weekly get-togethers, potlucks with games and movies. The holidays and the theme parties we created, that used all of our creative brains to imagine an outcome, will never leave my heart. It felt like it was one large family that all loved one another unconditionally. Sometimes I stop and feel this effortless magic some twenty years ago that was shared, and wonder why all of life relationships cannot equal these moments in time. I guess they were the people that were only meant to grace my life and deepest heart in divine time and Susie was one of them.

My daughter Kellie, who lives in Washington, has helped to create this same kind of friend connection with three other families. They call themselves the Communes. Several times a year they go camping at the coast and every New Years Eve they go away to the mountains and stay in a cabin. This is a family trip and all the kids and parents play in the snow during the day and sit by the fire in the evening. The women exercise and diet together and have done marathons in the past. Kellie tells me that because she lives so far away from her real family, that the communes have become her Washington family. "It feels like the old days," she says.

The following recipes represent the meals we all shared, and these are the recipes Susie gave to me. When you enjoy cooking with someone as much as I did with Suzie, making the recipe brings back the friendship and becomes far more important than the food itself.

Chocolate Mousse Pie - Sweet Treat Chapter<br>
Cuban Flan - South of the Border Chapter<br>
Potatoes Anna - Farmers Harvest Chapter<br>
Walnut Salad - Delightful Salads Chapter<br>
Cilantro Chicken – Caterer's Pride Gets its Due Chapter<br>
Black-Eyed Peas and Avocado – Beloved Veggie Meals Chapter<br>
Stuffed Green Peppers – Beloved Veggie Meals Chapter

# Company with History

There I was, standing at the fabric store checkout line waiting to pay for the fabric in my arms, when I turned around and there was Beck. I asked, "Is that you Beck?" She smiled and then walked over and gave me a really big hug, the kind you get when you haven't seen someone in a really long time. Becky had moved away for two years and had recently moved back to our area. I was so happy to be talking to her again that even though we both have aged it seemed like it was fifteen years ago that we were looking each other in the eyes. We gathered up our packages and off we went to dinner together.

We have not stopped spending time together since our meeting. We try to get a movie and dinner in at least once a month and it feels like time has never separated our friendship. One of our discussions over dinner was about how far we go back and the good and bad times we shared together that made our history. That is when we came to the conclusion why it was so easy for the two of us to just pick up and do the friendship circle again, is because we have so much history together. The history that was built fifteen years ago never left our hearts or the trust we share within the friendship.

To me Beck is comfortable to be with and good company to have by your side and that is truly a warm feeling. In 1992 the night before I opened the doors to my restaurant I had a private opening and about 25 guests graced the launching of the new business. Beck brought me a gift of 25 blue and white mugs. I used them every morning serving my guests their coffee in the pretty ceramic cups. After all these years I have one of those cups left. It is my favorite cup in the morning and for tea in the afternoon. The cup's handle is thin and the mug is light and feels comfortable in my hand. That is just how I feel about my friendship with Beck, light, comfortable and good company, continuing to make our friendship history together.

*How rare and wonderful
is that flash of a moment when we
realize we have discovered
a friend.
~ William Roaster ~*

# SASSY-SPUNKY-DORA

Dora, Dora, Dora. There is only one of you. Dora and her husband George live in what he calls, "Dora's house." It's a large, beautiful log cabin home nestled between pine trees and blue skies. George has to be the greatest husband in life, because he puts up with Dora, and because he wants to. He is a good man!!

I first met Dora and her clan when I moved into the cottage and became her neighbor. There were only three of us tucked back in the woods it seemed. We had our private little homes far enough away from one another and yet close enough for warm visiting. Warm is what it was. Dora was the kind of neighbor that never bothered you, and when you knocked on her door, she opened it wide with love and so much laughter that my side would ache. She loved looking at all of my junk in my home and I loved even more her treasures.

Dora wanted to get her eyes on the inside of the cottage from the day I moved in. Her mother had invited all of her church friends to come and take a tour of the cottage and I made some snacks and served them on the old patio. The first person to show up for the tour early was Dora. She had some kind of a housewarming gift and just smiled at me when I opened the door. She told me she wasn't part of the group, but since I was offering the house for a tour, she thought she would take advantage of it. What happened next created the bond we still share. She became very quiet as she looked around and felt the magic she saw. After the tour was finished she stayed and we talked for a long time. I think Dora was really the only person to ever fully understand how I was connected spiritually to that little old place. I do believe she felt that spirit.

Dora loved my cooking and one of her favorite foods I made was the Squaw Bread at least once a month. I would show up on her doorstep with a loaf of it and she would just look at me and say, "YOU know how much I love this and this one loaf could never be enough, even for me." I would tell her to just thank me and say no more and she did. One day after making about 900 muffins I came home to the cottage to find a large old sign in black lettering that read, "Bakery," hanging from my front porch. I had no idea who hung it there and for days I just wondered who the cohorts were.

Dora has spunk in every thing she does and says. She always made me laugh until it hurt and stop and pay attention when she needed to get her point across. She is direct and to the point and I adore her authentic confidence. But mostly, I love her heart and I know why George adores her… she is adorable.

For all of my friendship memories that lie in front of me, I will never forget our talks and that sign that represented the real meaning of Dora's friendship; love.

I celebrate Dora by including the Squaw Bread recipe that she wanted and I never gave to her until now.

Happy baking Dora, you will find this recipe in the Breads We Love Chapter.

*If instead of a gem, or even a flower,
we should cast the gift of a loving thought into
the heart of a friend that would be giving as the angles give.
~ George MacDonald ~*

# THE BELOVED SHERIFF

*It's the one's you can call all up
At 4:00 a.m. that matter.*

May 4, 1992. I have never forgotten this date because it is when I first met Mindy and began a life long mother, daughter, and work relationship. Today she is my beloved friend.

It was a month before my friend Cynthia died. I left her home early that morning after taking care of her the night before and drove to my catering job of which I was going to feed 350 guests. I was already tired and weary thinking about Cynthia. One of my best employees who I counted on to do the table, bar and room set up could not help me. I was devastated, but he assured me that he had someone covering him that knew as much as he did because he had trained her. That was the day Mindy arrived 15 minutes early in crisp black and whites. She smiled big and looked familiar, but I was too stressed to figure it out. She immediately went right to business and asked what the plan was. We completed this wedding successfully and everyone after that for the next 7 years together.

We have laughed over the years at some of the jobs we did and the memories we have been left with. Like one Saturday we had 7 jobs in one day and how did we even keep the food straight. Or the time we had to throw away the pie boxes so no one would figure out we really didn't make the pies for 400 people. I think of another time when I made her cut flowers in the dark from my neighbor's yard because we needed them for our garnish on the tray. The nights we never went to bed and our feet hurt for days after that. How we knew anyone who ever thought about wanting to be a carter was crazy. The hours and hours we spent planning, shopping, decorating and cooking together to make every job perfect. And how we didn't know then that the love we were putting into this was going to come back to us some day.

I remember about a year after Mindy started working for me I booked two weddings on the same day. I knew I had to train her to be able to decorate a crudités table and everything else, because to her surprise she was going to do the job by herself. She was a nervous wreck for a long time at the thought of I was going to actually leave her alone. I never had any doubts. I still remember the wedding, it was near Thanksgiving and all the colors were brilliant falls. I let her do her own thing and she did. Every time I look at the pictures of her standing next to the buffet table I am reminded of her fear before the event, and her confidence after. Mindy didn't know it then, but it was the start of her own future.

Not long after this Mindy became the boss (she thought) and we nick named her the "Sheriff." But to me, she was more than bossy or determined. She was loyal, beautiful and brilliant in many things she did. The beautiful thing about what Mindy and I possessed together was an incredible balance and trust and that is rare to find in a working relationship. She had the better organizational skills, set up and managing of the employees. I had the decorating, cooking and people – client skills. We learned and gleaned from one another. It was so beautiful that out of it grew a bond that can never be replaced. She became my daughter and friend and I her mother and friend. In all the years we worked 'at the hip,' we never had an argument. It was total respect and love.

Later on through the years I figured three things out. First, she was not an accident to come into my life. Second, she looked familiar because she looked just like Loretta Swift – 'hot lips' on the television show "Mash." And third, my worker did not train Mindy, come to find out, she trained him.

Years later when I am not home and she leaves me a message she starts out with, "This is your beloved." Mindy today has her own very successful catering business. I am nothing but proud of her. She amazed me a long time ago.

# Laguna Beach

Laguna is home to my heart. Each time I return to this blissful community, I am drawn to the aura that makes my soul feel good. I step away from life and feel who I am. It is these days, these moments I come home to my heart…and I listen.

I found Laguna Beach in southern California in the 1960's as a teenager. In the 70's I brought my daughter's Kellie and Korrie when they were toddlers to play in the sand and watch the waves, while I took a deep breath from motherhood. In the 80's I came back as a single mom discovering myself for the first time inside. This is when I brought Diana.

Diana was raised in a small community and like me walked down the high school steps into married life and motherhood. She probably found her heartbeat for the first time in Laguna.

I know that Diana and I were not an accident in meeting. I know we were brought together to share in friendship, and in helping one another discover our own selves and our spirituality. That growth always took place in Laguna. To this day we find it hard to explain, and now we don't even need to. All we have to say is, "Laguna" and we both understand.

I think every deep friendship have a story to tell. In my office a picture hangs of Diana and me taken in Laguna. When I look at it I smile from the inside out. Little did I know at that moment the picture was taken, that 15 years later I would be blessed by that moment in Laguna? That picture tells a story, our story.

I would say to every woman, there is no better time than now to write your story with your friend of the heart.

# Peacocks

1989. My 20-year reunion in southern California. This meant every woman had to work even harder than the first reunion to look better than the last time they saw you…or so the ego said.

One thing for sure, you can't show up at a reunion alone. Diana, was my date even if she complained about the meal ticket, she was still going. I enticed her with the magical idea that if she came along we would stay in Laguna and then drive to my reunion.

As I drove the 500 miles she read to us all the way there from the book, "Feel the Fear and Do It Anyway." We were into "Self help" of any kind we could get our hands on.

The day of the reunion we played make up and dress up for at least 5 hours. I must admit, she was generous with her time in helping me look the best; after all it was my reunion.

We arrived in time to stand in line and talk about food. We were hungry because we had not taken away from our beauty time to eat. Diana is a Taurus and traditionally they are careful people, especially when it comes to money. The one thing you don't want to do is starve a Taurus who is about to pay for her meal. Every few steps toward the door, Diana began to complain about how hungry she was and she just bet that we were going to be served roast beef and peas. I tried to convince her that for twenty- five dollars we would be eating something elegant. She would look at me through her sun glasses and say, "Trust me, it will be roast beef." Whenever she tells you, "Trust me," I get nervous.

There should have been appetizers, but there wasn't. By the time dinner was served we would have eaten anything we were that hungry. Wouldn't you know it, as the waiter set our plates down Diana looked up at me and said, "I told you," meaning it was roast beef and peas! By now I was feeling like a second-class friend. I took all the attention in the day, starved my best friend, and made her pay for her own ticket and she had to eat roast beef, not to mention neither she nor I were having an outstanding time.

As soon as we finished dinner we stepped out side of the banquet room and walked around. I said, "This is really boring and I'm ready to leave, how about you?" The look on her face was reason to believe she agreed.

We went over to the bar and asked a couple of people if there was a nice place to go dancing. Immediately the bartender told us that there was a brand new place called the Green Onion and how to get there. As we walked back to the car Di and I knew we had not wasted our time getting ready for nothing.

In no time we were turning into the parking lot of the Green Onion. It was a little hard to find a parking place so we knew it was going to be packed inside.

We re-did our lipstick and began walking towards the front door where we saw a doorman taking money. The music was loud indicating this was the happening place. Just before we got to the door Diana stopped and looked at me and said, "You know… we just aren't two peacocks sitting on a bar stool." I stood there and looked at her for just a second and said, "You are right, let's go." And we did.

When we got back to our room we changed into our sweats and grabbed blankets and our books. It was about 2 am and we had been reading quietly by the moon light on the patio, serenaded by the ocean waves below us. I looked over at Diana and very quietly asked her, "Hey, it was the cover charge – right?" She whispered back, "Yea."

# Recipes From Diana

All the years Diana and I have been friends we have shared the love of food and recipes. When I was contemplating over what to serve for a dinner party, family gathering or catering job, Diana always came to the rescue.

We savored recipes like they were holly. We added and subtracted from them to make them perfect in our eyes and our own creations.

I remember the two of us making 50 pounds of potato salad and adding shredded carrots and zucchini to our pasta sauce and all the stress she put on herself whenever she had to entertain guests. The time I dragged her to Fort Brag and made her help me cook for a biology class on the coast and the fun we had behind the scenes in the kitchen. When she showed up the day of a catering event after the night before I was spared my life after a nearly fatal accident. When I asked her why she was there she just looked at me for a moment and then said, "I drove home last night and thanked God that he did not take you, because I am not ready for you to leave me. I took a day off of work to come and help you because I am so grateful you are here." I don't remember what I served at that catering event; I only remember her hugging me in the kitchen and feeling her love for me the rest of the day.

The following are some of my favorites she has given me through the years. Most of them were used in my catering business and still asked for 19 years later. She always said, "Trust me," as she handed the recipe to me and I knew right then it was a winner!

Chocolate Cheese Cake – Simply Sandarella's Chapter
Seafood Dip – Caterer's Pride Gets its Due Chapter
Spinach Cauliflower Toss – Caterer's Pride Gets It's Due Chapter
Miniature Pecan Tarts – Simply Handmade Giving Chapter
Swisse Venigreate Dressing – Sassy Sauces and Dressings Chapter
Tortilla Tidbits – Sensational Starters Chapter
Zucchini Sesame Chocolate Bread – Brunch Celebrations Chapter

*No love, no friendship
can cross the path of our destiny
without leaving some mark on
it forever.*
~ Francois Muriac ~

# Friends Old and New
# Sandy and Sandy

I met Sandy about seventeen years ago when I first started catering and she worked as a professional florist. We had one thing in common back then and that was the catering and nurturing to brides and events. I saw Sandy often, but it was always revolved around work and our hectic schedules didn't allow us the time we needed to grow a friendship. I do remember that I was very drawn to her kindness and charitable heart. And one more thing, she is what she is and that is authentic and that quality kept me always drawn to her.

Years have passed, and as everything in my life it comes when I need it, and along came Sandy. It was January and as I was mentally assessing my heart's center, I began the ring in and welcome the new list. It seems as though I had just finished writing and a few days later, in walks Sandy into my life again.

In the past months that I have gotten to know Sandy I realize that the second time around is gold to me. Besides our forename, I have learned that we are alike in many ways. Both of us adore vintage jewelry, old photographs, timeless movies, photography, cooking and family. The two of us share passion for the same things and like she always says, "That puts me in a spell," and we act like we are in one! The icing on the cake or to top it off, Sandy retired from the florist business and started a catering business many years ago. I have learned that Sandy, like myself will travel by herself, but I have a feeling we are going to be doing a lot of that together in the years to come. Sandy has such a dry sense of humor; it's a wit that keeps me laughing like one of her spells.

She honors family and connection as I do and marvels in the opportunities to serve them. This year Sandy's daughter is getting married and she has asked for my hand in helping with this event. She is grateful for the assistance and I feel honored to be asked. My heart center feels gratitude for it's tending, listening and for the blessing God gave in answering.

Very recently I was a guest at my friend Sandy's home and I was introduced to what a wonderful cook she is. She definitely put a spell on me when I took the first bight of her basil bites. I was relentless; eating the very last basil toast and hardly had enough room to enjoy the rest of the meal. For dessert she served her mother's prune cake, a recipe she made up in the 1930's.

I am honored to share both of these recipes with you.
Basil Spread on Baguettes – Caterer's Pride Gets It's Due Chapter
　　The Prune Cake - Sweet Retreat Chapter.

*We are shaped and fashioned by what we love.*
*~Goethe ~*

# Understated Elegance

Once upon a family: my friend Susan has written the book on rising up children with character and big hearts like herself. When I asked Susan's daughter Heather for the recipe of the birthday cake they made for me as well as a little information about the two of them, Heather wrote:

"Hey Sandy, my mom and I had to find our recipe…go figure - that's where our story should start. My mom and I complete each other. I love her dearly; she is the most supporting person I know. My mom is my best friend who will always be there for me. This is just an altered recipe that was from a standard cook book but we made it our own."

I wish I could bottle her words of feelings for her mother and spread it upon every young mother today so that they could engage for even a moment their future with their children. Ah, if only I could…

Susan is a woman of unspoken talent and understated elegance in every step she takes in life. She is a role model, a signature of love gifts freely given. And she is one of the most unusual dedicated friends I have experienced. Now that is where we come together. When we met so long ago, she was captivated with something about me; getting to know one another at the health club we worked out at and finally one day we just settled in and became each others good friends. I truly love this woman for the mother and friend she is to all. I am honored to know her; honored to love her and blessed to do both. I celebrate Susan the friend and the mother.

Enjoy the recipe for Baked Alaska Cake that Susan and Heather made me for a special birthday in the Sweet Retreat Chapter.

*Chapter 5*

# Five Roses Catering

# The Catering Years

*You cannot have a party of a lifetime without
a lifetime of work.*

I have always thought of myself as a food and entertaining specialist; I have an insatiable enthusiasm for good food and preparation and, somewhere along the way, I became a caterer. It just happened. It grew out of my passion for parties and my desire to make people's dreams come true.

The year was 1989: pesto sauce, paella, and the food processor were no longer novelties, and I stepped out in faith and visited other business in the wedding industry. I passed out business cards and shared my small portfolio with anyone who would listen to me. It wasn't really what I had planned to do with my career, but now I was faced with providing for my daughter by myself, and what I knew most in my heart was that I was a person who inspired others and respected the power of their ideas. I had a way of taking a client's dream and expanding upon it and giving it back. I was self taught and believed that every meal, gathering, or party I had ever hosted had been an learning opportunity and now, with a step of faith, I was about to grow a business that I would look back upon years later with the knowledge that my work had made a difference in many lives and many hearts.

It started small, but by the end of the first year, I had performed two large weddings, birthday parties, open houses, and endless customized sit-down dinner parties. It didn't stop. One event led to another, and another, until I was catering three weddings a weekend. Throughout this catering career I developed an expertise in weddings. From small intimate gatherings to extravagant celebrations for seven hundred, the settings and choices varied, as did the personalities of the bride and groom and their families.

People have always been my business first. So when I met with a potential client, it was extremely important to learn about them so I could design their party personally around them. One of the first questions I would ask was, "What do you want to remember most about this day?" From that moment on, the setup, the timing of the toast or the first dance, the color of the table linens were not the most important things for me—it was how all these things worked together to create a whole the family could look back on with joy. It was my business to help create a memory.

When I look back at all of the brides and grooms I worked with and the weddings I completed, I don't know where I mustered the creative energy to create inspirational ideas over and over again, never the same twice. No matter how tired I felt, somehow every wedding was in my body, in my mind; each became a part of me. The work was a dance with a craft that became a gift. And after all of the months and months of planning, when each wedding was over, I always drove home with a sense of gratitude, and also a bit of loss.

Two messages in particular kept me going through all the sleepless nights and endless planning. The first was when a bride put the note in my hand that thanked me for giving her dream come true. The second was when another bride's parents drove away at the end of the night while I was still cleaning up; then they turned around and the father came back into the room. He approached me and I thought I had done something wrong. Instead, he put a $100 bill in my hand and said, "Thank you, you made us look like we spent a million dollars." Those moments reminded me that this was truly a business of service.

I have chosen to share some of my favorite catering stories in the following pages. I could never write them all, but what I have chosen will illustrate all those years of work and love; stories that are meant to inspire. They present a rich painting of my experiences and a decade of different events. But most importantly, it's an invitation to feel, from beginning to end, the love I have been privileged to share with these people.

*When we follow our bliss, doors will open where you would not have thought there would be doors; and where there wouldn't be a door for anyone else.*
  ~Joseph Cambell~

# BLISSFUL AMAZEMENT

Bob and Suzanne were my first real wedding in Paradise as an official caterer. They were a wonderful couple, helpful, and trusted that everything would be perfect. I knew that it would be, no matter what, and it was.

A few days before Bob and Suzanne's wedding, I was catering an open house for a doctor in town. Everything was going according to plan and on time until the ice-cold punch was poured into a very warm antique punch bowl. I saw the crack on the side of the bowl, and without thinking, put my arms around it, trying to remove it from the table before it broke into many pieces. I did just that, but didn't expect it to explode in my arms. I was left with a large piece of thick glass sticking out of my right arm and had to stop and have it taken care of. My arm was wrapped up, and I was told not to use it at all. This would have been fine with me, except that I am right handed—now the prep for Bob and Suzanne's wedding in the following days ahead would have to be completed with my left hand.

There were tiny tarts to be filled with custard and time-consuming appetizers to be prepared in advance. I guess I was being tested from the very beginning. I think I was either so filled with fear or so overconfident that I made the choice to get this work done one handed.

The wedding day arrived, and there I was in this picturesque setting among pine trees, tables, and strangers. I remember that I was tired, working on only a couple of hours sleep, and yet something was moving through me like fire. Somehow I was able to project what was really in my heart and willing spirit that day. No one around me seemed to have any doubt about my ability to create a beautiful wedding, even with only one hand. I remember that the women joined in and offered to help and seemed to encircle me with their joy. All the while, I was in my own little world, yet working towards the same celebration as everyone else. The flowers, the garnishes, the fruit, and all of the food came together like a perfect melody. When I look back, it seems like part of me was there and part of me was above the bustling scene, observing this entire situation.

When the food was served and the guests stood in the buffet line, I stepped back. I walked far away from the tables, the food, the guests, and found my own safe place to feel. The sounds of music and laughter seemed to come from far away. I stood with a tearful smile on my face, engulfed in a wave of emotion. I didn't know I was feeling, but I wanted to. So I stood there even longer until I heard my inner voice say, "You've done it. You did this…you created this masterpiece." I allowed myself to feel what I had done, and more than feel it, to touch the wonderfulness. I had been creating this same beauty all of my life, but it was not until this moment that I owned it. It was magic, and it was my gift from God to be given to many more brides and families to make happy with food and flowers and fantasy as time went by.

Lemon Ricotta Tarts are in the Caterer's Pride Gets It's Due Chapter.

*We must nurture our dreams like we would a child. They are God-Given and just as precious. Without ambition how would a child learn to ride a bicycle, play an instrument or whistle? We deny the spirit of God when we as adults settle for less than our dreams!*
*~Conway Stone ~*

# Dream Wedding My Mother and Daughter Story

The "dream wedding" means something different to every bride. For some, it is all in the dress or the honeymoon. Some find it is in the pace at which the bride and her attendants walk down the aisle, while for others, it's in the timing of the toast. My daughter Kellie cared most about the ambiance that would encircle the gathering. It was extremely important for Kellie to experience a connection with each guest and create an atmosphere that felt warm to all.

I remember several conversations with Kellie during our planning. She would confess, "Mom, it means everything to me that my guests feel *love* at my wedding." Kellie, my oldest daughter, and I both share the same passion—the desire to make people feel special.

Kellie and her finance, Jim, who lived in Washington State, wanted to have their wedding along the California coast. All three of my daughters, Kellie, Korrie, Katie, and I set out to find the wedding site. We met in Mendocino, and for two days, we drove up and down the coast visiting every restaurant and bed and breakfast we could find. The experience of driving along the coast brought back memories of their childhood days and the passion the four of us shared for the ocean. If we could find the perfect place that would meet all of our needs, our dream would come true.

Like a group of treasure seekers searching for a lost galleon, we scoured the coast for the ideal place in which to create wedding magic. The intuitive feelings harbored by four women—a mom and three daughters—told us that Kellie's wedding was supposed to be celebrated in this very location, and somehow it would just come to us. The large part of the dream for me was that I had brought the girls to this location for many yeas and had often come to write. The love of the ocean and the sentiment I felt here was flowing through me as we drove.

We felt the grandeur in a gift form when Marsha, the event coordinator working for the Little River Inn, gave us permission to not only book the wedding, the reception, the rehearsal, and guest's rooms, but also to use of their kitchen and for me to cater my own daughter's wedding.

From the very first meeting every dream we had just fell into place. She was like the greatest gift I could have received in this wedding. For some reason, Marsha listened to me and understood that I had to keep the promise I made to my girls, and myself, years before. I had looked forward to catering one of my own daughter's weddings since I had begun my own business. This was truly a dream come true. Most everyone I knew thought I was nuts and felt sorry for me. They did not understand what a blessing I was receiving from such an opportunity of service. For years I had visualized and designed fairylike and romantic dreams for the most extravagant weddings imaginable—and now I just wanted to give again for at least one of my daughters.

The date was set: August 23, 1997. In four months, we put together one of the most beautiful weddings I had ever undertaken. In one more trip from Washington and to the coast, we took care of all the arrangements and sent out the invitations. I remember each day going to the mailbox and finding another RSVP card. I felt many emotions and tears of happiness filled my eyes each time I opened another one. I would pick up the phone and call Kellie, "You won't believe who is coming." Then we would both be in tears.

The week of the wedding came. Anxious to get to the coast and feeling like I was going to burst with excitement, I arrived to warm sunshine. It was Wednesday, and the wedding would take place in three days. The next two days were used for food preparation and the welcoming of guests. Friday was busy and spirited, and I found myself filled with anticipation. By that evening, the wedding food preparation was complete and guests were arriving in time for the rehearsal dinner. The rehearsal dinner was always my favorite occasion before the wedding—when all the pretense and nervousness was set aside. This dinner was no different. It was casual, outside on the picnic tables overlooking the blue ocean. I ordered oodles of pizza and served an antipasti platter; sliced, homegrown yellow tomatoes with a basil-garlic sauce and plenty of Italian breadsticks.

While Kellie's sister Korrie was giving Kellie a surprise bridal shower in the bridal suite, I was busy starting the decorating with Mindy, which turned into an all-night regimen. As the sun was rising, the decorating of the reception room was complete. The buffet tables stood in front of the mahogany fireplace; the seating tables were dressed with ivory linen that fell to the floor; on each table were gold pots, some lying on their sides and spilling out peach and ivory Ecuadorian roses. Each table featured pictures of Jim and Kellie and rose petals scattered near the place settings. Truffle boxes were tied with organza ribbon and placed above each plate, and a place card sat at every place setting. Outside on the patio stood tall pillars of overflowing flower arrangements under a white canopy that was outlined in twinkle lights for the evening. The round appetizer table and bar marked the patio, where the sounds of the ocean could be heard. The appetizers were presented in three-foot heights, cascading down to the table; the bar was outlined with honeysuckle and freshly picked grapevine and held an antique barrel for beverages.

The room was magical and awaited its bride for the viewing. Hardly able to keep my eyes open, I somehow made breakfast for my three girls and carried it upstairs on a silver tray. After they ate and before Kellie had her makeup and hair done, she came downstairs to look at the room. She entered, looking slowly around trying to take it all in. She got to the center of the room and began to cry, and then she said, "How did you know?"

Little girls, big girls don't realize how well their moms know them and pay attention to their life-long dream requests. Kellie sat down in the seat awaiting her later in the day, and for a moment felt what it was going to feel like in just a few hours. Just for that moment my little girl was sitting in the seat in front of me. That was my magical-momentous experience, my mother-of-the-bride moment.

The wedding ceremony took place overlooking the blue ocean, and the evening ended with the glamour of the now-empty room. The guests had drifted outside under the stars and sounds of the waves. A hint of music was heard from inside while those few left seemed to be lingering on and on. I sat back and took it all in one last time. So this is what every mother had felt before me. It was a combination of bliss and sentiment. My heart felt like it could not hold any more or it would burst.

The next morning we celebrated one last time over coffee and brunch on the same patio while Kellie and Jim opened gifts. As I was sitting and enjoying it all, someone approached me and handed me a small gift and a letter. The letter thanked me for making the inn the most beautiful it had ever been. I was deeply moved by the message, but what no one knew was that that letter was the hallmark of my work, the fever, the passion, and the zest and that defines for me what is possible as a parent.

*Judges 5:7: The inhabitants of the villages ceased, they ceased in Israel, until that I Deborah arose, that I arose a mother in Israel.*

# CHRISTIAN MISSIONARY ALLIANCE WOMEN

For the last fourteen years I have been blessed to work with a good hearted group of loving women whom I have catered their daughters weddings. Each wedding has a different theme that matches the personality of the bride and included in that is another wonderful mom and family I am allowed to embrace and give service to.

For me the reason these women stand out is their appreciation level and the helping hand and emotional support they give one another. Every wedding the same gals show up for the entire day with the gift of surrendering hands to transform a gym into a fabulous banquet room effect. I've worked with Betty and her daughter Jessica for months to create a Cinderella ballroom. Both of Karen's daughter's weddings converted the gym into a magical afternoon with miraculous decorating touches that led their guest to forget they were in a gymnasium. And then my favorite was the Swell wedding. A November harvest that included an apple pie table replacing the traditional wedding cake, minestrone soup and antipasto plates served as the appetizer on 30 guest tables; a Mom who looked at every aspect of the wedding to the reception as a miracle. And so many other weddings and events from this church congregation that took place in their homes. Each and all play a deep part on my hearts scrapbook page of your unwavering commitment to one another and to making your friends dreams come true.

These are spirited hearts that really get what I create and feel what I give in my work and their appreciation is soft and humble and goes to the heart where a dollar cannot. When I finished Karen's daughter's wedding she took my tired hands in hers looking at me and said, "You blessed us."

That blessed part is what these women do for one another and once in a while I get to be a part of it. I am blessed.

The Pumpkin Butter that the Swell wedding loved so much is in the Caterer's Pride Gets It's Due chapter.

# Cinderella Wedding

Betty and Jessica came to me in the most beautiful way and that is gratitude. They were thankful before they even hired me.

Jessica had a dream of marrying the young man she so loved and Betty, her mom wanted what ever Jessica felt and both looked to God as their advisor.

Every little girl grows up in a fairy tale world and Jessica was no exception. She was marring her prince and intended to have the real Cinderella wedding.

It was a match made in heaven the day I met Betty. A caterer's dream is a mother like Betty. The three of us worked together for so long that I knew it would be a lasting friendship as well as a business agreement.

I don't remember the exact guest count, but I think it was something like 400. The reception room was set just like a scene out of a movie or a page from a book. Each table was covered with white linen and a piece of organza and topped with a castle. Everywhere you looked there was enchantment and another food table. The stage was the focal point and made a statement like none I have ever seen. It started with a red carpet up the steps and at top, yards and yards of white organza was ruffled resembling layers of clouds. To the right was an arch where the cake table was placed. And to the left sat an authentic Cinderella carriage that was lit up. The entire stage looked amazing. All of the decorating ideas came from the bride. She knew what she wanted and somehow created it.

This was a dream come true wedding and one I loved helping create. I remember Betty's friends arrived with irons in their arms and some had snacks while others were already on ladders hanging fabric. There they were again, the same friendship circle ironing tablecloths the entire day. They helped balance work and nerves and in the end, just as always this group of women came through for their friend Betty.

When I run into Jessica in town she is still the same glowing bride as that Cinderella who arrived at her ball some time ago.

# Four Weddings and Broke

*Giving love is the true measure of a true artist.*
*Diane Keaton*

I don't remember when I first met Margaret, but it was just one of those meetings when you know instantly that you and this person will have an always-heart connection. Margaret, I soon learned, has one of the biggest hearts a woman can have. It's a heart that never stops giving or thinking of ways to give again.

In 1996, Margaret hired me to cater a wedding for Jolene, her first daughter. During this planning, Margaret and I really got to know one another. Jolene's wedding and reception was held at a bed and breakfast, and I served a brunch menu. Everything went according to schedule, and the day came and went smoothly, but Margaret and I were far from done.

While planning Jolene's wedding, Margaret and I were already talking about the next daughter's wedding, just a month away. It seemed like we hardly got to take a breath before we were right in the middle of another wedding.

Wendy's wedding was held at a very beautiful estate. It was different from Jolene's, but the guest list was the same. I really don't know how Margaret pulled this off. How could any family have two daughters get married with such individual detail and unique decor just a month apart? Well, the only thing that would be harder would be having a third wedding, and that is what happened.

Tina, thankfully, waited ten months, just enough time to plan all over again. Margaret and I were back in motion. Having many daughters who value individuality makes for a lot of work—each wedding could be nothing like the last. Well, Tina's wedding was different from the start—the guest's list was around four- hundred. Once again we pulled it off, and the same guests enjoyed different food, different music, different trimming, with the same love.

By this time Margaret and her steadfast husband, Chuck, were out of breath and out of money. This would have been OK, except that there was one last child to marry off. Maybe they were secretly hoping that the last daughter, Laura, would change her mind or change the date…but she didn't. In two months, Laura and Jason were to be married, but it wasn't figured out yet how it was going to be paid for.

Margaret knew that I was in the middle of planning my first daughter's wedding, to take place on the Northern coast of California. I didn't know how I was going to do it all and still enjoy my role as mother-of-the-bride. I was really focused on this, and nothing else seemed as important until Margaret showed up again with the problem of another daughter's wedding. She could hardly get the words out, but finally the word "trade" spilled slowly over her lips. She proposed to me that if I would cater Laura's wedding, she would trade her labor for mine and come to the coast and be my slave.

This was one of those moments when two people don't know how or haven't figured out how to make a situation work, and the answer just shows up.

Laura's wedding took place on Margaret and Chuck's front lawn with 225 white chairs, and in the backyard about thirty round tables waited to seat the guests for the reception. In the long driveway, a beautiful canopy covered the food tables where I served the Mexican buffet. An array of sunflowers, Gerber daisies, and delphinium filled up the tall containers that added to the Southwestern flare. Somehow, this budget wedding was made to once again share in this family's continuing celebration. Through all of the four weddings, it was always about Margaret's love, and Chuck's now-empty pockets, that made it happen. But Margaret's love didn't stop there.

Then, if you can imagine, one week after Laura's wedding, my daughter Kellie would be married near Mendocino, California. That meant that, without taking a breath, I went to work on my own dream wedding for my first child. Margaret never took a breath either. The day after Laura's wedding, she showed up at my doorstep with the antique barrel I had noticed at her neighbor's house. I wanted to borrow it for Kellie's wedding, so Margaret bought it for me.

During this week, while I was at the coast preparing for Kellie and her guests, Margaret called me every day and went over her to-do list, adding what I had forgotten to bring. She made trips to my home and to the store and worked through the late evening hours. Margaret stayed up all night helping the florist arrange the flowers and then, with a smile on her face, helped in every step of food preparation that was left for that day. I made her cut tedious cheesecake squares and layer them with a strawberry on top, just because she made me do the same for one of those four weddings. She never complained.

When Kellie's guests finished the buffet, Margaret and Chuck cleared all of the plates and then washed the dishes and cleaned the kitchen. They would not let me in the kitchen and told me I was going to have to think of myself as a guest; it was hard, but I followed the order. As I look back at the pictures of myself on Kellie's wedding day, I am reminded that I was able to cater and decorate my daughter's entire wedding *and* enjoy being a guest because of Margaret. Years later we look back and smile, wondering how we did it, but in our hearts we know it was because we had each other to depend on.

# Humble Dip

Tantalizing! Yes, that's the word I would use to describe the experience of tasting, but not quite having, one of the most amazing culinary delights known to the tongue. Imagine a lemon dip so exquisite that it actually dresses strawberries in robes of royalty. This dip of which I speak I have used for many receptions in my work as a caterer. In fact, the majority of my clients have actually come to expect it.

Marsha was no exception. She not only wanted me to serve this delicacy at her parents' fiftieth wedding anniversary, but she wanted even more. When we designed the menu, she hinted that having the recipe would make her life complete. Little did she know at the time that I never give out such information. When I broke this news to her, she was crestfallen. She gave me a look that screamed disappointment, yet she recognized that I was a professional and that my creations were a secret of my trade. Still, she hadn't given up altogether.

Two years later, Marsha asked me to help with her daughter's wedding reception. Other friends were responsible for most of the food. However, Marsha had other ideas for me.

"I don't really want you to have to work too hard at the reception," announced Marsha a few days before the long-awaited event. "Tell you what, you could give me the recipe, and I could just make it myself." She was speaking, of course, of the lemon dip.

I smiled and replied, "Marsha, you know I don't give out my recipes. But I am going to be publishing a cookbook and it will certainly contain the recipe you desire."

"How can I get my hands on this book?" she inquired, a look of strong determination on her face, seemingly more concerned about the recipe than the reception.

I thought that was the end of the matter, but an hour later, Marsha called me on the phone. "I promise, Sandy, that I will never give out your recipe to anyone else if you'll just give it to me this once." I could actually feel the sincerity in her voice; so keen was her desire to have the secret formula. I still could not give her what she wanted, but I vowed that day to get to work on the book.

A few more years went by, and I was still working on the book when I got another call from Marsha, again wanting my catering services, this time for her son's wedding and, yes, the lemon dip recipe. This time, as we met over wedding plans, Marsha and I just joked about the recipe. Just before the wedding, she asked me to cater the rehearsal dinner to be given at their home. Everything went as planned: I arrived and got the dinner nearly ready to serve while family and friends were at the rehearsal. Soon the guests started to filter in while my friend Vicky and I were working in the kitchen. Marsha came in to check on us, and just as she came around the corner, Vicky spotted her and asked where she had gotten the two beautiful bowls she was holding. My back was to them, yet somehow I felt Marsha's finagling aura about her. I knew there was a maneuver in the makings. Marsha's response was not a hint or request; she got right to the point: "Tell you what, Vicky, I have two bowls you like, and you have two recipes that I want—what do you say we make a deal?"

I nearly choked on the ice water I was sipping. "So, now it's two recipes?" I declared in shock. I recovered, smiled, and said, "OK Marsha, you win, but the ingredients are a secret until the book is published. Deal?" She said the quickest yes you have ever heard and had the biggest grin ever on her face. The three of us broke into laughter that brought tears to my eyes.

I am proud to tell this story because it shows the determination of a woman, and Marsha is just that kind of determined gal. She is an amazing person that gets more done in life than most people ever hope of doing. So, it made perfect sense that after years of coveting my food, she would get what she wanted in the end! I am honored to have such a talented women love what I do.

So, for all of you out there who have ever gone to a restaurant and coveted a chef's recipe, or for all of you who have been to a catered function and were dying to know what was behind one of the greatest dips you have ever tasted, I now divulge the secret to one of my most desired yet simple creations:

Lemon Bavarian Dip that is found in the Caterer's Pride Gets It's Due Chapter.

# International Luncheon

Kurt and Gaylene were planning a wedding when they called me in 1991. Anxious to get started on the plans, they could hardly wait to meet with me. I remember their enthusiasm and zeal for their event. It wasn't often that the groom was just as excited about the wedding details as the bride, so this was going to be fun.

The wedding and reception was to be held at the home of Mr. and Mrs. Hadley. Their patio and back yard is one of the most spectacular in this area due to Mrs. Hadley's garden expertise. The ceremony would face the stunning flower garden and view of the Feather River Canyon. I remember that the flowers that would be staged behind them were brilliant in color. They planned a ceremony that would include all of the wedding party in a full circle. The circle represented the connectedness of love among them.

Their wedding luncheon and rehearsal dinner needed to be catered, so there was a lot of planning to be done. One of the most important factors to them was the wedding menu. Most of the guests were Vegetarians and they wanted to create a meal that was mainly veggie friendly, yet impressive with a subtle sophistication to it. We decided on dishes that were from different cultures and still meatless. There was a certain sway in the menu I created; that read "International Luncheon." The meaning that the new Bower's wanted their guests to feel, all-embracing and satisfying. The menu stood framed on the Buffet table while the garden wedding was spectacular and all enjoyed the Luncheon.

From the moment I met this couple, I realized that Gaylene was a huge life cheerleader to everyone that came her way. She was always interested in my work, children, up's and downs and always had a hand out to help. She has a way of celebrating every individual she meets, and her heart is in all of her endeavors. Sixteen years later and Gaylene's heart has grown larger. She and Kurt still celebrate that beautiful wedding memory.

The Mushroom Strudel I made for their wedding can be found in the Beloved Veggie Meals Chapter. Their wedding menu is found in the Treasure Trove of Menus chapter.

# Rain or Shine We'll Take Em' Both

    Ramona and Doug's wedding was scheduled for the end of May, a beautiful time for a garden wedding or they hoped. I met with the couple many times and I remember Doug was focused on the stuffed red potato appetizer and Ramona's attention surrounded the ceremony. She often mentioned what a blessing it was to have found a minister to marry them who wasn't going to read a script of formal Biblical wife rules, like the man is your boss and you are his slave, etc. And now that she had that figured out all she and Doug had to do was decide on where the ceremony would actually take place. They had found the wedding site, but Doug wanted the indoor ceremony while Rhonda's dream was outside. Doug succumbed to his bride's wishes and everything was ready for the big day except the sunshine.

    The night before Rhonda was awake nearly the entire night as she paced the floor listening to the rain pound against her window. She had envisioned her dream garden wedding for so long and thought about the amount of money they had put up for this special outdoor place. It was time to go and face the day, rain or shine. When I arrived to start setting up, Rhonda was still crying. After a few rainy hours she settled into the idea of walking down an indoor staircase instead of strolling on the lush lawn. The buffet tables had to be moved to the balcony instead of the lawn gracing the river behind them. Everyone changed plans like changing hats and managed to be on time, well at least everyone. The guests stood waiting in the overcrowded living room, listening to the background music while the bride waited for the minister to arrive. They waited and waited for at least forty-five minutes, until someone in the audience announced there was a minister in the room. Desperate and doomed to the fated weather and minister, Rhonda made the decision to take advantage of the mystery Clergy. He joined center with the groom and Rhonda walked to the music down the stairway. Sure enough there was one more obstacle for her to overcome. As the minister opened the Bible he began reading the very scripture she had planned not to hear. She said, "I do" and kissed the groom when the doorbell rang and the sun came out. It was the hired minister who thought he was on time for the wedding. Rhonda sighed, looked at her husband and said, "We are doing this again." So the guests stayed on the balcony and ate while the wedding party walked the wet grass and partook in the second ceremony of the day. Both Doug and Rhonda were able to experience their desired expectations as the guests looked on from the balcony.

    The Stuffed Potato recipe can be found in the Sensational Starters Chapter.

# Over-the-Edge Bride and Over-the-Top Wedding

Laura and I began planning her wedding months before the December Christmas-theme wedding. I knew from the very beginning that Laura was not sure what she wanted as far as the decorating, except that she wanted a Christmas theme. We met quite often, and each time I had added to the idea list of creations. Laura was not a visual person, so it was frustrating for both of us. I knew she trusted me completely, but couldn't see what I was trying to show her; we just were not on the same page.

The guest list started at 250. They planned for the reception to be held in a lovely banquet room in the next town. As the date grew closer, she and her fiancée began to get more and more response cards back. After sitting down and going over the growing guest list, they found their 250 guests had risen to 400.

A few weeks later, Laura called with a bit more than just concern in her voice, explaining that the list was still growing. Finally I asked her just how many guests they sent invitations to. It was quiet for a moment on the other end of the phone until I heard a soft-spoken response that I wasn't sure I heard right. "How many did you say Laura?" Seven hundred was her answer. Now I took a breath. I told her there was no way we could put even 500 in the original room she had rented, because the room capacity was only 400.

I took another even deeper breath and said, "Laura, I think we are going to have to move the reception to the church school gym." With the event just a few weeks away, and nowhere else available in the middle of the busiest season of the year, Laura had no choice. She began to cry. I explained to her that no matter where we had the reception, it was going to be the most amazing event anyone in this town had ever been to. She didn't hear anything I was telling her. I knew she was thinking about basketball hoops and a wooden floor and bare walls. I knew that I had pushed her over the edge. She still could not comprehend that seven hundred guests would ever RSVP, let alone show up.

In the next two weeks, the list continued to grow and Laura stopped talking about the reception. She would just leave me a count about every two days. The list never went down. Now that I had the gym, I could create just about anything I wanted, and I needed to in order to make Laura's dream come true.

In the middle of the gym, I created an enormous long oval table by using connectors and putting oblong tables together. The middle was hollow, so I placed the largest Christmas tree I could find in it and decorated around it with white linen and heights, setting about thirty white poinsettias in place. This was just the appetizer table! Two large urns about five feet in height held white roses, lilies, and large mums. Two smaller trees decorated with white lights and gold embellishments sat on the tables opposite the urns. It was a huge, complete circle, and every inch of the tables, from one end to the other, was covered with appetizers. It was an extraordinary extravaganza of delight and beauty.

On each side of the center oblong table I placed about forty round tables. All were covered in white linen and topped with tree cuttings and white candles. The cake was held up on a small round table. It was one of the largest attractions of the night. There were nine layers going straight up like a building, twelve feet high. The dinner buffet tables consisted of six long tables, white lights, tree trimmings, and poinsettias. Christmas trees surrounded the room, all lit up with twinkle lights. There were so many tables and decoration that there was no room for the eye to go anywhere other than the beauty of it all.

Laura never came to the gym while we worked, and I knew she just did not think it could be beautiful. When the wedding ceremony was over, someone called and told us the bride and groom were on their way. We turned all the lights out, and the room was lit with candle and twinkle magic. Classical music was playing and there was an awesome feeling in the room. I stood across the room and waited for Laura to enter. She got to the door and gasped, quickly putting her hand over her mouth. She stood there for quite some time in silence, taking it all in. I think she cried, and I know she did on the inside. At the end of the evening, and every time I have seen her since, she hugged me and said, "I just couldn't see what you were trying to tell me; it was the most beautiful sight I have ever seen, and it took my breath away." She was blessed, and I was grateful to be blessed to create and to do it with such love.

# SEAFOOD CREPES?

One of the dreams every mother of a daughter holds in her heart is their daughter's wedding day. For most of her daughter's childhood, a mother plans that all-too-special, bittersweet day, sometimes with great sacrifice. She gives her precious angel away and is left with what she hopes is one of her grandest memories of her life—the wedding.

Gail Prince was no exception to the traditional rule. Gail, a Paradise resident for many years, visited my restaurant, Sandarella's, for lunch quite often and found out that I also had a catering establishment. A little less than a year before her daughter Mary's wedding day, Gail hired me as the caterer, and we started planning the occasion.

One afternoon Gail, Mary, and I sat down at the restaurant and discussed weddings. We covered every subject possible: the photographer, florist, cake decorator, DJ, and finally, the menu. If I had known ahead of time that Gail had a hard time making up her mind, I would have skipped the shop talk and got right to the heart of the matter—what we were going to serve her guests for dinner. I did not know that this decision would continue nearly a year.

For the next ten months, Gail and I, and sometimes Mary, the bride, met at the CARD center in Chico, California, where the wedding and reception would take place. At the first meeting, I asked Gail if she had a chance to look over the menu ideas I had sent home with her, and she told me she did but was not certain on any of the choices. She asked me again what each entree contained and how it would be served; I was not sure if she had forgotten, hadn't heard me the first time, or was testing me. After many such meetings, I realized Gail was going to ask the same questions at each meeting and during each phone conversation and what I was dealing with was a nervous mother of the bride who was also a perfectionist. This was my first experience with such a client, and I knew I could not spend all of my time on the entree for the reception: there was still the rental, the set-up and decor, the service, the help, and buffet presentation to worry about, and all of it was always overwhelming. How could I get Gail to focus and make just one decision?

I decided I was going to have to bend and just use and display patience with this wedding. Finally, Gail came to a decision to have the seafood crepes as the main entree in her daughter's wedding menu. I thought an angel had come down and worked out this business deal for me, finally.

Too good to be true: a few weeks before the big event I get a call from Gail. I knew instantly she was nervous and whatever she was about to suggest was not going to be a suggestion, but rather a handful for me. And, oh, it was!

Gail had decided she did not want the seafood crepes after all and would like instead for me to make a different entree each day for her to come by the restaurant and pick up so she and her husband could try them and then make the decision. I remember wanting to strangle her at first, but that same angel must have whispered "patience" in my ear because I mustered the shreds of it I had left and made the selections Gail asked for. They were ready each afternoon when she arrived.

About a week before the wedding, I got a call from Gail: "I've made my decision." Oh happy day, I thought as I waited, holding my breath for her answer. "My husband, Gill, and I have decided on the seafood crepes." I was still holding my breath when I heard her answer, and I can't believe I didn't pass out. What could I say but "Thank you, Gail, for your decision. You have made a wonderful choice…you're going to love them."

Love the crepes she did, and everything else on the buffet table. About two months after the wedding, I received a formal thank-you letter from Gail expressing her most heartfelt gratitude and apologies. She wrote, "If I would have had any idea how easy everything would have gone, I would have relaxed a lot sooner." In her letter she talked much of what she remembered, and most of it was about the attention to detail I put into everything, the experiences her guests talked about, and those unforgettable crepes.

To me, this experience was much larger than the seafood crepes or even the patience I had to practice. I learned to listen, to stop and look inside each client, each bride, and each mom and hear what was important to them—sometimes it's everything, and sometimes it's simply seafood crepes. Whatever it is, it's their dream, and my job is to make it come true.

Patience is a quality within each of our hearts that, when put into practice, creates a more loving and peaceful self. When we open our hearts to what is, we become more accepting of the needs of others around us. Gail taught me the value a mother puts into a daughter's wedding and to pay attention to every mother thereafter, which I did. I also reaped the blessing of Gail's friendship, and for that, I am grateful!

And yes, those Seafood Crepes can be found in
Caterer's Pride Gets It's Due Chapter.

# The Flower Girl

Once again Katie managed to pull it off, meaning she finagled a way to get what she wanted, one way or another! Katie grew up as a caterer's daughter and experienced weddings every weekend of her life for many years. Somewhere along the line, she got the notion that she was going to be a flower girl: she just had to find the bride. Finally, someone who knew us asked Katie to be her flower girl. Katie was overjoyed and looked forward to the big day, talking about it daily and wondering what her dress would look like. The bride had told us we could pick out the dress ourselves, so after catering a reception in San Luis Obispo, Katie and I took the time to shop for her dress. There in the older part of town, we found the dress of her dreams. She stood in front of the three-way mirror just like a bride and held the sides of the dress out as she turned around and around. The dress she had on was for display only, and we had to order her dress in her size and wait for it to arrive in Paradise.

Every day when she walked through the doors of the restaurant, she asked if the dress had arrived, which it hadn't, and I told her she would have to be patient. Finally, the dress was delivered, and I put it on the top shelf of my office at the restaurant. Before the day was over and before Katie arrived after her third-grade school day, I got the call. It was a call from the bride: the wedding had been canceled. "Not postponed, but not going to happen," were the words I used to describe it to Katie later that evening. I was prepared for her disappointment and her tears, but not for her fixed determination to keep the dress. Katie pleaded with me for the entire evening, trying to convince me that she could use the dress for her dress-up collection. I was firm and told her I had to return the dress and that was that.

The next day, I had meetings on into the evening; while Katie was at the library with friends, I met with my last mother and bride. We just started talking about a menu for the reception when Katie was dropped off by a friend and walked through the restaurant door. I stopped and introduced my potential clients to Katie, and from there she took over with the same resolution I had seen the night before. She took one step towards Jenny and asked, "Are you the bride?"

"Yes I am," replied Jenny.

"Do you have a flower girl for your wedding?" When Jenny told her no, Katie looked her in the eyes and asked, "Well, do you want one?"

Jenny started to ask when I interrupted, only because I couldn't reach over and strangle Katie in front of these people. Her mother said Jenny would love to have Katie as a flower girl, and Jenny agreed with her mother. I argued that they didn't even know Katie. Jenny said, "It doesn't matter, we would love to have Katie in the wedding."

Katie's final response was "Good. I'll get the dress!"

When she returned from my office with the dress, she wouldn't look at me, and Jenny and her mom didn't seem to need any explanation of why we had a flower girl's dress in the restaurant. They were delighted to have me cater the food and to have Katie walk down the aisle. It all worked out, and even I calmed down after saying goodbye to my clients that evening and finally looking Miss Katie in the eyes and asking her the big question, "Was that planned?"

# The Pasture Will Never Be the Same

Sharon called me to discuss her daughter's wedding reception. I instantly liked her because I could feel what a wonderful mom she was and the love she was putting into this event.

Sharon was a single mom and she was taking care of every detail of this wedding on her own including the cost by herself. I understood this desire she had to give her daughter her dream wedding completely. After meeting with her, I hoped she would choose me as the caterer, because I wanted to help her fulfill her dream.

The wedding became like a hobby for Sharon. Every extra moment she had was put into details, planning for and dreaming of the wonderful day. I often wondered if her daughter or anyone around fully understood what she was giving and creating.

She started with the location, a pasture on her sister's property. Her sister's husband had given his permission and even allowed Sharon to plant wildflowers and get the grass into shape. The grounds began to take on a beautiful park-like atmosphere. Sharon outlined every detail, from a white baby grand piano delivered to the pasture to a horse and buggy driving the guest to the wedding site. There was iced lemon water and fruit when the guests stepped off of the carriage on their way to putting the gifts in an old buggy draped with organza and pink roses. Next to the buggy was an antique table that held the guest book. Sharon had an arch with a seat underneath it made for the ceremony. Everything in the pasture was white. As the guests set down their gifts and walked towards the wedding site, they saw white chairs, the white piano, and white linen covering the tables. A wooden dance floor was made, umbrellas covered the food tables that held large urns of overflowing flowers, and the food beckoned to hungry mouths. And last, but not least by any means, was the tempting dessert table displaying a delicious, tantalizing course of sweet foods that awaited delight from Sharon's guests. And on that table were the heart-shaped cookies she baked and decorated with the bride and groom's name in pink icing.

I think it was the time Sharon put into every detail that I felt all the way through the planning to the wedding day. This was truly a mother whose heart was displayed throughout the entire wedding.

The day of the wedding, while setting up the guest and buffet tables, I heard Sharon's brother-in-law talking to himself, saying, "I don't think this is ever going to be a pasture again."

Late into the evening, when the stars became almost as bright as the twinkle lights, Sharon came up to me and held out her arms and embraced me and whispered "thank you" in my ear. We both had an unspoken understanding for what she needed to do. Sharon was an ambassador who was worthy of this dream. She deserved this beautiful night as much as her daughter for all the years of service in taking care of her children. I have never been back to her sister's property, and even if it is once again a pasture with grazing sheep, it will always be a ground that was blessed with a mother's love.

The Pork Tenderloin with Blackberry Sauce is found in the
Caterer's Pride Gets It's Due Chapter.

# The Princess Arrives at the Ball

After my first daughter Kellie's wedding, her sister Korrie told me she did not want me catering hers. "It's too much work, Mom, and you should be able to just enjoy the day as the mother of the bride." I really believed she meant that, except women do change their minds and Korrie has been known to take this female trait to extremes.

Brian and Korrie's wedding was planned for June 24, 2000. I had three years to recover from Kellie's wedding before I began helping Korrie with hers. The two of us visited every country club in her area, but we just couldn't seem to find the rapport we were looking for with any of the event coordinators we met. Finally, the day came when everything we needed just fell into place, including our connection with and the determination behind the person in charge. As we looked over menus and talked about décor, Korrie grew a little nervous; wondering if this wedding was going to look like her sister's or better, or possibly worse. As the meeting went on she kind of slipped it in that her mother was a professional caterer. She made sure to get the word "professional" in. After some discussion and then some…they agreed to allow me to prepare the appetizer table and to decorate entire room.

By this time, Korrie had forgotten all about her original request, and I was glad. I wouldn't know what to do without being able to get my hands on one of my children's weddings. We spent many months planning and creating new ideas and passing on old ones. I bought yards and yards of exquisite fabric for shirting and draping the food, cake, and head tables. I approached the design of the appetizer table in an artsy way, including a water fountain in the middle and a succession of round mirrors about four feet in height, each stage derived from the last, holding fresh fruit. The two of us met often with the event coordinator, photographer, florist, and singer. It was time well spent together as we approached the big day.

The day Korrie had dreamed of all her life finally arrived. As the guests entered the gorgeous room, they stopped to sign the guest book under an umbrella, where they were offered a glass of fruited water and a program with Brian and Korrie's personal romantic love story inside. The reception room sat in a splendor of stateliness waiting for the princess and guests to arrive.

Korrie had spent the day in a fairytale dream state as she was pampered and attended to—this too was a large part of her wedding dream. When the limo drove up to the country club, "That's when everything happened for me. As I stepped out of the limo, it was like the princess had arrived at the ball," she remembers. And it was just that. A few minutes later, she and her father walked down a spiral staircase that seemed like it was the longest bridal entrance in history. But Korrie had planned it that way, making sure everyone's eyes were on her for as long as the walk took. She was magnificently beautiful, and everyone felt her and Brian's joy for the rest of the night. Sometime during the reception, Korrie put her arm around me and said, "Mom, this is my dream, thank you." It was my dream, too.

# Royalty Tree
# Made for a King and Queen

The Robbins's son was planning to be married, and this was not just an everyday affair—to the Robbins, it was the event of the year in our small town. They wanted a wedding fit for royalty, so I took my job very seriously as I planned for the event. I wanted to present something unique that made a statement to this family and their friends. After many months, I came up with a grand idea so unusual that I was sure no one in this community had ever set their eyes on such a creation.

I found a gentleman who built two wooden cones for me. They were five feet and four feet tall. The day before the wedding, Mindy and I made two hundred and fifty cream puffs, or maybe more. All of the batter was mixed by hand and then piped through a pastry tube. Our hands were so sore; we could hardly squeeze the last batches of cream puffs. When they had cooled, we attached each one to one of the wooden cones. In between the cream puffs, we placed red roses that had fully opened. At the top of the tree sat a white cherub. The second tree was covered with fruit, white lilies, and yellow roses and had a pineapple at the top. The two trees were such a royal statement that they almost took the guests' breath away.

This was the first and last time I have ever made a royalty tree. I knew ahead of time what kind of work it was going to take, but it was worth it just to see the look of awe on the faces of the wedding family.

# Mellow Meadow Wedding

A lovely bride named Karen called from San Francisco one day and made arrangements to meet with me at the Mineral Ranch valley where her wedding and reception would soon take place.

Driving into the meadow, I instantly knew why she wanted to create a celebration here. It was away from everywhere that was busy and focused on the world. Nothing could happen here except to feel and experience beauty. So we got busy and in one meeting designed the menu and decorating plans.

The guest list was small, only about sixty guests. We lined long tables down the center of the meadow with chairs on both sides. White linen covered the tables, and champagne flutes with folded napkins enhanced the place settings. Antique glass lanterns were placed in the center of the table from one end to the other. The creek and the birds chirping were the only sounds that could be heard while we were setting up. This was not just another wedding. As I stood back and looked at this long table in the meadow, I realized it was an exquisite, yet modest welcome to dine in the celebration of love. Looking at it from a guest's perspective, it represented the importance of your presence, the realization that without the guest, there can be no celebration. Here the guests were welcomed and honored.

My second favorite memory was the menu. I was just crazy about the idea of serving grilled polenta. Polenta is one of my top five foods. I could eat it for three meals a day. And what could go better with this than grilled trout? Every sense was touched that day, including the taste of outdoors.

The Meadow menu can be found in the Treasure Trove of Menus Chapter
and the Polenta is in the Italian Dining Chapter.

# Lights Out

It was about 1989 or so when I got a phone call from Tom about his daughter's wedding. The wedding reception was taking place at a country club, but the family wanted to enjoy brunch the morning after the wedding in Tom's beautiful backyard.

I arrived at Tom's home after our phone chat with pictures, menus, pencil and paper in hand. We discussed the menu; he showed me the kitchen and the backyard. All the while I sensed he was not sure about hiring me. He said goodbye with, "I'll get back to you." I really didn't think I would hear from him, but a few weeks later his wife Donna called and told me they had decided to use my services.

In August, when the wedding was approaching, I made another visit to Tom's backyard, and we decided where to place the buffet for the morning brunch. Tom was beginning to remind me of a nervous mom who wanted everything in place and nothing out of order.

A few days before the event, I got a call from Tom asking me to consider skirting and decorating the buffet table the night before, while they were at the wedding. "Consider" meant "do" in Tom's vocabulary. What was a caterer to do? Argue; explain that I needed that time to do my prep? No, I told him I would be glad to come over and set everything up. I didn't tell Tom I would have to stop my production because I figured he already didn't believe that I was capable of getting it all done by early morning. Why throw more fuel into the fire of his fear and nervousness? I thought

That night, I stopped my work and drove to Tom's house, noticing for the first time that day some very large clouds coalescing above me. I worked for about two hours unloading containers of decorations and tablecloths. When I left, the buffet table was skirted with muslin fabric and topped with white and pink covers. All of the decorations, flowers were perfectly placed on the table, including an array of silk vegetables. As I left, I looked back to make sure that Tom would be happy with what I was looking at.

I continued my prep work on into the evening, thinking of this family and their celebration and feeling relieved the decorating was over and all I would have to do in the morning was walk in the door with the food. I was so busy that I didn't hear the raindrops falling until a very large crack outside got my attention. I stopped and looked out of nearest window and saw hail coming down and lighting flashing, and all I could do was think of the buffet table in Tom's backyard. Another cracking sound came from outside, and the lights were out! I stood there in the dark and said to myself, "Is this a catering nightmare?"

Indeed it was. I could not use my machines, nor could I even see to make sure I was not cutting off my fingers, now that the knife was going to be my chopping machine for the rest of this job. The storm got worse as I lit lanterns and candles. I prepared the food into the morning hours, and got only two or so hours of sleep.

I arrived at Tom and Donna's lovely home at 8 A.M., just as planned. When Tom opened the door, the look on his face frightened me. Walking towards the backyard, I could only imagine what the table looked like. To my dismay and panic, the entire skirting was now dripping with colors from the dye in the silk vegetables, looking like a long piece of tie-dye fabric. It was not the table, but the horror in Tom's face that frightened me. Surely he knew I did not order this storm. But it did not matter to him what I was thinking; he just knew it was my job to fix it. And I did.

In less than one hour, the guests would arrive. Donna and I took the fabric off of the table, washed, dried, and ironed it, and re-skirted the table. When the doorbell rang, the food and presentation were just as Tom had pictured.

This near-disaster grew a very long and trusting relationship with the family. On many occasions, I saw Tom other catering jobs I was doing and he always put his arm around me and thanked me for coming through for them. It took a sense of urgency and pride to complete the job, but it was worth it. That was the only job I ever did in the dark— in fact, after that brunch, it seemed like everything got brighter.

# June and Jamie: Mother and Bride

In fifteen years of catering, I have worked with some wonderful people, but the most amazing mother and daughter duo was June and Jamie.

As their home was being transformed in preparation for a backyard wedding, the three of us were making plans. We would meet in the evenings on the unfinished patio and envision how the end product would look, while planning menus, decorating, seating—every last detail down to a science.

Jamie is June's only daughter, and this long-awaited day was a one-time event in June's heart. I felt this passion in June from the very first meeting. And from Jamie, I immediately understood that she knew just what she wanted and the most important thing for her was to realize the evening of bliss she had waited for her whole life.

We spent months planning and meeting and laughing and connecting over glasses of wine. My job, although a lot of work, was easy because of whom I was working for. These two women gave me respect and trust and something more. I knew they really understood who I was. I felt appreciation in everything I did. I have never counted how many weddings I have catered in the last nineteen years, but this had to have been one of my top five. And June and Jamie are my favorite mom and daughter of all time.

I catered the rehearsal dinner the night before with down-home flare, serving barbequed ribs, corn on the cob, cornbread, potato salad, and baked beans. The lights that June and Jamie had so patiently and artistically strung were turned on for the special guests like a preview of the evening to come. It was a joyous evening; the love was truly felt at that table.

And the next evening, the love doubled under the lights. Jamie and her father stood on the patio waiting to make their walk down the aisle. The music started; Etta James singing "At Last." There was a sigh from the audience and everyone felt chills. There was gush of tears from the bride before she even made it down the aisle. And I had a lump in my throat as I held my breath. Somehow the words of this song rang true as the perfect beginning of the night. I felt blessed to meet and work with and love such wonderful people.

The following is the secret marinade recipe I use on the tri-tip. In fact, at this wedding, a gentleman who had just graduated from a culinary art school in San Francisco approached me and nearly begged me for this recipe.

I told him it would be in my cookbook, it can be found in the Caterer's Pride Gets It's Due Chapter.

# Cowboy Scott

When I think about all of the wonderful people I was blessed to have worked with, I always think of Scott. I called him one day and asked for his help, and he said, "Sure, I'll be there." And he was, for the next seven years.

In seven years, we never had a bad time together; no matter what the job had in store for us; Scott was positive, positive, and positive.

He did anything from set up to take down to barbecuing to prepping food, but mostly he became the bartender. We all finally figured out that Scott loved the attention he got from the women who hung out at the bar.

Poor Scott—the things he did for me! Once I made him wear a grass skirt and a coconut bra and kneel under a short grass hut for a Hawaiian theme party. And at every job, just before show time, I would make him go over the plan for the evening. It was the same plan we always had, but he just stood there patiently waiting for me to get the words out, letting me go over it all again, just so I felt less nervous.

Scott always came to work wearing Wrangler jeans and a tall hat. Before the guests arrived, he had his bow tie on and a cummerbund around his waist. He started bringing his own bar kit and developed some professional ideas of his own on the job. Scott is a tease and full of life. He always kept us happy, light, and joyful. On some of the worst jobs, he made me smile, and on the best jobs, he always made me feel the goodness. We were like family and worked as one.

During the time I was remodeling the restaurant; Scott came day after day and sanded all of the tables for me. I never forgot this. On his wedding day, I gave him the gift of food and service, and it was my highest pleasure. Scott is one of those guys you wish your daughters would marry, and even if they don't, he still feels like a son to you. I was blessed to share every catering job I did with him. He brought so much joy into my work. Thank you, Scott!

# Big Beautiful Spirits

I was introduced to a wonderful world of high-quality business people when I was hired to do the catering for Financial Title in Sacramento, California. The Financial Title team is a first-class, big-hearted thinker for their clients and employees. I believe their success is do to the way they care for everyone involved.

When I arrive for an open house I immediately sense the excitement in the air and feel the joy in the office for the party that is going to take place. The office girls are scrambling to get the beverage table and ice ready; several are decorating and laying out the red carpet. What impress me the most is even after a hard day's work and then all this party fuss, the way their customers are greeted is with a kind of old fashioned welcoming that feels like family. Clients are lavished with food and drinks, music, gifts and attention. But behind all of this generous flattering is abundant, kind spirits that are not afraid to give.

My favorite part of planning these parties are the different office event themes, this is where I watch the excitement build for months with the staff. The office manager and myself work the details out and then I get to work creating their themes. Some of the best have been: "Reaching for the Stars", "Fall Harvest", "Fall in Love with Financial Title", and "Cinco de Mayo".

At the end of every open house I'm feeling exhausted from the work, but smiling with gratitude for how I have been treated kindly and with respect. Financial Title is a company that teaches that old-fashioned service is still in our business world today.

You will find menus for these events in the Treasure Trove of Menus Chapter.

# Another Stupid Wedding: That's Why I'm Having a Potluck

At Katie's sister Korrie's bridal shower, Katie determined the theme of her own wedding.

About three years before that day, she met Margaret for the first time when Margaret came over to our house to discuss her daughter's wedding. Katie was thirteen, and like most girls that age, didn't often get up on the right side of the bed. And that's how it started that day. When our voices woke her up, she was not too happy, and then to top it off, I handed her a list of duties I wanted done that same day. Katie just had to add her two cents to the conversation.

She had never met Margaret, so when she walked out of her room and I introduced her, she said, "Oh brother. Are you working on another stupid wedding?" Margaret looked up at her and answered, "Yes, my daughter's." Katie woke up quick and knew she had put her foot in her mouth. Margaret laughed, I didn't, and Katie just tried to get herself out of that one. For the next couple of years, we all teased her about how she met Margaret.

She still hadn't quite learned to think before she spoke when seated outside at Korrie's shower. She spoke up and said, "This is too fancy for me. When I get married someday, I just want a potluck." The few of us that heard her held our breath for a moment and then said, "That's a really good idea, Katie, and we'll do that."

A few years have gone by, and Katie is not yet married, but her family has not forgotten about her potluck. We remind her about it every chance we get. She thinks we are kidding. We'll see!

# The Best Salmon You'll Ever Eat

This is an impeccable fish story, but not the storytelling of catching the fish, rather the preparing of it. It's a story about perfection, a man named Bill and the "best tasting salmon you'll ever eat!

I met Bill on October 1, 1994 at Bill's home where I did the catering for his friends Lynnda and Doug Leiker's wedding, Bill's best friends. Lynnda and I had spent months of wonderful connection while planning for her special day. She was just one of those brides that made my job easier because she trusted me and allowed my creativity to unfold.

On the day of the wedding Bill sat back and took the whole experience in. He told me later…he, being the skeptic, did not believe I would just show up and be able to create such a masterpiece. "I just didn't know how you were going to do it." Much to Bill's surprise and amazement everything turned out just the way it was supposed to, just the way the bride dreamed. Bill must have been impressed, because two months later he called me to ask if I would consider doing his office Christmas party.

I met with Bill one evening and we worked on a menu. I gave him lots of choices, but had a hard time visualizing the selections. After lots of brainstorming and enthusiasm Bill arrived at the place in his mind that he was sure he wanted this meal to be the state of art presentation. It was important for his guest to feel catered to, but not uncomfortable.    About the time Bill's wife Lana arrived home we were finished discussing the importance of the event and on to the menu. After another forty-five minutes of soulful searching and food chit-chatting the three of us had created an interesting and appealing menu, except that Bill felt something was still missing. He said we needed just one more item and thinking that I had this man all figured out…I knew that no matter how enticing the food sounded to him or how desirable it looked to his guest, it was not enough. Bill wanted just one more specialty…something they had never tasted before, like a decoy that was the bait waiting for those office boys to grab!

Well, it was now or never, no matter how tired I was I had better make this next suggestion; the last entrée believable or I was never going to get home or get the job! I had remembered the cover of a magazine with a picture of a salmon fillet presented on a beautiful platter and the recipe was inside. Wanting to try it, but hadn't found the time, somehow I knew this was going to be the one for Bill. Within the next few minutes I thought I had convinced Bill that the salmon was the final touch to his upcoming party, until he hesitated, and then I got really serious and said, "Trust me, it's the best salmon you will ever eat." I think at that moment what I was doing was convincing my self, since I had never prepared it, only glanced at the recipe. The conclusion of Bill's decision showed me his trust and his zealous anticipation for the upcoming office event, and even the outlook of the mystery salmon.

Two weeks had gone by and in just twenty-four hours I would be on Bill's front door step ready to unload my colorful food pageant. Something told me I had better find that salmon recipe and start rehearsing.

I arrived at Sandarella's, turned on the lights, music to set the cooking mood and began looking for the magazine with the salmon platter on the cover. Hum…I couldn't find it. I look in every possible place I could have put the recipe aside, but it was not to be found. I turned off the lights, the music and drove home, hoping it was there. Nope, it had disappeared; I drove back to Sandarella's and started my prep. I poured a glass of red wine, put on the music and decided I would make up my own recipe.

The day of the event I felt confident in everything I served, even the salmon. But I was hoping for that euphoric taste I had so proclaimed would happen with the first bight.

Bill's guests gave me good and great reviews, but Bill was still not sure it was perfect. Standing near the buffet table to assist guests I saw this: two co-workers walked up with their empty plates to refill them and as they scraped the last of the salmon off the plate one of them said to the other, "This is the best salmon I have ever had." To my delight Bill was standing on the other end of that buffet table across from me. At that moment he looked up at me and I gave him the biggest haughty…self-important look on my face followed by a large grin, not a smile…a grin. He got it! I was thinking, "Don't doubt me again." At the end of the evening Bill was more than happy, believed in me and was no longer a challenge. I said goodnight with a smile, a tip and trying to remember what were the ingredients in the salmon sauce…sometime later I remembered.

The recipe for the Boston Glazed Salmon is
found in the Caterer's Pride Gets It's Due Chapter.

*Chapter 6*

# *Simply Sandarella's*

*With a scrap of fabric,*
*A cherished recipe,*
*And a call of inspiration,*
*Begins a dream...called*

# SIMPLY SANDARELLA'S

*It started as a dream to open the restaurant doors in 1992, and it happened. I set a goal of six weeks of renovation and in six weeks to the day, October 6, 1992 a little old fashioned store front holding nine small round tables with fabric table cloths and antique chairs sat waiting for it's opening.*

Diana called me about a month before the sign was to be hung and said, "Well, I was thinking again... and I think you should name the restaurant, "Simply" Sandarella's because everyone that walks in will look around and remark that is looks just like what you would do." So I took her advise once again, and added the Simply.

About thirty minutes before the doors opened; outside stood about ten people waiting. I was bit nervous, making sure everything was in place just like all the times guest were about to arrive at my home. I put a CD on and unlocked the door. Welcoming these people was not like greeting a customer, but rather a friend. As I was making my way back to the kitchen, I heard some women chatting, and one of them said, "This looks just like her," someone else remarked, "like a bit of Mendocino." I smiled thinking of Diana and how well she knew me.

It was fall, just a slight chill was in the air and as the winter months came more and more guests came to Sandarella's. Some for the first time and others were weekly guests becoming part of the quaint establishment. Winter's cold welcomed the hot cup of homemade soup nearly everyone wanted. The blackboard menu changed daily and offered a different soup, entrée, quiche and sandwich selection each day. The entrée might be stuffed shells, seafood crepes, or chili-tomato quiche. Each meal was generously served with two kinds of fresh salads, bread and a smile. All the menu items were made with lots of love and the best ingredients. It was a celebration luncheon fare for your pleasure, with all the charm of a nostalgic country inn; while guests enjoyed a magical feeling of "Coming home."

The value I gained each day was the feeling of family in my own town. Cooking for strangers and putting love into it was like cooking for my own loved ones in my home. I embraced that feeling each day and added it to their plates.

During the years of Sandarella's open doors I found myself immersed in a life-changing adventure filled with unexpected warmth, surprises, challenges and lessons. I found through this experience that life offers us thousand and thousands of chances...and I took one. What I gleaned was the gift of embracing all of it.

The following stories are about some of the people and who helped create and sustain the magic... the best ingredient used there.

# Jen

I met Jen around her fourth grade in school. She grew into an eccentric, bold, individual. She is a gal whom I would say has a rare case of women grit! I love everything about her, especially her wit and that other part that goes with it, her sense of humor and a bit of Kate Hepburn the great actress of our time.

When Jen came to work at Sandarella's she brought her vintage diva style, cheerfulness and dash!

Every day was a new challenge and Jen flowed with all of it. She showed up always about ten minutes early and you knew when she walked through the door she was a different diva than the day before. Jen loved playing with Nostalgia and the wistfulness that came with it was playfulness for the guest and me. No matter how hard a day I was having she made me not just smile, but laugh until it hurt.

Two of my favorite memories of Jen are how she answered the phone every day, "Sandarella's- happy lunch!" And because we celebrated every holiday at Sandarella's, Jen always got into it as well. One October she came to work with a large trash sack over her shoulder. She carried it right into the dining room area and the next thing I knew – I was watching autumn leaves spilling out of this bag onto the floor. Jen suggested as she spread the leaves over the entire floor because this would be a fun way to bring in and stir up the season. I wasn't sure about this, but as the days went by I realized the guests loved it and soon word had gotten out about the leaves and people were visiting just to add to the crunchy sound.

Besides the joy of working with Jen I have the memories of our daily, weekly long philosophical conversations that would immense in profound and insightful reflections of the ordinary and unusual. Jen is an old soul that gave on a deeper level than most ever do. She was truly a woman that was not afraid to embrace everything in life, even pain.

Jen made a difference every day she worked at Sandarella's; it wouldn't have been the same without her. Jen helped birth the spirit and beauty of an aged building into a charming adventure with her special gifts.

# Doris

Doris arrived every morning about five am and started the baking. She had studied the night before for her college classes and I know she was tired when she arrived, but chatter, chatter, chatter, some giggles and stories about yesterdays events, and that's how I started off my early mornings at Sandarella's. Who ever arrived first would start the coffee, while I think she drank hot chocolate, she still made the coffee for me. She only had a few hours before she had to leave for school so she quickly started her pastries, the coffee cake and croissants.

Doris had a good amount of sass in her step, always letting me know if I had pushed her button and smiling if she had pushed mine. The same steps were taken each morning when she was doing her winding down dance out the door. She quickly put her pastries in the oven, set the timer (because she knew I would forget and burn the pastries), stroll to the sink and start running the water to soak the mixing bowl. As I heard the water I would start to ask her to please wash out the bowl and she gave me the giddy-up response, "Sorry, I gotta go or I'll be late." I smiled every day and said, "Brat" as she drove away.

The coffee cake recipe called for Cream of Tarter and I don't know what she would do with it, and she would ask about it's missing like I did something with it, but every time I looked at the shopping list; Cream of Tarter was on it again. I own about 8 containers of Cream of Tarter.

Doris is one of the most loving, loyal and hard working women I have ever known. She gave me so much of herself with her stories, her wonderful laughter, cheerful giggles and such a good heart. She became a big sister to my youngest daughter Katie, a memory that now is a cherished treasure to me. The time we spent together baking for holidays and making gift baskets and just listening to her share her boy friend woes and heart aches and good times. If she had been out with the girls the night before I could count on there was going to be a story in the morning and they were detailed so I had to be on my toes not to forget yesterdays accounts because it was going to be a part of this one. And there is one tale or rather a few tales we share only between us, but all of it combined is the fiber and thread of history together.

Mornings with Doris made me smile each day and proud to have her by my side in the wee early mornings…a smile that lingered after the door closed behind her. Working with Doris was not just a privilege, rather if felt like working with a daughter.

So much time has passed and Doris is married and has four daughters. Domestic, creative, giving, resourceful and beautiful inside and out, giving of herself to her family, doing what she does best…an open hand to help and an open heart to love. My life has been blessed to carry our memories.

In honor of Doris and cream of tarter I share my
favorite coffee cake with you in the Brunch Chapter.

The Orange Poppy-Seed Scones Doris made every morning
are in the Sandarella's Chapter.

# Soup Dragons

*If you cook*
*They will come*

    Eleven A.M. and soups on; every day anywhere from three to five women who worked just down the street at the elementary school stood waiting for the doors of Sandarella's restaurant to open.

    Jen would holler to me in the kitchen, "The soup dragons are here, are you ready?" I was always ready for these Paradise teachers who needed some energy, peace and quiet and a place to re-group before they returned to the classroom. Jen named them the dragons because they were ready to blow the door down if we didn't open it and feed them right then. The only thing they ever ordered was the homemade soup of the day, sometimes having a second cup. It didn't take long to realize these gals appreciated homemade soup, and soon it was because of these ladies that I started making a second soup of the day so they would have a choice. I loved every minute of cooking for them.

    I enjoyed watching them wind down for one hour of their day, enjoying themselves and the food. Like all teachers everywhere they have a job that is one only a certain kind of person can do. It was my privilege to feed them and one of them every year was my daughter Katie's teacher. I remember how kind and thankful they were to visit my restaurant. It was one on these teachers, Mrs. Lafferty, that left me the note on her plate expressing her gratitude for her meals and it was her words that titled this book. It's such a blessing when we appreciate each other. Some of those teachers are still teaching at the same elementary school and I think of the difference they have made in so many children's lives and our family life.

# Egg Heaven

Jen unlocked the door exactly at eleven am as she did every day and in walked the start of our regulars; we called them. Jen brought back a couple of orders and I got started on them while she served the beverages and took more orders. I noticed one of our best customers I will call Mr. Jones, walked through the door and taking one look at him I realized I had forgotten to do something that morning.

Jen put some more orders on the clip above me, I handed her a couple of completed orders and more customers walked through the door. Every time I tried to get Jen's attention, she was off again attending to another table. Finally I was able to tell her that the special loaf of sweet bread I usually make for one of our customers with out eggs; I had forgotten to leave the egg out. She picked up another order and on her way out she said, "Too late, I already told him it was made." When she came back in and snagged his plate, I told her she couldn't serve him the bread with the egg in it and as she quickly walked away from me she whispered…ok, so he's not going to egg heaven…not a big deal!!

This was a typical lighthearted scheme of Jens that kept me going day to day. Mr. Jones did come back every other day and brought a guest with him. I made sure not to forget to make his loaf of sweet bread without the egg!!

# Good Sport

Jim Brown kind of just showed up in my life thorough and about catering and some other good friends. One day he was the janitor for the elementary school and the next he is traveling the world taking pictures of cats at animal shows. But somewhere in between we became buddies. For years we were hired for the same events and were growing our business at the same time. By the time I opened the restaurant doors we were old friends.

Jim is a nice guy. How many really nice people do you know? This Jim is solid, authentic, funny and talks a lot like me, so we hit it off from the beginning. He was as excited as I was for the doors of Sandarella's to open, but that's because he and his lovely wife Barb wanted to dine there. When I explained to Jim that the menu was different each day and would be written on the black board every morning, he suggested that I have a small menu designed each week and that he would be glad to create this menu on his computer and have the copies made in exchange for a meal. I thought he was crazy for being responsible for this, but I agreed.

Every Monday he showed up and grabbed my list from me and ran home, put it on his computer and then off to have them copied and before lunch was served he was back at the restaurant with the creative menus. Poor Jim had been ripped off - he had waited all weekend for a good meal and now there was a line out the door, which meant he had an hour wait. This man was hungry and I felt bad and knew I needed to feed him. I told him to slip into the kitchen since he was family anyway. He did, but there wasn't a lot of room for him so we told him to take a seat on the ladder that happened to be near the door and he did. Jim was such a good sport. He waited patiently for his food and enjoyed it on a ladder step. He chattered and drove Jen crazy, but he never bothered me ever! I loved having him hang around as long as he went home eventually.

I miss those days with Jim after catering a wedding and then sharing our stories together. Jim has moved on to become a successful photographer. I will forever treasure our talks and gut laughing stories and his humor. "Hey Jim, I've got to go."

The Potato Chili Cheese Soup was Jim's favorite
and can be found in Soup Comforts Chapter.

*Chapter 7*

# Covered In Grace

# Covered In Grace

*To the hungry soul every bitter thing is sweet. Proverbs 27:7*

What made Mother Teresa a woman before her time? Was it the strength of her tenacity to not give up until she was granted permission to start a mission? Was it her quest to serve God by serving the poor? Or was it God bestowing his order upon her before the church was ready to fully understand the divine in the calling?

I believe that God handpicked Mother Teresa because of her selfless heart. He knew that she would be recorded in history for her servant work, but what he knew more is that her work would be a legacy for all of mankind to call upon in the long days to come. God knew that she understood the calling was not just to feed the leper, but also to work with the poverty of the spirit. It was Mother Teresa like Jesus who felt the yearnings of the human soul and so he placed her on the streets of Calcutta to be a mother to all people, straight from his heart.

During her joyous walk with us here she went beyond touching the flesh of the sick and pour. Her calling was to bring us home to our hearts; our spirit over and over again. She was one of the great teachers of our time whose wisdom we should all study, cultivate, embrace and use on the home front. Through God she taught us to restore and to re build the human being and the family. (Proverbs: Better is a dry morsel, and quietness therewith, than and house full of sacrifices with strife. Children's children are the crowns of men; and the glory of children are their fathers.)

How could Mother Teresa look past the flaws of mankind? Did you ever have a grandmother, parent or someone who looked at you with eyes of love and not judgment? Remember how different that felt when you were a child compared to how you fee when people look at you now as an adult? Mother Teresa looked not just into the faces of the poor but also into the faces of the world with eyes of love, with the eyes of God. That is why she gave of herself to the world to give us God. God blessed her character with a virtue coming straight from him called Grace. (St. John 1: 16 "And of his fullness have we all received, and grace for grace.") This tiny woman, this five feet frame was covered in grace. Every person she met, she embraced them with a state of grace and therefore her work was of grace and not works.

Every American in our country will never forget the pictures in our minds of the people standing in the background looking up at the World Trade Center on 9-11. Every eye watching, every body standing was covered in grace. What did it take for us to come together, connect, and see each other as one body and one family? It took tragedy. Whenever tragedy strikes we all infinitely feel it together as a whole.

We have to face up to the unfortunate growing amount of rage demonstrated in the world today. The amount of unaccountability and blame for personal suffering that pushes a person past a point of conscious emotions to the other side of tragedy; inner hunger screaming to get a fix.

What can we do to strengthen and prepare our children for the streets of life before we send them there and why would I use Mother Teresa's life as an example to draw from? Because she taught us that holiness aspires at home. We recognize that the greatest gift we possess is our children on the day of their birth and yet what we value the most seems to slip away until hindsight brings wisdom staring us in the face. Children need to feel that the family union is their heart's resting place like an oasis for their soul. Connecting with family to a child should feel not just safe but like the warmth of a circle of fire all bundled up clutching a warm cup and really sharing. This impression seems almost sacred to me like a mold that is pinned to the heart forever and ever.

Gratitude, charity and forgiveness are other virtues we need to keep us whole and undivided in a family and the world. They have all been talked about many times probably because they are fundamental in the seriousness of raising a child.

All of my three children would tell you they could hardly get the gift opened before they had to start writing a thank you note. I probably did this because of the value in appreciation that was instilled in me as a child. I never have taken anything for granted in my life and I wanted my children to experience this. I wanted them to stop and look and feel every time someone did a favor, gave a gift, said a kind word or went out of their way for them. I pushed them to look for the gift in every experience and to never ever take anything for granite. By doing this I opened up a world of positive thinking and acting. It taught them to always look at what they have and not just focus on what they do not have and opened a door of taking responsibility. I can remember times that I have been so grateful that I actually felt like God had just touched me and the state of Grace was exuding from my soul.

I found a note scribbled on a piece of paper tucked in a book that I had read about 15 years ago and it read, "Thank you God for my tears of the depth of me like no one else can cry and fall to her knees over a sunset." For me gratitude is a state of fullness, a state of grace. In the Jewish faith the essence of being a Jew is to be thankful. In their prayer, Modeh Ani: "I am grateful to God for bringing life to me each and every day," expresses the grace of gratitude. Having a grateful heart creates a giving state of mind. I believe that gratitude is one of the greatest gifts we can receive and pass onto our children and even more than that I deeply believe it is our responsibility to teach our children this benevolent gift. It is the first step in creating a servant's heart in our families.

You will find, as you look back upon your life, that the moments that stand out are the moments when you have done things for others.
~ *Albert Drummond* ~

Giving starts in the heart of all humans. We all have something to give even when we think we have nothing. Mother Teresa's life taught us that every person we reach out and give to be a gift of love to God. This is charity and adding a charitable element to all aspects of our lives keeps us connected and binds us to one another. Living and teaching the spiritual language of giving to our children is like sowing is to reaping. And believe me when I tell you that what our children see what we give, what we put into our families is what they learn to give back.

*Giving is a necessity sometimes more urgent, indeed, than having.*
~ *Margaret Lee Runbeck* ~

Forgiveness is the secret to life yet probably the hardest work we will ever do. We were not created perfect beings and not with out error and therefore the simplest act of letting go of grievance cuts between heart and ego. There is such power in forgiveness in that it not only sets you free and opens doors, but it is one of the highest places spiritually we can go. Many years ago, when I choose forgiveness, that moment seemed like the first day of my life, in that I was linked with grace and a miracle as though I was handed a new heart as my soul was washed of pain. I never looked back. My therapist told me, it was my choice and it didn't matter to him, it was my decision. That's just it; it's a choice to take our relationships to the highest level and demonstrate in our children's safe haven, their homes, that forgiveness is natural, necessary and life changing. When forgiveness is apart of a family life it becomes a lesson that is remembered in the heart of a child and easily accessible as an adult.

*The weak can never forgive.*
*Forgiveness is the attribute of the strong.*
*~ Mohandas Gandhi ~*

Families come in different packages, not always being the traditional mother and father situation. I know that single moms today face one of the largest challenges in this life. I was a single mom, I was the only parent on duty with two business and most of the time the only thing I felt was the pain inside of me while going through my divorce. But something snagged at me daily to keep our family together and never give up. I had to finally face the shame I felt of failing and then I realized the good stuff was flying by and if I rose to the occasion I could make something of the good stuff that was still flying in. I grabbed the only thing worth living for, the good, knowing that something is going to get passed on…I'm going to find a way to make it good. It was years of hard work in rebuilding our union and finding a way to balance work and the mother and father role. I kept making mistakes, but somehow my children forgave me and we became a new, stronger family. We are the parent on duty and we are what makes the good stuff, like it or not, want it or not, it is our job. One day when the kids leave and you look around at all the other families and then back at yours you can feel proud. It's an inner knowing that of all the work and accomplishments you have obtained in your life, none is far greater than the job of raising your child.

What's your history? Are the seeds you are about to plant feel like they are from scratch? Are you faced with the responsibility of raising children and creating a family and you don't have the recipe because no one ever gave it to you? Everyone in your new family is hungry and it's your job to feed them, but you have been starved your entire life and you are still living on inner hunger. You try to follow the recipe in the book, but there isn't even a measuring cup and you don't trust you're self to eyeball the amount of ingredients. Finally you give up. You don't leave but you just coast through your job like driving in the fog; you never see or know where you are going. Sometimes you wonder how you got to this place and begin to feel angry, sad and detached. So what is the answer? Do you continue to drive in the fog or do you reach down so deep inside, to a place that no one ever took you to and look at the child in front of you from eyes of the child inside of you? Would you want this child to feel what you have felt all of your life or would you be willing to let go, forgive and never look back in order for this precious part of you- your child to have what you did not; a home with love, without shame and fear. If you can see this picture then you can change the recipe and write your own, you can create your very own tapestry of family values and your own history and no one will ever know because you have taken the greatest step in your child's life; leaving your past behind and live in the now with your family. You have done the soul and solitary greatest accomplishment in your life and what couldn't be done for you. It is your gift; you have graciously changed history and now possess great love. Your legacy is unwavering hope.

On the thirteenth day of the Chinese New Year preparations are made for the Lantern Festival, which is to be held on the day of the fifteenth. The evening of the fourteenth is a celebration of family reunion and thanksgiving. It is a time of sacrifice to the ancestors, uniting the loving members with whom have passed away. Those who have passed are remembered with great respect for they laid the foundations for the family's fortune and glory of the family. The ancestors are honored with a dinner arranged for them at the family banquet table. They celebrate the onset of the New Year as one great community. The communal feast called "surrounding the stove," symbolizes family unity.

Christians symbolize bread as the Holy Communion with God. The Jewish share a spiritual feast called the Passover, symbolizing God's presence and love. The Hindu's holly food called Prasada is shared among worshippers as a form of grace. And the Buddhist practices a ritual of sharing a spiritual meal, using only one bowl. Eating should be a divine gift that is symbolic of receiving God's grace.

Does your table invoke the presence of love? Is your table sharing more than a meal...is it sharing an experience? Is your table set with sacred honor? Your family table is a canvas, how are you painting your picture? Close your eyes for a moment and envision that table. Can you feel the emotions of those seated around you? Do you hear the request your children are asking: I want you to show me what love is? Feel this emotion; those seated around you have come home to their hearts. Your family's plates are served with love and your table is covered in grace.

*What lies behind us and what lies before us are small matters compared to what lies within us.*
*~ Ralph Waldo Emerson ~*

You might ask yourself why I would write about the people I know in a simple small town that I live in and how would these stories impact or make a difference in the lives of others around the world. We are all one and all connected as a whole and the nourishments we give and receive becomes a circle that is defined not by how much is given, but how much love we put into the giving. We are all mentoring something to one another. May we mentor to our children the passion of love in the petitioning of their lives so that we can experience the sentiment at the end of our life?

The following stories are about giving, gratitude and grace.

*The place to improve the world is first in one's*
*own heart and head and hands.*
*~ Robert M. Pirsig ~*

# A Voyage To Home

Suffering. It's within every one of us and it is also within our human suffering the courage to transcend our thinking, our living and our hearts into miracles beyond our burning grief.

Why does it take a tragedy to look at our world or at our neighbor's hunger physically and emotionally? Why does it take war, episodes of disaster and anguish like 911 and Hurricane Katrina before we stop and look around and within? Does God use these disasters as a wake up call? Because we have gone from personal communication to the information age we have lost touch with old-fashioned deep living. Even though every detail and task in our lives is simplified by pushing a button, yet we have no time. When will we ever get to "enoughness"? When will we realize that the most important values we can teach our children are wisdom, character and compassion, not wealth? When will we look around at our country and see the starving families and deeply care enough for each of us to help at least one family?

If God asked you to pay deep attention to just one person in need - would you? If he told you your salvation depended upon it - would you? I was fifteen years old and stepped off of the school bus and there sat Maria in her car waiting at the stop sign for the bus to move on. She called my name and I moved towards her and we talked. That was the day my life changed and she is my hero. She grabbed a hold of that unexpected feeling inside her that told her what to do and she acted on her gut that said "take a chance." I wish I could tell her how her bravery gave me unconquerable courage and helped me take the first big step in my life. And how out of her actions, was the first time I knew that God had really heard my prayers. Maria gave me an idea to think about that felt like hope, and there is nothing that can stop an idea inside of someone.

Our children are growing up today with a sense of polluted confidence. The inherent nurturing that mushrooms into self-love and self-validation is missed. As adults some of us are still waiting for the world to validate us. And as adults we give up trying and you find us homeless, hungry and angry. What would happen if each of us found one hungry person and gave them an idea that no one had ever given before? Would your idea help them touch their own suffering and began to dismiss the past? Would they learn that through our suffering we are being taught a valuable lesson? What if the miracle caused this person to finally get to the point in their life that they were done with anger; choosing grace is loving them and seeing it in everyone else? And most important, the possibility of learning that they don't belong in yesterday anymore; it is coming home, a place some have never been. Could your leadership and strength be a model spirit and moral fiber to change the mindset of what life do I have to what life can I build?

Are we blinded by living the American dream behind glass and coddled by what money gives us that we close our eyes and avoid the homeless and the abused child around the corner? For every act of courage we give, an influence of change will occur in the heart. Every unfortunate person we look straight in the eye and share our light with, is the possibility they will hear, feel and see integrity.  Put your hand before them and watch them slowly embrace yours.  If you think the look on their face is puzzled, it's only because it feels like they have touched a velvet cloth.

*"I'm just trying to matter."*
*June Carter*

    Los Angles California has one of the highest rates of homeless people in the United States. Cardboard boxes hide the shame of those living within the containers where their lives come to an end.  It is at the coroners office that the identification process begins on mummified hands to uncover the fingerprints of these lost souls.  What happens to make a person give up?  Why are good lives wasted?

    Most feel the humanitarian spirit within our hearts. We all look up at the same sky and we are all connected to people we don't know. The moment we listen to the love task that God is waiting for our surrender in, you'll feel bigger than you are, like stepping into the land of Shangri-La.  Making a difference makes a difference and lies in your blood.

*You cannot do a kindness too soon,*
*for you never know how soon*
*it will be too late.*
*~ Ralph Waldo Emerson ~*

# CHARITY

Selfless giving is not hard. Turn on Oprah daily and you will see stories of ordinary people who have found a way to make someone's life more excellent. Watch Extreme Make - Over Home Addition and with in the first five minutes of the show you feel your heart in your throat and chills moving over your body. These are real people who make a difference in the lives of others in need of help. They are not heroes except to the needing person; they are ordinary people with extraordinary hearts. They have learned how to step out and give a hand.

*"We ourselves feel what we are doing is just a drop in the ocean.*
*But the ocean would be less because of that missing drop."*
*~ Mother Teresa ~*

Several years ago I was impressed to help a family at Christmas time and the feeling wouldn't leave me until I acted on it. I called the Salvation Army and ask if they had a name of a needy family and the voice on the other end of the phone became very excited. The gentleman told me that just a few days ago they had given out the entire donated items that had come in to as many families as they could. The next day a woman came in and needed their help and they had nothing left. As she was leaving in tears, the man told me he got her phone number just in case anything else showed up. He said that her husband's sister came to live with them to get away from her abusive husband. Her husband had a job, but now there were five more people to feed and they just didn't have the money to buy six children gifts. I was so happy to get this phone number and started planning how I was going to go about my giving. I first called the mother and told her who I was and what I would like to do for them when she burst into tears. She gave me all the children's names and ages and we made plans to meet on Christmas Eve early in the morning.

I had a Christmas party planned for my seniors that I had written their life stories for. I sent out invitations and requested everyone to bring food and one toy. I could hardly believe how much these good people shared. I had boxes and boxes of food and toys to give this family. One senior gentleman brought a one hundred dollar check and food. I added to the food by buying the turkey and all the trimmings. I made one of my gift baskets filled with cookies, breads, jams, candies, hot chocolate and candles. I wrapped all of the toys and put the kid's names on them and I had a gift for each one of the adults too. The most fun was making stockings for every child and stuffing them, which I laid in a beautiful basket. Now the best part is when I drove up in my car that was over flowing with joy. Both the mother and father walked towards my car and shook my hand. When I opened up the back of my SUV they took one look and the dad started crying. All he could do in thank me and tell me that now his kids would have a Christmas. Of course I started crying along with his wife. This was my greatest gift I gave myself that year.

Ever since I told my daughter Kellie this story she has wanted to take the time to create the same magic with her family. Last year she was impressed just like I was to seek out a needy family. She approached the counselor at her children's school and she gave Kellie the name of a gentleman who worked on a dairy farm and raising his two children by himself. He is Hispanic and speaks very little English. Someone explained to him what Kellie and her family was going to do and the man was overjoyed. Kellie asked the man to have his children make a list of the things they wanted and the son's list was quite long and the daughter said she would like a Barbie and anything would be just fine with her. So Kellie told one of her friends about what she was doing and she joined in and bought toys and wrapping paper and wrapped all of the gifts. Kellie and her family joyfully put the gifts, food and a food gift certificate in the car and drove to the family's home. The father came out side to greet them and all he could say was thank you. The children were so excited, but the ones who got the real blessing were Kellie's children, my grandchildren Nikki and Alec. What an experience for them to learn first hand about charity.

Since then Kellie told me about one of her good friends who gives like this every year to about ten families and spends nearly five-hundred dollars of their money towards this project and uses her living room for the set-up like Santa's work shop. Kellie plans to do her giving again and this year ask all of her good friends to help her out by bringing items to their annual family Christmas party, which inspires me to make plans to start some charity work again my self. So my plan is to let the other half of my family know that the admission into Thanksgiving dinner is canned goods or no food. I know I'll have a good show!

If you can't help needy families, try not to forget to drop off a canned good or two at a neighborhood store collecting donations and always drop that dollar into the can next to the ringing bell and make sure and return your shopping cart. Charity comes in lots of packages.

Charity is ministering to, caring for and serving. Serving together creates true success in progress toward not just helping our fellow man, but opening our eyes to our brothers and sisters, to the "We" of our world, a work of the heart right next to what God created and started. The closest thing to God's heart is our giving; help me be a miracle to someone.

Charity is one more thing…what it can do for you.

*All we see of someone at any moment is a snapshot of their life;*
*They're in riches or poverty, in joy or despair. Snapshots don't show*
*the million decisions that led to that moment.*
*~ Richard Bach~*

*To speak gratitude is courteous and pleasant. To enact gratitude is generous and noble, but to live gratitude is to touch Heaven.*
~ Johannes A. Gaertner ~

# CUSTOM OF THE ORDINARY

Customs in families can be fun, routine, serious and sometimes feel like rituals of their own. As a little girl I remember things like handing my mother the clothespins as she pinned the laundry on the clothesline, ironing the pillowcases and folding them into thirds, making a pot of soup for a sick neighbor or taking flowers to my teacher.

The memory that rings the loudest was the word thank you used in our home. There was a point to it that my mother was surly going to drive home, one I wouldn't get until I was an adult and that was gratitude.

Every birthday my grandmother and my Aunt would send me birthday cards and presents in the mail. From my Aunt June there was always a crisp five-dollar bill inside the sweetest Happy Birthday Niece card signed the, "Seven J's." And my dear Nana's gifts were always surprises of money and a new or old hanky tucked into a birthday card or a new dress. Whatever the gift, it always made me feel special and important and loved.

After opening the gift, I knew what my mother's custom was and that was the thank you note. I sat at kitchen table and began,

"Dear Nana, how are you? I hope you are fine and happy.

Thank you for all of my gifts, I loved them."

And then I would tell her what I did for my birthday or Christmas and what gifts mommy gave me. I never minded sitting down and thanking others for their kindness and I think it was at that young age I developed a sense of what it felt like to be grateful and that gratitude has stayed with me my entire life.

Long after my grandmother had passed on and I had been given the hanky collection of hers that I begged her for all through my childhood, I decided to take a look at it. My granddaughter Nikki was coming for a visit and she was excited to see Nana's old hankies. As I took each one out of the old box they took me back to my childhood remembering Nana sharing where each of these treasures were from. When I got to the bottom of the box, I lifted up the very old tissue paper and there before my eyes were all of my old letters and cards I had written to Nana. I was filled with a humble pride in my heart and a lot of tears filled my eyes. She knew how much I adored those hankies and someday would find every letter she saved of mine. Our gratitude for one another was still in motion, and I am thankful that my mother taught me to stop and feel the gift.

It is incredible to think about all the tools God hands to parents to use in raising their children and how poised it is for a parent to bring goals of virtue into perspective in the growing years of a child's life.

Hand written notes are almost an outdated fashion, but not to a senior. Ask your child to write a note to their grandparent even if they live in the same town and watch what happens.

*The moments of happiness we enjoy take us by surprise.*
*It is not that we seize them, but that they seize us.*
*~Unknown~*

# Heart Bellows

Our memories of life's strongest moments are patterns of experiences to savor until the end. They are the moments when we open our hearts and listen to the voice of stillness and feel the sacred around us.

Finding the sacred is not easy and often feels like a task, when it should come naturally. Our lives are over the edge with urgent matters that seem the most important things in a day to be completed. Seldom do we look at time spent together, not flashing moments, but time together without a schedule. How often do we sit around the table together and not a timetable?

We are born each day and new life and new breath is born out of it if we allow the blessing to take place. Around the time that ancient man discovered the secret of making fire, he found that a squall of wind made the burning process come to life. And so the earliest forms of bellows were born. A closed container in a heart shape design was made to collect air and then oust it through a valve that helped to start the fire. Our families impart sharing that builds strength; power and staying together called sacred foundations. Who is bellowing the sacred air into your families fire?

*"The family fireside is the best of schools."*
*~ Arnold Glasgow ~*

Take some time to sit down to a meal and feel the blessing by honoring food and family together and feel the sacred gratitude and realize that our families are the most urgent and important things on our daily list.

# THE ANCIENT LAW

*We make a living by what we get.*
*We make a life by what we give.*
*Winston Churchill*

In the late 1980's I was very drawn to the laws of prosperity, so I studied the ancient law of the number ten. The law states that prosperity has a spiritual basis, meaning that God is the source of your supply. Every talent we possess is instruments of our prosperity that are channeled from God who is the source of it all. Sharing is a way of keeping in touch with the rich source, and begins a way of opening a system of receiving.

After tithing faithfully in a church for over 11 years I was accustomed to giving money, but never really looked at it as giving back as a way of expressing gratitude for what I had already received. So as I studied, I began to look at tithing in a different light. I had made a decision to leave the church and find God. In my search I held a reverence in my heart and wanted now more than ever to draw close to him on my own. What I found was peace of mind, health, wholeness, plenty and love.

I found a small church near San Louis Obispo that I had never been to but felt drawn by the spirit to help. I began sending regular checks to the address of this tiny congregation and after about a year I received a letter in the mail from the pastor of this church. The letter stated that the unexpected checks that had been received were a large blessing and was much appreciated especially since it was from someone who was not a member of the congregation or anyone they personally knew. It was signed, " Reverend Jean." After I read the letter I picked up the phone and called the number on the printed stationary. A woman answered, "Hello, this is Reverend Jean." I introduced my self and Jean was elated to talk to me. This was the beginning of a very long relationship.

Over the years I never told anyone I was sending money to Jean's church except my bookkeeper and she did not understand why. Years later Jean called me one evening and told me she was going to retire as the minister of the church, but not from the ministry. She planned on ministering and helping people over the phone daily and through the mail by sending enlightening and inspirational literature to those in need. A few more years passed and I got a call from Jean and she told me her health was failing and she wanted me to know that although we had never met, she felt the blessing from God through our connection. She went on to say that there were times that she didn't know how she was going to make it and then a check from me would always show up in the mail. I told her it wasn't from me it was from God and the real blessing was in trusting and letting go. I was the beneficiary of wealth in this situation, a wealth of knowledge and wisdom gained by trusting and letting go to God. In that time my business flourished and I was always able to pay my bills and provide for my daughter.

*"The Lord commanded us to obey…so that we might always prosper…"*
*Deuteronomy 6:24*

*God moves through doors to bring you the joy that you desire.*

*They who love an old house*
*will never love in vain.*
*For how can any old house*
*used to sun and rain*
*to lilac and to larkspur*
*and arching trees above,*
*fail to give it's answer*
*to the hearts that give it love.*
*~Author Unknown~*

# The Cottage

*Call on fate when the doors of destiny don't seem to open. When we lose one job, we seek another.*
*When we lose our partner and what feels like our hearts, we start over and go back to the beginning.*

It was January of 1989. I remember the cold. I was leaving my husband, my life—the only one I knew. Have you ever had to do something because deep inside you knew you would die if you didn't? It felt like no one understood me on this cold January day, yet the call from the deepest place inside of me had to be answered. I needed to find a new home for my daughter and myself. I had looked all day. While driving, I noticed the beauty of the snow, yet I could not seem to embrace its rare tranquility. As I wiped the tears away I turned on a narrow dirt road. I drove slowly following the curve of the road to the front of a little old house. There among the pine and oak trees stood a haven all by itself.

There I sat the very aloneness of me in my car. I became very still, gazing out the window of my car at what seemed to be my heart's desire. Could this little home be God's signature, a gesture that spoke louder than words? Without a speech, without a note, this little old house conveyed a message. All of my senses were touching what was right in front of me. I was pulled toward the house, that light in the darkness, that warm place I wanted to be. I saw an older gentleman inside. He looked kind. I began to cry and talk to God. "Oh Father, how will I ever be able to tell this man that this is where I am supposed to be, this is your gift to me, that this is your love?"

I went inside, and as I entered, I felt such emotion that I had to fight back the tears. I did not understand all that was going on at that moment, but I knew I was supposed to live here. I gave Mr. Wright my phone number and asked if I could bring my five-year-old daughter back to see the house in the morning. He said of course. He told me he would make his decision within a couple of days and call me. I felt like I was going to have to hold my breath.

The next morning before taking Katie to school, I drove her over to the house. We both sat there for a moment in silence, staring. Katie looked up at me, and in an almost a whisper, she said, "Mom, it's a cottage." We went inside, and this time a smell hit me. It was a combination of old and familiar, like a perfume that I had worn before. I knew this was going to be our home, and so did Katie.

On Monday Mr. Wright called and said, "How would you like to be our neighbor?" I could hardly speak; I was filled with such gratitude.

We lived in the cottage for a long time. We filled it with our antiques and our love. Over the years, the cottage was blessed with stories of a family who shared many, many happy times and many, many meals fixed with loving care.

I now realize the cottage that became my home knows the most of my soul. It was where I healed and yearned to become whole. In the quiet of that winter day, I did not know that this little old house waited to give me love. It loved me. Today the memories that fill that abode linger in my heart. My gratitude is immeasurable.

*Journal entry:*
*This old house, this small cottage has waited for me… the place my heart calls home. God and his splendor opened this door of love for me. I lie in bed and watch the sun open the day. I see the green of the new grass growing… my heart widens and the faith that rests in my soul, the kind that has taught me to believe in the unseen, deepens to my core. I am here to stir the magic in my soul and follow the road to this old house that leads to love.*

*I am home.*

*The best portion of a good man's life,*
*his little, nameless, unremembered acts of kindness*
*and love.*
　　*~ William Wordsworth ~*

# Labor of Love

It was December of 1994. Our little old house glistened outside with lights and all the Christmas cheer I could add to a front porch. Inside, the antique tables displayed the many old decorations I had treasured through the years. It was just our Christmas tree that waited to be put up and decorated. Katie and I had picked it out together, like we had every year. I just hadn't found the time to put it up in my flurry of activities.

My restaurant was in its third year, and during this particular December, I had thirty-six catering jobs. I don't know how I kept all the details straight without losing my head. Each night that month if I was not catering a client's Christmas party, I was still at the restaurant preparing for the next day. Katie was at home waiting for me. As Christmas approached, I promised Katie I would put up the tree. Each night I lingered on the porch. Inside, Katie was waiting to greet me with the question, "Are we going to put the tree up tonight?" I finally decided that no matter how tired I was, I could not come up with any more excuses. I smiled and told her to help me bring in the boxes of tree decorations while I looked for the tree stand.

Now we were ready. This was not the first year Katie and I had put up a tree without a man in the house. We could do it again, because we were a team. I carefully carried the tree past all of our treasures while Katie helped guide the trunk right into the tree stand. Next she stood on a chair and held the tree up while I lay on the floor and began to tighten the screws into the trunk.

"Mom, what's taking so long?" Katie repeatedly asked me.

"I don't know. It worked last year," I told her.

"How much longer, Mom?" I heard for the next fifteen minutes or so. Finally, I gave up, took hold of the tree, and said, "Katie, this is not working, and I am too tired to figure it out. We will do it tomorrow night." She was not happy, but refrained from showing too much disappointment. She kissed me goodnight.

The next night, we labored again without getting any farther than the night before. I told Katie I would go to the store and buy new hardware for the tree stand and we would be successful the next evening. I kept my promise and brought home the new hardware. It was late, and Katie and I were both tired. I would have much rather been relaxing in a hot bath or watching TV, or just plain sleeping. But I had promised, and I was going to get what was turning into a miserable task over with!

I approached the situation positively, pretending to be excited to decorate our tree. I put on a Christmas CD and poured us some warm cider. I decided after that night that our problem was not the tree stand or hardware. I was the problem. I just could not get the thing to work again. Katie went to bed crying and mumbling, "Why can't we be like other families? All their Christmas trees are up." Now, not only was I completely stressed out, I felt like the only mom in America who was a tree failure.

The next day Katie did not mention the tree before leaving for school. I figured she had given up. The rest of the day was very hectic for me, and I didn't think much about our problem. I arrived home late and tired from a catering job. When I got to the door, I was greeted with a large piece of white paper. In ten-year-old, large handwriting, I read, "MOM, THE TREE IS UP- BUT BE CAREFUL."

I studied the note and could not imagine what I was in for. All the lights were out and Katie was asleep. I quietly stepped into the family room. There I saw our Christmas tree with beautiful lights glowing. I just stood there for the longest moment and took it all in. I stepped back and saw that the entire tree was decorated and that there were presents under the tree. I knelt down, pushed the gifts aside, and saw that the tree was secured around the base with old rags. I shook my head with disbelief as I stood back up and saw that the top of the tree was tied with a piece of string over to a cupboard door. As tears began to fall, I felt a joy sweep over me that I had not felt in a long time. I stood and admired the entire scene in silence. I decided it was the most beautiful tree I had ever seen.

The tree gave me the spirit to complete the rest of the jobs I had filled with peace. I was able to prepare a wonderful Christmas meal and share it with family and friends. I even found the time to prepare Beef Wellington for our guests.

Katie does not realize what she gave me that Christmas. It was a huge gift of love and a message: "Don't give up." At the top of that tree, where the string held everything up, there was hope.

*"The giving of love is an education in itself."*
*~ Eleanor Roosevelt ~*

# Home Sent in a Box

It was 1990 and my oldest daughter, Kellie, had moved to Washington State. She was enjoying her new life, but was so homesick. Christmas was approaching, and it was so important to me to send just the perfect gifts to Kellie to make up for some of her loneliness.

By chance somewhere, I came upon a book designed to hold recipes called "Mom's Five-Star Recipes." I knew instantly this was a perfect gift for Kellie. It reminded me of all the phone calls I had gotten in the previous months asking for one of my recipes. She had called more than once for the same ones. When I asked her, "Didn't I just give you that one?" Kellie told me she had scratched it down on something and lost the piece of paper. Now I had the perfect solution.

About a month before Christmas, I started writing out the recipes by hand. I kept adding and adding. One night I thought I would look through them to make sure I hadn't forgotten any. I grabbed a pen and made a note on one of them, and then another note, and soon the notes became the theme of the book. I made notations on every page about that particular dish—where we had shared it or what family celebration it was connected to. I wrapped all of her gifts and mailed them in a very large box.

On Christmas Eve, Kellie called, sobbing. I tried to wish her Merry Christmas and cheer her up. "What's wrong, Kellie?" I asked her. She sniffed a little and then said, "Mom, the book is the greatest gift you could ever give me—it's our family in a recipe book. Everything I remember about food and our celebrations is right here."

It was after this conversation that I first decided to write a cookbook. The idea seemed vague at the time, but grew the more I shared it with others; the more I realized that it would be no ordinary book. I could send a box of gifts over the miles to my daughter, and she could receive it as pure love. I could write real stories and share our family's love with those who needed it. Most of all, I could encourage other mothers and daughters to start recording the emotions and love within their families' recipes.

*"The soul should always stand ajar,*
*ready to welcome the ecstatic experience."*
*~ Emily Dickinson~*

*"Love is the warmth that devours
your pain, when all else dies love will remain."*

*~ Ronnie Young Jr.~*

# Time Passing

It had seemed then that since I had started my catering business and opened my restaurant's doors, I had not stopped. Of course, it only seemed that way. Every moment of every day was so full, there wasn't a pause to take a breath and look around. I had forgotten what the life I once had at home felt like.

One day I just decided I needed to let go of everything called work. Not for very long, just an afternoon. I came in to the restaurant even earlier than usual, and by 11 A.M. I was ready to head home. It felt so good, like I was sneaking off to an island.

I remember it was fall. The leaves were just starting to turn color. This was my favorite time of year. It was always the time that I felt the most emotion stir inside of me. For some reason, I seemed to be more open to what my spirit was whispering…always just a kind whisper. And when I listened, there was a lesson waiting for me.

As my car turned into the driveway, tears began to slip down my tired face. I had only driven about half a mile from the restaurant, yet I felt like no one could get to me for just a few hours. This was my time in my home. Now what was I going to do?

I thought of starting a new book. It had been so long since I'd taken the time for pleasure reading. Did I even know how? I just did not know what to do with myself. I looked outside and realized I wanted to be a part of the autumn air. I decided to go to the garage and start going through some boxes I needed to organize.

I got through a few of the falling apart ones and threw out lots of stuff I didn't need. Then I came across a particular box. I had no idea what it was, so I took it over to a chair in the backyard and opened it up. The sun's warmth resting on my back was just enough to fortify me against the morning chill. I reached into the box and pulled out papers and cards that I had not read in years.

This was a box of sentiment that had been moved around and shoved in a corner as though it had very little importance. After a while of looking through it, however, I was overwhelmed with its contents. This was my life, I thought. They were the experiences I once shared. Inside the box were the times I cherished and the memories I so desperately missed. I wept. I think I finally stopped long enough to feel the pain I had tried so hard to keep myself too busy to feel.

I picked up the box and carried it to the garage. I came inside, picked up a pen, and wrote these words.

*The leaves fall today
as quickly as the years pass.
I feel time.
I feel time, as I clear through boxes that bring the past to me.*

*I miss my children; I miss my girls.*
*I miss taking care of them, our togetherness ~ our ways.*
*I wait.*
*I wait for my life to change, to move away from too much work.*
*I love the bird's song, the sound of the laundry,*
*the cat and the cracks in this old house.*
*It brings home to me…*
*a place my heart belongs.*

*I miss friends; I miss commitment and the way things are*
*supposed to be…the magic of togetherness and time-shared.*
*I miss time.*

When I finished writing, I decided to fix a nice meal for Katie and me at home. After all, it was the domestic life that I was missing. I thought that a fall soup and vegetable would be perfect to celebrate the coming of winter and to honor the bittersweet blessing I had just received. My heart overflowed with gratitude.

*"Challenges make you discover things about yourself that you never really knew. They're what make the instrument stretch, what make you go beyond the norm."*
*~ Cicely Tyson ~*

# Recipe for Joy

At one time in my life I realized that I did not know what joy was and that I had actually never really experienced it. It's not that I am unhappy or that I have not experienced happiness. I just stopped and asked myself what does real joy feel like? I could not answer that question so I pondered on it for quite sometime.

To me, feeling good was when I was on a vacation or sharing a moment with family or friends, but it was never absolute joy, not completely like a sigh feels. There was always something hanging over me or something undone outside and inside of me.

During this brainstorm searching I had asked God to bring to me more joy (whatever that is), more friends that felt joyful and so on. It was about that time that Yvette really showed up in my life. I was drawn to her strength and character. I was drawn to love her and share friendship with her; I wanted to be her friend…I chose her.

Yvette lost her daughter; her only child in a car accident who was only was 17 years old. I have known many people with losses, but I have never known anyone to move forward like Yvette has. So I began to study her and want to know what has made her still live life well. After a few years I realized the answer is that she made a choice. She took what she had left and made another recipe. It wasn't the one she wanted, but the first one, the best recipe was gone like ashes sprinkled over water that are not humanly possible to put back together. And so she started mixing new ingredients one at a time until she has made a new recipe to live by. What I marveled at was that I found joy in her and her life and yet how can that be? Yvette has separated herself from what she does not have and what she has and wants.

I began to realize that was the formula I was not using. Along with the happy moments, I never stopped focusing on what I didn't have, didn't like and didn't give focus to what I really wanted. I couldn't get to the joy, because I was stuck in not feeling enough because of what I hadn't accomplished. I was living in past instead of present. Yvette silently taught me I needed a new recipe.

Now I focus on what I want and the ingredients that are needed to make this happen. For the first time in my life I feel joy because I am making joy. Once again God has shown me the answer through one of his own created beings and her loss. I am grateful and look at this as God's grace.

Yvette is one of the best friends I have. A true person of her word; someone I look up to and love to have fun with. I look forward to amazing times and memories with her. I'm blessed. Thank you Yvette.

*"The heart, like a grape, is prone
to delivering it's harvest in the
same moment it appears
to be crushed."*
*~ Roger Houseden ~*

# Ruby: The Golden Soul

There is something about an older person that makes them willing to listen. Maybe they have the time, maybe they have heard it all, but if you want to be heard, just find yourself an old soul. When they leave our earth; our lesson is that their souls are really golden, and the final blessing comes when we realize they are still listening.

Ruby came to me through and by grace as I was starting my historian business. I was speaking to a hospice group of senior guests who had each lost a loved one to cancer. The next day I received a phone call from one of the guests who had attended the presentation. When I answered, I heard a magical British accent on the other end of the phone—it was Ruby Kidd.

Ruby inquired more about the process and the prospect of leaving her written legacy for her only child, Ruby Jr. We talked for quite a while and instantly connected. At the end of the conversation, she asked about the cost of the book. When I told her, she very graciously replied, "Oh, the work is so beautiful, but I just can't afford that amount." She thanked me for my time and nearly said goodbye when, for some reason, I stepped in and said, "Wait, Ruby. How much can you afford?" She really felt uncomfortable and hesitated to answer. So I said, "I don't know why, Ruby, but I know I am supposed to write your story—please let me help you with this." A strange feeling came over me, and I knew I should not let her hang up the phone.

*"Giving is a necessity sometimes…
more urgent, indeed, than having."*
*~ Margaret Lee Runbeck ~*

Ruby agreed on a small amount that she could make payments on over a period of time. We began meeting at her home where she served me English tea and hot soup every visit. We started with her childhood in England and the memories of real candles lit on her grandmother's Christmas tree. She remembered the magic of making steamed pudding and how it was her job to stir the mixture. We worked up to the time of the war when she met Malcolm at a dance where American soldiers had been posted. It was at that dance that the two fell in love. They were married, and Malcolm left for war—they never knew if they would see one another again.

As I have with all of my seniors, I began to grow to love Ruby as the weeks went by. Each week I knew a little more about her life, her dreams, and her fears. I learned how Malcolm returned from war to find his daughter in Ruby's arms. And that the day Malcolm took his last breath, just after Ruby and Ruby Jr. sang to him, as he lay unconscious, a tear fell down his face, just like the ones Ruby cried as she told me this story. We became friends and mother and daughter at that table week after week.

Ruby called me nearly every week. If I wasn't home, I received an uplifting message that always ended with "I love you." After we had finished the book, we became even closer. I realized I could talk to Ruby about anything, as she could me. Now that the book was completed, I did most of the talking, and she listened and listened and listened. But her listening was from her heart. She never interrupted; she was silent and experienced each situation or experience as I told it. In all the time I knew her, she never so much uttered a negative word about anyone.

I am so thankful that I listened to my heart the day I heard her voice for the first time. She always thought I gave her something special, but she was my gift. The most beautiful part of the gift is I know she is still listening to me—I feel it.

*"Nothing splendid has ever been achieved expect by those who
dared believe that something inside of them was superior to circumstances."*
*~ Bruce Barton ~*

# TAKE A CHANCE

I have always felt a sense of guidance and purpose behind and before me. There is some kind of trust beneath all the doubt, the anxiety, and the fear we humans feel. I am surrounded and filled with the reality that can never be named, which I therefore call God.

We all have felt the kind of despair that separates us from life itself. God has given me many of these times, either as lessons, character builders, or because he needed to use me as the instrument in an experience.

One particular despairing day I felt alone. Not the kind of alone like no one is paying attention to you, but rather alone inside. I was invited to a great party at a wonderful friend's airport hanger. "Yes I'm going; no, I'm not," I argued with myself all day. Not wanting to get dressed and step out of my comfort zone, I played this game with myself until finally I rose to the occasion and dressed for the party.

I arrived alone and not knowing anyone. I kept my sunglasses on and walked around looking for my friend Sue. After about an hour with my heart in my throat because I brought my pain with me, I was ready to leave. I headed towards the gate I entered and, to my surprise, there was Sue, now I knew there was no turning back.

Sue took me under her wing and introduced me to many lovely people that day, including Gary, her brother-in-law. Gary and I shared in conversation, and he took me on a tour of the airport hanger. I still had my sunglasses on because I thought I would start crying any minute. I think even though Gary never saw my eyes, he could sense the sadness behind my smile.

I was thinking I had spent long enough in my pretence when Gary approached me and asked if I would like to take a sunset flight. I paused, not sure what he really meant. I asked what a sunset flight was, and he smiled and then pointed to a beautiful old airplane, a two-seated 1930 plane. "See that plane over there? I would like to take you up for a sunset tour." I really wanted to cry now, because the thought of doing this frightened me and I was so emotionally drained that I had no energy to even think, let alone answer and get myself out of this. I just stared at Gary and smiled back at him and said, "You're kidding, right?" He took me by the hand and walked me over to the plane. He began telling me how long he had been using this plane and what incredible condition it was in, but all I could see was that it had no top above the seats. I looked at Gary and finally said, "Thank you, Gary, but I could never risk going up in a plane like this, not me."

*"As soon as you trust yourself,
you will know how to live."*
*~ Johann Wolfgang von Goethe ~*

Now that I look back on that day, I see that God used Gary as an instrument—just like the engine in the plane—to help me fly past fear, pain, and change. Gary helped me climb up to the seat in the back. My hands began to sweat as this man who thought he was an old hat with this piece of history I was sitting in handed me the historic goggles to cover my eyes. I placed the goggles over my eyes and a brown leather hat on my head. I still could not move; I was holding back the tears for the hundredth time that day.

Gary started the plane's engine, which sounded like the pounding of my heart. Slowly, the old timer began its short journey down the runway and turned itself around for take off just like all of the commercial planes I had flown in. I think as the plane picked up speed I was holding my breath, and just as it lifted off of the ground, I finally began to cry. Deep inside, I wanted to do this, but at the moment I was so full of fear that I just wanted the plane to turn around and land and take me back to my comfort zone.

Gary's plane continued to climb. When it finally reached the altitude he wanted, the engine became quieter; the view became my focus as I looked down and saw perfect rows of crops and farmhouses and old buildings. There were rows of trees and roads without any cars on them. I sat back and took a deep breath. My attention was drawn to the sky above me as a few birds soared past us. The sky seemed so large and so close, as though I could reach and touch what was in front of me; larger than anything was the sun that was about to descend into the backdrop of the day. The sky took on a glimmer of colors, as though an artist was painting a brilliant masterpiece in front of my eyes. Tints of umber, shades of bronze, and flushes of ocher made casts of golden orange. The colors painted the cirrus clouds teasing those skies of blue. Blushing, this flamboyant luster performed like glitter lighting the sky for this sunset flight.

The plane began to feel lighter, as did my heart, as though it were soaring like a bird in flight. Just as I started to speak, the sky pressed closer and the sun rushed down—descending, larger, almost touchable. Just for a moment, larger than life and blazing with color. In what seemed like an eerie hush, this sunset was captured in my heart forever.

I looked down again at what was beneath us, now darker; it seemed like a large puzzle. Above me was a resplendent place that swept everything I was carrying away. I felt like I was the plane or the distant birds soaring effortlessly through the half-lit night. I reached up and pulled the cap off of my head, allowing my yellow-blond hair to sweep with the breeze as the air tickled my skin and made me shiver just as we returned and began to land.

I was and am still so amazed at what I learned that day. The experience taught me that I could do anything if only I took the chance. Long since the flight, I have come to realize that God stepped in and used Gary to lift me right out of my depression and sadness. God knew that if I were ever to see the fulfillment of my desires, I would have to be taken upward and feel the face of God—and I did. God gives our lives grace because he is the state of grace that causes us to feel loved and cared for inside. Through grace, I was moved, and like a forgotten child, I was found.

*"Practice generosity, share your wealth  
and share your self. Without a rich heart,  
wealth is an ugly beggar."*  
*~ Ralph Waldo Emerson ~*

# GIFT BASKET

For as many Christmas memories I have, I can remember giving some sort of jam, bread, chutney or an assorted gift basket and always my quiche. Sometime close to Christmas we would all pile in the car after I had loaded the goodies carefully inside. We drove and enjoyed the lights as we delivered the gifts to friends. I liked the girls to be apart of the spirit of giving. When Katie and I were on our own she would help me assemble the baskets and tie the ribbons to secure the plastic wrap. There were always a friend or two of hers she enjoyed giving to their families so she made most of the choices that went into their baskets and I think that made her feel like this was a gift from her.

One particular year I got the idea to make the classic English pudding. I knew this old fashioned dessert is synonymous with the holiday season, like jingle belles and Christmas trees. I went to the library and bookstores and read about the history and gathered many recipes. I used old crock bowls to steam the magic ingredients in. Then I wrapped the bowls in cheesecloth and tied them with string to secure. I made 17 of them. Each pudding was then put in a brown bag with a traditional lemon hard sauce and the recipe and history of English pudding. I covered the outside of the bag with an old fashioned picture of a family in the 1800's standing over a wood burning stove surrounding an old pot as the pudding was taken out. I secured the handles of the bag with gold ribbon that added the last touch. I made loaves of sweet bread and several quiches. When Kellie and my grand daughter Nicole arrived from Washington, we delivered all the steamed puddings while Nikki awed over the Christmas lights. This was a lot of work, but fun to step back into history and share it with so many people.

Another important memory of our family gift giving was a year when Katie had a friend whose family was having financial hardships. Together Katie and I had made it our project to give to this family. We bought many gifts and made a couple of meals along with a dessert gift basket. We found out when they were planning to be gone. Katie used the excuse that she left something there of hers and would they please leave the door unlocked. This was a wonderful opportunity to teach my daughter the joy of giving. We snuck in the house and Katie had the pleasure of lining their empty tree with many gifts while I carried all the food into the kitchen. We got back in the car and smiled at each other. We didn't have a lot that year ourselves, but after that delivery we had more than when we arrived.

About four years ago Katie called me and asked if we could bake together, because she had some friends she would like to give a little something to. We had so much fun together. When she was ready to leave she had a list and in her hand and all of the baskets in the back seat of her car. She went home and got the baby and as a family they gave in love.

One of the ladies who Katie worked with lived alone and seemed to have no family. This year Katie felt it was important to take Bee a gift basket. When she showed up at her door on

Christmas Eve, Bee stood at the door looking at the gift in Katie's arms and could hardly speak. She was all alone and accepted the gift with a big hug. The next week at work she told Katie that was the first visitor she had had in years on Christmas Eve. For about three more years Katie made sure that Bee was on her delivery list and Bee told her she looked forward to it every year. Last year Bee didn't show up for work because she had died in her small apartment. Twenty-one year old Katie called me and told me the sad news and then she said, "Mom, I am so glad I took the time each year to give Bee a little happiness and make her feel special."

*"You can easily judge the character of a man*
*by how he treats those who can do*
*nothing for him."*
*~ James D. Miles ~*

It's important what we are teaching our children. Giving is sustaining in the heart and continues and maintains in the hands.

Chapter 8

# Soup Comforts

*I would have to say that soup is my favorite food to make. My grandmother taught me that from the old days when a pot of soup was made from leftover vegetables and a soup bone that was practically given to you by the neighborhood butcher; that was homemade soup. I loved this theory of hers and brought it to my own kitchen every Friday where my girls arrived home from school and smelled home cooking in a pot of soup. Our souls were warmed with the comfort it brought.*

# Wild Rice Soup

3 tbsp. butter
1 cup sliced celery
¾ cup coarsely chopped carrot
½ cup chopped onion
½ cup sliced mushrooms
3 tbsp. flour
  Salt and ground pepper to taste
1 ½ cups cooked wild rice
1 ¼ cups water
1 ½ cans chicken broth
1 cup half and half or cream
½ cup toasted slivered almonds
1/3 cup chopped fresh parsley

Cook vegetables except mushrooms, in butter about 3 minutes, stir in flour, salt and pepper and cook for another 3 minutes on low heat. Mix in rice, water, broth and heat to boiling; reduce heat. Add mushrooms and cook 10-15 minutes. Add almonds, parsley and cream. Heat just until hot, do not boil.
Serves 6

# Crab Chowder

1 6-ounce can crabmeat, drained and cleaned
1 large potato, cubed, cooked, with skin left on
1 ½ cups sliced fresh mushrooms
½ cup sliced celery
½ cup minced onion
2 garlic cloves, minced
¼ cup clam juice
   Salt and freshly ground pepper
1/3 cup flour
3 cups milk
1 cup light cream
1 tbsp. fresh dill weed

In soup pot cook garlic, mushrooms, celery and onion in butter (adding a little salt) until vegetables are tender. Add flour and cook for 2 minutes; adding milk and cream and stir over medium heat until mixture is thick. Stir in clam juice, potatoes, crab and dill. Heat through on low.

Serves 4-6

# Cream of Acorn Soup

2 large acorn squash
4 cups vegetable or
   chicken broth
1 ½ cups whipping cream
   Freshly grated nutmeg
2 granny smith apples, grated
½ cup chopped pecans, toasted
   Salt and pepper to taste

    Cut squash in half and remove seeds and cut each piece in half. Place squash in steamer and add 2 cups of the broth for the liquid. Steam for 30 minutes or till squash is tender. Remove and cool a bit and reserve the broth.

    Scoop out the squash and place in blender or food processor. Cover and puree, adding the reserved steaming liquid as needed.

    Pour pureed squash into a saucepan and add the reserved steam liquid as needed. Return the puree to a sauce pan and add the remaining steaming liquid and broth, salt and pepper. Bring squash mixture to a boil and reduce heat. Add 1 cup of the whipping cream and nutmeg. Heat on low for about 15 minutes; stirring. Beat the ½ cup of whipping cream to soft peaks and add to soup.

    Place some of the grated apple in each soup bowl and ladle the soup over apple. Garnish with chopped pecans, nutmeg and a dollop of sour cream.

# Cream of Asparagus Soup

1 pound asparagus, cut into 2-inch pieces
1 onion, chopped
1 celery stalk, chopped
2 tbsp. flour
3 tbsp. butter
4 cups chicken or vegetable broth
1 cup cream
1 tbsp. fresh lemon juice
½ tsp. lemon zest
   Salt and pepper to taste
½ tsp. tamari

   Sauté onion, celery and butter for 3 minutes. Stir in flour and cook for 2 minutes. Add broth while stirring. Add asparagus and cover and simmer for 30 minutes. Cool and puree mixture in blender.
   Return to soup pot and add cream, lemon juice, zest, salt and pepper and tamari.

Serves 4

# Cream of Chicken Wild Rice Soup

½ cup wild rice
2 14-ounce cans chicken broth
1 cup water
½ cup chopped carrot
½ cup chopped celery
½ cup chopped onion
2 cups sliced mushrooms
2 tbsp. butter
¼ cup flour
　Salt and freshly ground pepper
½ tsp. dried basil, crushed
¼ cup snipped parsley
2 tbsp. fresh chives
1 cup whipping cream
2 cups chopped cooked chicken

　In Dutch oven combine 1 ½ cans of chicken broth, carrot, celery, onion, and uncooked rice. Bring to a boil; reduce heat and simmer, covered for 30-40 minutes or until rice is tender. Add mushrooms the last 5 minutes of cooking.

　In a sauce pan, melt butter and add flour, salt and pepper and cook for 1 minute. Add remaining broth and whip cream and cook until bubbly on low heat about 1 minute. Add cream mixture to rice mixture and stir in chicken, basil, parsley and heat through. Top with chopped chives.

Serves 4-6

# Curried Carrot Cream Cheese Soup

3 tbsp. olive oil
1 pound carrots, sliced
1 small onion, cut up
1 10-ounce can chicken broth
1 tsp. curry powder
½ tsp. dried thyme and oregano, crushed
1 clove garlic, minced
1 3-ounce package cream cheese, cubed at room temperature
½ cup milk
½ cup cream

In soup pot combine carrots, onion, curry, thyme and oregano, and garlic, and oil and sauté for 4 minutes. Add broth and bring to a boil, reduce heat and simmer 20 minutes or until vegetables are tender.

Cool slightly and place half of mixture in blender and process about 30 seconds. Repeat with remaining mixture and add cream cheese. Pour into soup pot and add milk and cream and simmer until cream cheese has blended, about 10 minutes.

# Fresh Mushroom Linguine Soup

4 cups chicken broth
2 tbsp. soy sauce
1 tbsp. fresh ginger, grated
3 garlic cloves, crushed
1 cup button, porcini, portobello and shiitake mushrooms, cleaned, discard stems
2 cups cabbage, chopped
1 cup carrots, sliced thin
½ cup chopped leeks
2 cups fresh spinach
1 cup green onion, sliced thin
2 cups cooked, shredded chicken
Salt and pepper to taste
1 tbsp. sherry
2 cups cooked linguine

Combine broth, soy, ginger, garlic, mushrooms, cabbage, carrots and chicken. Bring to a boil; cover and simmer for 5 minutes. Stir in noodles, green onion, spinach and sherry, simmer 2-3 minutes. Season to taste.

Serves 6

# Garlic Cream Soup

1 stick butter
4 heads garlic, separated and peeled
3 tbsp. flour
1 can chicken broth
2 cups water
¼ cup champagne or dry white wine
1 cup cream
  Salt and freshly ground pepper
  Homemade rustic baguette croutons

Sauté garlic pieces in butter on low heat until softened. Add the flour and cook for 5 minutes. Add water, broth salt and pepper, cover the soup pot and cook on low for about 30 minutes. Add the wine and cream and continue to simmer for 10 minutes. Season again to taste and serve with croutons on top.

Rustic Croutons:
Dice one baguette into small cubes. Melt a little butter, olive oil and garlic in sauté pan and add croutons. Mix on moderate heat, stirring occasionally. Drain and cool on paper towels.

# Mom's Potato Soup

3 potatoes, peeled and cubed
3 stalks celery, sliced fine
1 small onion, chopped fine
2 cups vegetable broth
2 cups milk
1 cup heavy cream
½ cube butter
¼ cup flour
   Salt and pepper
½ cup chopped fresh parsley

   Melt butter and sauté onions and celery. Gradually add flour and cook for 3 minutes on low heat. Whisk in vegetable broth and milk. Add potatoes and cook on low heat for 20-30 minutes; stirring often. Add cream, salt and pepper and parsley; continue cooking for about 5 minutes. If desired add cooked crumbled bacon or imitation bacon bits in serving bowls.
   Sometimes I cook potatoes in a separate pan and then add them to soup and a little of the potato water.

Serves 6

# Pumpkin Bisque

1 15 ounce can pumpkin
1 can chicken broth
2 tbsp. butter
1 celery stalk, chopped
½ small onion, chopped
2 cups cream
3 tbsp. almond flavored liqueur
1 tsp. nutmeg
1 tbsp. catsup
   Salt and pepper to taste
½ cup toasted slivered almonds

Sauté onion and celery in butter. Transfer vegetables to food processor or blender and puree with pumpkin and broth until smooth. Return to a soup pot and simmer on low heat for about 30 minutes. Add cream, nutmeg, liqueur and catsup. Season with salt and pepper. Garnish with toasted almonds.

Makes 6-8 servings

# Pumpkin Soup With Apple Relish

3 tbsp butter
½ cup chopped onion
2 cloves garlic, minced
2 cups chicken broth
1 16 ounce can pumpkin
3 tbsp brown sugar
½ tsp. each fresh rosemary,
    thyme, chopped
    Salt and pepper
2 cups half and half
½ cup toasted chopped pecans

Sauté onion and garlic in butter for about 5 minutes, add chopped toasted pecans and stir on low heat for another 2 minutes.

Add remaining ingredients except half and half and cook for 15 minutes on low heat, stirring. Cool, and pour into food processor or blender. Blend on low and return to soup pot. Warm and top with apple relish.

Apple Relish:
1 green apple, peeled and chopped
¼ red onion, finely chopped
½ cup dried cranberries
3 tbsp. lemon juice
1 tsp. lemon zest
¼ tsp. allspice
Mix all ingredients and chill.

# Pumpkin Soup with Ginger Cream

3 tbsp. butter
1 yellow onion, diced
1 celery stalk, diced
1 ½ tsp. fresh gingerroot, minced
3 garlic cloves, minced
1 15 ounce can pumpkin
1 cup sweet potatoes, peeled and sliced
5 cup vegetable broth
½ tsp. cinnamon
¼ tsp. nutmeg
1 tsp. salt
3 tsp. fresh lime juice
½ cup white wine
½ cup milk
½ cup cream or half and half
1 cup heavy cream
1 tsp. fresh gingerroot, minced

Sauté onion, celery, garlic and gingerroot in butter for about 10 minutes. Add the sweet potatoes, broth and spices. Simmer until the potatoes are tender. Remove soup from heat and cool slightly. Puree in blender or food processor. Pour into soup pot and add the pumpkin, lime juice, wine, milk and cream. Combine well and reheat soup to warm.

Beat cream and fresh ginger until stiff peaks form. Garnish soup with ginger cream.

*One Christmas season I invited several of my girl friends for a festive friendship gathering. I wanted to treat my friends to an evening of relaxing, connection, warmth and a sense of comfort from the inside out in such a busy season. To make them stop and feel the magic I surprised them with a massage therapist and a reflexologist therapist waiting in another room for each of them to have a turn of comfort. Meanwhile, the other girls listened to soothing music, laughed, connected, and amongst the Christmas glitter, they shared a warm bowl of one of the best soup I ever made.*

# Pumpkin-Potato-Leek and Roasted Sweet Potato Soup

2 cups half and half
1 cup canned pumpkin
1 can cream of potato soup
1 cup chopped leeks
1 medium sweet potato
   cut into bite-size pieces
2 tbsp. olive oil
   Salt and pepper
   Dash of cinnamon and
   nutmeg

Toss sweet potato pieces in one tbsp. of olive oil, salt and pepper and pour into a greased casserole dish. Roast uncovered in a 375 degree oven for about 30-45 minutes. Take out and let set for 10 minutes.

While sweet potatoes are roasting, sauté leeks in 1 tbsp. olive oil for about three minutes. In saucepan combine half and half, soup, pumpkin, leeks and spices; salt and pepper to taste. Bring to a slow boil, stirring. Reduce heat to low. Simmer covered for 3-5 minutes. When sweet potatoes are finished roasting and set, add to soup. Garnish with chopped chives.

Serves 4-6

# Roasted Vegetable Chicken Chowder

1 onion, chopped
½ cup leeks, sliced
1 cups parsnips, carrots, turnips, peeled and chopped
¼ cup olive oil
   Salt and ground pepper
2 cans chicken broth
2 14 ½ can diced tomatoes
3 garlic cloves, minced
1 can corn, drained
1 tsp. chopped fresh rosemary
4 boneless chicken breasts, cut into 1- inch pieces

   Toss all vegetables in 2 tablespoons of oil, salt and pepper. Transfer vegetables to a casserole dish or baking sheet. Bake in a 450 degree oven for about 30 minutes or until browned, turn over a few times.
   After vegetables have roasted puree 2 cups of vegetables with 1 can of broth.
   Toss chicken pieces with salt and pepper. Cook garlic in remaining oil about 1 minute. Add chicken and brown for about 8-10 minutes. Mix in tomatoes, 1 can of broth, corn, roasted vegetables, pureed vegetables and cook for abut 30 minutes on low heat. Mix in rosemary.

Makes 10 cups

# Sherried Brie Soup

1 pound fresh mushrooms, sliced
2 tbsp. butter
3 tbsp. flour
8 ounces shitake mushrooms
½ cup minced onion
1 garlic clove, minced
2 cans beef broth
½ cup cream of sherry wine
6 ounces Brie cheese
1 cup milk
1 ½ cup cream
   Salt and freshly ground pepper

   Soak shitake mushrooms in warm water and let set for 5 minutes, drain and dry. Heat butter and sauté onion, garlic and mushrooms for 2 minutes. Add flour and cook 2 more minutes. Add broth and sherry . Bring to a boil; reduce heat and simmer for 30 minutes.
   Trim rind from brie and cut into cubes. Add cheese to soup mixture, milk and cream; season. Warm, do not boil.

# Vegetable Asparagus Soup

3 lb. leeks, sliced into ½ inch pieces
1 large onion, chopped fine
4 tbsp. butter
3 medium potatoes, peeled and diced
3 medium carrots, sliced thin
  Salt and pepper
½ cup uncooked long grain rice
1 pound fresh asparagus cut into
  1-inch pieces
½ pound fresh spinach torn into small pieces
2 quarts chicken or vegetable broth
1 cup heavy cream

Sauté leeks and onions in butter. Add potatoes, carrots, salt and pepper, broth and rice. Simmer for 25 minutes, stirring occasionally. Add asparagus, cover and simmer for 10 minutes or until vegetables are tender. Add spinach and cream.

Serves 12-16

# Wild Rice Soup

3 tbsp. butter
1 cup sliced celery
¾ cup coarsely chopped carrot
½ cup chopped onion
½ cup sliced mushrooms
3 tbsp. flour
   Salt and ground pepper to taste
1 ½ cups cooked wild rice
1 ¼ cups water
1 ½ cans chicken broth
1 cup half and half or cream
½ cup toasted slivered almonds
1/3 cup chopped fresh parsley

Cook vegetables except mushrooms, in butter about 3 minutes, stir in flour, salt and pepper and cook for another 3 minutes on low heat. Mix in rice, water, broth and heat to boiling; reduce heat. Add mushrooms and cook 10-15 minutes. Add almonds, parsley and cream. Heat just until hot, do not boil.

Serves 6

*Chapter 9*

# Sensational Starters

*Treats, snacks, delicacy; all delightful pleasures we indulge in before the main course. Music, glass of wine and appetizers start the party and bring to the celebration a tasty experience.*

*For 19 years I have been making and creating my own appetizers. The guests are the critics that provide the review; if it's good, you know you'll make it again. The following recipes have been tested many times and are favored well.*

# Asparagus and Artichoke Mini Crêpes

20 crêpes
   Garlic cream cheese spread
40 slender asparagus
2 tbsp. olive oil
2 Gars marinated artichokes,
   drained and chopped
   Sea salt and pepper

    Cut ends from asparagus and toss with oil and salt. Place in microwave dish, cover and cook for 1 minute; let set with cover on top.
    Spread cream cheese over each crêpe and sprinkle a little artichoke in each and add 2 asparagus at each end; sprinkle with pepper. Wrap and cut in half and lay on platter. Refrigerate until serving.

Makes 40 mini appetizers

# Baked Brie

1 8-10-inch round wheel of Brie
¼ cup red pepper jelly
2 tbsp. honey
1 tbsp. Grand Marnier
½ cup slivered almonds
½ cup fresh sliced strawberries
1 17-ounce package frozen puff
   pastry sheets, thawed
   Egg white and water

Put Brie in freezer for 30 minutes. Take out of freezer and slice in half horizontally; set aside. In sauce pan mix jelly, honey and liqueur on low heat until bubbly; cool and set aside.

On a floured surface, roll both sheets of puff pastry into 12-inch squares. Trim each to a 9-inch circle.

Spread one half of jelly and fruit over inside of Brie and top with other half, cut side down. Top with remaining jelly and place on pastry and pull sides up. Place second pastry on top of brie folding edges down and crimping into bottom pastry.

Mix egg white with a drop of water and brush top of Brie. Bake in a 400 degree oven for 30 minutes or until golden. Let stand for 20 minutes before serving.

12 servings

# Apricot filling:

¼ cup apricot brandy
Canned chopped apricots
Slivered toasted almonds

Mix brandy and apricots in sauce pan and bring to boil; cool. Spread over Brie and add almonds.

# Walnut filling:

1 tbsp. softened butter
2 garlic cloves, minced
1 cup chopped toasted walnuts
¼ cup chopped Kalamata olives
Mix all ingredients and spread over Brie

# Brie and Apricots

1 15-ounce round Brie
1 10-ounce cans whole apricots
¼ cup apricot brandy
1 tbsp. brown sugar
¼ cup apricot jam
¼ cup toasted slivered almonds

    Drain apricots and reserve syrup in a saucepan. Cook syrup until reduced by half. Add brown sugar, brandy, jam and cook for 1 minute, remove from heat and add apricots and cool. Top brie with apricot mixture and sprinkle with slivered almonds.

# Champagne Stuffed Mushrooms

8-10 large mushrooms
¼ cup finely chopped onion
2 tbsp. finely chopped green onion
2 cloves garlic, minced
1 ½ cups sour dough bread crumbs
4 tbsp. butter
¼ cup champagne
2 small cans crab meat, drained and flaked
1 tbsp. Dijon mustard
2 tbsp. chopped fresh parsley
¼ cup grated Swiss cheese
   Favorite hollandaise sauce
   recipe or package mix

    Clean mushrooms with damp towel and remove stems. Melt 2 tbsp. butter and sauté garlic for about 1 minute. Add both onions and champagne and continue cooking for 3 minutes. Add crab, mustard, cheese and parsley, mix until combined. Remove from heat and add bread crumbs. Melt remaining butter and dip mushrooms in butter to cover. Stuff mushrooms full and set in casserole dish and top with hollandaise sauce. Bake in a 350 degree oven for 10 minutes.

Serves 4-6

# Chicken Cashew Canapés

2-3 chicken breasts, cooked and chopped
½ cups chopped celery
3 tbsp. red onion, chopped fine
½ cup mayonnaise
1 tsp. orange zest
½ tsp. tarragon
   Salt and pepper
1 8-ounce container whipped cream cheese
1 tsp. lemon juice or cream
   Chopped cashews or pecans
   Bread slices

Mix chicken with next 6 ingredients. Spread mixture over trimmed bread slices. Mix whipped cream cheese with lemon or cream and spread over all sides of bread. Dip bread into cashews or pecans and place on platter.

Put bread in freezer, as it makes it easier to cut crusts off. I assemble sandwiches while bread is still a bit frozen, making the cream cheese spread easier and cutting into triangles go faster and easier.

Makes about 16 canapés

# Crabmeat Canapés

1 8-oz. container whipped cream cheese
3 garlic cloves, minced
1 tsp. fresh lemon juice
1 tbsp. minced onion
   Dash of Tabasco
   Salt and cracked pepper
1 7-oz. can crabmeat, drained and flaked
¼ cup chopped radishes
¼ cup chopped green onions
   Toasted baguettes slices

    Mix softened cream cheese with remaining ingredients and spread on toasted baguette slices.

Makes 25 appetizers

# Crème de Brie Pastry Triangles

1 box frozen phyllo dough
1 3-ounce package cream cheese
2 garlic cloves
½ small onion, minced
1 small brie triangle, softened
½ box frozen chopped spinach
1 egg white
2 tbsp. cream
   Pinch nutmeg
   Salt and pepper

    In food processor chop garlic and onion and add egg. Add remaining ingredients and pulse until blended. Chill for 1 hour.
    Lay dough on counter and cover with towel. Lay two sheets on working surface and spray with non stick spray or brush with melted butter. With knife make 6 slices in length; making 6 long strips. Place ½ tsp. of filling on each strip and wrap in a flag design to top of strip. Brush each triangle with melted butter and place on baking sheet. Bake in a 350 degree oven for 20-25 minutes or until golden.

# Curried Chicken

6 chicken breasts
2 cups half-and-half
2 cups mayonnaise
¼ cup apricot jam
3 tbsp. dry sherry
3 tbsp. curry powder
½ tsp. coriander
   Salt and pepper to taste
2-3 cups coarsely chopped salted peanuts
1 jar bottled green curry sauce
   Chopped cilantro

    Cut chicken into 1-2 inch pieces and place in a large skillet with the half-and-half. Cover chicken and cook for about 30 minutes on low heat; cool. Whisk together the mayonnaise, jam, sherry, curry, coriander, salt and pepper. Mix chicken in sauce and refrigerate for 2 hours or more. When ready to serve, roll chicken pieces in peanuts and place on a platter that has bottled curry sauce drizzled on the platter. After all chicken pieces have been placed on platter, drizzle more curry sauce over chicken and sprinkle chopped cilantro on top; place took pick in each piece.

# Feta and Fruit

Block of feta cheese
Kiwi fruit
Sliced mango, papaya, tangerines,
Pineapple
3  tbsp. honey
1  tbsp. brown sugar
peach liqueur
Slivered almonds

    Hollow out middle of feta block; place fruit inside.  Warm honey and brown sugar in saucepan and add a few drops liqueur, cook until bubbly, remove from heat.  Drizzle over feta and fruit.

# Figs in Merlot Reduction

1 16-ounce container figs, chopped
2 cups Merlot wine
2 tbsp. sugar
  Goat cheese
1 baguette, sliced

    In sauce pan simmer figs, wine and sugar on low heat for 30 minutes; remove and cool for several hours until thick syrup has been made.
    Spread cheese over sliced baguette, add figs and drizzle sauce over top.

# Frosted Brie

1 15-ounce wheel of Brie
1-2 8-ounce containers whipped
   cream cheese
1-2 tsp. cream
1 tsp. almond liqueur
   Pinch of nutmeg
   Slivered almonds, dried cranberries,
   Toasted pecans, golden raisins

Add to softened cream cheese; almond liqueur, nutmeg and cream, mixing well. Spread frosting over top and sides of Brie. Arrange each topping in sections on top of Brie. Refrigerate until serving.

Serves 25 guests

# Gingered Teriyaki Tri-Tip with Roasted Red Peppers

1 package trimmed tri-tip
1 cup teriyaki sauce
½ cup teriyaki glaze
½ cup red wine
2 tbsp. minced fresh ginger
2 garlic cloves, minced
1 cup herbed goat cheese
1 jar roasted red and yellow
   peppers, drained and chopped
1-2 baguette sliced and toasted

Whisk together sauce, glaze, ginger, garlic and wine. Marinate meat in sauce up to 24 hours. Bake tri-tip in a 400 degree oven for 30-45 minutes; cool and slice.

Slice bread and spread olive oil on each slice and bake on a baking sheet in a 350-400 degree oven until brown, about 8 minutes; cool.

Spread goat cheese on baguettes, a slice of tri-tip and pieces of pepper, lay on platter. Serve at room temperature.

Makes about 30 appetizers

*This is a beautiful presentation with little work. The strawberries can be placed whole with flat side down and points up; using small strawberries is best for this.*

## Glazed Brie

1 15-ounce Brie cheese
½ cup currant jelly
1 tbsp. white wine
   pinch of cinnamon
   and nutmeg
   Fresh strawberries,
   raspberries and blueberries,
   washed and dried

Remove stems from strawberries and cut in half; set aside. Warm jelly, spices and wine in sauce pan until jelly has melted, remove from heat and cool slightly. Spread a bit of jelly on top of brie and lay fruit over brie. There is no certain pattern, be creative. Before jelly hardens, pour over fruit. Jelly will return to its original consistency and hold fruit together.

# Italian Stuffed Endive

12-15 endive leaves, separated
1 ½ 8-ounce container whipped
   cream cheese
2 garlic cloves, minced
3 tbsp. chopped sun dried tomatoes
   in oil
3 tbsp. pine nuts, sautéed in olive oil
½ cup grated Parmesan cheese
1 tsp. each dried oregano and basil
2 tbsp. chopped Italian parsley

   In a skillet sauté pine nuts and garlic for 3-5 minutes until golden brown, stirring often. Mix nuts and remaining ingredients into cream cheese. Spread endive leaves with spread, cover with plastic wrap and refrigerate to blend flavors.

Makes 8 servings

# Marinated Goat Cheese

2- packages soft herbed
   goat cheese
4 garlic cloves whole
1 tbsp. capers
2 garlic cloves minced
2 tbsp. lemon zest
¼ cup fresh lemon juice
1 cup extra virgin olive oil
1 bay leaf
   Italian parsley,
1 tsp. each oregano, basil
   thyme

Carefully cube cheese into about 2 inch pieces. Whisk together lemon juice, zest, garlic, herbs and olive oil. Pour dressing over cheese and add whole garlic and capers. Let cheese marinate in Frig for 24 hours before serving. Serve at room temperature.

# Marinated Shrimp

2 pounds peeled, de-veined large fresh shrimp
5 garlic cloves, minced
1 ½ tsp. salt
½ tsp. fresh thyme
1 tsp. freshly ground pepper
3-4 tbsp olive oil
½ cup champagne vinegar
¾ cup extra virgin olive oil
3 tbsp. fresh rosemary, chopped
2 lbs. smoked cheddar cheese,
   cut into 2- inch cubes

Sauté shrimp and garlic in oil add salt, pepper and thyme and stir for about 4 minutes. While shrimp is cooking make dressing by whisking the vinegar, rosemary and olive oil. Toss cooled shrimp in marinate and refrigerate until ready to serve. Serve each on top of cheddar cube holding with a toothpick.

Makes about 50 shrimps; serves 25 guests

# Mushroom Pâté Turnovers

2 garlic cloves, minced
½ cup onions, chopped fine
2 tbsp. olive oil
1 ½ cups chopped fresh mushrooms
1 tsp. salt and cracked pepper
2 3-ounce packages cream cheese
1 package piecrust mix
½ sour cream
2 egg whites

    Sauté onion and garlic in oil for 1 minute. Add mushrooms and sauté 3 minutes. Mix in salt, pepper, and cream cheese. Cool
    Combine piecrust, sour cream and egg white until ball forms. Refrigerate for 30 minutes. Divide dough in half. Roll out on a floured surface to a 1/8-inch thickness. Using a cookie cutter cut dough into rounds. Spoon a ½ teaspoon of filling onto half of circle. Fold round dough over filling and press edges together. Using a fork dipped into flour, crimp edges. Poke holes on top of turnover. Mix remaining egg white with a drop of water and brush tops of dough.
    Bake in a 400-degree oven for 12-15 minutes or until golden.

Makes about 40-50 turnovers.

# Pecan and Pear Wraps

1 pkg. garlic flavored tortillas (count of 8-10)
1 container whipped cream cheese
¼ tsp. nutmeg
1/8 tsp. pumpkin spice
2 fresh pears, skin removed and diced
1 ½ cups chopped, toasted pecans
1 small bag fresh baby spinach, stems removed
1 ½ cups cook bacon, crumbled
   (optional)

At room temperature mix spices in cream cheese. Spread cheese over each tortilla and add small amount of remaining ingredients at end of each tortilla. Roll tightly. Wrap and store in refrigerator for 2 hours before slicing. Each tortilla makes about 7 slices.

Makes approximately 70 slices

*This is the magical pizza recipe from my dear friend Cynthia. I made this nearly as often as I said the title out loud, because I loved the sound of the French word ringing in my mind. I would have never tried to make this, but watching Cynthia's mother made it seen effortless.*

# Pissaladiera

2 cups whole wheat flour
1 cup all purpose flour
1-egg
2 tbsp. olive oil
1 tsp. salt
1-package dry yeast
1 ½ cups warm water
2 tbsp. honey

# Filling

4 garlic cloves, minced
4 lbs. onions
8 filet anchovies
2 cups *Olives noires de Nice,*
   (black olives)
4 tbsp. olive oil
2 tbsp. thyme
   Salt and pepper

Slice onions and chop anchovies and olives. Sauté onions with garlic, thyme, salt and pepper and olive oil in large covered skillet for 1 hour on low heat; onions will caramelize. Add anchovies and olives and combine.

While onions are cooking prepare pizza crust. In small bowl dissolve the yeast and 1 teaspoon of the honey in ½ cup of the lukewarm water. Let it sit until it just begins to foam, about 3-5minutes.

Put both flours and salt in a food processor fitted with metal blade; turning the machine on pulse several times to blend flours. With machine running, add the yeast mixture, remaining honey and oil through the feed tube. Add enough of the water to form smooth dough. Dough will form a ball and will be kneaded. Remove dough and place in a large oiled bowl. Cover with a damp cloth and let rise for 30-45 minutes or doubled in size.

Remove dough and separate into 4 balls. Shape dough onto pizza stone and add filling. Bake in a 400-degree oven for 30 minutes. If dough is browning too fast, turn oven down to 350 degrees. Remaining dough can be wrapped in plastic wrap and frozen for up to 4 weeks. Defrost in refrigerator.

## Smoked Gouda Cheesecake

3 8-ounce packages cream cheese
4 eggs
½ cup whipping cream
2 tbsp. white wine
1 cup grated smoked Gouda cheese
½ cup grated Swiss cheese
½ cup grated Parmesan cheese
3 garlic cloves, minced
1 cup chopped roasted red peppers
1 tbsp. oregano and basil leaves
1 tsp. fresh chopped thyme
1 cup fresh chopped Italian parsley

In food processor mince the garlic. Add the cream cheese and blend. With machine running add one egg at a time and then the cream and continue blending. Add the peppers, herbs, wine and cheeses; blending well. Pour into a prepared springform pan and set on a baking sheet. Bake in a 300 degree oven for 1 ½ hours. Reduce heat to 200 degrees and bake for 30 minutes. Turn off oven and leave cheesecake in oven for 30 minutes. Remove and cool completely; several hours. Refrigerate overnight

# Spinach Pecan Mushrooms

2 cup fresh spinach, stems removed, chopped
2 8-ounce packages cream cheese, softened
1 cup grated Parmesan cheese
1 can water chestnuts, chopped
1 cup finely chopped pecans
10 slices bacon, fried and crumbled
1 cup chopped sun dried tomatoes
½ cup sliced green onions
3 cloves garlic, minced
2 tbsp. olive oil
2 cups sour dough bread crumbs
3 tbsp. white wine
25-30 medium mushrooms, wiped clean
   Melted butter

Sauté green onion and garlic in olive oil for 1 minute, add bread crumbs, stirring and cook for 2 minutes, cool.

Mix onion mixture and all other ingredients until well blended. Clean mushrooms with dry cloth and remove tops. Stuff with mushroom mixture; sprinkle more Parmesan cheese on top.

*Here is another great recipe from my friend Diana. I can't remember how many years I have been making these wraps, but as I look at the original recipe jotted down by Di; I am looking at a very faded crimped piece of paper. Diana reminds me of Rachel Ray because they both have a secret language of their own. I notice at the end of this recipe she writes, "Yum." Now what is Rachel known for? Yum-O...Hum...I think we all have a twin somewhere.*

# Tortilla Tidbits

2-8oz. pkg. cream cheese
1 small can chopped green chilies
1 small can crushed olives
3-4 green onions
   Few drops Tabasco,
   (I use more than a few)
2-3 tbsp. mayonnaise
   Little dry mustard
½ tsp. seasoning salt
   Little garlic powder

Mix all together and refrigerate over night. Take one dozen flour tortillas and spread thinly all the way to the edges and roll up and slice diagonally.

Makes about 100 wraps

Yum!

## Chapter 10

# *Delightful Salads*

*I stick to asparagus, which still seems to inspire gentle thought.*
*Charles Lamb (1775-1834) English writer*

*Dine or graze? Today's unique salad combinations reflect the American cook making a meal out of a salad and a change from rushed meals.*

# Apple Pecan Salad

2 heads butter lettuce,
   cleaned and torn
2 Granny Smith apples,
   cored and sliced thin
½ cup toasted chopped
   pecan and walnuts
¼ cup dried cranberries

Line 4 salad plates with lettuce leaves. Top with toasted nuts, apples and cranberries. Drizzle dressing over salad.

# Dressing:

4 tbsp. mayonnaise
4 tbsp. sour cream
4 oz. Gorgonzola cheese
2 tbsp. cream
3 tsp. white wine vinegar
2-3 tbsp. chopped chives
1 tsp. chopped Italian parsley
   Freshly ground pepper

Puree all ingredients in food processor. Makes 1 cup

*This is a down home Southern-style salad that goes great with fried chicken*

# Black-Eyed Peas and corn Salad

3 tbsp cider vinegar
1 tsp Dijon mustard
1 tsp salt
½ tsp sugar
½ tsp ground pepper
4 tbsp olive oil
2 cups cooked fresh corn or
　canned corn
1 package 10 oz frozen black-eyed peas
　cooked according to package directions
½ cup finely chopped red onion
¼ pound smoked ham or turkey,
　diced (optional)

　Mix vinegar, mustard, salt, pepper and sugar in bowl; whisk in oil.
　Add remaining ingredients.

Serves 12

*Eileen and I made this salad for years together and for a catered wedding we did together in 1982.*

# Cold Artichoke Salad

1 pkg. chicken Rice A Roni
3 green onions, sliced
2 6 oz. jars marinated artichoke hearts, chopped
¼ tsp. curry powder
½ cup mayonnaise

Cook rice as directed on package omitting butter step. Remove from heat and let stand until cool. Add chopped onion and green pepper to rice. Drain artichoke hearts reserving juice. Add curry powder and mayonnaise to artichoke juice and mix well. Add this dressing to rice mix and add artichoke hearts. Arrange in a salad bowl. Chill at least 4 hours.

# Cranberry Slaw

1 cup fresh or frozen cranberries, chopped
1/3 cup sugar
3 cups shredded cabbage
1 10-ounce can mandarian orange sections, drained
1/3 cup plain yogurt
1 tsp orange zest
2 tbsp orange juice
½ cup chopped walnuts

Combine cranberries and sugar. Cover and chill. Combine cabbage and orange sections, cover and chill. Mix yogurt, orange peel, juice and cranberry mixture. Pour over cabbage and toss.

Serves 6

# Fruit and Pasta Salad

8- ounce package
   tortellini, uncooked
2 cups broccoli flowerets
2 cups cubed cheddar cheese
¼ honey
1- 15 oz. can pineapple chunks,
   drained
1- 11 oz. can Mandarin oranges,
   drained
½ tsp. celery seed

Cook tortellini according to package directions. Rinse and drain well. In large bowl mix remaining ingredients with tortellini. Chill 2 hours.

Serves 8

# Italian Chicken Salad

1 small red onion thinly sliced
2 tbsp capers
1 red pepper, grilled
1 yellow pepper, grilled
5 cups shredded roasted chicken from deli
¼ cup chopped fresh parsley
¼ cup toasted slivered almonds
Salt and pepper to taste
¼ cup red wine vinegar
1/3 cup fresh lemon juice
2 tsp honey
Salt and pepper to taste
    1-1 ½ cup olive oil

Mix first 6 ingredients and set aside. In blender mix vinegar, lemon juice, honey, salt and pepper. Add oil slowly. Pour over chicken mixture and toss. Refrigerate for 2 hours before serving, toss again.

Serves 6-8

Clean out peppers and cut in half. Lay over medium flame on stove, turning until entire pepper in cooked. Cool and slice into long slices for salad.

# Marinated Mushroom Salad

6 cups fresh mushrooms, sliced
3 tbsp finely chopped onion
2 tbsp lemon juice
2 tbsp sugar
¼ tbsp ground pepper
½ cup whipping cream, whipped
¼ cup sour cream
¼ cup dry mustard
   salt and pepper
   romaine lettuce

Toss mushrooms, onions, lemon juice, and ¼ teaspoon pepper. Chill for up to one hour. Beat whipping cream. Mix sour cream, salt, dry mustard and fold in whipped cream. Stir into mushroom mixture. Spoon onto individual salad plates lined with romaine lettuce leaves or one platter. Garnish with tomato wedges and black pepper.

# Minty Shrimp Salad With Lime Dressing

1 pound cooked shrimp
  tails removed
2 cups small broccoli florets,
  cooked
2 seedless oranges, cut into
  chunks
1 ½ cup sliced mushrooms
¼ cup chopped fresh mint leaves
½ cup toasted sliced almonds
6 ounces lime yogurt
3 tbsp fresh lime juice
Salt and pepper to taste.

   Combine all ingredients and refrigerate.

Serves 4-6

*The secret is in the handling. For perfect potato salad, don't cube cooked potatoes; crumble with hands.*

# Mom's Potato Salad

8 potatoes
1 cup or more good mayonnaise
½ cup Miracle Whip salad dressing
1 small onion finely chopped
5 celery stalks sliced thin
1 large carrot, shredded
1 small jar sweet pickles,
   drained well and chopped or sliced
A few dill pickles, drained and chopped
1 bunch fresh parsley, chopped
1 can sliced olives, drained well
1 tsp garlic powder
2 tsp dill weed
1 or more tbsp salt
1 tsp pepper

Cook potatoes until tender, drain and let cool. Peel skins off and crumble with hands into bowl. Add spices and toss over potatoes. Add remaining ingredients and mix well. Refrigerate for a few hours, but take out 30 minutes before serving.

# Poppy Seed Cole Slaw

1 medium head cabbage, chopped or produce package slaw
3 carrots, grated
1 medium onion, chopped
1 green pepper, chopped
¼ cup chopped parsley
1 tsp poppy seed
½ tsp celery seed
 salt and pepper
½ lb. bacon, browned and chopped

Mix all ingredients together with dressing and chill for 1 hour. Bacon may be omitted.

# Dressing:

¼ tsp pepper
1 cup sour cream
½ cup mayonnaise
1 ½ tbsp horseradish
1 tsp lemon juice
¼ cup cider vinegar

# Potato, Celery and Ham Salad with Tarragon

1 pound red potatoes
1 tbsp tarragon white-wine vinegar
1 ½ cups thinly sliced celery
4 ounces Black Forest ham, cut into 1 inch strips (optional)
½ cup mayonnaise or crème fraiche
3 tbsp chopped fresh tarragon

Cook potatoes in boiling water until tender, drain. Cool to lukewarm. Peel potatoes and cut into ½ inch thick slices and put in bowl. Drizzle vinegar over potatoes and toss. Cool completely.

Add celery, ham, mayonnaise and chopped tarragon. Season with salt and pepper.

Serves 4

# Red Potato and Green Bean Salad

## Dressing:

¼ cup balsamic vinegar
2 tbsp Dijon mustard
2 tbsp fresh lemon juice
2 cloves garlic minced
　Dash of salt
½ cup extra-virgin olive oil

## Salad:

1½ pounds small red potatoes
½ pound fresh thin green beans,
　trimmed and cut in half
1 red onion, coarsely chopped
½ cup chopped fresh basil

　Whisk first 5 ingredients in bowl. Gradually whisk in oil. Season with salt and pepper. May be made 1 day ahead, cover and refrigerate. Bring to room temperature.
　Steam potatoes until tender, cool and cut into quarters. Cook green beans in boiling salted water, about 5 minutes and drain and put in ice water bath. Combine green beans, potatoes, onion and basil in large bowl. Add dressing and toss. Season with salt and pepper.

Serves 6

*If you are looking for a summer salad for a Hawaiian Party this is one to try.*

# Rice Mingle

3 cups cooked, cooled white rice
2 green onions, chopped fine
2 green peppers, chopped
¼ cup chopped pimento
2 tomatoes peeled and cubed
¼ cup chopped fresh parsley

Mix all ingredients with dressing and refrigerate for 2 hours before serving.

Dressing:
¾ cup olive oil
½ tsp. white pepper
1 ½ tsp. salt
¼ cup white wine vinegar
2 cloves garlic, minced

Whisk garlic, salt and pepper with vinegar. Whisk in oil and toss over rice.

Fall in love with eggplant! The hint of rosemary in the sauce melodiously lingers. Serve just the eggplant slightly warm with a dollop of sauce and not as a salad; makes an attractive platter.

# Roasted Eggplant Salad

2 medium eggplants, cut into ½ inch slices
4 tbsp. olive oil
1 garlic clove, crushed
½ tsp. oregano
   Salt and pepper
   Tossed greens
2 large tomatoes, sliced

　　Mix olive oil, oregano and garlic together and brush both sides of eggplant slices.  Place slices in a greased baking sheet and bake for about 20 minutes (10-12 minutes each side) or until brown in a 400 degree oven.  Sprinkle with salt and pepper and let cool.  Divide lettuce among 4 salad plates or all on a platter.  Top greens with eggplant and tomato slices.  Drizzle dressing over salad.

# Dressing:

½ cup mayonnaise
½ cup sour cream
2/3 cup grated Parmesan cheese
2 garlic cloves, crushed
15-20 fresh basil leaves
1 tbsp. chopped fresh rosemary
3 tsp. balsamic vinegar
¼ tsp. salt and pepper

　　Puree all ingredients in blender or food processor.

Makes 1 cup

# Smoked Mozzarella Tomato Salad

5 ripe tomatoes, sliced
6-8 oz. fresh smoked mozzarella
   cheese, sliced
3 tbsp. extra-virgin olive oil
3 tbsp. balsamic vinegar
1-2 garlic cloves, minced
¼ cup fresh basil, snipped
1 tsp. cracked pepper
   Fresh spinach leaves or
   lettuce

Line a platter with fresh spinach leaves. Arrange tomato and cheese slices on top of spinach. Combine vinegar and garlic and whisk in oil. Drizzle over salad and top with basil and pepper.

Makes 4 main-dish servings.

*This is another recipe that recalls friendship and memories for my children. My friend Eileen and I started making this salad around 1980. Every family picnic we experienced I brought along this salad. As the girls became teenagers, it was the most requested food their friends ask me to make for school, scouting and church events. It's simple and you can feed an army with it for pennies...and I did; my kind of treasure!*

## Spaghetti Salad

1 4-ounce can chopped olives
3 green onions, chopped
1 green pepper, chopped
1 tsp. sesame and poppy seeds
1 tbsp. paprika
1 tsp. garlic and onion powder
1 bottle Italian dressing
1 cup grated parmesan cheese
1 pound package vermicelli,
   cooked and drained

Add all ingredients and mix well, ending in dressing. Refrigerate a few hours before serving. If too dry- add more dressing.

*This salad is beautiful and perfect for Christmas*

# Toss Pine Nut Salad

½ cup pine nuts
3 tbsp lemon juice
½ tsp[ salt
¼ cup olive oil
1/8 tsp lemon zest
    dash of nutmeg

    Combine and mix well. Then add baby spinach leaves. Top with ¾ cup pomegranate seeds.

# Walnut Salad

¼ cup red wine vinegar
2 tsp mustard
½ cup walnut oil
½ cup broken walnuts
1 cups celery
2 cloves garlic, crushed
2 cups seeded, chopped tomatoes
1 cup cubed or shredded mozzarella cheese
½ cup chopped fresh basil leaves

Mix vinegar, garlic, mustard and pour oil in while mixing dressing. Toss remaining ingredients and add dressing.

## Chapter 11

# *Casseroles from Scratch*

*Memories of cooking from scratch for my family takes me back to my own childhood. When thumbing through my old recipes the feelings of sentiment roll off my heart like a sentimental tale that emerges from a stained and faded piece of paper.*

*A timeless classic.... true comfort food*

# Baked Macaroni and Cheese

6 cups water
  Salt
2 cups elbow macaroni
2 ½ cups grated sharp
  cheddar cheese
3 tbsp. butter
2 tbsp. flour
2 cups milk
½ onion, minced
  Salt and pepper to taste
1 tbsp. butter
½ cup breadcrumbs

    Bring water and salt to a boil and cook macaroni until tender, drain and place in a large bowl.
    Melt butter and add flour whisking for 2-3 minutes over low heat. Gradually whisk in milk, onion and cook for 10 minutes. Remove from heat and stir in one-half of the cheese, salt and pepper.
    Melt one-tablespoon butter and add to breadcrumbs and toss. Pour half of macaroni into a casserole dish and top with half of remaining cheese. Top with remaining macaroni and cheese. Sprinkle breadcrumbs over macaroni and bake in a 375-degree oven for about 30 minutes or until crumbs have browned. Let set before serving.

# Best Tuna Casserole

2 cans chunk-style tuna,
6 oz. cooked, rinsed egg noodles
½ cup sliced thin celery
1/3 cup sliced green onions
1 small pkg. frozen peas,
 (optional)
½ cup dairy sour cream
2 tbsp. Dijon mustard
½ cup mayonnaise
½ tsp. dried thyme leaves
½ tsp. dried oregano
½ tsp. salt and pepper
1 zucchini, washed and grated
2 carrots washed and grated
2 tbsp. olive oil
1 clove garlic, minced
1 cup each grated Jack and cheddar cheese
1 large chopped tomato
2 cups bread crumbs
 tossed in melted butter

Sauté zucchini, carrot and garlic in oil on low heat for 2-3 minutes, set aside.

Combine noodles with tuna, celery, peas and green onions. Blend in sour cream, mustard, mayonnaise, thyme, oregano and salt and pepper and one-half of cheese.

Spoon half of the mixture into a buttered 2-quart casserole dish. Top with zucchini and carrots. Spread remaining noodle mixture on top.

Cover and bake in a 350-degree oven for 35 minutes. Uncover and sprinkle remaining cheese, tomato and breadcrumbs on top. Bake 15 minutes or until golden.

# Candy's Noodles

1- 10 ounce box frozen chopped spinach, drained well
1  3 oz. pkg. Cream cheese
2  cups small curd cottage cheese
1  cup sour cream
½ cup chopped fine onion
1  cup jack cheese
    Salt and pepper
1  8 ounce pkg. wide noodles, cooked and drained
1-2 tbsp. olive oil

Sauté onions in olive oil for 3-5 minutes and add cream cheese. Warm cream cheese over low heat while stirring for about 2 minutes. Add cream cheese, onion and remaining ingredients to hot noodles and mix well. Pour into buttered casserole dish and bake for 30 minutes in a 350-degree oven.

Serves 6-8

*There always will be a passion for mixing and matching flavors and calling it a casserole. And noodles are American's great contribution to American cooking. This recipe is by far one of the best homemade Mac and cheese dishes I have ever discovered. My friend Candy gave it to me to make for the lunch program I was responsible for. Children ranging from k-12 grades never turned it down and I rarely saw any left on their plates. Two years ago I made this for one of my granddaughter's birthday lunches for the kids, but it was the parents that gobbled it down and asked to take home the leftovers.*

# Mac and Cheese

8  cups cooked elbow macaroni
2  quarts cottage cheese
1  quart sour cream
4  eggs, beaten
4-6 cups grated cheddar cheese
2  cans mushroom soup
½ - ¾ cup dehydrated onion
1-2 tbsp. Lawry salt

Mix noodles with sauce ingredients. Pour in large casserole or several dishes. Add more cheese on top. Bake in a 350-degree oven for 1 ½ hours, uncovered.

If desired, mix crushed cornflakes with melted butter and cover top of casserole dish before baking.

Serves 20

# Poppy Seed Noodle Casserole

1 ½ cups soft bread crumbs
6 tbsp. butter
1 cups finely chopped onion
5 hard boiled eggs, chopped
2 cups small curd cottage cheese
1 cup plain yogurt
½ cup grated Parmesan cheese
1 tbsp. poppy seeds
1 tsp. Worchester sauce
½ tsp. salt and pepper or to taste
8 ounces wide noodles, cooked and drained

Melt 3 tablespoons of butter in a skillet. Add breadcrumbs and toss. Remove crumbs and sauté onion in remaining butter over medium heat, about 5 minutes.

Combine onion, cooked noodles and eggs in large bowl; stir in remaining ingredients. Pour into a buttered casserole dish and sprinkle with breadcrumbs on top. Bake in a 350-degree oven for 30 minutes.

*Oh my goodness! This is another one of those easy, toss it and bake it casseroles that comes out tasting amazing and everyone wants to know what is in this dish! This is too good to turn the page and not try it....trust me!*

# Southern Potato Casserole

In a large bowl mix:
1 cube melted butter
2 cups sour cream
2-3 cups grated cheddar cheese
½ cup diced onion
1 can cream of chicken soup
1 tsp. salt and pepper
1- 2 lb. pkg. frozen Southern style hash browns

Mix ingredients well and add hash browns. Pour into a buttered casserole dish and bake for 1 hour in a 350 degree oven.

# Tamale Pie

1 ½ pounds ground beef
   or turkey
2 cloves garlic, minced
1-2 tbsp. tomato paste
1- 8 ounce can corn, drained
2 large tomatoes, chopped
½ cup chopped green olives
1 tbsp. each chili powder
   and cumin
1 tsp. ground cinnamon
   Salt and pepper to taste
3 cups sharp grated cheddar cheese
2 cups chicken stock
1 ½ cups yellow cornmeal
1 tsp. salt
½ tsp. pepper
1 tsp. baking powder

    Brown meat and drain. Add garlic, corn, tomato paste, tomatoes, olives and spices. Mix in 1 cup of grated cheese and combine well. Pour into a buttered casserole dish and top with remaining cheese.

    Mix cornmeal, salt and pepper and baking powder and add to boiling stock. Reduce heat to medium low and using a whisk, stirring constantly until thickened. If too thick add some hot water to mixture. Pour on top of casserole and cheese. Bake in a 400-degree oven for 40 to 50 minutes or until browned. Let rest for 15 minutes before serving.

*This is not real Hungarian Goulash; rather it's a family mixture of leftovers and ground beef. When I was first married I probably made this once a week. Today, the store's shelves are lined with boxed hamburger dinners. I don't think this one takes any more time to put on the table. Years later I started adding paprika and a cup of beer to the mixture. If you are on a budget and have a lot of little people sitting around your table, this is a good dish to double and serve leftovers later in the week. This recipe is now three generations strong!*

# Terry's Goulash

2 – lb. ground beef
½ onion, chopped fine
1 green pepper, chopped
2 garlic cloves, minced
½ can tomato paste
1 14oz. can diced tomatoes
1 13 oz. can corn, drained
2 cups cooked macaroni noodles
1 4 oz. can sliced olives, drained
2 cups grated cheddar cheese
   Salt and pepper to taste

Brown beef and drain grease. Add onion, green pepper and garlic and cook with meat for 3 minutes. Add remaining ingredients and toss well. Cook on low heat for about 10 minutes. Let set for a few minutes before serving.

Serves 6-8

# Zucchini Corn Bread Casserole

1- 8oz. can whole corn, drained
1 medium onion, chopped
1 cup chopped green and red pepper
1 ½ cup chopped fresh tomatoes
2 small zucchini, diced
2 cups grated cheddar cheese
1 cup chicken broth
½ cup cornmeal
3 eggs, beaten
¾ cup milk
½ tsp. dried thyme and oregano
   Salt and pepper

    Combine corn, peppers, onion and broth in a sauce pan and simmer for 3-5 minutes. Add zucchini, tomatoes, cheese and cornmeal. Set aside.
    Whip together eggs, milk and spices. Add egg mixture to cornmeal and combine. Pour into a buttered casserole dish. Bake, uncovered in a 350 degree oven for 40-50 minutes or until set. Let set for about 5-10 minutes.

Serves 6-8

# Vegetable-Chicken Casserole

2 cups chicken broth
2/3 cups cooking sherry
1 pkg. long grain and wild rice mix
1 small onion, chopped
2 small carrots, grated
1 small green pepper, chopped
½ cup butter
1 4oz. can sliced mushrooms
3 cups diced cooked chicken
1 8 oz. pkg. cream cheese
2 cups grated cheddar cheese
1 cup evaporated milk
1/3 cup grated Parmesan cheese
¾ cup sliced almonds
   Salt and pepper to taste

Bring broth and 1/3 cup of Sherry to a boil. Add contents of rice package to broth, cover and simmer on low for 25-30 minutes.

Sauté onion and carrots and green pepper in butter until soft, about 5 minutes. Add rice, chicken and mushrooms, mixing well.

Place cream cheese, cheddar and milk in sauce pan and melt over medium heat, stirring until smooth. Add to onion with remaining sherry and mix thoroughly. Pour into buttered 13x9 casserole dish. Top with Parmesan cheese and almonds.

Cover and bake in a 350 degree oven for 35 minutes. Uncover and bake about 15 minutes longer or until bubbly.

May be refrigerated over night before baking; bake 45 minutes covered and 15 minutes uncovered.

*Chapter 12*

# Farmer's Harvest

*For anyone who has grown their own vegetables know the fragrance that lingers in the early morning as they walk through the garden: the ripening of tomatoes, the smell of fresh herbs and the flavors all awaiting the experiences of their garden. Arrangement of vegetables is like choosing colors from a paint pallet: from egg plant of purple, beets of red to the most golden squash and accents of imagination all combine the edifice of enjoyment and nourishment.*

# Baked Yams with Yogurt Creme

Yams
Butter
1 cup Yogurt Creme Cheese or
plain low-fat yogurt
2 tbsp honey
1 tsp grated orange rind
1 tbsp orange juice
pinch ground coriander

Wash skins of yams and dry. Bake in a 350 oven until done. Make a slit and fluff up yam and add a dot of butter. Top with yogurt cream.

## Creme Topping:

Mix yogurt, honey, orange rind, orange juice and coriander well. Refrigerate until used. May be used on fruit salads or topping for other desserts.

# Broccoli with Cream Sauce

4 tomatoes
2 tbsp hot olive oil
Fresh or dried marjoram and parsley, chopped
3 cups fresh broccoli steamed
2 egg yolks
salt and pepper
¼ tsp cayenne pepper
1 tbsp tarragon vinegar
2 tbsp cream
2 tbsp butter
1 tbsp fresh herbs
½ tsp lemon juice

Chop tomatoes and cook in hot olive oil, set aside. Steam broccoli and keep covered while making the sauce.

Whisk together the yolks, salt, cayenne pepper and vinegar; add the cream and turn into a double boiler or bowl with pan of water under it. Cook until thicken and add butter in small pieces, followed by the herbs and lemon juice.

Place broccoli on platter with sautéed tomatoes on top and then pour sauce over broccoli.

# Creamed Carrots

6 large carrots
lemon juice
4 tbsp butter
3 tbsp flour
salt
cayenne pepper
2 cups chicken or vegetarian stock
½ cup cream
1 tbsp chopped parsley
1 tbsp chopped chives
2 eggs
1 tbsp milk

    Peel carrots, cut in small slices and cook in salted water with a bit of lemon juice until tender.
    For sauce: Melt half of butter and stir in flour and cook for 2 minutes on low flame, stirring. Add salt and cayenne pepper. Pour in stock and stir until sauce comes to a boil, add cream and the other half of butter in small pieces. Mix in the parsley, chives, egg yolk and milk. Add carrots and mix thoroughly.

# Creamed Swiss Chard

2 tbsp unsalted butter
¼ cup coarsely chopped shallots
1 tbsp flour
1 cup milk
½ tsp ground nutmeg
1 tsp salt
¼ tsp freshly ground black pepper
1 large bunch green Swiss chard,
ribs removed and leaves chopped.

    In a large skittle melt butter over medium heat. Add shallots and cook until translucent. Add flour and cook, stirring constantly for 1 minute. Add milk, nutmeg, salt and pepper. Cook until mixture is reduced by half, about 2 minutes. Add chard and cook until tender and coated with milk mixture, about 3 to 4 minutes. Serve immediately.

# Creamy Brussels sprouts

1 cup shallots thinly sliced
2 tbsp olive oil
1 pound Brussels sprouts, trimmed, cut in half
1/3 cup white wine
½ tsp salt
¼ tsp fresh-ground pepper
2 cups low-sodium chicken broth
½ cup Gruyere cheese, finely grated

Sauté the shallots and Brussels sprouts and cook over medium heat until the shallots are soft and the Brussels sprouts have begun to turn golden, about 10 minutes. Add the chicken stock and stir. Reduce heat to low and cook until Brussels sprouts are tender and liquid is syrupy and reduced by half, about 20 minutes. Transfer to an 8 by 10 inch casserole dish. Add the cream and sprinkle with the cheese. Bake until the liquid is bubbling, the cheese has melted, and the top is golden brown, about 20 minutes.

Makes 6 servings

# Green Chili Pesto with Grated Zucchini Squash

Pesto Sauce:
2  cloves garlic peeled
4  oz. parmesan cheese grated
2  4oz. cans mild chopped green chilies drained
¾ cup pumpkin seeds or pine nuts
½ cup fresh parsley sprigs
5-6 tablespoons olive oil
¼-1 tablespoon salt to taste

    Process ingredients with metal blade in food processor making a smooth paste while adding oil last with machine running.

2-4 medium/large grated zucchini
2/3 cup green chili pesto
½ cup sour cream or cream
1/3 cup chicken stock
Salt and pepper

    In a medium skillet combine pesto, cream and stock to thin mixture.  Set over medium heat to warm through.  Add squash and stir over heat.  Add salt and pepper to taste.

# Grilled Vegetables with Garlic Sauce

Assorted vegetables, washed, halved, sliced or quartered
½ cup olive oil
2 cloves garlic, minced
1 tbsp. each fresh rosemary,
   thyme and sage
Salt and fresh ground pepper
1/3 cup maple syrup
1 tbsp. balsamic vinegar

Whisk together the oil, vinegar and syrup. Add spices and garlic and toss all vegetables in sauce. Grill, basting with sauce for about 12 minutes. Be careful not to burn vegetables.

# Old Fashioned Corn Cakes Dressed with a Spicy Sauce

2 cups canned whole-kernel corn, drained.
1 tbsp curry powder
3 tbsp flour
3 tbsp cornstarch
4 green onions finely chopped
1 egg, beaten
salt and pepper

## Salsa:

2 fresh pears, finely diced
1 small tomato chopped
½ cup chopped red onion
2 green onions finely chopped
¼ cup chopped fine cilantro
¼ cup chopped red pepper
4 tbsp fresh lime juice
1 tbsp olive oil
1 tsp ground cumin
½ tsp white pepper
½ tsp sugar
¼ tsp salt

## Sauce:

2 pears, cored and diced
1 tbsp shallot, minced
1 tbsp olive oil
2 tbsp fresh ginger root, minced
2 tbsp dry sherry
   tbsp sesame oil

Put corn in blender and add curry, flour, cornstarch, green onions and eggs. Mix until corn is chopped. Add oil to sauté pan on medium high heat. Add 2 tablespoons for each cake. Grill until cake is golden brown on both sides. Makes about 15 cakes.

Salsa:

Combine fruits, onions, red pepper, cilantro, lime juice, oil, cumin, white pepper, salt and sugar. Mix and refrigerate for 2 hours.

Sauce:

Sauté the shallots in oil for one minute. Add the pears and the rest of the ingredients and cook until fruit is soft. Cool and transfer to a blender. Puree the mixture into sauce consistency.

To serve cakes:

Spoon 2 tablespoons of sauce in the center of plate and lay 2-3 corn cakes on top. Spoon salsa on top of corn cakes with a small amount of chopped cilantro.

*This recipe comes from Washington State. My daughter Kellie's best friend Holly gave me this recipe; or rather she e-mailed it to me so that I could make it for her on Thanksgiving Day at Kellie's home in Washington.*

# Potato-Apple Gratin

3  eggs
3  cups buttermilk
2  tsp salt
½ tsp pepper
1  tbsp fresh thyme
1  tbsp flour
4  large baking potatoes,
   peeled and sliced into 1/8 inch slices
3  Granny Smith apples,
   peeled and sliced into 1/8 inch slices
2 ½ cups grated Swiss cheese
1  cup grated Parmesan cheese

Heat oven to 400 degrees. Spray cooking spray in a deep casserole dish. Beat eggs, buttermilk, thyme, salt, pepper, and flour, set aside. Arrange a layer of potatoes in casserole dish. Cover with a layer of apples and sprinkle with a third of both cheeses. Pour a third of the egg mixture on top. Repeat and make two more layers ending with cheeses. Bake, covered for 15 minutes and turn oven down to 350 degrees. Continue to bake for 45 minutes and uncover and bake for another 10 minutes or until golden on top. Remove from oven and let set for about 10 minutes before serving.

*I nearly did jumping jacks the first time I tasted these potatoes after Suzie made them for several of our families at a get-together. I have made them ever since.*

# Potatoes Anna

2 pounds of baking potatoes,
  peeled and sliced.
Olive oil
Dots of butter
Salt and pepper
Pinch of oregano
Pinch of fresh parsley
1 cup sour cream
2 cups grated cheddar cheese
1 cup grated Parmesan cheese

    Heat cast iron skillet with olive oil and place potato rounds in pan, overlapping to make a second layer. Add spices and turn potatoes to make sure all potatoes have been sautéed. Remove potatoes from heat. Add a bit more salt and pepper and dots of butter. Spread the sour cream on top of potatoes and then both of the cheeses. Bake in skillet in a 350 oven uncovered for 30-45 minutes or until potatoes are tender. Let set for a few minutes and then slide a knife around the sides of the pan, turn out on a dish or serve in skillet. Serve sour cream as a topping.

# Roasted Sweet Potatoes and Onions

2 large sweet potatoes, peeled and
cut into 1-inch chunks
2 medium sweet onions cut into
1 –inch chunks
3 tbsp olive oil
¼ cup amaretto liqueur
1 tsp dried thyme
1 tsp dried oregano
salt and pepper to taste
½ cup sliced almonds, toasted

Heat oven to 425 degrees. Toss everything except almonds in a baking dish. Cover and bake for 30 minutes. Uncover and sprinkle almonds on top of potatoes and bake uncovered for another 20 minutes.

Serves 6

# Succulent Carrots

1 bunch carrots peeled
2 cups water
¼ tsp salt
1 tsp orange flavoring
1 tbsp orange zest
1 tbsp cornstarch
¼ tsp ground nutmeg
1 tbsp chopped parsley
1 tbsp sugar
3 tbsp butter
2 tbsp orange liqueur
chopped watercress for garnish

    Slice carrots ¼ inch and cook in covered pot for 10 to 12 minutes until tender but crisp. Drain and reserve liquid. Place liquid, flavoring, cornstarch and nutmeg in same pan and bring to boil until thick, stirring constantly. Add parsley, sugar, butter and orange liqueur. Cook 4 minutes over low heat, serve hot and sprinkle with parsley before serving.

# Sweet Potato Puff with Sage and Pecans

2- 30 ounce canned sweet potatoes or yams
1 1/3 cups finely chopped shallots
2 tbsp olive oil
1 egg beaten
2 tbsp freshly chopped sage
1 1/3 cups low-fat cottage cheese
1 tsp salt
½ tsp pepper
¼ tsp nutmeg
½ cup coarsely chopped pecans

Chop the shallots in food processor and sauté in oil. Add the sage and cook for about 1 minute more. Drain the canned potatoes and place in food processor and puree. Put the potatoes in a mixing bowl and mix in egg. Add the cottage cheese, salt and pepper to processor and puree. Add cottage cheese to sweet potatoes and the shallots, sage, nutmeg and mix well. Put mixture in a casserole dish and bake for about 45 minutes and then top with pecans. Bake 10 more minutes.

# Swiss String Beans

4 cups string beans cut into ½ inch pieces
½ cup minced onions
2 tbsp whole wheat flour
½ tsp salt
1 cup plain yogurt
1 tbsp honey
2 cups grated Swiss cheese
¼ cups sesame toasted sesame seeds, ground
Butter

Steam string beans in a small amount of water for about 3 minutes and drain. Combine the beans, minced onions, whole-wheat flour and salt. Stir well so that the flour coats the vegetables. Stir in the yogurt and honey. Put the mixture into and deep-dish casserole dish. Cover the bean mixture with the grated cheese and top with the ground sesame seeds and a few dots of butter.

Bake at 325 degrees for 30 minutes.

*This recipe was shared with me from a gal who was planning to attend Culinary Cooking School. It was her mom's recipe and we used it for years in dinner and buffet menus.*

# Tarragon Green Beans with Celery Puree

4 cups fresh green beans
olive oil and butter
2 tbsp fresh tarragon and parsley
1 cup pureed celery
1 cup pureed onion
salt and white pepper

Place green beans in boiling water for about 3 minutes, drain and place in ice water bath for another 3 minutes. Drain and dry beans. Chop onion in food processor to a paste and do the same with the celery. Heat a little olive oil and butter in sauté pan; add some of the puree and green beans. Sauté beans, turning until tender and coated with oil and puree. Add some of the herbs and salt and pepper to taste. Do beans in batches if pan is small.

*Chapter 13*

# *Best Sunday Family Dinners*

*Meat and potatoes are the quintessential of a Sunday Supper;
to grandmother's house we go…*

# Broiled Chuck Roast

3 pound boneless chuck roast
1 onion, chopped
3 tbsp olive oil
3 garlic cloves, crushed
½ cup soy sauce
1 tsp ground ginger, allspice
1 tsp dried rosemary
¼ cup red wine
3 tbsp dark brown sugar
1 cup beef broth

    Sauté onions in oil and add remaining ingredients and bring to a boil. Remove from heat and cool. Place roast in a plastic container and pour marinade over roast; refrigerate covered for 24 hours.
    Bake in a 450 degree oven for 20-30 minutes or broil on high for 10 minutes each side.

Serves 6-8

# Buttermilk Biscuit Topped Pie

3 cups cooked and shredded chicken
½ cup chopped onion
2 garlic cloves, minced
2 tbsp butter
1 10-ounce frozen chopped spinach, thawed and drained
1 cup sour cream
1 egg, beaten
½ tsp salt and pepper
¼ tsp nutmeg

Sauté onion and garlic in butter, add spinach and salt and pepper and cook for 1 minute. In a bowl mix all ingredients and pour into a casserole dish.

# Biscuit Mixture:

1 2/3 cup flour
¼ cup butter, melted
¾ cup buttermilk
2 tsp baking powder
½ tsp salt

Stir together all ingredients. Drop dough by tablespoons onto chicken mixture. Bake in a 350 degree oven for 30-40 minutes.

# Chicken Pot Pie

3 cups cubed cooked chicken
½ cup chopped onion
1 cup fresh sliced mushrooms
1 celery rib, sliced
2 carrots, sliced
1 small potato, peeled, cubed 1 inch pieces
½ cup frozen peas
¼ cup dry white wine
½ tsp dried marjoram, thyme, tarragon, crushed
2 tbsp fresh chopped parsley
1 ½ cups whipping cream
2 tbsp flour
½ tsp salt and pepper
½ cup chicken broth
2 tablespoons butter

Place chicken in a 2-quart casserole dish. Melt butter in large skillet over low heat. Add onion, mushrooms and increase heat to medium; sauté until browned and liquid evaporates, about 5 minutes. Add herbs and wine; cook until almost evaporated. Pour over chicken. Add all vegetables to chicken and carefully mix. In a saucepan, whisk together cream, flour, salt and pepper and cook over low heat for 5 minutes. Whisk in broth and add to chicken mixture.

Roll out favorite pie dough recipe on floured surface to fit the top of casserole dish. Place on top of pie; trim and seal edges. Beat one egg till fluffy with 1 tsp water. Brush top of crust with egg glaze. Bake in a 375 degree for 40-50 minutes or till browned and bubbly. Cool slightly, serve warm.

Serves 6-8

# Corn Pudding

½ cup cornmeal
1 15-ounce can whole kernel corn, drained
1 15-ounce can cream-style corn
1 cup half-and-half
3 eggs, beaten
¼ cup butter, melted
½ tsp pepper
½ tsp salt
1 tsp sugar
1 tbsp flour
½ cup cornmeal

In mixing bowl combine corns, half-and-half, eggs, butter, salt, pepper and sugar. Add corn meal and flour and blend. Pour mixture into a casserole dish and bake in a 350 degree oven for 1 hour or until browned and set in the center.

Serves 8

# Creamed Biscuits

2 cups flour
1 tbsp baking powder
1 tsp salt
1-1 ½ cups whipping cream
1/3 cup butter, melted

Combine flour, baking powder and salt in a large bowl and stir to combine. Slowly stir in 1 cup of cream; if dough appears dry; slowly add enough additional cream to form dough into a ball. Do not overwork. Knead dough 1 minute. Pat dough into ½ inch-thick square. Cut out 16 rounds and dip each into melted butter, coating completely. Place on ungreased baking sheet about 1 inch apart. Bake in a 400-425 degree oven for 12 minutes or golden. Serve hot.

# Dutch-Oven Chicken and Beans

2 tbsp. oil
10 chicken thighs
2 tbsp. brown sugar
1 tbsp. cider vinegar
¾ tsp. fennel seeds, crushed
½ tsp. cracked black pepper
  Salt
½ pounds green beans
½ pound wax beans
1 15 ounce can red
  kidney beans, drained

In a Dutch oven over medium heat, sauté the chicken thighs until well browned on all sides. Remove chicken and drain all oil but 1 tablespoon from Dutch oven. Return chicken and add brown sugar, vinegar, fennel, pepper, salt and ¼ cup water. Heat to boiling and reduce to low; cover and simmer 15-20 minutes until chicken is tender.

Cook green and wax beans in 1 inch salted, boiling water. Cook 5 minutes until tender and drain.

When chicken is done, add all three beans and heat through.

Makes 4 servings

# Five-Hour Stew

1  3-pound chuck roast or
   2 pounds stew meat
1  large bag frozen vegetables with potatoes, celery, carrots
½ onion, chopped
2  garlic cloves chopped
1-2 35-ounce canned chopped tomatoes and juice
½ cup red wine
½ cup instant tapioca
   salt and pepper

Cut roast into 1/4 inch chunks and season with salt and pepper. Put into large roasting pan or casserole dish. Add vegetables, onion, garlic, canned tomatoes, wine and tapioca and more salt and pepper. Mix in pan and cover tightly. Bake in a 250 oven for 5 hours without lifting cover. Stew will be tender with lots of gravy. Serve with salad and biscuits.

*This was one of my favorite memories growing up. I loved chocolate cake and thought nothing could ever compare, until one Sunday years ago, Grandma Stella made this cake for us. She dressed it with her old fashioned butter cream frosting, the kind our mother's made before frosting was sold in a can on the grocery shelf. Since then I have iced the cake with a cream cheese frosting. Both are wonderful.*

## Grandma Stella's Sunday Spice Cake

1 stick unsalted butter
1/3 cup shortening
4 eggs
1 ½ cups buttermilk
3 tbsp sour cream
1 tsp vanilla
1 cup brown sugar
1 cup sugar
2 ½ cups flour
1 tsp baking soda
1 ½ tsp baking powder
2 tsp cinnamon
1 tsp nutmeg
½ tsp allspice

In an electric mixer bowl cream butter and shortening until smooth. Add the sugars and blend. Add the eggs, one at a time, beating well after each egg. In separate bowl, mix the buttermilk with the sour cream and vanilla; set aside. In another bowl, sift the flour, baking soda, powder and spices. Add the buttermilk to the egg mixture and then the flour mixture.

Pour cake batter into 2 greased and flour dusted prepared cake pans. Bake cake in a 350 degree oven for 45 minutes or until a toothpick comes out clean from center of cake. Cool on wire rack.

## Butter Cream Frosting

Cream 1 stick softened butter with 1 tsp vanilla. Add 2-3 cups powdered sugar and 1-2 tbsp milk. Mix until smooth and all lumps are gone. Ice cake with first layer of icing and let set and finish with second layer.

## Cream Cheese Frosting

Cream 2 8-ounce packages cream cheese (softened) with 1 stick unsalted butter (softened). Add 1 tsp vanilla and 1 tbsp orange extract, 2 tbsp fresh orange zest. Add 3-4 cups powdered sugar; using a mixer blend all ingredients until creamy, about 5 minutes. Frost cake as above.

*Oh how I remember this meal of scalloped potatoes, Swiss steak and homemade biscuits. The meat was so tender and melted in your mouth. From the depression era, I am sure this was a dish Nana made only on Sunday's or special occasions.*

# Grandma Stella's Swiss Steak

1 large packaged round steak, tenderized
½ cup flour or more olive oil
1 large green pepper, sliced
½ onion chopped
3 garlic cloves chopped
1 cup sliced celery
1 35-ounce can diced tomatoes
1 4- ounce can tomato sauce
¼ cup water
   salt and pepper

Slice meat into 6-8 pieces. Salt and pepper them and dust them generously with flour. Heat skillet, adding good amount of oil and the garlic and sauté meat on both sides; about 2-3 minutes. Transfer meat to a baking dish, salt and pepper again and sprinkle vegetables on top of meat, canned tomatoes (with juice), water and tomato sauce. Add a little flour in the corners of dish for a thickener. Cover and bake in a 300 degree oven for about 3 hours or until meat is very tender. If it looks like sauce is evaporating, add more water while cooking.

## Lima Beans in Cream

3  cups frozen lima beans
1  cup cream
1  ounce cooked ham, cubed
2  tsp. butter
   Salt and freshly ground Pepper

Cook lima beans according to package directions.  Drain liquid.  Add cream, ham, butter, salt and pepper to lima beans.  Heat through but do not boil.

Makes 6 servings

*I remember my mother putting the flour mixture in a brown bag and coating the chicken pieces by shaking the bag. When I heard the bag shaking, I knew we were having Fried Chicken for Sunday dinner.*

# Old Fashioned Buttermilk Southern-Fried Chicken

1   3 pound chicken, cut into 8 pieces
1 ½ cups buttermilk
1   tbsp Dijon-style mustard
1   tsp salt
1   tsp pepper
2 ½ cups flour
1   tbsp baking powder
2   tsp salt
1   tsp pepper
1   tsp garlic powder
1   tbsp paprika

Combine the buttermilk, mustard, salt and pepper in a large dish and add chicken pieces and turn to coat. Refrigerate 3 hours or overnight.

Mix together the flour, baking powder, salt, pepper, garlic salt and paprika. Add the chicken to flour mixture and turn to coat on all sides. Leave chicken in dish for about 10-15 minutes before frying. Shake off excess flour and place in a cast iron or other skillet with heated vegetable oil. Cook, covered, over medium-high heat for about 20 minutes and chicken is crispy. Transfer to paper towels and serve hot.

Serve with mashed potatoes and gravy.

## Roasted Chicken

1 whole roasting chicken
1 lemon
4 garlic cloves, crushed
1 tsp dried sage
1 tsp dried thyme
1 tsp oregano
½ tsp pepper
½ tsp salt
1 tbsp sesame seeds
2 tbsp olive oil
½ cup dry white wine

    Clean chicken and pat dry. Squeeze juice of lemon and mix with one tbsp olive oil and rub over chicken. Place the lemon rinds inside the chicken. Mix the other tbsp of oil with dried herbs, salt and pepper, sesame seeds and garlic. Sprinkle and rub over chicken; place in a cast iron skillet or baking dish. Pour wine in bottom of dish and bake uncovered in a 375 degree oven for 1 hour and chicken is golden and drumsticks move easily. Cover chicken and let stand for 15 minutes.

**Makes 6 servings**

# Oven-Fried Chicken

1 fryer chicken, cut into 8 pieces
1 cup light mayonnaise
¼ cup cider vinegar
½ tsp pepper
1 tsp onion powder
1 cup crushed corn flakes
½ cup seasoned bread crumbs
1/3 cup parmesan cheese

    Mix together the mayonnaise, vinegar, pepper and onion powder. Remove skin from chicken and place in a storage bag with first 4 ingredients. Refrigerate for 2 hours, turning once.

    In food processor with metal blade grind the corn flakes. Mix corn flakes with bread crumbs and cheese and put into plastic storage bag. Place chicken pieces 2 at a time in bag, seal and shake to coat chicken evenly.

    Cover a baking sheet with foil and preheat oven to 400 degrees. Place chicken on a metal rack on top of covered baking sheet. Bake 40-45 minutes or until chicken is cooked through and brown.

# Savory Corn Pie

1 8-9 inch prepared pie shell
4 eggs
1 cup half-and-half
1 tsp flour
  salt and pepper
2 cups fresh corn kernels or canned corn, drained
½ cup finely chopped onion, sautéed in a little olive oil
8 slices bacon, fried and drained
1 cup shredded cheddar cheese

Combine all ingredients except the cheese and bacon in a bowl and mix well. Process half of mixture in a food processor until smooth. Return mixture to bowl and blend in cheese and bacon. Pour into the pie shell and bake in a 350 oven for 40-50 minutes or until puffy and set.

# Sunday Biscuits

2 cups flour
1 tbsp baking powder
2 tsp sugar
½ tsp cream of tartar
½ tsp salt
½ cup butter, chilled
1 cup buttermilk

    In mixing bowl, mix together flour, baking powder, sugar, tartar, and salt.
    Using a pastry blender or fork, cut in butter into flour mixture till mixture resembles coarse crumbs. Push mixture against sides of bowl, making a well in the center. Pour milk into the well all at once. Using a fork, stir just till the mixture follows fork around bowl and forms soft dough.
    Turn onto a floured surface. Knead gently 12 strokes. Pat dough on floured board to ½ inch thickness. Using a biscuit cutter cut out biscuit rounds and place on baking sheet. Bake in a 400 degree oven for 12-14 minutes or until browned.

*We don't like fancy dinners. We like a family dinner....all of us together.*

# Yankee Pot Roast

1 boneless chuck roast
3 tbsp olive oil
2 cups chopped onion
2 cups chopped fresh
   plum tomatoes or
   1 35- ounce canned
2 cups small red potatoes,
   cubed into 1-inch pieces
½ cup peeled carrots, sliced
½ cup chopped fresh
   Italian parsley
1 tsp oregano
   salt and pepper
2 tbsp flour
2 cups beef broth
¼ cup red wine
¼ cups ketchup
2 tbsp Worcestershire sauce

Heat oil in large pot; season roast with salt, pepper and flour. Add roast to pot and brown on all sides. Remove from pan and sauté onion for a few minutes. Place roast in baking dish. Combine broth, wine, ketchup and Worcestershire, tomatoes, onion and pour over roast. Bake covered in a 300 degree oven for 1 hour. Add carrots, potatoes, parsley and oregano and bake for an additional 1 ½ to 2 hours.

## Chapter 14

# *Soufflé Fluff*

*Rise to the occasion; that's what the pure fluff of a soufflé does for a dinner or dessert presentation. The forthcoming of such a spectacular, elegant dish; with the airy magic that goes in and comes out like a whisper of a breath, could have been named only by the French. But not only can the French culinary genius make a soufflé. If patience is used in the folding and timing in the completion than you will be serving a masterpiece your guests sit up and pay attention to.*

*The first soufflé I made was a lime soufflé for dessert. It was one of the most refreshing desserts I had ever made. After that I tried several savory versions to go with the main course for dinner and received great reviews.*

# Crab and Cheese Soufflé

3 tbsp. butter
3 tbsp. flour
¾ cup milk
¼ cup half and half
¼ tsp. white pepper
½ tsp. salt
½ tsp. Dijon mustard
4 eggs, separated
¾ cup grated Swiss cheese
6 ounces crabmeat, picked over
1/8 tsp. cream of tartar

Grease a 4 cup soufflé dish. Melt butter in medium saucepan over medium heat. Stir in flour; cook until bubbly, stirring constantly. Gradually stir in milk and half and half; cook until thickened, stirring constantly. Stir in pepper, salt and mustard. Remove from heat. Beat in egg yolks, one at a time. Stir in crabmeat. Beat egg whites with cream of tartar in large bowl until stiff peaks form. Stir ¼ of the egg whites into cheese mixture to lighten. Fold in remaining egg whites. Pour mixture into soufflé dish. Bake in a 375 degree oven for 30 minutes or until puffed and lightly browned on top. Serve immediately.

Serves 4-6

# Breakfast Grits Soufflé

1 pound breakfast turkey sausage
2 14 ounce cans chicken broth
1 cup quick cooking grits
1 tbsp. Dijon mustard
1/8 tsp. paprika
Salt and pepper
2 tbsp. chopped fresh parsley
3 ounce package cream cheese
½ cup grated parmesan cheese
4 eggs, separated
½ tsp. cream of tarter

Brown sausage until brown, remove and crumble, remove. Bring broth to a boil and add grits, cover and reduce heat, simmer for 5 minutes. Remove from heat; add sausage, mustard, salt, pepper, cheeses, paprika, and parsley. Mix until cheese melts.

Add grit mixture to egg yolks in large bowl and stir with whisk constantly. Beat egg whites with cream of tarter until stiff peaks form. Gently fold one-fourth of whites into the grits and then the remaining whites, mix carefully.

Carefully pour mixture into prepared soufflé dish. Bake in a 400 degree oven for 10 minutes. Reduce oven to 350 degrees and bake for 55 minutes or until golden and puffed. Remove collar and serve warm.

Serves 6

# Lemon Soufflé

3 envelopes unflavored gelatin
¾ cup water
6 eggs
1 ½ cups sugar
1 ½ tbsp. lemon zest
2 ½ cups heavy cream
¾ cup lemon juice
   Lemon slices, strawberries

   Sprinkle gelatin over water in small saucepan. Let stand until softened, about 1 minute. Place over low heat, stirring until gelatin is melted. Let cool slightly.
   Fold a length of heavy-duty foil long enough to go around a 4-cup soufflé dish, in half lengthwise. Fasten around dish to make a collar 2 inches above rim.
   Beat eggs and sugar with electric mixer on high speed until very thick and light, about 7 minutes. Beat 1 ½ cups of the cream in a bowl until stiff; refrigerate.
   Stir lemon zest and juice into cooled gelatin and pour mixture into egg mixture. Beat at low speed until well blended.
   Chill mixture over ice water until it mounds softly when spooned.
   Fold in whipped cream until no streaks of white remain. Pour into prepared dish. Refrigerate at least 3-4 hours or until set. Remove collar gently; whip remaining cream. Garnish soufflé with cream, lemon slices and strawberry halves.

Serves- 8

   A lime soufflé can be made following the same directions by exchanging lime juice and lime zest for the lemon.

# Raspberry Soufflé

3 envelopes unflavored gelatin
1 ¼  each orange and lemon juice
4  cups raspberries, rinsed
   and drained
6  large eggs whites
1  cup sugar
1 ½ cups whipping cream,
   whipped to soft peaks

In saucepan mix gelatin with orange and lemon juices; let stand until liquid is absorbed. Heat gelatin over medium heat; stirring until melted.  Puree raspberries in a blender or food processor; add gelatin mixture.  Rub puree through a fine strainer into a bowl and discard seeds.  Chill stirring often, just until mixture barely thickens, about 10 to 15 minutes.

With high speed of mixer, whip egg whites until foamy.  Slowly add sugar, beating until soft peaks form.  Fold whites and whipping cream into puree. Form a 3-inch wide foil collar on the rim of a 5 to 6 cup soufflé dish.  Pour mixture in and cover and chill until firm, about 3-4 hours or next day.

Serves 10

# Savory Artichoke-Asparagus Soufflé

1 bunch fresh asparagus
   ends removed
1- 14 ounce can artichoke
   hearts, drained
¼ cup finely chopped onion
¼ cup grated parmesan cheese
¾ cup grated Gruyere or
   Swiss cheese
4 large eggs separated
4 bacon slices,
   cooked and crumbled
1 ½ cups half and half
2 tbsp. flour
   Salt and white pepper
1 tsp. dried oregano
1 ½ tsp. cream of tarter

Steam the asparagus covered until tender. After cooking bacon, reserve one tablespoon of fat. Cook chopped onion and sauté for 2 minutes. Whisk in flour and cook 1 minute. Gradually add half and half, stirring constantly. Bring to a boil over medium heat and cook until thickened. Gradually add hot mixture to egg yolks stirring constantly with a whisk. Mix in crumbled bacon, artichokes, asparagus, cheeses, salt and pepper and oregano.

Beat egg whites and cream of tartar at high speed of mixer until stiff peaks form. Gently fold in small amount of egg white mixture into milk mixture. Gently fold remaining egg white.

Prepare soufflé dish by cutting a piece of foil long enough to fit around a 2- quart dish, allowing a 1-inch overlap. Fold foil into thirds and coat one side of foil and bottom of dish with cooking spray. Wrap foil around dish with coated side against dish. Foil needs to be extended 4 inches above rim to form a collar; secure with string.

Carefully pour mixture into prepared dish. Bake in a 400 degree oven for 10 minutes. Reduce oven to 350 degrees and bake an additional 45 minutes and golden and puffed. Carefully remove collar and serve immediately.

Makes 6 servings

# Spinach Soufflé

1 10-ounce package
 frozen spinach, squeezed dry
2 cups shredded smoked
 Gouda cheese
½ tsp. Dijon mustard
1 cup onion, chopped fine
1 tsp. salt
½ tsp. freshly ground pepper
1 tsp. nutmeg
2 cups milk
½ cup cream
6 tbsp. butter
¼ cup flour
5 eggs, separated,
 room temperature

In a saucepan warm milk and cream; set aside. Sauté onion with butter in a saucepan. Add flour, stir and simmer for 2 minutes. Gradually add warm milk, stirring over medium heat until mixture thickens, about 5 minutes. Whisk in egg yolks. Cool.

Pour mixture into a large bowl and add spinach, 1 ½ cup cheese, salt, pepper and nutmeg.

In mixing bowl beat egg whites in until stiff, but not dry. Fold whites into spinach mixture. Pour into a prepared soufflé dish and sprinkle remaining cheese over soufflé. Bake in a 350 degree oven for 45 minutes or till puffed and set.

Makes 8 servings


# Soufflé Suggestions

Leave the soufflé undisturbed while baking. Don't open the oven door; rather look through the oven window.

The soufflé can be tested when the top is turning brown. Inserting a knife in the center of the soufflé that comes out clean means it's done.

Never over beat the egg whites by whipping too long. Always use cream of tarter when beating the whites on high speed just until they are stiff.

Carefully stir in one-fourth of the egg white mixture into the base mixture.

Make sure the remaining egg whites are gently folded in and stop folding as soon as mixture is blended.

## Chapter 15

# Beloved Veggie Meals

*To me, the rudiments of vegetarian cooking are blending flavors, imagination and passion. Our family ate a vegetarian diet most of the time and what an experience for me to learn the art of it and share with my family - the absence of meat was not missed. The town I live in has a large vegetarian population so I have enjoyed creating tasteful, yummy, veggie dishes that screamed rave reviews. I have a respect and love for real healthy food and following recipes from the vegetable and casserole file as well as this file are all recipes a vegetarian can use. Any of these recipes containing chicken or meat can be omitted and will cook up wonderfully on their own. Vegetarian cooking has been truly a loving experience in my life. Enjoy!*

# Baked Lentils

1 cup lentils
½ cup brown rice
  Garlic powder,
  Salt and pepper
3 cups water
1 cup tomato sauce
1 cup vegetable broth

    Combine broth, tomato sauce, and water along with rice and lentils.
    Sauté sliced carrots, celery, and onion, green peppers in 2 tsp. minced garlic and olive oil. Add to liquid along with potatoes and spices.
    Bake at 350 - cook about 3 hours or until liquid is absorbed.

# Barley Mushroom Pilaf

3 cups fat-free, less sodium chicken broth
1/3 cup dried porcini mushrooms, chopped
1 ½ cups uncooked quick-cooking barley
2 tablespoons olive oil
3 cups quartered shiitake mushrooms caps
2 cups chopped onion
¾ teaspoon salt
½ teaspoon dried rosemary
1 package pre-sliced mushrooms
¼ cup dry Marsala
2 teaspoon sherry vinegar

 Combine the broth and porcinis in a large saucepan. Bring to a boil, and stir in barley. Cover, reduce heat, and simmer 12 minutes or until tender.
 While the barley cooks, heat oil in a Dutch oven over medium-high heat. Add shiitakes, onion, salt, rosemary, and pre sliced mushrooms; sauté 5 minutes. Stir in Marsala, and cook 1 minute. Stir in barley mixture and vinegar; cook 2 minutes or until thoroughly heated, stirring frequently.

Serves 4.

*I am happy to share another recipe from my friend Suzie who eats vegetarian most of the time.*

## Black-Eyed Peas & Avocado

2 cans black-eyed peas,
  drained and rinsed
1 onion, chopped fine
1 tbsp. butter
½ cup rice, cooked
1-2 avocados
½ cup cheddar cheese

Sauté onion in butter and add to peas. Mix in rice, avocados and cheese. May be served warm or as a cold salad.

# Buffet Bean Bake

1 cup brown sugar
½ cup vinegar
½ teaspoon salt
1 tablespoon Dijon mustard
1 can butter beans, drained
1 can onion rings
1 can vegetarian baked bean
1 can lima beans
1 can yellow wax, drained
1 can kidney beans, drained
1 can French cut green beans

Preheat to 350.
Drain all beans. Mix sugar, vinegar, salt and mustard. Simmer uncovered 10 minutes. In large bowl combine drained beans ½ cup of onion rings and hot sugar mixture. Spoon beans mix into 9 by 13 bake dish. Bake uncovered at 350 for 30 minutes or until heated through. Top with remaining onion rings. Bake uncovered for 5 minutes until golden brown.

# Carrot-Mushroom Loaf

1 cup chopped onion
4 ½ cups grated carrots
1-lb. Chopped mushrooms
5 eggs
2 cloves garlic
1 cup fresh, whole wheat breadcrumbs
2 cups grated cheddar cheese
¼ cup butter
½ teaspoon salt
½ teaspoon pepper
½ teaspoon basil
½ teaspoon thyme
½ teaspoon oregano

Crush garlic into melting butter. Add onions and mushrooms and sauté till soft.
Combine all ingredients (saving half the breadcrumbs and cheese for the top). Season to taste. Spread into buttered oblong baking pan. Sprinkle with reaming breadcrumbs and cheese; dot with butter. Bake at 350 for 30 minutes covered, 5 minutes uncovered until browned.

Serves 4-6.

*This is another recipe from my friend Lorraine and again my girls loved it.*

## Cottage Cheese Roast

¼ cup butter
1 large onion
5 well-beaten eggs
4 cups cottage cheese
1 ½ cups walnuts
5 cups Special K cereal
1 teaspoon poultry seasoning
   Salt and pepper

Sauté onion in butter.  Beat eggs and add 1 cup of the nuts (ground) and ½ cup chopped.  Add remaining ingredients, adding the cereal last.

Pour into buttered casserole dish, 9 x 9 pan or 9 x 13 pan.  Smaller pans make large moist roast.  1 ½ recipe fills it.  Bake at 350 for 45 minutes to and hour.

Serves 8-10.

# Cranberry-Walnut Couscous

½ cup dried cranberries
2 ½ cups vegetable broth
1 tablespoon olive oil
½ cup chopped onions (about 1 small onion)
1 tablespoon minced garlic
1 teaspoon kosher salt
¼ teaspoon fresh-ground black pepper
1 ¼ cups couscous
½ cup chopped walnuts, toasted
¼ cup chopped mint

Re-hydrate the cranberries: Bring cranberries and ½ cup vegetable broth to a boil in a small saucepan over medium-high heat. Remove from heat and allow to steep until cranberries are plump—about 10 minutes. Set aside.

Make the couscous: Heat oil in a medium saucepan over medium-high heat. Add the onions and cook until translucent—about 5 minutes. Add garlic and cook until golden—about 2 minutes. Add the remaining broth, salt, pepper, and bring to a boil. Immediately stir in the couscous, cover, and remove from heat. Let the couscous stand 5 minutes. Remove cover and use a fork to separate and fluff the couscous grains. Stir in the walnuts and chopped mint.

*I made this amazing dish for my friends Kurt and Gaylene's wedding. The menu was an International Vegetarian Luncheon.*

# Mushroom Strudel

8 ounces fresh shiitake mushrooms
8 ounces fresh button mushroom
6 green onions, sliced
3 tablespoons butter
3 tablespoons dry white wine
2 tablespoons snipped parsley
¼ teaspoon dried sage, crushed
¼ teaspoon pepper
1/8 teaspoon dried thyme, crushed
1 egg yolk
6 sheets frozen phyllo dough, thawed
¼ cup margarine, melted
2 tablespoons fine dry bread crumbs
  Assorted fresh mushrooms (optional)
  Lemon leaves (optional)

    Remove any woody stems from mushrooms; discard. Coarsely chop mushrooms. You should have about 2 cups of shiitake and 3 cups of button mushrooms.
    In a 10-inch skillet cook mushrooms and onions in the 3 tablespoons or butter for 4 to 5 or till tender. Add wine and cook on high for 2 to 3 minutes or till liquid has evaporated; Remove from heat. Stir in parsley, sage, pepper and thyme. Cool about 10 minutes.
    In a blender container or food processor bowl place half of the mushroom mixture and egg yolk. Cover and blend or process till finely chopped. Combine the chopped mushroom mixture with the remaining mushroom mixture.
    Cut the sheets of phyllo dough in half crosswise. Cover the sheets with a damp towel. Layer six half sheets of the phyllo on a large un-greased baking sheet, brushing some of the ¼ cup melted butter between the sheets. Sprinkle half of the breadcrumbs down the length of one side of phyllo within 3 inches from long edge and 1-½ inches of short edges.
    Spoon half of the mushroom mixture over breadcrumbs. Fold short edges of phyllo toward center; roll jellyroll style from long side nearest filling. Brush roll with melted butter. Cut diagonal slits about 1 inch apart to, but not through, mushroom mixture.
    Repeat with remaining phyllo, butter, breadcrumbs, and mushroom mixture to make a second roll.
    Bake in 400-degree oven, 15 to 18 minutes or till golden. Cool 5 minutes; cut. Using a serrated knife, cut rolls completely through at diagonal slits. Arrange slices on a serving platter lined with lemon leaves. Garnish with additional mushrooms, if desired. Makes 2 strudels.

*My girls grew up on these at every get together, church or school function. I guess they loved them; they ask for more. How many times did this easy, put together snack happen in my home, at least once a month?*

# French Roll Stuffing

2 Boiled eggs, chopped
1 lb. Sharp cheese, grated (Jack)
1 green pepper, chopped
20-30 stuffed olives, chopped
½ cup olive oil
1 small onion, minced

Combine ingredients. Stuff into French rolls. Wrap each roll in foil and freeze or bake immediately. Bake at 400 degrees 20-30 minutes if frozen, less if not.

# Fresh Spring Rolls with Dipping Sauce

Dipping Sauce:
2 cloves garlic, peeled
      1-1Inch piece ginger, unpeeled
      ½ teaspoon Vietnamese chili sauce
      2 tablespoons Vietnamese sauce
      2 tablespoons lime juice
      1 teaspoon sugar

Spring Roll filling:
      1-2Carrots, peeled and cut into 1/4 by 3 inch slices
1 teaspoon sugar
1 package 6-inch (preferable) or 8 ½ inch rice papers
  Fresh mint leaves
6-8 soft lettuce leaves, thick stems removed, torn into large pieces
1 yellow pepper, cut into ¼ by 3 inch slices
1 cucumber, peeled, seeded, and cut into ¼ by 3 inch slices
1 box sprouts, such as radish
  Small bunch of chives (optional)

Mix the dipping sauce ingredients with 1 tablespoon water in a food processor. Set aside in a small bowl. Combine the carrots and sugar. Set aside to soften. Lay the rest of the ingredients in front of you including a tea towel and a Pyrex pie plate filled with hot water. You may have to replenish hot water as it cools. Working with one rice paper at a time, place a sheet into the water for about 10 seconds, carefully turning over once. Drain briefly over plate and lay the paper on the towel. Let it sit till it becomes pliable (about 30 seconds). Assemble spring rolls in the following order: lay a mint leaf on the bottom third of the paper. On the left edge place a piece of lettuce horizontally and top with a few piece of each of carrot, pepper, cucumber, some sprouts, and 2 optional chives so the vegetables hang over the of paper by an inch or so. Place another mint leaf near the top of the paper. Fold the right half of the paper over to cover at least half of the vegetables. Roll the paper up into a cylinder from the bottom. Moisten the edge with a dab of water if it doesn't stick together. Place finished rolls on serving plate; cover with damp towel. Refrigerate until ready to serve. Serve with dipping sauce and lots of napkins. Makes 12 rolls.

*This is just one of Katie's best recipes she has shared with me. I used this recipe for a vegetarian menu and made 400 of them. They were the first thing eaten and gone!*

# Katie's Meat Balls

4 cups grated cheddar (1 lb)
2 cups cracker crumbs (2 tubes)
1 large onion (chop fine)
1 cup walnuts (chop fine)
8 eggs (beat)
1 teaspoon salt

Sauce:
½ can cream of mushroom soup
½ cup water
½ cup sour cream
   Salt and pepper
2cups sliced mushrooms

   Whisk all ingredients together and simmer for 10 minutes on low.

   Mix all together to deep fry in oil. When ready to use, place in a casserole dish; pour sauce over and cover and bake for 40 minutes in a 350-400 oven for 15-20 minutes.
   These are delicious without the sauce and the frying can be replaced with just baking them.

*I don't know why, but these patties were one of my girl's favorite foods when they were young. I would never have thought they would ask me to make it over and again.*

# Mushroom Patties

3 slightly beaten eggs
3 cups coarsely chopped fresh mushrooms (8 ounces)
½ cup all purpose flour
½ cup seasoned fine dry bread crumbs
1/3 cup finely chopped onion
1 T. dried parsley flakes
¼ teaspoon pepper
3 T. cooking oil

In large mixing bowl combine eggs, mushrooms, flour, breadcrumbs, onion, parsley, and pepper; mix well. In a 10-inch skillet heat oil over medium-high heat. Using 1/3-cup mixture for each patty, shape mixture into 3 ½ inch patties; sprinkle a little more bread crumbs on patties. Using spatula, place 4 patties at a time into hot oil in skillet. Cook 3 to 4 minutes per side until done (brown). Remove from skillet; drain on paper towel. Keep warm in oven. Cook and drain remaining patties. Serve with Walnut Sauce found in the Oatmeal-Wheat Germ Patties recipe.

Makes 8 patties.

# Oatmeal-Wheat Germ Patties with Walnut Sauce

1 ½ cups quick cooking oats
1 cup wheat germ
1 pkg. dry yeast-dissolve in ¼ cup warm water
4 teaspoons soy sauce
1 teaspoon salt
¼ teaspoon poultry seasoning
1 teaspoon sage
  Dash garlic salt
1 onion finely chopped
2 eggs
½ cup finely chopped nuts,
  roasted
1 large can evaporated milk
1 cup

  Mix all ingredients and let sand 5 minutes. Make into patties, fry-put into casserole. Bake at 350 for 30-40 minutes. Pour walnut sauce over patties and serve.

Walnut Sauce:
1 cup milk
1 cup cream
3 garlic cloves, minced
½ cup chopped toasted walnuts
1 tbsp. butter
1 tbsp. flour
½ tsp. nutmeg
½ tsp. salt
½ tsp. white pepper

  Sauté walnuts in skillet with a drop of olive oil over medium heat, stirring; about 4-5 minutes. Add garlic and cook 1 minute. Turn heat off and add milk; set aside.
  Melt butter and add flour whisking to make a roux; cooking 2 minutes. On low heat add the milk, cream and seasonings and simmer, stirring for about 5 minutes.

*This strudel is the best I have ever made or tasted. It's truly a brilliant combination of sweetness with onions.*

# Onion and Fig Strudel

½ cup raisins
1 ½ cups dried figs
2/3 cup sugar
½ cup red merlot wine
2 cups finely chopped
   sweet onion
2 tbsp. olive oil
2 tbsp. balsamic vinegar
½ cup crumbled blue cheese
2 tsp. powdered sugar
8 sheets phyllo pastry

Combine first 4 ingredients in a small saucepan. Bring to a boil and cook for 5 minutes. Remove from heat, cover and let stand 40 minutes.
In skillet over medium-high heat, add onion and vinegar; cook 15-20 minutes or until golden, stirring. Remove from heat; stir in fig mixture and cheese. Set aside.
Place 1 phyllo sheet on work surface (cover remaining dough). Brush with butter and continue adding until all 7 are buttered. Spoon onion mixture along 1 long edge of phyllo, leaving a 2-inch border. Fold over the short edges to cover 2 inches of onion mixture on each end.
Starting at long edge with 2-inch border, roll strudel up jelly-roll style. Place strudel on sprayed baking sheet. Slice diagonal slits into top of strudel using a sharp knife. Brush strudel with butter.
Bake in a 350 degree oven for 30 minutes or until brown. Sprinkle powdered sugar over top. Serve warm.
Makes 8 main dish servings.

*This was one of Kellie and Korrie's favorite dishes their best friends mom Lorraine would make for them*

# Yugoslavian Style Peas and Potatoes

Peas

Sauté small amount chopped onion in a tablespoon of oil. (May add a little water and cover so onions cook soft. Sprinkle with about ¾ teaspoon sweet paprika and a tablespoon of flour. Stir so flour is mixed well with oil. Add one package frozen peas and enough water to almost cover peas. Salt slightly. Cook slowly over low heat, stirring occasionally to avoid burning. These reheat well if made ahead. Use more or less flour and water amount to make sauce thin or thicker as desired.

Potatoes

Wash small red potatoes well. Cut in halves and place flat side down in flat baking dish. Drizzle with 2-3 tablespoon of oil, sprinkle fresh chopped parsley or dry dill weed over potatoes, a little salt or seasoning salt, and add a small amount of water to just cover bottom of dish. Cover with foil and bake at 350-400 for ½- 1 hour depending on size of potatoes and temp of oven. Allow potatoes to brown a little if desired on side next to pan but add small amounts water to loosen potatoes.

*Diana and I experienced these veggie burgers in a little vegetarian restaurant one evening. We begged the waiter to get the recipe from the cook who was making the next days soup. Finally by the end of the evening we walked out with the ingredients scribbled on the back of the waiter's ticket. The pinto beans make the burger! Enjoy.*

# Pinto Burgers

Approx.
2 cups whole wheat flour
¼ cup wheat germ
½ teaspoon salt
½ teaspoon pepper
½ teaspoon chili powder
¼ cup finely chopped onions
¼ cup chopped carrots
¼ cup chopped bell peppers
1 teaspoon Soy Sauce
½ cup Brown Rice
1 cup canned, drained smashed pinto beans
2 eggs, beaten well

Mix all ingredients well, chill for one hour. Shape into patties and sprinkle with salt and pepper and a little bread crumbs. Sauté in skillet with a little olive oil on both sides until done, about 4-5 minutes on each side. Serve with a whole wheat bun, lettuce, tomato and a slice of red onion.

# Pumpkin-Stuffed Shells with Jalapeno-Rosemary Sauce

For the Filling:
2 tablespoons dry sherry
2 tablespoons olive oil
3 cloves garlic, minced
2 tablespoons fresh rosemary leaves, minced
1 3-ounce package cream cheese
1 bunch fresh spinach leaves, chopped
1 16 ounce can pumpkin puree
½ teaspoon salt
   Pinch fresh ground black pepper

For the Sauce:
3 tablespoons olive oil
2 cloves garlic, minced
1 tablespoon fresh rosemary leaves, minced
3 tablespoons unbleached white flour
1 ½ cups plain rice or soymilk
1 tablespoon pickled jalapeno peppers, minced

For the shells:
12 ounces dried jumbo pasta shells
½ teaspoon olive oil
6 lemon wedges

    To make filling, heat the sherry, oil, garlic and rosemary over a low flame in a large sauté pan for about 30 seconds.  Add the cream cheese and smash and mix together with garlic mixture. Add the spinach and cover the pan. Cook for about 3 minutes, or until the spinach wilts.  Stir occasionally. Add the pumpkin, salt and pepper, and stir to combine.  Remove from the heat and set aside.
    To make the sauce, heat the oil in a heavy-bottomed skillet over a medium flame.  Add the garlic and rosemary and cook for 1 minute.  Sprinkle in the flour and cook for 1 minute, stirring constantly. Whisk in the milk ½ cup at a time, then bring to a simmer and cook for about 6 minutes, or until slightly thickened. Stir in the jalapenos and set aside.
    Meanwhile, bring several quarts of water to a boil in a large stockpot. Add the pasta shells and cook until al dente, tender but still slightly chewy, about 6 minutes.  Drain the pasta and rinse with cold water.
    Preheat the oven to 350 degrees and use remaining 1/2 teaspoon of olive oil to lightly coat the bottom of an 8 by 12 inch baking dish.  To stuff the shells, hold one at a time in your hand and stuff mounded teaspoon of the pumpkin filling and place in the baking dish.  Pour the sauce over the shells, cover and bake for 20 minutes.

Makes 6 servings.

# Rice, Green Chiles-Cheese Bake

1 cup uncooked rice
3 medium zucchinis, sliced thinly
1 4oz. Can diced green chilies
12 oz jack cheese
1 large tomato, thinly sliced
   Salt

Combine the following:
2 cups sour cream
1 teaspoon oregano
¼ cup chopped green pepper
¼ cup chopped green onion
2 tablespoon chopped parsley

   Cook rice. Cook zucchini until crisp tender set aside.  In 3 qt. Casserole place cook rice; cover with chilies, sprinkle on half of cheese. Arrange zucchini slices on cheese.  Layer tomato slices. Sprinkle on salt.  Spread sour cream mixture on top.  Sprinkle remaining cheese on top. Bake 350 for 35-45 minutes.

# Spaghetti Casserole

4 ounces cooked spaghetti
1 egg
1 cup sour cream
¼ cup Parmesan cheese
   Garlic Powder
2 cups shredded jack cheese
1 pkg. frozen spinach
1 can french onion rings

Pre heat oven to 350.

In bowl combine egg, sour cream, Parmesan cheese, and garlic. Stir in jack cheese, spinach, and ½ can onion rings. Pour into 8-inch square baking dish. Bake covered 350 for 30 minutes or until heated through. Top with onion rings, bake uncovered 5 minutes or until golden brown.

# Spinach-Cheese Dumplings

Dumplings:
1 ½ cups ricotta cheese
1 ¼ cups Italian cheese
1 ¼ cups Italian flavored breadcrumbs
1 cup chopped spinach cooked and drained
½ cup grated Parmesan cheese
¼ cup wheat germ
2 eggs
½ teaspoon baking power
1 clove garlic
¼ teaspoon salt
1 teaspoon basil
¼ teaspoon nutmeg

Combine all ingredients. Roll into 36 balls. Drop into simmering water and poach –7 minutes. When they float to top remove with slotted spoon to baking dish

Sauce:
1 cup tomato sauce
1 cup vegetarian beef broth
½ cup lemon juice
½ cup chopped onion
2 clove garlic crushed
1 teaspoon oregano
¼ teaspoon pepper

Combine all sauce ingredients. Pour over dumplings. Bake at 350 for 30 minutes.

# Stuffed Green Peppers

3 cups cooked pinto and kidney beans-drained
1 cup cooked wheat berries or barley
1 chopped onion
2 cloves garlic
6 tomatoes canned or fresh

Sauté onion, garlic, tomatoes, then add

1 tsp. Sweet basil
1 tsp. Oregano
1 tsp. Salt

Mix with beans and wheat. Add 1 cup shredded jack cheese (I also add cheddar) Fill green peppers with prepared mixture. Bake at 350 for 30 minutes.

Makes 6 servings.

# Two-Grain Salad with Red Lentils and Yellow Pepper

3 ½ - 4 ½ cups low-sodium vegetable broth
½ cup pearl barley, washed, drained
½ cup green, brown or red lentils,
　washed, drained
¾ cup couscous
1-2 tablespoons olive oil
2 tablespoons lemon juice plus additional
　as needed (1-2 lemons)
½ cup cubed yellow pepper
1 cup peeled, chopped cucumber
6 dried apricots, slivered
1 teaspoon capers
2 tablespoons shredded fresh mint
2 tablespoons shredded fresh basil
　Salt and pepper

　Bring 1 ½ cups broth to a boil in a medium-size saucepan. Add barley. Cover and simmer until tender, about 25 minutes. Drain and spread out in a jellyroll pan to cool quickly.
　Bring ½ cup broth to a boil in a saucepan. Add lentils. Cover and simmer for 12-20 minutes, depending on kind of lentil, until tender. Drain and add to pan.
　Bring 1 ½ cups broth to a boil. Add couscous. Cover and remove from heat, let sit for 5 minutes. Fluff with a fork and add to pan.
　Toss the grains and lentils together with 1-2 tablespoons of olive oil and 2 tablespoons of lemon juice. Add the yellow pepper, cucumber, apricots, capers, and herbs. Add more lemon juice if desired. Salt and pepper to taste.
　Serve salad at room temperature or refrigerate and serve cold. If you serve it cold, be sure to taste it again for seasoning, as foods lose flavor when chilled. Add more lemon juice, salt, pepper if necessary. Serves 3-4 (makes 4-5 cups).

# Vegetable Strudel

1 medium carrot, red pepper, and onion
3 garlic cloves, minced
½ pound mushrooms
1 head escarole
1 tbsp. butter
¼ tsp. black pepper
¼ tsp. thyme
Salt
1 15-ounce can red kidney beans
1 cup shredded Jack cheese
6 sheets phyllo pastry
2 tbsp. dried bread crumbs
Paprika

Cut carrots and red pepper into thin strips. Dice onion and mushrooms; coarsely slice escarole.

In a nonstick skillet over medium heat, sauté garlic, carrot, red pepper and onion in butter 3 minutes. Add escarole, black pepper, thyme and salt. Cook 2-3 minutes until tender. Remove to a bowl.

In same skillet over high heat in 1 tablespoon butter cook mushrooms and ¼ teaspoon salt until all juices are absorbed. Remove mushroom to same bowl.

Rinse beans; drain well. Stir beans and cheese into vegetable mixture.

Preheat oven to 375 degrees. Melt butter. On work surface, place 1 sheet of phyllo and brush with butter; sprinkle with 2 teaspoons of bread crumbs. Continue layering phyllo, butter and every other sheet dust with bread crumbs.

Starting at long side of phyllo spoon vegetable mixture to about ½ inch from edges to cover half of phyllo. From vegetable side, roll phyllo jelly-roll fashion.

Place roll seam side down on baking sheet. Brush with butter and sprinkle with paprika. Cut 12 slashes on top of strudel. Bake 25-30 minutes and golden.

Cool in pan 5 minutes. Slice to serve.

Makes 6 main dish servings.

# Vegetarian Bean Burritos

4 flour tortillas (10 inches each)
2 teaspoons vegetable oil
4 medium zucchini, each cut lengthwise
   in half, then sliced crosswise
¼ teaspoon salt
¼ teaspoon ground cinnamon
1 can (15 ounces) Spanish style red kidney beans
1 can (15-19 ounces) black beans, rinsed and drained
½ (8 ounce) package shredded Monterey Jack cheese (1 cup)
½ cup loosely packed fresh cilantro leaves
1 jar (16 ounces) chunky style salsa

Warm tortillas as label directs, keep warm.

In nonstick 12-inch skillet, heat oil over medium-high heat. Add zucchini, salt, and cinnamon and cook until zucchini is tender-crisp, about 5 minutes.

Meanwhile, in 2-quart saucepan, heat kidney beans with their sauce and black beans just to simmering over medium heat; keep warm.

To serve, allow each person to assemble burrito as desired, using a warm flour tortilla, zucchini, bean mixture, cheese, and cilantro leaves. Pass salsa to serve with burritos.

Makes 4 main dish servings.

# Vegetarian Soufflé

1 onion, finely diced
1 to 2 cloves garlic, peeled
　and finely diced
2 to3 sage leaves
1 sprig rosemary, washed, stems discarded,
　needles finely chopped
2 zucchini grated or cut into fine strips
2 tablespoons olive oil
½ cup cream
4 eggs, separated
½ cup Parmesan cheese
　Salt
　Pepper
1 pinch fresh grated nutmeg
　Oil for soufflé dish

　　Preheat oven to 350. Oil a shallow soufflé dish. In a medium skillet, heat the oil over medium heat. Fry onion and garlic until golden and yellow. Add rosemary or thyme, sage and zucchini and cook for 1-2 minutes. Pour in the cream; cook, stirring, until all is reduced by about half. Take off the stove and allow to cool a little.
　　Place a shallow pan (such as a broiler pan, deep enough to hold the soufflé dish) in the oven and fill with enough water to make a water bath coming about 2/3 of the way up to top of soufflé dish. Stir the egg yolks and Parmesan cheese into the zucchini mixture. Season to taste with salt, pepper and nutmeg.
　　Beat egg whites to stiff peaks; carefully fold into zucchini mixture. Spoon mixture into the oiled soufflé dish; set the soufflé dish into the hot water bath in to oven and bake for 30-35 minutes until soufflé's top is golden brown.

# Veggie Meatballs

2 ½ cup cracker crumbs
1 ½ cup groundnuts
1 tsp. salt
1 large onion (finely chopped)
2 tsp. Poultry seasoning
1 ½ cup grated cheese
3 garlic cloves (pressed)
1 tbsp. parsley (more if fresh)
8 eggs

Make walnut size balls. Bake on cookie sheet about 10 minutes or till cheese melts and sets. Ready to use or freeze.

Gravy:

1 can cream of mushroom soup
½ cup water
1 tbsp. kitchen Bouquet
½ cup sour cream
Mix all ingredients and thin
to desired consistency.

Also good with sweet and sour sauce:
½ chili sauce
½ grape jelly

Also wonderful with King Sauce and can be found in the Caterer's Pride Gets it's Due Chapter.

# Chapter 16

# Brunch Celebrations

## Pleased As Punch to Have You for My Brunch

*Brunch is my favorite meal theme to plan for. It makes an ordinary Sunday breakfast seem special and the special, extraordinary. Enjoy!*

# Apple Cobbler French Toast

1 French bread baguette
4 eggs
1 cup half and half
½ tsp baking powder
1 ½ tsp vanilla extract
5 apples, peeled, cored and sliced
¾ cup brown sugar
1 tsp cinnamon
½ tsp nutmeg
2 tbsp melted butter

Slice baguettes into 1-inch slices. In a bowl whisk together the eggs, half and half, baking powder, and vanilla. Pour over the bread, turning to coat. Cover and let stand until all of the liquid has been absorbed.

Grease a 9x13-inch baking dish. Place the sliced apples in the bottom of dish. Sprinkle brown sugar, cinnamon and nutmeg over the apples. Arrange the soaked bread over the top. Brush with melted butter. Bake in a 450 degree oven for 25 minutes.

Serves 8

*This is a unique recipe my friend Terry gave me and it's from her good friend Bam who she met on a recipe chat room on the internet. Bam is another woman with cookery passion. The recipe comes from a Bed and Breakfast Inn in Arkansas. A breakfast dish that makes a statement!*

# Apple Pecan Baked Pancake

1 ½ cup pancake batter (not bisquick)
2 tbsp. butter, melted
1 cup Granny Smith apples,
   peeled and sliced
1/3 cup pecans, chopped
3 tbsp. maple syrup
½ tsp. cinnamon

Heat oven to 350 degrees. Prepare pancake mix according to package directions, set aside.

Pour melted butter in a 9-inch pie plate. Place apple slices in bottom of pie plate, sprinkle cinnamon and pecans over apples. Drizzle maple syrup over top.

Carefully spoon pancake batter over top. 30-35 minutes or until top springs back when touched. Loosen edges and invert onto serving plate. Cut in wedges and serve with warm maple syrup and fresh apple butter.

# Apple Strudel

½ cup golden raisins
3 tbsp amaretto liqueur
3 cups peeled, chopped, apples
1 ½ cups sugar
½ cup butter
1 cup fine, plain breadcrumbs
1 tbsp flour
1 tsp cinnamon
2 tsp lemon zest
3 tbsp fresh lemon juice
8 sheets phyllo dough, thawed
melted butter

    Mix raisins and amaretto in saucepan over low heat for about 10 minutes, set aside. In skillet melt butter and add breadcrumbs and sauté until browned. In a large bowl combine apples, sugar, lemon zest and juice, raisins, flour and bread crumbs. Toss well and set aside.

    Place one sheet of dough on work surface (cover remaining dough). Brush dough with melted butter using pastry brush. Continue until last sheet is in place. Spoon apple mixture along edge of dough leaving a 2 inch border on each side. Fold over the edges of dough to cover filling on each end. Roll in a jelly-roll fashion. Cut several diagonal slits into top of strudel. Place on a greased cookie sheet and bake in a 350-375 degree oven for 30 minutes. If top seems to get to dark, turn oven down to 350 degrees.

# Applesauce Date Nut Bread

1 cup chopped walnuts
1 cup chopped pitted dates
1 ½ tsp baking soda
½ tsp salt
3 tbsp butter
1 cup hot applesauce
3 eggs
1 tsp vanilla
1 cup sugar
1 ¾ cup flour

Mix walnuts, dates, soda and salt with a fork. Add butter and applesauce. Let stand for 25 minutes. Beat eggs; add sugar, vanilla and flour. Add walnut mixture and mix just until blended. Pour into a 9x5 loaf pan and bake in a 350 degree oven for 60 minutes or until center is firm. Cool in pan before removing to wire rack. Cool completely and wrap in plastic wrap. Best when made day before slicing.

# Artichoke Bake

5- 6 ounce jars marinated
   artichoke hearts
1 pound ricotta cheese
5 eggs
½ cup sour cream
½ cup chopped green onions
1 cup sliced fresh mushrooms
1 ½ cup shredded Swiss cheese
½ cup chopped fresh basil
½ tsp dry mustard
   salt and pepper
1 stick butter, melted
10 sheets phyllo dough

Drain artichokes and chop into small pieces. In mixing bowl beat eggs until fluffy and add ricotta, sour cream, green onions, mushrooms, cheeses, spices and artichokes.

Butter a 9x13-inch baking dish. Unroll phyllo and keep covered with heavy towel. Use 5 phyllo sheets and cover the remaining dough. Brush each sheet with butter and place each in the baking dish, one at a time. Pour artichoke filling and spread evenly. Butter remaining filo sheets one at a time, laying them on top of the other. Fold the pile in half and place on top of filling and then fold extended edges over to top. Brush top with melted butter. Bake at a 400 degrees for 25-35 minutes or until dough is golden. Let set 10 minutes before cutting into squares.

Makes 8 main dish servings

# Baked Pecan French Toast

½ cup melted butter
1/3 cup real maple syrup
1 cup chopped pecans,
   toasted
6-8 1 inch-thick slices
   French bread
4 eggs, beaten
1 ½ cup milk or cream
1 tsp nutmeg
1 tsp cinnamon

   In a bowl mix the melted butter and maple syrup and pour into a 9x13 baking dish. Sprinkle ½ cup of the chopped pecans over the butter mixture. Arrange bread slices in a single layer on top of the nuts.
   Whip eggs well add milk and spices. Pour egg mixture over bread in baking dish. Sprinkle the remaining ½ cup pecans over bread. Cover and refrigerate the dish for 24 hours.
   Remove cover and bake in a 350 degree oven for 35 minutes and is lightly browned. Let the toast stand about 10 minutes before serving. Serve with slice bananas and blueberries and real maple syrup.

Serves 8-10

# Blueberry-Lemon Muffins

2 1/3 cups flour
½ cup sugar
1 ½ tbsp baking powder
1 tsp salt
2 eggs, beaten
¾ cup sour cream
½ cup unsalted butter, melted
1/3 cup milk
4 tbsp lemon juice
2 tbsp lemon zest
1 ½ cups fresh blueberries, washed and drained
2 tbsp flour
4 tbsp sugar

Mix dry ingredients and set aside. Whisk eggs, sour cream, butter, milk, lemon juice and zest. Carefully stir egg mixture into flour just until combined. In another bowl combine 2 tablespoons flour and berries and fold into batter.

Spoon into greased muffin cups, sprinkling tops with sugar. Bake in a 350-400 degree oven for 30 minutes and tops are golden. Cool on wire rack.

# Breakfast Strata

1 ½ pounds turkey sausage
or breakfast sausage, cooked,
drained and crumbled
5 eggs
2 egg whites
4 cups milk
½ cup green onion,
chopped fine
1 tsp dried sage
1 tsp dried oregano
½ tsp dried thyme
1 tsp dried parsley
salt and pepper
1- 8 ounce package cream cheese,
softened and cut up
1 cup shredded Parmesan cheese
½ cup cottage cheese
½ cup shredded Parmesan cheese
½ cup green onion,
chopped fine
6-8 slices white bread,
crusts removed

Butter a 13x9- inch-baking dish. Arrange bread slices to fit in baking dish. Sprinkle sausage over bread. Set aside.

In mixer bowl beat eggs, egg whites and milk. Add herbs, salt and pepper, cream cheese, green onion and ½ cup Parmesan cheese mixing until cream cheese is in form of small balls. Puree cottage cheese in food processor and add to egg mixture. Pour egg mixture over bread and sausage. Push bread down with spatula to keep it immersed. Sprinkle remaining Parmesan cheese on top followed by green onion. Cover and refrigerate overnight.

Place on a cookie sheet and bake in a 350-degree oven uncovered for 1 hour and 15 minutes or until set in center.

Makes 12 servings

*A little like hot apple pie with a little melted cheese!*

# Buttermilk Apple Cheese Muffins

1 stick butter, room temperature
¾ cup sugar
2 eggs
¼ cup butter milk
¼ cup apple juice
2 cups flour
1 tsp baking soda
1 tsp baking powder
½ tsp salt
1 tsp cinnamon
½ tsp nutmeg
1 green apple, peeled cored and chopped
½ cup chopped pecans
1 cup brown sugar
2 ½ cups shredded cheddar cheese

In a mixing bowl cream butter and sugar until fluffy. Add eggs and mix well. Mix in apple juice and buttermilk.

Combine all dry ingredients and add to egg mixture, do not over mix. Stir in apples and pecans and 1 cup cheese. Spoon batter into greased muffin cups. Sprinkle with brown sugar and then remaining cheese. Bake in a 375-degree oven for 20-25 minutes or until knife inserted in center comes out clean. Serve warm with butter.

Makes 20 muffins

# Buttermilk Waffles

3 cups buttermilk
1 cup flour
½ cup yellow cornmeal
1 cup rolled oats
2 tbsp baking powder
½ tsp salt
2 eggs
½ tsp oil

    Put all dry ingredients in a large bowl.  Add eggs and mix well.  Add oil and buttermilk.  Let stand for 15-30 minutes or until it doubles in size.
    Pour about 1 cup of batter into waffle iron.  Serve with syrup or jam.

# Cheddar Apple Breakfast Bake

2  9-ounce packages frozen
    French toast
8  ounces sliced thin deli ham
2 ½ cups shredded cheddar cheese
1  20 ounce can apple pie filling
1  cup sour cream
½ cup brown sugar

    Grease a 9x13-inch baking dish.  Prepare French toast and place 6 slices in the bottom of baking dish.  Top with layers of ham, 2 cups of cheese and remaining French toast.  Spread the pie filling over the toast and top with ½ cup cheese and bake in a 350 oven for 25 minutes.  Mix sour cream and brown sugar and refrigerate.  Let bake set for about 2-3 minutes to set and serve with sour cream mixture.

Serves 8

# Cherry-Almond Scones

2 cups flour
½ cup sugar
1 tsp baking powder
¼ tsp baking soda
½ tsp salt
1 stick unsalted butter
½ cup dried cherries
½ cup sour cream
½ cup almond extract
1 egg

In a bowl mix flour, sugar, salt, baking powder and soda. Mix in butter until it resembles coarse crumbs. Mix in cherries.

Mix sour cream, almond extract and egg together and using a fork add to flour mixture until large clumps form. Press into a ball. Place on a lightly floured surface and pat into an 8-inch circle. Sprinkle with 1 tsp sugar. With sharp knife cut dough into 8 triangles and place on a cookie sheet. Bake in a 375-400 degree oven for about 15-17 minutes or golden. Cool for 5 minutes.

## Amaretto Butter:

1 stick unsalted butter,
   room temperature
1 tbsp honey
2 ½ tbsp honey
½ tsp almond extract

    Mix butter and honey until smooth. Add amaretto and almond extract and blend well.

Makes ¾ cup butter.

# Chocolate Coffee Ring

½ cup butter, softened
1 ½ cup sugar
2 eggs
2 cups sour cream
1 tsp vanilla
2 cups flour
1 tsp baking powder
1 tsp baking soda
¼ tsp salt
1 cup chocolate chips
Topping:
½ cup flour
½ cup brown sugar
2 tbsp baking cocoa
¼ cup cold butter
½ cup chopped pecans
½ cup semisweet chocolate chips

Cream butter and sugar until fluffy; beat in eggs, add sour cream and vanilla; mix just to combine. Set aside. Combine flour, baking powder, baking soda and salt; add to creamed mixture. Stir in chocolate chips. Pour into a greased 8-cup bunt pan. For topping, combine flour, sugar and cocoa; cut in butter until mixture resembles coarse crumbs. Stir in pecans and chocolate chips. Sprinkle over batter. Bake in a 350 degree oven for 55-60 minutes or until cake is set in center. Cool in pan 15-20 minutes and remove to wire rack to cool completely.

Serves 8-10

# Chocolate Croissant Bread Pudding

6 baked croissants
½ cup sugar
3 eggs
½ cup melted butter
½ cup cream
½ cup milk
½ tsp nutmeg
1 tsp cinnamon
¼ cup orange marmalade
1 tsp orange liqueur
small bag chocolate chips

Tear croissants into cubes and place in a greased 9x13 baking dish and mix in chocolate chips.
Beat eggs until fluffy and add cream, milk, butter, spices, marmalade and liqueur. Pour egg mixture over croissants, refrigerate for 2 hours. Bring to room temperature. Bake in a 350-degree oven for 45-55 minutes and fluffy on top.

Serves 8

*Any decent Southerner would never use anything but real stone grits. Try and tell a tempestuous Southern personality anything different and you'll get a stare of ill-conceived contempt!*

# Creamed Grits

2 cups whipping cream
2 cloves garlic, minced
2 tbsp unsalted butter
1 ½ cups chicken broth
¾ cup hominy grits
½ cup cream cheese
¼ cup grated Parmigiano Reggiano cheese
Salt and pepper to taste

Melt butter in heavy saucepan over medium heat; add garlic and cook 2 minutes. Stir in the cream and broth. Bring to a boil and reduce heat. Stir in grits and cook; stirring constantly over low heat until creamy, about 10 minutes. Add cream cheese and Parmigiano; continue cooking for 4 minutes. Season with salt and pepper.

Serves 6

# Crepes

3 eggs
1 tsp salt
2 cups milk
2 cups flour
¼ cup melted butter

Beat eggs and salt in a mixer until fluffy. Alternate milk and flour and mix well. Add butter and mix. Pour into a large measuring cup, cover and refrigerate for at least two hours.

To make crepes, use a non stick skillet or crepe pan. Hold pan in one hand while pouring crepe batter enough to swirl over bottom of pan. Heat over medium flame for about 2 minutes or less and then turn to other side. Cool on wax paper. Stuff crepes with chicken, vegetables and cheese.

Makes about 22 crepes

# Fillings:

Apple Mint Crepes
1 ½ cups ricotta cheese
2 cups chopped apples
2 tsp chopped fresh mint
¼ tsp cinnamon
2 cups grated jack cheese

Mix all ingredients except jack cheese. Spread about a tablespoon or so of filling in each crepe and end with the jack cheese. Roll up and lay in a lightly greased casserole dish. Bake for 15 minutes in a 325 degree oven.

# Artichoke Asparagus Crepes

2 bunches fresh thin asparagus
2 jars marinated artichokes,
   drained and chopped
1 ½ cups sliced mushrooms
2 containers of spreadable cheese
   Olive oil
   Salt

Wash and dry asparagus, cut ends off leaving only short pieces of asparagus tips. Pour a little olive oil and salt over asparagus in a small container - cover and microwave for 2 minutes. Spread cheese on each crepe and follow with vegetables. Roll up and place in bottom of lightly greased casserole dish. Bake 15 minutes in a 325-degree oven.

# Crumb Coffee Cake Superb

2 cups flour
1 cup sugar
½ tsp ginger
½ tsp cinnamon
¼ tsp nutmeg
½ cup butter
½ cup chopped dates
½ cup chopped nuts
1 egg, beaten
¾ cup buttermilk
1 tsp baking powder
½ tsp baking soda

Combine flour, sugar and spices in bowl. Cut in butter until mixture is crumbly like cornmeal. Take out 1 cup of crumbly mixture and set aside. Stir dates and nuts into remaining crumbly mixture. Mix together the egg, milk, baking powder and soda; stir into the flour mixture containing dates and nuts, just until mixed. Spread half of the reserved crumbs in the bottom of a greased 8x8 baking dish. Pour in the batter, spread evenly and top with remaining crumbs over the top. Bake in a 375 degree oven for 40 minutes. Cool in pan.

Makes 8 servings

# Fruit Cobbler Supreme

½ cup flour
½ cup sugar
½ cup milk
1 tsp baking powder
½ cube butter
2 cups fresh fruit, sliced peaches

    Put butter in a baking dish and bake in a 350-degree oven until melted. Mix the flour, sugar, milk and baking powder and add to melted butter in dish, but do not stir. Add the fruit in the center of pan and do not stir. Bake for 45 minutes. Enjoy!

# Grandma Stella's Banana Nut Sweet Bread

2 ¼ cups flour
1 tsp baking soda
1 tsp baking powder
½ tsp salt
2 eggs
1 cup sugar
1 cup butter softened
3 bananas
1 cup chopped walnuts
½ cup ground chocolate chips

    Sift flour, salt soda, baking powder and baking soda slowly, set aside.
    In mixer add eggs and beat until fluffy, add butter and sugar and mix until creamy. Put bananas in food processor until mashed and creamy. Add to egg mixture.
    Slowly add flour to wet mixture, mixing until combined. Add nuts and chocolate chips. Pour into loaf pan and bake at 350 for 45-55 minutes.

# Glazed Smoked Ham

1 5-8 pound smoked ham, shank end
1 large onion, sliced in chunks
1 tsp dried thyme salt and pepper
2 cups orange juice
1 cup brown sugar
½ cup canned whole cranberry sauce
2 tbsp currant jelly
2 tbsp cooking sherry
½ tsp ground allspice pinch of ground cloves
1-2 tbsp corn starch
¼ cup water

Place onion on bottom of baking pan. Mix thyme, salt and pepper and then rum over ham and place in baking pan. Bake covered for 1 hour at 350 degrees.

Mix together in sauce pan remaining ingredients except cornstarch and water. Heat glaze mixture for about 10 minutes stirring. Mix water and cornstarch until lumps are gone and add to glaze mixture until thickened.

Uncover foil from ham and brush with glaze mixture every 15 minutes for another 45 minutes.

# Hash Brown Quiche

Grease 9-inch pie pan and press 1 24 oz package shredded hash brown potatoes (thawed) into pan. Brush with 1/3 cup melted butter and bake at 425 degrees for 25 minutes. Reduce temperature to 350 degrees.

Fill crust with 1 cup shredded Cheddar and Monterey jack cheese and 1 cup diced cooked ham. Whisk 2 large eggs, ½ cup milk and ¼ tsp salt and pepper together and pour on top. Bake 30-40 minutes.

# Lemon Curd Mascarpone Tart

1 sheet frozen puff pastry
8 ounces mascarpone cheese
1 10 oz jar lemon curd, at room temperature
2 tbsp honey
2 tbsp lemon zest
½ cup sour cream
2 cups fresh fruit
 sugar

    Roll out one puff pastry sheet on a lightly floured surface into about an 8 inch square. Place in a baking dish and bake for 10-15 minutes or until golden. Remove from oven and let cool on a wire rack.
    Mix remaining ingredients and spread in cooled pastry. Top with blueberries, mixed berries or mixed fresh fruit. Sprinkle top of fruit with a bit of sugar. Refrigerate until ready to serve.

*My dear friend Terry served me these scones with fruit and homemade jam while visiting her. Absolutely superb scones, served with lemon curd.*

# Orange Oatmeal Scones

1 cup flour
3 tbsp. baking powder
1 tsp. orange zest
1/3 cup chilled butter
1 cup quick cooking oats
2 slightly beaten egg whites
2 tbsp. orange juice
  Nonstick cooking spray
  Milk and sugar for top

Stir together flour, sugar, baking powder and orange peel. Cut in butter till mixture resembles coarse crumbs. Stir in oats. Combine egg whites and orange juice and stir into oat mixture. Mixture will be sticky.

On floured surface, roll or pat dough into a 7-inch circle. With floured knife cut circle into 12 or 6 wedges.

Spray baking sheet with nonstick spray. Place wedges on baking sheet. Brush tops with milk and sprinkle sugar on top. Bake at 400 degrees for 20 minutes if making 6 wedges and 12-15 minutes for 12 wedges, or until golden brown.

Serve with orange or lemon curd or jam of choice.

# Pear Butter

8 medium pears, cored and chopped
1/3 cup water
½ cup sugar
1 cinnamon stick
2 tbsp grated fresh gingerroot
½ tsp nutmeg
½ cup dried cranberries

In saucepan combine pears, water, sugar, cinnamon stick, gingerroot and nutmeg. Cook, covered over medium heat for 25 minutes, stirring occasionally. Add cranberries and cook, uncovered 25-30 minutes until mixture is thick and chunky. Cool to room temperature; remove and discard the cinnamon stick. Transfer pear mixture to container, cover and refrigerate until ready to use. Perfect for scones, muffins and pancakes.

# Sandra's Quiche

pie shell
5 eggs beaten
8 oz container whipping cream or half and half or milk
1 tbsp nutmeg
2 cups shredded cheddar cheese
½ cup shredded Parmesan cheese
½ cup vegetables of choice, such as sliced mushrooms, broccoli, zucchini, red pepper, artichokes, spinach
½ tsp garlic

 Sauté vegetables in a little olive oil and garlic for about 3 minutes. Pour into prepared pie shell and add cheeses and lightly mix. Beat eggs in mixer or blender and add cream or milk, and nutmeg. Bake in a 350-degree oven for about an hour or until top is golden and puffs up. Let cool for about 10 minutes before slicing.
 Anything can be added to a quiche, which makes it like a meal. I add turkey ham, turkey, bacon and whatever is on hand or keep it vegetarian.

Serves 8

*I remember watching my mother and grandmother make this dish. I would stand and watch them put together the layers and out of memory made it when I was 17. It tasted just like my mother's potatoes sitting on her table. I was fortunate to learn the craft of making a real potato dish that a box version can never replace the real thing! This is our favorite side dish at Easter and for brunches.*

## Scalloped Potatoes

4-5 russet potatoes, peeled and sliced thin
3 cups shredded cheddar cheese
1 small onion chopped fine
butter and milk
flour, salt and pepper

Pour some milk in a casserole dish and layer potatoes over milk. Dust potatoes with flour, salt and pepper, dots of butter, some of the onion and cheese. Repeat again and pour milk slowly over top and sides, making sure there is enough milk to cook potatoes. Add a little more flour in the corners of dish. Cover with foil and bake in a 350 oven for 50-60 minutes or until potatoes are tender. Let set for 20 minutes covered to thicken before serving.

I use a food processor to slice the potatoes very thin. They can be put in the microwave before assembling the dish to speed up cooking.

# Seafood Brunch

2 tbsp butter
3 cups sliced leeks,
  white ends only
12 slices white bread
1 pounds cooked small shrimp
4 cups shredded Swiss cheese
3 tbsp chopped fresh dill
1 tsp dried oregano
5 eggs
2 cups milk
1 cup heavy cream
  salt and pepper to taste

Butter a 9x13-inch casserole dish. Melt butter in skillet and sauté leeks until they are tender. Remove crusts from bread and arrange half in the casserole dish. Top with half of the leeks, shrimp, cheese and dill. Repeat the layers. In a bowl beat the eggs, milk, salt and pepper and oregano. Pour the eggs over the casserole, cover and refrigerate overnight.

Bake in a 350 degrees oven for 50-60 minutes.

Serves 8

# Strawberry Mandarin Mousse

2 cups fresh strawberries, hulled and sliced
1 can mandarin oranges, drained
1 tsp orange zest
1 ½ envelopes unflavored gelatin
½ cup sugar
1 ½ cups heavy cream, whipped

Process oranges and strawberries in food processor until smooth. In a sauce pan sprinkle gelatin over liqueur and let stand until gelatin is softened. Add fruit mixture and sugar and combine with gelatin. Cook on medium heat until sugar has dissolved. Remove from heat and set aside, cooling completely. Fold whipped cream into fruit mixture. Spoon into a 6 cup mold and refrigerate over night. Place on decorative plate and serve with fig sauce around the mousse.

Serves 6-8

# Fig Sauce:

1 ½ cups chopped,
    dried figs
1 cup sugar
¼ cup sherry
1 tsp honey

Place all ingredients in a saucepan and simmer until fruit has softened and thickened. Set aside to cool. Serve at room temperature.

# Stuffed French Toast

1 cup brown sugar
¾ cup butter
3 tbsp corn syrup
8 eggs
1 ½ cups milk
2 tsp vanilla
1 tsp cinnamon
2-8oz. whipped cream cheese, softened
2 tbsp brown sugar
1 loaf French bread, sliced into ¾ inch pieces

Begin melting butter in saucepan, adding corn syrup and then the brown sugar. Cook on medium heat until all ingredients are well blended and begins to bubble. Do not boil.

Pour mixture into a greased 9x13 casserole dish. Place one layer of bread on the caramel sauce without overlapping. Spread the softened cream cheese on bread and sprinkle 2 tbsp of the brown sugar over cream cheese. Top the first layer of bread with a second layer, directly on top of bottom piece.

Beat eggs well adding milk, vanilla and cinnamon. Pour over bread making sure to coat all bread pieces. Cover and refrigerate over night. Bake in a 350 degree oven for 40 minutes. Serve warm with caramel side on top. Serve with whipped cream and fresh fruit.

# Marmalade Stuffed French Toast

8 slices sourdough bread
½ cup whipped cream cheese
6 tsp orange marmalade
4 eggs
¼ cup milk
1 tsp vanilla
2 tsp cinnamon

    Make a sandwich spread with the cream cheese and marmalade. Spread over 4 slices of bread and top with remaining 4 bread slices. Beat eggs and add milk, vanilla and cinnamon.
    Dip sandwiches in egg mixture and heat on buttered skillet or griddle until lightly browned on both sides. Sprinkle with powdered sugar and warm syrup.
    Syrup: boil together 2 cups brown sugar, 1 cup orange juice and 1 tbsp butter.

*This is my girls all time favorite bread recipe. I have served this wonderful sweet bread for many catering jobs, gift baskets and brunches. With a slice in one hand and munching on a bite of this amazing bread I am asked...what is this? I have to say, I probably would not have ever tried this except that once again my best bud Diana made me taste, experience and bake it. The recipe did not include the chocolate chips, but she added them and I don't think it would be as good without them. Enjoy!*

# Zucchini Sesame Chocolate Bread

3 eggs
1 cup salad oil
1 cup sugar
1 cup firmly packed
   brown sugar
3 tsp maple flavoring
2 cups shredded unpeeled
   zucchini
2 ½ cups flour
½ cup toasted wheat germ
2 tsp soda
2 tsp salt
½ tsp baking powder
1 cup chopped nuts
1 ½ cups mini chocolate
   chips, ground
½ cup sesame seeds

Beat eggs until frothy and add oil, sugars and maple flavoring beating until mixture is foamy. Stir in zucchini.

In separate bowl combine flour, wheat germ, soda, salt, baking powder. Mix until dry ingredients are well blended. Stir gently into zucchini mixture just to blend. Mix in walnuts and chocolate chips. Pour batter into 2 greased 9x5-inch loaf pans. Sprinkle sesame seeds evenly over top of each loaf. Bake in a 350 degree oven for 1 hour or until a skewer comes out clean from center of loaf. Let cool in pans for 10 minutes and cool on a rack.

Makes 2 loaves

## Chapter 17

# *Breads We Love*

*All of the bread and muffin recipes in this chapter were made for our traditional Friday night soup and bread meals. There is something wholesome, natural, warm and welcoming about bread. It was a treat to try new recipes and then add them to my collection. The pleasures of watching my family at our dinner table scoop up a new or favorite slice of bread and dip it in their soup, while sharing their day, was indulging my heart in that wholesome sentiment. Homemade bread made at home is something of the past that feels like a warm hug on a cold day.*

# Bubbling Cheese Bread

½ cup shredded mozzarella cheese
½ cup shredded cheddarcheese
1/3 cup mayonnaise
1/8 tsp onion powder
1/3 cup grated Parmesan cheese
1 loaf French bread, halved lengthwise

    Combine first four ingredients and spread mixture on bread halves. Sprinkle with Parmesan cheese. Place on rack in broiler pan; broil 4 inches from heat for 3 minutes or until bubbly and lightly browned. Cut into 1-inch slices. Makes 28 slices.

# Cheddar and Date Nut Quick Bread

½ cup chopped dried dates
1 cup hot strong tea
2 cups self-rising flour
1 tbsp sugar
1 tbsp baking soda
½ tsp salt
¼ cup butter
½ cup shredded cheddar cheese
¾ cup chopped walnuts
1 egg, beaten

Soak dates in hot tea for 1 hour. Sift flour, salt, sugar and baking soda into a large bowl. With a pastry blender, cut in butter until mixture resembles coarse meal. Add cheese and walnuts and mix. Set aside.

Drain dates, reserving tea. Mix dates with flour mixture.

In small bowl whisk together reserved tea and egg. Add to flour mixture, stirring quickly just until blended. Spread batter into a prepared 9x5x3 loaf pan. Bake at 325 for 45-60 minutes.

# Creamy Corn Spoon Bread
- Shirley Rea 1988

1 can whole kernel corn, drained
1 can creamed corn
¾ cup melted butter
1 cup sour cream
2 eggs beaten
1-8 ½ once box Jiffy Corn Muffin Mix
¼ cup grated cheddar cheese

    Stir corn and melted butter, fold in sour cream and eggs and corn bread mix and blend. Place in a casserole dish or a loaf pan and bake at 375 degrees for 1 hour.

*This bread is one of my girl's favorite reminders of family dinners. I made this for many of our Friday night soup and bread meals. The crust is hearty and the round shape adds character. If there is any leftover the next morning; toasted for breakfast is a hit too.*

# Dill Bread

1 pkg. active dry yeast
¼ cup warm water
1 tbs. sugar
1 cup cream-style cottage cheese
1 tbsp. sugar
1 tbsp. minced onion
1 tbsp. minced dry onion
1 tbsp. butter
2 tbsp. dried dill weed
1 tsp. salt
¼ tsp. baking soda
1 slightly beaten egg
2 ¼ to 2 ½ cups flour
½ tsp. dried dillseed

In small bowl combine the yeast, warm water and the 1 tablespoon sugar. Set aside.

In a saucepan combine cottage cheese, sugar, dried onion, fresh onion, butter, dill weed, salt, and baking soda. Heat and stir just till mixture is warm. Remove from heat.

In large bowl combine the dissolved yeast mixture, cottage cheese mixture and egg. Stir in the flour a little at a time.

Turn dough onto a floured surface. Knead for 3-5 minutes to make a soft dough. Shape into a ball. Turn dough in a greased bowl to cover the ball.

Cover and let dough rise in a warm place for about 50 minutes or till double in size. Punch down and place in a round buttered casserole dish. Cover and let rise in warm place till nearly double in size, about 30 minutes.

Brush dough with 1 teaspoon of melted butter and sprinkle with the dill seed. Bake bread in a 350 degree oven for 40-45 minutes or till golden brown. Cool on wire rack.

Makes 16 servings.

# Greek Biscuits

½ cup butter
1 cup feta cheese, crumbled
½ cup pitted and chopped Kalamata olives
2 tbsp black olives, chopped
1 tbsp finely chopped onion
¼ cup sun dried tomatoes,
    drained and chopped
¾ cup cream
2 ¼ cups flour
1 tbsp baking powder
1 tbsp sugar
1 tsp oregano, basil and thyme, crushed
2 tbsp dried onion
½ tsp salt
1 egg, beaten

    Stir together flour, baking powder, sugar, herbs and dried onion. Using a pastry blender, cut in butter until mixture resembles crumbs. Mix in feta, onion, olives and tomatoes. Make well in center of dry ingredients. Add cream and stir just to moisten.

    Turn dough on floured surface. Knead dough 10 to 12 strokes. Carefully roll out dough into a ½ inch thickness. Cut dough into 1 ½ -2 inch squares. Place on ungreased baking sheet and brush with beaten egg. Bake in a 400 degree oven for 10-12 minutes or golden on top.

# Oatmeal and Nut Bread

2 packages active dry yeast
½ cup very warm water,
(100 to 115 degrees)
1 tbsp honey
1 cup oatmeal
1 cup water
¼ cup honey
2 tbsp butter
1 tsp salt
2 tbsp brown sugar
3 ½ - 4 cups flour
½ cup chopped toasted pecans
or walnuts
¼ cup roasted sunflower seeds
2 egg whites beaten
with 2 tbsp water

    Dissolve yeast in warm water. Add the one-tablespoon of honey and let stand 10 minutes.
    Combine the oatmeal and water in a saucepan and bring to a boil and cook for 3 minutes. Stir in the honey, butter and salt. Remove from heat. Add the yeast to oatmeal mixture.
    Mix flour, brown sugar, walnuts, and sunflower seeds. Fold into yeast-oatmeal mixture and add the egg white. Turn out on floured surface and knead for 3-6 minutes. Place in round deep casserole dish or large loaf pan. Let rise for 45-60 minutes. Punch down and reshape, cover and let rise again for 25-30 minutes. Bake at 350 for 45 minutes. Makes one large loaf.

# Southern Cornmeal Smoked Cheddar Muffins

1 cup flour
1 cup cornmeal
¼ cup sugar
1 tbsp baking powder
½ tsp salt pinch of cayenne pepper
2 eggs beaten
1 cup buttermilk
¼ cup butter, melted
1 ¼ cup shredded smoked cheddar cheese sesame seeds additional cheese

Combine flour, cornmeal, sugar, baking powder, salt, and cayenne pepper. Beat eggs in separate bowl and add milk and butter and then add to flour mixture. Add cheese and stir until batter is smooth.

Spoon batter into greased muffin cups. Top with additional cheese and sesame seeds. Bake in a 425 degrees for 12 to 15 minutes or until golden brown. Let cool in pan for 5 minutes. Serve warm.

Makes 12 muffins

# Squaw Bread

2 cups water
1/3 cup oil
¼ cup honey
¼ cup raisins
5 tbsp brown sugar
2 packages active dry yeast
¼ cup warm water
2 ½ cups flour
3 cups whole wheat flour
1 ½ cups rye flour
½ cup dry nonfat milk
2 ½ tsp salt melted butter

   Combine in blender container or mixer the water, oil, honey, and ¼ cup brown sugar. Soften yeast in warm water with remaining 1 tbsp brown sugar.
   Sift together in a large bowl 1 cup unbleached flour, 2 cups whole wheat flour, non fat milk, and salt. Add oil and honey mixture with yeast to flour mixture. Beat with mixer at medium speed until smooth, about 2 minutes. Gradually stir in enough remaining flour to make soft dough that leaves the side of bowl. Turn out onto floured surface and knead until smooth and satin texture, about 10 to 15 minutes.
   Place dough in lightly greased bowl and turn to grease other side. Cover and let rise until doubled about 1 ½ hours. Punch down and let rest 10 minutes. Shape into 4 round loaves. Place 2 loaves on each of 2 lightly greased baking sheets sprinkled with cornmeal. Cover and let rise in warm place until light and doubled in size, about 1 hour. Bake at 375 degrees 30 to 35 minutes. Cool on racks while still hot, brush with melted butter.

   Makes 4 loaves.

# Tomato Cheese Muffins

1 ½ cups flower
2 tsp sugar
1 tsp dried basil and oregano
½ tsp dried thyme
1 tsp baking powder
1/2 tsp baking soda
½ salt
½ cup butter milk
1/3 cup melted butter
1 egg, beaten
10 sun-dried tomatoes, well drained and chopped
½ cup soft goat cheese

    Mix together flour, sugar, seasonings, baking powder and soda. Combine egg, butter, milk, butter, and tomatoes; mix with dry ingredients just to moisten. Fold in crumbled goat cheese.
    Fill muffin cups ¾ full and bake in a 400-degree oven 10-12 minutes. Let muffins cool and remove from muffin pan.

Makes 6 muffins

Chapter 18

# Ideal Fish Recipes

*Good for you; learn to love fish!*

# Baked Champagne Salmon

2 ½ pounds salmon fillets
1 cup champagne
¼ cup finely chopped onion
1 tbsp fresh rosemary
juice of 1 lemon
salt and pepper
½ cup melted butter
½ cup sour cream
½ cup whipping cream
2 tbsp champagne
3 tbsp sugar
1 tbsp lemon zest
1 tbsp Dijon mustard

Combine butter, 1 cup champagne, onion, rosemary, lemon juice and salt and pepper. Pour over fillets in baking dish. Bake for 30-40 minutes uncovered in a 350 degree oven. Remove and let set for about 5 minutes. Place on platter and add sauce on top or to the side.

For sauce mix sour cream, whipping cream, 2 tbsp champagne, sugar, lemon zest and Dijon mustard with wire whisk until smooth and spoon over salmon.

Makes 6 servings

# Flounder Fillets with Papaya

1 firm ripe papaya
1 lb. flounder fillets
¼ cup fresh lime juice
¼ tsp salt
½ cup flour
¼ cup butter
1 tbsp olive oil
¼ tsp cinnamon
1 tbsp dark brown sugar

    Cut papaya lengthwise in half, scoop out seeds. Cut into ½ inch thick slices. Sprinkle fish with 1 tbsp lime juice; let stand 5 minutes.
    Sprinkle fish with salt. Place flour on waxed paper, dip fish in flour to coat both sides. Add 2 tbsp butter, olive oil and heat skillet on medium-high heat until foamy. Add as many fillets as will fit in a single layer. Cook fish turning once, until golden brown on outside and opaque throughout; about 1 ½ - 2 minutes per side. Remove to warm platter.
    Heat remaining butter and add papaya and sprinkle with cinnamon. Sauté papaya, turning over gently just until heated through. Remove papaya with slotted spatula and arrange on platter with fish.
    Sprinkle brown sugar over drippings in skillet. Stir in the 3 tbsp lime juice and cook over medium heat to boiling until sauce is slightly thickened; about 1 ½ minutes. Spoon sauce over fish and serve immediately.

Makes 3-4 servings

# Red Snapper with Coconut Cream Sauce

4 red snapper fillets
olive oil
salt and pepper
½ onion sliced

Brush olive oil over fillets and add salt and pepper. Place onion rings on top of fillets. Bake uncovered for 25 minutes in a 350-degree oven. Pour sauce over fillets and continue to bake 10 minutes.

# Coconut Sauce:

3 tbsp butter
1 onion chopped
1 cup heavy cream
2 cans coconut milk, unsweetened
2 tbsp corn starch
1 tbsp water
salt and pepper

Sauté onions in butter and add cream, milk, salt and pepper. Mix cornstarch and water well and add to sauce. Bring to a boil and reduce and cook for 2 minutes. Let set a bit before pouring over fish.

# Shrimp Curry Fettuccini

1 pound fresh, cleaned shrimp
2 tbsp butter
3 cloves garlic, crushed
2 tbsp curry powder
¼ cup white wine
cooked fettuccini
Parmesan cheese

Sauté shrimp in butter, garlic and curry. Add wine and sauté until almost evaporated. Add to cooked fettuccini with lots of Parmesan on top.

# Snapper with Ginger Pesto Sauce

4 red snapper fillets
olive oil
salt and pepper

Brush olive oil over fillets and salt and pepper. Bake covered in a 350 oven for 30 minutes. Uncover and spread pesto sauce on top of fillets and continue baking uncovered for 10 minutes in a 400-degree oven.

# Ginger-Pesto Sauce:

½ cup cilantro
½ cup sliced green onion
¼ cup grated fresh ginger
¾ cup peanut oil salt and pepper

Chop cilantro and ginger in food processor. Add oil while machine is running. Transfer to a small bowl and mix in green onion, salt and pepper.

*I have been making this for years; great dish!*

## Stuffed Flounder

½ cup chopped onion
¼ cup butter
1 3-ounce can broiled sliced mushrooms
1 7 ½ ounce can crab meat, drained
¾ cup saltine cracker crumbs
¼ cup fresh snipped parsley
½ tsp salt
4 tbsp butter
3 tbsp flour salt
1 ½ cup milk
¼ cup dry white wine
1 ½ cup shredded Swiss cheese
½ tsp paprika
8 flounder fillets

    Cook onion in a skillet in ¼ cup butter till tender. Add mushrooms, crab, cracker crumbs, parsley, ½ cup cheese, ½ tsp salt and dash of pepper. Spread mixture over flounder fillets and roll fillets and place in a 9x13 baking dish.

    In saucepan, melt 3 tbsp butter. Blend in flour and salt. Add milk and wine to saucepan, cook and stir until mixture thickens and bubbles. Pour over fillets.

    Bake in a 400-degree oven for 25 minutes. Sprinkle with cheese and paprika and return to oven for 10 minutes longer.

Serves 8

*Chapter 19*

# Italian Dinning

*Some of my most meaningful connections were shared with a fine Italian dinner, a glass of red wine and good conversation.*

# Angle Hair Pasta With Feta Cheese

½ cup walnuts
2 tbsp olive oil
½ onion, chopped
2 cloves garlic, chopped
1 tsp dried basil
½ tsp cumin
1 14-ounce can chicken broth
1 14-ounce can diced tomatoes
½ cup crumbles feta cheese chopped parsley feta cheese
1 5-ounce package angel hair pasta

    Sauté walnuts over medium heat for 5 minutes, set aside. Sauté onion, garlic in olive oil for 3 minutes. Add broth, tomatoes, basil, cumin and pasta to onion and garlic. Cover and reduce heat to low. Simmer until pasta is tender. (If liquid evaporates before pasta is done, stir in a little water). Mix feta cheese in pasta and serve. Garnish with parsley, walnuts and feta on top.

Serves 4

*I remember years ago being guests of an Italian family for a Thanksgiving meal. I was quite surprised as we were seated at the family dinning table, to see a small dish of pasta sitting on top of the dinner plate. It contained gnocchi, known as Italian dumplings with a little sauce covering them. I was later told that in Italy, pasta is served between the antipasto and the main course. Years latter while helping cook for an Elderhostel group at the coast, I made my first batch of gnocchi and through the years have come up with my own favorite recipe. Absolutely delicious!*

# Gnocchi Italian Dumplings

2 cups ricotta cheese
2 eggs, beaten
1 10-ounce package frozen spinach, thoroughly squeezed and dry
½ cup freshly grated Parmigiano Reggiano cheese
1 clove garlic, crushed
3 tbsp fresh basil, chopped
1/3 cup minced green onion
½ tsp nutmeg salt and pepper
1 cup Italian bread crumbs
½ cup flour

    Mix all ingredients well. Roll into 3-inch logs between palms until firm. Roll each in flour and lay slightly apart on a baking sheet. Cover and refrigerate 6 hours or over night. In a large pot of boiling salted water, reduce heat and drop dumplings in one at a time and simmer for 5-10 minutes. Remove with a slotted spoon and transfer to a buttered baking dish or cookie sheet. Drizzle melted butter across the tops of dumplings and sprinkle with Parmesan cheese. Broil until the cheese is golden and crisp.
    Serve with favorite pasta sauce, melted parsley butter, warm cream and chopped basil or over pasta with sauce and finish with Parmesan cheese.

Serves 6

# Clam Fettuccini Bake

1 6-ounce package fettuccini noodles
¾ cup half and half
½ finely chopped onion
2 garlic cloves minced
1 can chopped clams, undrained
1 cup shredded Parmigano Reggiano
1 tbsp parsley flakes
1 tbsp flour
1 cup fresh sliced mushrooms
2 tbsp diced pimento

    In saucepan cook noodles to package directions, drain and return to sauce pan. Sauté garlic, onion and mushrooms in a little olive oil for about 2 minutes. Add half and half, flour, clams, ½ of cheese, parsley and pimento. Heat and stir for 3 minutes until bubbly. Mix with fettuccini and pour into a 9x13-baking dish. Bake in a 375-degree oven and bake covered for 30 minutes or till thickened. Sprinkle remaining cheese and bake uncovered for 3-5 more minutes.

*Polenta is an age-old, traditional dish of northern Italy. Simple cornmeal, making it a humble dish is dressed up with herbs, cheeses, vegetables and sauces. I was introduced to polenta in the 1970's at an Italian restaurant. After ordering my meal, a dish of yellow cornmeal with a little sauce and cheese was set in front of me. I had no idea what I was eating, but I would have been happy to have more than just a taste. It was another 10 years before I started cooking one of my now favorite dishes.*

*Cooking a successful batch of polenta requires patience, attention and lots of stirring, but it is truly a slice of Italy!*

# Herbed Polenta

2 ¾ cup whole milk or water
¾ cup polenta (coarse cornmeal)
1 tbsp salt
5 garlic cloves, crushed or chopped
2 tbsp chopped fresh Thyme, Oregano, Rosemary
1 cup chopped fresh Italian parsley
2 cups grated Parmesan cheese

Heat milk or water, and salt to boiling and add polenta, garlic, herbs and parsley. Reduce heat and simmer stirring constantly until thickened. Stir in cheese. (I use a whisk and heavy large metal spoon). Remove from heat and pour into a buttered baking dish, sprinkle with Parmesan cheese. Let cool to room temperature and refrigerate until set.

Slice into rectangle or squares and place on a hot grill or skillet and grill for about 5 minutes on each side. Top with favorite sauce or grilled vegetables.

# Baked Crusty Polenta

2 tbsp minced garlic
1/3 cup chopped onion
3 tbsp olive oil
1 cup polenta
3 cups canned vegetable broth
1 tsp dried oregano and basil
¼ cup chopped fresh Italian parsley
1 cup grated Parmesan cheese

Sauté garlic and onion in oil over medium heat. Add polenta and sauté 1 minute. Add broth and bring to a boil. Simmer, stirring until very thick. Pour into a shallow buttered baking dish. Sprinkle with cheese. Bake in a 400-degree oven for 20-30 minutes or until crusty.

# Broiled Polenta

2 14-ounce cans chicken broth
1 cup yellow cornmeal
½ cup sun dried tomatoes, chopped (in bulk section of store)
½ cup grated Parmesan cheese
3 tbsp olive oil

Bring broth to a boil. Whisk in cornmeal and tomato pieces. Reduce heat and simmer, whisking constantly about 5 minutes or until mixture is thick and creamy. Remove from heat and whisk in cheese. Spread in a greased, lined 9x13-baking dish. Cover loosely with plastic wrap and refrigerate 2 hours or overnight. Remove polenta from pan and cut into squares.

Heat broiler and place polenta on baking sheet, brush with olive oil. Broil for 1 minute just until lightly browned, watching closely, serve hot.

# Italian Sausage Basil Casserole

1 lb. fusilli pasta, cooked,
   drained and set aside
1/3 cup extra-virgin olive oil
2 cups fresh basil, chopped
1 red pepper cut into strips
1 onion sliced
3 garlic cloves, chopped
1 15-ounce can white cannelloni beans,
   rinsed and drained
¾ pound Italian sausage links
1 cup dry white wine
1/3 cup heavy cream
1 cup freshly grated Parmesan cheese

Heat skilled and add sausage and cook until all pink is gone inside links. Cool and slice thin, set aside. Sauté in olive oil the garlic, onion, red pepper, for 3 minutes and add wine. Continue cooking until wine evaporates slightly and add cream and blend. Add beans, sausage and 1 cup of basil and combine. Pour over pasta and add 1-cup cheese. Pour into a greased casserole dish and top with breadcrumb topping. Bake in a 350-375 degree oven for 30 minutes and crumbs are golden. Top with remaining basil.

Serves 6-8

# Bread Crumb Topping:

1 cup Italian bread crumbs
½ cup Parmesan cheese
3 tbsp butter, melted
2 cloves garlic, minced

Mix ingredients and top casserole.

*Although it's rare to find anyone who stops and makes a spaghetti sauce from scratch these days, I felt I needed to include my mother's recipe. I remember the aroma floated outside of the house and when I walked home from school, nearing home I knew we were having spaghetti for dinner. When we have a large family gathering I still take the time to make this, because there is no replacement like it in a bottle. This year for my granddaughter Kamille's birthday I am fixing Italian lasagna with roasted red pepper sauce, polenta and of course Mother's sauce over pasta noodles.*

# Mother's Italian Sauce

2 lbs. ground beef
1 lb. Italian bulk sausage
2 1- lb. can Italian diced tomatoes
1 1- lb. can tomato sauce
1 small can tomato paste
5 garlic cloves, crushed olive oil
1 medium onion finely chopped
3 cups fresh sliced mushrooms
2 cups grated carrots
2 cups grated zucchini
1 cup dry red wine
1 cup chopped fresh basil
1 tbsp dried oregano and thyme
½ cup chopped fresh Italian parsley
1 bay leaf
3 tbsp sugar
½ cup grated fresh Parmesan cheese

Brown meats together- drain liquid and mix in the tomato paste, set aside. In separate pan sauté garlic in olive oil, add onion, mushrooms and cook on medium heat for 3 minutes. Add wine and simmer for three minutes. Transfer to large pot and add the carrots, zucchini, meat mixture, canned tomatoes, tomato sauce and combine. Add herbs, sugar, bay leaf and cheese. Simmer on low for 2 hours or more, stirring often. Turn off and let set for an hour or so before serving. May be made the day before and taste even better the next day.

Sauce cooks well in a crock-pot. You may substitute store bought pasta sauce in place of tomato sauce. Replace meat with more vegetables for veggie lovers.

# Orange-Marsala Sauce

2 35-ounce cans chopped plum tomatoes, liquid reserved
1 cup Marsala wine
1 cup fresh basil leaves, chopped
3 tbsp olive oil
¾ cup chopped red onion
6 garlic cloves, finely chopped zest from one orange, cut into strips
1 tbsp fresh rosemary, chopped
1 tsp dried thyme
1 bay leaf salt and pepper to taste
1 tsp sugar

Heat oil and sauté onion, garlic and zest for 3 minutes. Add thyme, rosemary, salt and pepper, tomatoes, wine, bay leaf, sugar, and half of the basil, bringing sauce to a boil and simmer for 30 minutes, stirring occasionally. Remove from heat and remove bay leaf and orange peel. Stir in remaining basil and season again. Let set a while before serving or overnight.

Makes 6-8 cups

# Pasta and Shrimp

½ cup chopped walnuts
2 cups frozen peas, cooked and set aside
½ chopped onion
1 garlic clove, chopped
2 tbsp olive oil
1 tbsp lemon zest
½ cup fresh chopped Italian parsley
1 tbsp fresh chopped basil
6- ounces shelled cooked tiny shrimp, rinsed salt and pepper
1 5- ounce package Radiatore pasta grated Parmesan cheese

 Sauté walnuts for 5 minutes over medium heat; set aside. Cook pasta, rinse and set aside.
 Sauté onion and garlic in oil and add shrimp, lemon zest, parsley and basil, for 3 minutes. Add cooked pasta and peas, salt and pepper and toss. Top with walnuts and Parmesan cheese.

# Pasta Turkey Bake

1 pound penne pasta
2 cups chopped fresh broccoli
½ cup chopped onion
½ cup chopped pimento
2 cups cooked smoked turkey, cut into chunks
2 cups smoked mozzarella, diced
½ stick unsalted butter
½ cup flour
3 cups milk
1 tsp salt
½ tsp pepper
¼ tsp nutmeg

    Cook pasta in salted boiling water and add broccoli last two minutes, drain. Melt butter and add flour and stir until blended. Add milk, salt and pepper, nutmeg, onion, and pimento. Cook stirring until bubbly and thickened. Remove from heat. Mix pasta and turkey, adding cheese and sauce and mix well. Place in a greased 13x9 baking dish. Bake in a 375-degree oven covered for 20 minutes. Uncover and bake for 10 minutes. Let set for 5 minutes before serving.

# Pasta with Vermouth Clam Sauce

2 cans chopped clams
¾ cup finely chopped onion
2 cloves garlic, minced or pressed
1 cup dry vermouth
2 tbsp capers, drained
10 ounces linguine
½ cup chopped parsley
½ cup shredded Parmigiano reggiano cheese

    Drain clams and reserve juice. Combine ½ cup of the clam juice, onion, and garlic and ¼ cup vermouth. Stir on high heat until about ¼ of liquid remains. Add remaining vermouth, clams, and capers; simmer 5 minutes, keep warm.
    Cook pasta and drain and mix with clam mixture. Mix until most of the liquid is absorbed. Top pasta with parsley and cheese and mix again.

# Pasta with Walnuts and Swiss Chard

½ cup coarsely chopped walnuts
½ pound Swiss chard
1 ½ tbsp extra-virgin olive oil
½ pound mushrooms, sliced
½ cup chopped onion
2 cloves garlic, pressed
1 tomato, chopped salt and pepper
1 cup grated Parmesan cheese
4, 6-ounces of pasta of choice

While pasta is cooking, brown walnuts over medium heat, set aside. Rinse chard and chop only the leaves. Sauté onions, mushrooms and garlic until liquid is almost evaporates, about 5 minutes. In bowl toss pasta in 1 tablespoon olive oil. Add chard mixture, walnuts, tomato, salt and pepper and cheese and toss again. Serve warm.

Serves 4

*If the thought of making Ravioli leaves you feeling tired, try this shortcut using won ton wrappers and then add this amazing stuffing and you may want to skip buying the packaged ravioli.*

# Ravioli with Basil Cream Sauce

½ cup finely chopped figs
½ cup ricotta cheese
4 ounces blue cheese, crumbled
¼ cup finely chopped walnuts
1 ½ tsp dry sherry
½ tsp dried thyme and basil
salt and pepper
1 14-ounce package prepared won ton wrappers
Basil Cream Sauce
 coarsely chopped walnuts, toasted

Combine cheeses, walnuts, sherry, thyme, salt and pepper to taste; mix well.  Place won ton wrappers on wax paper and fill each with 2-3 teaspoons of filling in center.  Moisten edges and place a wrapper over each, press edges to seal, crimp with fork.

Cook in salted boiling water until ravioli floats.  Drain well and top with basil cream sauce.  Sprinkle toasted walnuts or Parmesan cheese over top.

# Basil Cream Sauce:

Melt 2 tablespoons butter in saucepan and stir in two tablespoons flour to make a paste.  Stir in ½ cup half and half and chicken stock; cook, stirring until mixture bubbles.  Stir in ½ cup chopped fresh basil, 3 tablespoons dry white wine, ½ teaspoon nutmeg, salt and pepper.

*Primavera is Italian for springtime, and this lasagna is packed with fresh vegetables. I have added Italian sausage, but it's wonderful with just the veggies, like I made it for my oldest daughter Kellie's 17th birthday lunch.*

## Roasted Red Pepper Primavera Lasagna

1 egg beaten
4 cups ricotta cheese
1 cup freshly grated Parmesan cheese
1 cup prepared basil pesto

8 ounces sweet Italian-style turkey sausage - cooked, cooled and crumbled
2 tbsp extra-virgin olive oil
1 medium onion, coarsely chopped
6 cloves garlic, pressed
1 tbsp dried oregano
1 tsp marjoram
½ cup fresh basil, finely chopped
1 cup fresh Italian parsley leaves, chopped
2 bunches fresh cleaned spinach
3 large red peppers, seeded and slightly pulsed in food processor
3 pounds fresh Italian plum tomatoes, coarsely chopped
1 7-ounce jar roasted red peppers, drained and pureed in food processor with metal blade
½ cup dry white wine
2 cups Parmesan cheese
1 lb. lasagna noodles, cooked, drained and tossed with olive oil

# Béchamel Sauce:

½ cup butter
½ cup flour
3 ½ cups milk salt and ground pepper
1 cup freshly grated parmesan cheese
½ tsp nutmeg

Melt butter in heavy saucepan over medium heat until bubbly. Add flour and cook for 1 minute. Add milk, stirring until smooth. Bring to a boil and reduce heat and simmer 5-8 minutes, add cheese and mix well and cook another 2 minutes. Pour in bowl and cover, set aside.

Sauce:
In large pan on medium heat add garlic and sauté for 1 minute and add onion and continue cooking on low heat for another minute. Add red peppers, plum tomatoes and roasted peppers and mix. Add all herbs, spices and salt and pepper, and wine. Cook for 10-15 minutes on low heat. Combine sausage with pepper mixture, set aside.

Mix beaten egg into ricotta, add pesto, nutmeg and cheese. In a large greased baking dish pour ½ cup red pepper sauce over bottom. Place a layer of noodles over sauce and spread one-half ricotta over noodles and ½ cup of béchamel sauce over ricotta mixture. Add one half of red pepper sauce and a layer of cheese and spinach. Repeat layers, ending with cheese and topping off with the rest of béchamel sauce.

Bake in a 350-degree oven for 30 minutes, covered. Take cover off and continue baking for 10-15 minutes or until lightly browned and bubbly. Let set for 10 minutes before cutting, sprinkle with fresh chopped Italian parsley and cut into squares.

*Fresh oregano, marjoram, basil or thyme may be used in place of rosemary or all together.*

## Rosemary Cream Sauce Over Ravioli

1 lb fresh or frozen cheese ravioli
1 cup heavy cream
1 ½ tsp fresh rosemary chopped
2 tbsp fresh lemon juice
½ tsp salt and pepper
3 tbsp chopped chives
    Parmesan cheese

Combine cream and rosemary and bring to boil, reduce the heat and simmer until reduced to ½ cup. Add fresh lemon juice, salt and pepper. Cook ravioli to package directions, drain and add to cream sauce and toss. Serve with chives and Parmesan cheese.

Serves 4

# Rustic Pasta Casserole

8 ounces fusilli pasta, cooked and drained
10 ounces sweet Italian turkey sausage
10-ounces cream cheese, softened
2 ½ cups cubed, rustic Artesian French bread
1 cup halved kalamata olives
2 cups grated mozzarella cheese
1 tbsp. butter
1 tbsp. olive oil
5 garlic cloves, minced
2 ½ cups heavy cream
1 tsp. dried sage
1 tsp. dried thyme
½ tsp. salt
½ tsp. cracked pepper
2 cups cherry tomatoes, halved
2 cup grated Asiago and Parmesan cheese

Sauté sausage in skillet and crumble, drain. Combine sausage, cooked pasta, cream cheese, bread, olives, cherry tomatoes, mozzarella cheese and 1 cup of the Parmesan cheese. Set aside.

In saucepan sauté garlic, herbs with butter and olive oil for 1 minute. Add cream and simmer on low for 5 minutes, stirring.

Pour sauce over sausage mixture and fold gently together. Put mixture into a buttered casserole dish and top with remaining cheese. Bake in a 350-degree oven uncovered for 30-45 minutes or until brown on top. Let rest 10-15 minutes before serving.

# Tortellini with Creamy Topping

2 9-ounce packages spinach-cheese tortellini
3 tbsp butter
2 tsp finely chopped fresh garlic
2 cups sour cream salt and pepper
½ tsp ground nutmeg
1 tbsp chicken stock
2 tbsp Parmesan cheese
½ cup Parmesan cheese

Cook tortellini according to package directions, drain and set aside. Melt butter and sauté garlic over medium heat for one minute. Stir in sour cream, salt and pepper, nutmeg, 2 tablespoons Parmesan cheese and stock. Cook until heated through, about 2 minutes. Pour over warm tortellini and top with Parmesan cheese.

# Toscana Soup

3 Italian sausage links
¾ cup chopped onions
2 slices bacon, diced
1 ¼ tsp minced garlic
1 14-ounce can chicken broth
2 cups water
2 medium potatoes, peeled and sliced
2 cups sliced fresh kale
1/3 cup whipping cream

    Heat oven to 300 degrees. Bake the links on cookie sheet for 15-20 minutes. Drain and cut into ¼ inch slices.
    Cook onions and bacon in a saucepan over medium heat 3-4 minutes. Stir in garlic and cook 1 minute. Add the chicken broth, water and potatoes. Bring to a boil; reduce heat to medium and simmer for 25 minutes or until potatoes are tender. Stir in kale, whipping cream and sausage and cook for 5 minutes.

Makes 6 servings

# Chapter 20

# *Sassy Sauces and Zesty Dressings*

*There is nothing better; no bottle of dressing compares to homemade.*

# Buttermilk Dressing

½ cup buttermilk
1 tbsp mayonnaise
½ tsp Dijon mustard
2 tsp lemon juice
¼ honey
¼ tsp salt  Freshly ground pepper

Place all ingredients in blender and process for 1 minute.  Refrigerate several hours before serving.

*I tasted this amazing dressing on a salad while eating outside in a wonderful little café in Placerville California years ago. I savored every bite trying to guess what the ingredients were. The waiter helped me out a bit and I quickly scribbled the ingredients on the back of a shopping bag. It's worth making; the experience is defined in the taste.*

## Chili Lime Dressing

1/3 cup rice vinegar
¼ cup fresh lime juice
1 tsp. lime zest
½ seeded and chopped jalapeño chili
1 tbsp. sugar
1 tsp. grated fresh ginger Salt and cracked pepper
1 cup olive oil

Whisk vinegar with lime juice and sugar. Add ginger, zest, jalapeno, salt and pepper and whisk in oil, mix well.

# Creamy Garlic Dressing Over Romaine Lettuce

4 cloves garlic, minced
½ tsp. salt
1 tbsp. lemon juice
1 egg
1/3 cup mayonnaise
2 tbsp. Worcestershire
3 tbsp. grated Parmesan cheese

Mash garlic and salt together into a paste with the back of a spoon. Mix garlic paste with juice and add egg and beat until foamy. Stir in mayonnaise and Worcestershire. Cover and chill if made ahead.

Salad:
Combine romaine lettuce, cherry tomatoes, diced avocado, green onions and croutons and toss with dressing.

Serves 6-8

# Cucumber Mint Dressing

½ cup yogurt
2 tbsp salad oil
2 tbsp fresh lemon juice
¼ tsp salt freshly ground pepper
½ cucumber , sliced
2 tbsp fresh mint leaves
2 tbsp chopped green onions

Place all ingredients in blender or food processor for a full 3 minutes.

# Easy Balsamic Dressing

2 cloves garlic, minced
1 tsp. ground mustard
1 tbsp. mayonnaise
¼ cup balsamic vinegar
3/4 cup olive oil

    Whisk together the first 4 ingredients. Whisk in the oil.

Makes about 1 cup dressing.

*While at an event I was catering, I met a woman who was a guest of the party and talked with her for a long time about the love of good food. She wanted to share a few of her favorite salad dressing recipes with me, and some time later I received three of them in the mail. This is one of them.*

## Favorite Salad Dressing

2 ¼  tsp. salt, coarse pepper, dry mustard
1  tsp. garlic powder
1  ½ tbsp. onion powder
6  tbsp. each- white, red and cider vinegar
2 ½ cups light olive oil

Mix all spices with cider vinegar and make a paste. Add remaining ingredients and whisk together.

# Ginger-Orange Sauce

½ cup butter
½ cup flour
2 tbsp. freshly grated ginger
2 garlic cloves, minced
½ cup milk
1 cup orange juice
2 tsp. orange zest
1 tsp. tamari Salt and pepper to taste

Melt butter and add ginger and garlic and sauté. Whisk in the flour; cook 4 minutes. Add milk while whisking on low heat about 4-5minutes. Add orange juice, tamari, salt and pepper and orange zest. Cook about 10 minutes longer.

Serve over baked fish.

# Honey Lime Dressing

½ cup fresh lime juice
4 tsp. honey
1 tbsp. rice vinegar
Salt and pepper

    Whisk all ingredients. Makes ½ cup.

# Lemon-Basil Dressing

½ cup fresh basil leaves
1 garlic clove, minced
1 tsp finely chopped fresh oregano
6 tbsp olive oil
1 ½ tbsp fresh lemon juice
½ Parmesan cheese
1/3 cup pine nuts Freshly ground pepper

Combine all ingredients except oil in food processor. Process briefly until blended; add oil while machine is running. Serve over greens.

Makes about 1 cup

# Orange Parsley Dressing

1 tbsp orange zest
1 orange, peeled and seeded
3 tbsp olive oil
1 tbsp champagne vinegar
1 tsp sugar
¼ tsp salt
2 tbsp chopped parsley

Blend orange zest, orange, vinegar, and salt for 1 minute in blender or food processor. While running add olive oil and process for 2 minutes.

# Orange Vinaigrette

2 tbsp. sherry vinegar
½ cup walnut oil
2 tsp. orange zest
3 tbsp. juice of fresh orange
1 tsp. salt and freshly ground pepper

    Whisk together all ingredients. Makes 1 cup of dressing.

# Orange-Butter Sauce

8 tbsp butter
1/3 cup minced shallots
1 tsp Dijon mustard
1 1/3 cup freshly squeezed orange juice
2 tsp orange zest

    Melt 1 tablespoon of butter and add shallots and cook, stirring for 1 minute. Add mustard, orange juice and 1 teaspoon of zest. Increase heat to high and boil, stirring until reduced to 2/3 cup. Add remaining butter and cook, stirring constantly until butter is melted and sauce is smooth. Spoon sauce over fresh asparagus and garnish with remaining 1 teaspoon of orange zest.

# Peach Vinaigrette

4 medium ripe peaches, peeled, and diced
3 tbsp. champagne vinegar
2 tbsp. honey ½ tsp. salt Freshly ground pepper
3 tbsp. olive oil

In bowl of food processor combine all ingredients except oil. After a few pulses, while machine is running, add oil and mix.

Makes 1 cup dressing.

# Roasted Garlic Sauce

2 whole heads garlic
1 tbsp. flour
1 cup chicken broth
2 tbsp. dry white wine
2 tsp. olive oil
½ tsp. salt

    Remove white shins from garlic, making sure not to separate the cloves. Wrap each head of garlic separately in foil. Bake in a 400-degree oven for 30 minutes. Let cool 10 minutes. Squeeze pulp, and discard shins. Mash garlic pulp; set aside.
    Place flour in saucepan and whisk in oil, broth and wine. Over medium heat, bring to a boil. Add pulp and salt and cook 1 minute or until thickened. Place in blender or food processor and blend until smooth.

Serve over pasta. Makes 1 ¼ cup.

*This is my dear French friend Cynthia's salad dressing recipe that I coveted.*

## Salade Dressing ala Tomatis

½ cup good olive oil
3 tbsp. Ume vinegar
3 tbsp. cider vinegar
1 tsp. mustard
2 garlic cloves crushed
Sea salt and ground pepper
Pinch of thyme or basil

Whisk vinegar with mustard and herbs, salt and pepper. Whisk while pouring in olive oil.

# Spinach Salad Dressing

6 Tbsp. olive oil
2 tbsp. cider vinegar
2 tbsp. Dijon mustard
2 tbsp. sesame seeds
2 tbsp. garlic powder
2 tbsp. lemon juice

Mix well and pour over spinach salad.

*Welsh Rarebit is a British dish, but traditionally served when the Welsh rabbit hunter came home empty-handed. I learned to make this dish from my grandmother who used a double boiler set over boiling water; to melt the cheese and then add the remaining ingredients. However, the same wonderful sauce can be created from a saucepan starting with flour to thicken it. Either way, it's not the pan that makes the sauce, it's the beer.*

# Welsh Rarebit

3  tbsp. butter
2  tbsp. flour
1  cup ale
1  tbsp. Milk at room temperature
1  lb. grated Cheddar or Colby cheese
1  tsp. English mustard
½ tsp. paprika
2  drops Tabasco sauce
Salt and ground pepper

Melt butter in medium saucepan, add the flour, mustard and milk and cook for 3-5 minutes. Whisk in the beer and cook for 10 minutes on low heat. Add the cheese and remaining ingredients and continue to cook on low heat stirring constantly with a wooden spoon for about 8 minutes.

Serve on toast, English muffin or cheddar scone with a slice of tomato. Great sauce served over fresh steamed vegetables.

My grandmother would pour sauce over toast and then place a slice of tomato on top and place them in the broiler for 1 to 2 minutes or until the cheese bubbles.

## Chapter 21

# Favorite Chicken Recipes

*I think every cook has a little recipe box with a couple dozen good chicken recipes. Most of them we remember and make over and over again, but we are always open to a new one. It may be the latest one found while flipping through a magazine or the best chicken you tasted all year in your favorite restaurant and try to duplicate, or the dinner at a friends' house that is written down for you before you leave. I think chicken recipes are so sought after because we prepare it for our families weekly and store it as a staple in our freezer.*

*The following chicken recipes are my favorites and on behalf of family and friends I will say they are really good recipes. You can never have too many chicken dishes to call upon.*

*This is my daughter Kellie's recipe and is a perfect dish and now a family recipe.*

## Chicken and Vegetables with Garlic Cream

2 tbsp. butter
4 chicken breasts
2 cups sliced zucchini
1 cup carrots, sliced thin
½ cup sliced green onions
2 tbsp. butter
3 garlic cloves, minced
3 tbsp. flour
1 3-ounce package cream cheese
1 10-ounce can chicken broth
Salt and pepper

In a large skillet over medium-high heat sauté chicken in the butter for 15 minutes. Remove from pan and add vegetables and cook until crispy about 5 minutes. Add chicken to vegetables.

Melt butter and add garlic; cook over medium heat, stirring for 1 minute. Add flour and stir until smooth. Add remaining ingredients and cook until sauce is thickened. Pour sauce over chicken and serve on a platter of hot rice.

Makes 4 servings

# Chicken Breasts in Mustard Sauce

4 large chicken breasts
1 tbsp. butter
1 tbsp. olive oil
1 shallot, minced
2 garlic cloves, minced
½ cups sliced green onion
1 tbsp. grain mustard
1 tbsp. Dijon mustard
1 tsp. dry mustard
½ cup dry white wine
1 cup heavy cream
Salt and pepper

    Rub salt and pepper into chicken breasts. Sauté chicken in 1 tbsp. oil and butter over medium heat. Cook chicken until well browned and no longer pink inside. Remove to a platter.
    In a bowl mix the mustards together. Mix the wine into pan drippings in the skillet; bring to a boil, scrapping bits from bottom of the pan. Stir in mustards and next whisk in the cream. Bring to a boil; whisking until reduced enough to coat a spoon. Season with salt and pepper. Return chicken to pan and heat through.

Makes 4 servings

*Another great recipe from my friend Terry; she made this for me in the 1980's and I still make it. The lemon makes the dish.*

# Chicken Picata

6 chicken breasts
¼ cup wheat flour
1 tsp. paprika Salt and pepper
2 tbsp. olive oil
2 tbsp. butter
½ cup dry white wine
½ cup lemon juice
Wheat flour to thicken

Mix flour, paprika, salt and pepper and coat chicken with flour mixture. Sauté for 4 minutes on each side in oil and butter. Place in a baking dish and bake uncovered in a 350 degree over for 30 minutes.

In same skillet add wine and lemon juice and flour to thicken sauce. Pour over chicken and place on a platter. Serve with lemon wedge garnish.

*I love tarragon and so this is one of my favorite dishes. It's good, classy, infectiously delicious and one of my friend Suzie's best recipes. I have been making this chicken dish since 1987.*

# Chicken with Tarragon and Orange

4 broiler-fryer chickens
¼ cup olive oil
2 tbsp. chopped shallots
1 tsp. salt
¼ tsp. cracked pepper
4 bay leaves
¼ cup butter
1/3 cup flour
1 tsp. salt
1 tbsp. dried tarragon leaves
3 cups chicken broth
1 cup dry white wine
½ cup whipping cream watercress sprigs
1 orange- cut into 8 wedges
1 tbsp. orange zest

Salt and pepper chicken and sauté lightly in a little olive oil in heavy skillet. Whisk together ¼ cup olive oil, shallots, 1 tsp. salt, and pepper in a small bowl. Place the chickens in a large shallow roasting pan and pour the sauce over chicken. Place the bay leaves on the chicken breasts. Bake uncovered, basting with the pan juices until tender in a 400 degree oven, about 1 hour and 15 minutes.

Melt the butter in a saucepan over medium heat; stir in flour, 1 tsp. salt and the tarragon. Cook and stir 2 minutes; add chicken broth, wine and gradually cook, stirring constantly till thick (about 10 minutes), reduce heat; stir in cream gradually and orange zest. Simmer uncovered, stirring frequently, about 10 minutes.

Transfer chicken to serving platter; pour about 2 cups of sauce over chickens. Garnish with watercress and orange wedges. Pass remaining sauce.

# Coconut-Basil Chicken

6 chicken breasts, cubed into 1-inch pieces
1 red onion, chopped
6 garlic cloves minced
 Olive oil
1 14-ounce can coconut milk
2 tsp. cornstarch
¼ cup finely chopped fresh basil
2 tbsp. minced fresh ginger root
½ tsp. each ground coriander, cumin, cloves, cinnamon
Salt and pepper
2 tsp. chopped cilantro
Cooked rice

     Combine all ground spices, salt and pepper and coast chicken breasts in spice mixture; cover and set aside for 2 hours.
     In skillet cook onion, garlic in olive oil, add chicken and sauté for 3 minutes; turning once. Remove chicken and set aside. Whisk together the coconut milk and cornstarch and pour into skillet. Cook while stirring till thick. Add basil, ginger, cilantro and chicken. Simmer on low for 5 minutes. Serve over rice.

Makes 6 servings

# Paprika Chicken

1 4-5 pound chicken, skinned and cut up
2 tbsp. butter
3 garlic cloves, minced
2 medium onions, chopped
1 green bell pepper, chopped
1 tbsp. paprika
1 tsp. salt and pepper
1 tbsp. dried basil leaves
1/8 tsp. cayenne pepper
½ can tomato paste
½ cup water
1 tbsp. cornstarch
½ cup sour cream
Hot cooked egg noodles

    Mix salt, pepper, paprika, cayenne and basil together and rub onto chicken and sauté in Dutch oven with garlic, onion and bell pepper; turn once and continue cooking for about 20 minutes.

    In bowl whisk water and cornstarch together; adding tomato paste salt and pepper and sour cream. Pour into pot, cover and simmer with chicken for 15 minutes. Serve over noodles.

# Mushroom Chicken

2 ounces mixed dried mushrooms
1-cup chicken broth
½ stick butter
4 boneless chicken breasts
　Salt and pepper
1 large shallot, minced
½ pound white mushrooms, sliced
½ cup whipping cream
½ cup brandy

　　Heat chicken broth and add dried mushrooms, remove from heat. Let stand while preparing the chicken.
　　Salt and pepper the chicken; melt butter in skillet over medium heat and sauté chicken for 5 minutes on both sides. Remove chicken.
　　Add white and dried mushrooms, shallots to same skillet. Sauté over medium heat until all liquid evaporates, about 10 minutes. Add cream, brandy and reserved broth. Bring to a boil and cook stirring until thickened, about 8 minutes. Add chicken and simmer on low for 5 minutes.

Makes 4 servings

# Mushroom Chicken

2 ounces mixed dried mushrooms
1 cup chicken broth
½ stick butter
4 boneless chicken breasts
   Salt and pepper
1 large shallot, minced
½ pounds white mushrooms, sliced
½ cup whipping cream
½ cup brandy

    Heat chicken broth and add dried mushrooms, remove from heat. Let stand while preparing the chicken.
    Salt and pepper the chicken; melt butter in skillet over medium heat and sauté chicken for 5 minutes on both sides. Remove chicken.
    Add white and dried mushrooms, shallots to same skillet. Sauté over medium heat until all liquid evaporates, about 10 minutes. Add cream, brandy and reserved broth. Bring to a boil and cook stirring until thickened, about 8 minutes. Add chicken and simmer on low for 5 minutes.

Makes 4 servings

# Tarragon Chicken

4 chicken breasts, skinned and boned
   Salt and pepper
2 tbsp. olive oil
2 tbsp. butter
6 shallots, finely chopped
3 cloves garlic, minced
1/3 cup chicken broth
½ cup dry white wine
½ cup brandy
2 tbsp. honey
2 tsp. Dijon mustard
1 tsp. dried tarragon
1 cup cream
1 egg yolk
½ lb. button mushrooms
2 tbsp. butter
1 tsp. chopped fresh tarragon

   Sauté garlic and shallots in olive oil for 1 minute. Salt and pepper chicken well and brown on both side for about 2 minutes. Remove to a platter.
   In a bowl whisk together the wine, broth, brandy, mustard, honey, and tarragon. Pour into skillet and simmer for 2 minutes; stirring. Whisk the egg yolk and add the cream and blend. Mix the cream into the wine mixture and continue simmering for 1 minute. Add chicken, cover and simmer for 10-15 minutes.
   In separate pan sauté mushrooms for 5 minutes. Put chicken and sauce on platter; arranging mushrooms around chicken and sprinkle fresh tarragon over chicken.

Serves 4

## Chapter 22

# South of the Border Cha-Cha-Cha

*Who do you know that doesn't love Mexican Food? Not only do we American's love the Latino cuisine, most of us have acquired our own collective home-cooking repertoire that we are proud to serve and show off to family and friends.*

*I was fortunate to have known a wonderful Hispanic family in the 1970's. For two Mother's Day weekends we traveled with Frank and Bell and their children to Fresno California. All day Saturday the women prepared a little and a lot of everything from Mexican Menudo soup to rice and beans to enchiladas. I learned to roast peppers, make sauces from scratch, shape a tortilla and be laughed at in Spanish for the shape of it. That is when Bell's mother caught me stirring the rice and screamed in Spanish not to ever stir the rice. I took what I learned including the connection of food, surrounded by family and began making my own sauces from scratch and over the years I have saved some good recipes that my family loves. There is nothing hard about any of these recipes, just easy good cooking and remembered as fondly by me as any Hispanic family. Enjoy!*

# Black Bean Salad

2 cups dried black beans, rinsed
Water and salt
1 can garbanzo beans, rinsed and drained
1 can navy beans, rinsed and drained
1 can white hominy, drained
1 cup finely chopped red onion
8 whole garlic cloves
2 cups extra virgin olive oil
1 ½ cups fresh lime juice
1 tbsp. lime zest
2 tbsp. cilantro
1 tsp. salt
Salt and cracked pepper
3 firm avocadoes, cubed
1-cup farmers cheese, crumbled

    Wash black beans and bring to a boil in pot of salted water; reduce heat and simmer until tender. Drain and rinse; cool. Add garbanzo, navy beans, hominy, red onion to black beans and toss. In food processor mince garlic, add zest and lime juice and blend. Pour olive oil in while machine is running; add salt and cilantro. Pour dressing over beans and mix well. Refrigerate overnight to mingle flavors. Serve at room temperature.
    Before serving toss in avocados and cheese.

Serves 15-20

# Carnitas

1 bone-in pork shoulder roast
5 garlic cloves, minced
1 onion, chopped
1 orange, quartered
1 lime, quartered
½ cup water
Juice of 1 lime
½ cup brown sugar
2 tbsp. chili powder
1 tsp. cinnamon
Salt and pepper
Flour tortillas

    Trim meat and place in slow cooker with remaining ingredients. Cover and cook on high for 5 hours. Cool and shred meat adding some of the liquid. Fill warm tortillas and add a variety of lettuce, cheese, sour cream and salsa.

# Calabasa - Black Bean Veggie Wrap

2 cans black beans, rinsed
1 8-ounce package cream cheese
½ small can chipolata sauce
Juice of 1 lime or more
2 tbsp. lime zest
3 garlic cloves, minced
2 tbsp. chopped cilantro
3 green onions, chopped
Deli smoked peppered turkey, sliced thin
8-10 flour tortillas

In food processor chop garlic and add beans and pulse until smooth. Add cream cheese, lime juice, zest, chipolata sauce, cilantro, and sliced green onions. Mix well and spread over each tortilla, add some peppered turkey and roll up; wrap in foil and refrigerate for 2 hours or more. Slice tortillas on an angle and lay on a platter garnished with cilantro, limes and peppers.

Makes about 60-75 slices

# Chicken Tostada with Mexican Slaw

5 chicken breasts boiled and cooled, or roasted whole chicken
2 tbsp. olive oil
1 package taco seasoning mix
1 7-ounce can salsa Verde
2 garlic cloves, minced
1 ½ cups shredded jack cheese
1 can refried beans  flour tortillas

# Slaw

1 package shredded cabbage-slaw mix
1 cup chopped tomato
½ cup crushed pineapple, drained
1 tbsp. chopped cilantro
½ pkg. taco mix
½ cup mayonnaise
¼ cup sour cream
4 tbsp. lime juice

Shred chicken and sauté with garlic in olive oil on high flame; add ½ of taco seasoning mix, cover and turn heat to a simmer. Add can of salsa Verde and cook for 5 minutes.

Combine cabbage, tomato, pineapple. Whisk together mayonnaise, sour cream, taco mix, cilantro, and lime juice together until smooth. Mix dressing into slaw until well blended.

Heat flour tortillas in skillet with a little oil or over flame until lightly brown. Spread beans over tortilla, chicken Verde, shredded cheese, slaw and top with remaining cheese.

This is a meal in itself, besides being colorful served by itself or on a platter with cilantro and halved tomato wedges.

# Chiles Rellenos

1 large can green whole chilies
Jack cheese cut into long strips
¼ cup tbsp. flour
4 eggs,
4 egg whites, room temperature
½ tsp. salt
dash of cumin
Flour
Oil for frying

    Open each chili and stuff with cheese strip; set aside. Beat egg whites until stiff. Whisk eggs, ¼ cup flour, cumin and salt; add egg whites and blend. Dip each chili in flour and then in egg mixture; lay in hot oil in skillet. Cook chili until brown underneath and turn over and finish cooking. Drain on paper towels and serve on a platter with cilantro leaves as a garnish.

*Years ago I would take the time to make homemade chilies rellenos, but when I found this recipe I would add this to my Mexican dinners and everyone else like it too. I can't remember who gave me this recipe, but it's easy and goes well with rice and beans.*

# Chile Relleno Casserole

1 13-ounce can whole green chilies
4 eggs
1 tbsp. flour
½ tsp. cumin
¼ cup cream
2 cups grated jack cheese,
1 cup grated cheddar cheese
1 small can tomato sauce

Open each chili and lie flat in a prepared baking dish; sprinkle half of the cheese over chilies. Whisk eggs and add cream, flour, and cumin. Pour the egg mixture over chilies and add remaining cheese. Drizzle the tomato sauce over the egg mixture and slowly mix into the top of the egg mixture. Bake uncovered in a 350-oven for about 50 minutes or until top is puffy and golden.

Serves 8-10

*This recipe is my favorite food that my friend Vicky has made for me. I love sharing it with you; sharing a friend's recipe is sharing the friendship!*

# Chile Verde

4 tbsp. cooking oil
4 lbs. boneless pork shoulder,
   cut into cubes
¼ cup flour
1 4-ounce can chopped green chilies
½ tsp. ground cumin
¼ tsp. salt
¼ tsp. pepper
3 garlic cloves, minced
½ cup chopped fresh cilantro
½ cup salsa
1 can chicken broth
   Flour tortillas

   Brown pork in large pot and flour after browning, mix well. Add remaining ingredients, cover and simmer until pork is tender, about 1-½ hours.
   Serve in warm tortillas. Add anything you like in tortillas or serve with just the meat mixture.

Serves 6-8

*This is another great recipe from my friend Suzie. She always seemed to have the best dessert recipes that I loved to follow. Suzie is an elegant cook and host.*

# Cuban Flan

½ cup sugar
1 13-ounce can coconut milk
2 cups heavy cream
1 8-ounce package cream cheese
3 eggs
1 tsp. vanilla
1 tsp. lime zest
½ cup sliced toasted almonds

    Caramelize sugar in saucepan on low heat and pour into a 9-inch cake pan; spreading evenly. Set cake pan in a roasting pan and add ½ inch water in the bottom.
    In food processor blend all ingredients and pour into the cake pan and bake in a 350-degree oven for 55-60 minutes. Cool, chill and invert onto a plate and sprinkle with almonds.

12 slices

# Easy Enchilada Sauce

1 can red Chile sauce
3-4 tbsp. vegetable oil
2 garlic cloves minced
2 tbsp. flour
1-cup water
   Salt

In skillet melt the oil and sauté the garlic; add flour and cook for 2 minutes; stirring constantly. Slowly add the red sauce and water; whisking until blended. Cook on high heat for 2 minutes, stirring constantly.  Salt to taste.

# Empanadas

1 package piecrust
1 egg white
1 tbsp. sour cream
½ pounds lean ground beef, pork,
　or shredded cooked pork roast
¼ cup golden raisins
¼ cup figs, chopped fine
¼ cup honey
¼ cup chopped green olives
2 cup onion, chopped fine
1 tomato, cored and chopped
2 garlic cloves, minced
2 tbsp. olive oil
¼ tsp. ground cloves
¼ tsp. cinnamon
1 tsp. dried oregano
　Salt and pepper
½ cup cooked rice

　In skillet sauté onion until caramelized; add garlic and sauté 1 minute. Add raisins, figs, green olives, tomato, honey, spices and rice. In separate skillet sauté the beef or pork until brown, drain grease and fold into onion mixture.
　Mix pie crust with egg white and sour cream. Roll out on a floured cutting board to a 1/8-inch thickness. Use a biscuit cutter to cut out small rounds. Fill each with about a teaspoon of filling. Fold each one in half, and press the edges together to enclose the filling. Use a fork pressed down on dough to decorate and seal the edges. Finish by poking a few holes in center with fork. Place on a baking sheet and brush with an egg and milk wash. Bake in a 400-degree oven for about 15 minutes.

# Enchilada Casserole

1 deli rotisserie chicken, shredded
1 cup sliced green onions
4 garlic cloves, minced olive oil
1 large tomato, diced
½ cup chicken stock
2 cans chopped green chilies,
1 can sliced olives
¼ tsp. red pepper flakes
2 tsp. cumin
¼ tsp. coriander
Salt and pepper
2 cups cream or half-and-half
2 tbsp. butter
3 tbsp. flour
1 cup each shredded cheddar and jack cheese
6 corn tortillas, torn

Add shredded chicken to hot skillet and sauté olive oil, garlic, 1 tsp. cumin for 2 minutes. Lower heat and add chilies, green onion, red pepper flakes, chicken stock and diced tomato. Cook until liquid has evaporated.

Melt butter in saucepan and whisk in flour and cook for 2 minutes. Add cream, remaining cumin, coriander and salt and pepper and continue to simmer until sauce is thick.

Spread ½ cup of white sauce in the bottom of a soufflé dish, coated with cooking spray. Arrange tortilla pieces over sauce; top with chicken mixture, white sauce and ½ of the cheeses. Repeat layers twice, ending with sauce. Sprinkle olives on top and bake in a 350-degree oven for 30-40 minutes. Let stand 10 minutes before serving.

Makes 8 servings

You may assemble the casserole ahead of time, cover and refrigerate overnight. May be frozen and thawed in refrigerator.

*My friend Diana's mom Carolyn introduced me to friendly, tasty noodles. They're similar to vermicelli with a kick of spices and a change from rice.*

# Fideo Noodles

1 15-ounce package fideo noodles
1 small can tomato sauce
½ cups water
2 garlic cloves, minced
½ cup chopped onion
1 red bell pepper, chopped
¼ tsp. cumin, chili powder
½ tsp. salt and pepper
3 tbsp. olive oil

Sauté onion, pepper and garlic in oil for 1 minute, add the noodles and stir frequently; noodles will brown quickly. Mix in the water, tomato sauce and spices; bring to a boil and reduce heat to a simmer and cover skillet and cook for 12 minutes or until all water has been absorbed.

Makes 6-8 servings

# Green Tomatillo Sauce

1 13-ounce can tomatillos, seeded and drained
1 jalapeño chili, seeds removed, diced
¼ cup chopped cilantro
1 onion, chopped
1 garlic clove
   Salt

   In food processor pulse onion and garlic; add tomatillos and chili and blend until sauce is a puree. Salt to taste.

# Marinated Zucchini Salad

3 Medium zucchini
½ tsp. salt
5 tbsp. white vinegar
1 clove garlic, minced
¼ tsp. dried thyme
½ cup olive oil
1 cup drained canned garbanzo beans
½ cup sliced, black olives
3 green onions, minced
1 canned chipotle chili, drained, and seeded
1 ripe avocado, cut into ½ inch cubes
½ crumbled farmer cheese

    Cut zucchini lengthwise into halves; cut halves crosswise into 1/4 inch thick slices. Place slices in bowl; sprinkle with salt, toss. Spread zucchini on several layers of paper towels; let stand at room temperature for 30 minutes to drain. Combine vinegar, garlic and thyme in a large bowl. Whisk in oil until dressing is thoroughly blended. Pat zucchini dry; add to dressing. Add beans, olives and onions; toss. Refrigerate covered, stirring occasionally up to 4 hours. Just before serving, add chili to salad, stirring gently; add avocado and cheese.

Makes 4-6 servings

# Mexican Cheese Corn Muffins

1 ¼ cups flour
¾ cup corn meal
3 tbsp. sugar
4 tbsp. baking powder
½ tsp. salt
½ cup butter milk
½ cup sour cream
¼ cup oil
1 egg
1 4-ounce can chopped green chilies, drained
½ cup grated cheddar cheese
¼ tsp. cumin

In large bowl combine flour, cornmeal, sugar, baking powder, and salt; mix well. In medium bowl combine milk, sour cream, oil, egg and chilies; beat well. Add to dry ingredients, stirring just until moistened. Fill muffin tins or paper cups inside muffin pan 2/3 full. Bake in a 400 degree oven for 20-25 minutes. Remove from pan.

Makes 12 muffins

# Mexican Meatballs

1 lb. ground beef
1 lb. ground pork or turkey
1 egg, beaten
2 garlic cloves, minced
½ cup finely chopped onion
1 cup bread crumbs
¼ cup raisins
¼ cup toasted pumpkin seeds
1 tbsp. finely chopped jalapeño chile, seeded
¼ tsp. cinnamon and cloves
¼ tsp. coriander and cumin
1 tsp. Mexican oregano
1 16-ounce jar mild salsa verde
1 cup chopped cilantro

Combine all ingredients except salsa and cilantro; mix well and shape into small round balls. Fry meatballs in skillet until tender. Add salsa verde to skillet and gently mix cooked meatballs. Serve on platter and sprinkle cilantro over meatballs.

Serves 25-30

# Mexican Mushrooms

2 cups stuffing mix (unseasoned)
10-12 mushrooms, wiped clean
½ cup thinly sliced green onions
2 cloves garlic, minced
½ tsp. each cumin and chili powder
1 4- ounce can diced green chilies
1 cup jalapeño jack cheese, grated
2 tbsp. olive oil
½ cup chicken broth

Remove mushroom stems and cut off dried ends, finely chop stems. In skillet over medium heat, combine stems, onions, garlic, cumin, chili powder and chicken broth. Cook for about 5 minutes, add the chilies, ½ half of cheese and the stuffing.

Brush mushrooms with olive oil and place in baking dish. Fill each mushroom with filling and sprinkle with remaining cheese.

Bake in a 375-degree oven for 12-15 minutes.

# Mexican Rice

1 cup long grain rice
2 tbsp. vegetable oil
1 ½ cups chicken or vegetable broth
1 cup finely chopped onion
2 garlic cloves, minced
1 large tomato, chopped
1 tsp. finely chopped cilantro
  (optional)
½ tsp. salt

    Sauté the onion, rice and garlic until lightly browned on low heat.  Add the broth, tomato, salt and cilantro; bring to a boil and reduce heat to low.  Simmer covered rice for about 15 minutes or until nearly all the broth is evaporated.  Turn off heat and let set for another 10-15 minutes; fluff with fork.

Makes 4 servings

# Red Chile Sauce

3 canned chipotle chilies
4 garlic cloves, peeled, whole
2 large tomatoes, peeled and chopped
½ tsp. salt
1 cup jarred, roasted red pepper

Place garlic in food processor and pulse until minced. Add remaining ingredients and pulse until blended. Use sauce to make Enchiladas.

# Seafood Filled Avocados

2 tbsp. fresh lime juice
1 tbsp. cider vinegar
2 garlic cloves, minced
1 tsp. lime zest
Salt and pepper
¼ tsp. finely diced jalapeño chili
¼ cup vegetable oil
4 ounces cooked crab meat
8 ounces tiny cooked shrimp
2 tbsp. chopped cilantro
2 large firm-ripe avocados
2 cups shredded Romaine lettuce
Red bell pepper strips
4 green olives
4 lime wedges

Combine lime juice, vinegar, garlic, lime zest and chilies in a small bowl; gradually whisk in oil until thoroughly blended.

Combine crab, shrimp and cilantro in medium bowl. Add dressing; toss lightly with 2 forks to mix. Refrigerate while you prepare avocados. Cut avocados lengthwise into halves. Remove pits and peel. Divide lettuce among 4 serving plates. Top each with 1 avocado half and fill seafood mixture into each hollow avocado.

Garnish with red pepper strips and lime wedges.

Makes 4 servings

# Sour Cream Enchiladas

1 large can green tomatillo sauce
3 cups grated jack cheese
3 cups grated cheddar cheese
1 small container sour cream
1 can cream of chicken soup
1 ½ cups sliced green onion
½ tsp. cumin and chili powder
salt and pepper
4 -5 chicken breasts, cooked and shredded
1 can chopped olives
8-10 corn tortillas, sautéed lightly in oil and drained on paper towels

    Sauté shredded chicken, spices and salt and pepper in olive oil on high heat until browned. Mix together the sour cream and soup until well blended. In each tortilla add some of the green sauce and spread over tortilla. Next add some of the chicken, green onion, both cheeses, olives and roll up; place in a baking dish that has a bit of the green sauce and the sour cream mixture. Repeat until all tortillas are rolled; spread remaining green sauce and sour cream mixture over rolled tortillas. Sprinkle with remaining cheeses, green onion and olives. Bake in a 350-degree oven for 35 minutes or until bubbly. Let stand for 5 minutes or so before serving.

Serves 8-10

# Southwestern Cheesecake Dip

3 8-ounce packages cream cheese, softened
1 cup cottage cheese
4 eggs
2 cups shredded cheddar cheese
1 cup shredded pepper jack cheese
1 4-ounce can diced green chiles
¼ cup finely sliced green onion
1 tbsp. fresh lime juice
1 tbsp. lime zest
1 tsp. cumin
½ tsp. chili powder
½ tsp. cinnamon
¼ cup chopped cilantro
¼ cup yellow corn meal
2 tbsp. flour
3 tbsp. melted butter

 Mix melted butter, flour and butter well and spread onto the bottom of a prepared 9-inch springform pan. Bake in a 325-degree oven for 15 minutes.
 In food processor pulse cream cheese and cottage cheese until smooth. With machine running add eggs one at a time and scrape bowl. Add lime juice, zest, cheeses, chilies, green onions and spices. Pour into pan and bake for 50-60 minutes. Remove and spread sour cream mixture over top and bake an additional 15 minutes. Turn oven off and let set for 15 minutes in oven. Cool on rack. Refrigerate overnight, top with more cheddar cheese, chopped tomatoes, green onion and sliced olives.

## Sauce:

1 container sour cream
½ can chipolata sauce
½ package taco seasoning

# Strawberry Salsa

2 cups strawberries, tops removed and cut into small pieces
1 cup red grapes cut in half
1 cup grape tomatoes, quartered
1 tbsp. finely chopped jalapeño, seeds removed
½ cup finely chopped red onion
¼ cup chopped fresh cilantro
½ cup chopped fresh mint
2 tbsp. lime juice
1 tbsp. lime zest
1 tbsp. balsamic vinegar
Salt and ground pepper

Combine strawberries, tomatoes, pepper, grapes, red onion, mint, cilantro and lime zest in bowl and set aside. Wisk balsamic, lime juice, salt and pepper in another bowl and pour over fruit. Toss and cover with plastic wrap and refrigerate for 2 hours.

Makes 3 cups

*These tacos were enjoyed once a week. Terri tried to stretch the beef mixture by adding the instant oats and to her surprise we were smitten with a taste for more of the good tacos.*

# Terri's Tacos

1 lb. lean ground beef
1 package taco seasoning
Water
½ cup instant oats
2 cups grated cheese
6-8 corn tortillas, pre-cooked, drained
Cooking oil
Chopped tomatoes, onions & olives
Shredded lettuce
Salsa

Brown meat; mash beef to a fine texture. Add seasoning package and a little water; stirring and continue to cook until water has been absorbed; mix in oats. Fill each tortilla shell with meat mixture and cheese and put back into hot oil; cook on both sides until lightly browned, drain well on paper towels. Add taco fixings or enjoy the twice-cooked tacos.

Makes 6-8

*Tropical fruit salsa is an art; a fusion of sweet and tangy flavors!*

# Tropical-Fruit Salsa/Peach Salsa

2 cups fresh peaches, peeled and chopped
¼ cup chopped red pepper
¼ cup chopped green onion
¼ cup finely chopped red onion
4 tbsp. fresh lime juice
1 tsp. lime zest
2 cloves garlic, minced
1 tbsp. seeded jalapeño pepper, finely chopped
2 tbsp. chopped fresh cilantro
1 tsp. sugar
½ tsp. coriander

Combine all ingredients and mix well. Refrigerate for 2 hours before serving.

Makes 2 cups

# Pineapple Salsa

2 cups fresh pineapple, sliced thin
2 tbsp. honey
2 tbsp. fresh lime juice
2 tbsp. pineapple juice
1 tsp. orange zest
2 green onions, finely chopped
1 tbsp. seeded and finely chopped jalapeño pepper
½ tsp. fresh oregano
½ tsp. salt
pinch of cinnamon

Combine all ingredients and mix well. Refrigerate for 1 hour, stirring occasionally to blend flavors. Serve at room temperature.

Makes 2 cups

*Chapter 23*

# Caterer's Pride Gets Its Due

*If I were asked the question, what is my greatest accomplishment in my life? I would have to say it is by far my children; they are my greatest joy. They are my pride and joy. The following recipes are similar to this pride. After years of testing and client request to recreate; how else can I relate to recipes that are sought after but to say, here is my pride and joy. Enjoy!*

# Baked Salmon with Boston Glaze

1 large salmon filet
2 cups maple syrup
1 cup brown sugar
¼ cup red wine
3 tbsp. Worcestershire sauce

    Whisk together all ingredients and pour over salmon. Bake in a 350 degree oven for 30-40 minutes; remove and let cool. Place salmon on a large platter and drizzle sauce on top. Sauce will be thick.

Serves 12

*My friend Sandy served these amazing slices of heaven with soup for dinner one evening and I can't even remember what else was served because my focus was on this new find! I have made them for the last year and every person that has tasted them has commented or asked what they are? What a great and simple appetizer at the last minute or bread for a meal; a must at every party.*

## Basil Spread on Baguettes

1 cup grated Parmesan cheese
1 cup mayonnaise
½ cup chopped fresh basil leaves
1 tsp. fresh minced garlic
1 baguette, sliced

    Mix all ingredients well and spread on French bread or baguette. Bake in a 350-degree oven for 12-15 minutes or until golden and bubbly; let set about 3 minutes before serving.

Makes about 20 slices

# Beef Wellington

3 pounds filet of beef, well trimmed
½ cups sliced fresh mushrooms
1 tbsp. Madeira wine
1 3-ounce package cream cheese
1 cup finely chopped onions
1 shallot, minced
2 garlic cloves, minced
1 tbsp. butter
1 tbsp. brandy
1 tbsp. cognac
1 tbsp. cream
1 tsp. nutmeg
1 cup chopped fresh mushrooms
   Salt and pepper
1 package of phillo pastry
   Melted butter

For the Pâté; in skillet sauté onions, shallots and garlic in butter, add mushrooms, salt and pepper, brandy, cognac, cream and nutmeg and cook for 1 minute. Add cream cheese and mix well; set aside.

Slice meat in small cubes, toss with salt and ground pepper and sauté for only 1 minute on high heat, mix in 1 tbsp. of Madeira wine. Unwrap fillo and lay on counter with towel covering fillo. Lay 2 pieces of the fillo at a time on working surface and brush with melted butter. Slice in half length wise; lay a few beef pieces, mushroom pâté and some of the 1 cup sliced mushrooms, salt and pepper. Wrap Wellingtons by folding sides in and starting at end nearest you fold over and wrap upward until completely wrapped. Brush with melted butter and lay in baking dish. Continue making 6 more Wellingtons. Bake in a 350-degree oven for 30-45 minutes or until golden.

Serve with king sauce also found in Caters Pride Chapter.

Makes 8 servings

*This is another one of those recipes that has been pleaded for quite some time. I created the honey effect as the glue that held the topping on while it adds a touch of sweetness that is unexpected and cannot be seen.*

## Brie with Walnut Topping

1 8-inch round Brie
1 cup chopped walnuts
2 tbsp. butter
3 tbsp. sugar
  Pinch of cinnamon
  Honey

Melt butter and add sugar, cinnamon and walnuts and mix well. Pour good amount of honey on top of Brie; followed by walnut mixture. Drizzle honey over top of walnuts; add strawberry in center and dried cranberries or blueberries.

Serves 15-20 guests

# Champagne Rice

3 cups wild rice
3 cups white rice
8 cups chicken or vegetable broth
4 cups champagne
2 cups chopped green onion
1 tbsp. salt
1 tsp. pepper
2 cups toasted slivered almonds
4 sticks butter

Sauté green onion and rice with butter in large skillet or pot, stirring not to burn. Warm broth and champagne in separate pan. Pour over rice and mix well. Pour into buttered baking dish and cover with foil and bake in a 350 degree oven for 35-45 minutes or until fluffy. Fluff rice with fork and add almonds.

Serves 30

## Champagne Walnuts

3 cups whole walnuts or pecans
1 egg white, beaten to fluff
   Dash cinnamon and nutmeg
¼ cup sugar
3 tbsp. champagne

Whisk egg white, add sugar, spices and champagne and fold into walnuts. Pour onto a greased baking sheet and bake in a 350 degree oven for 20 minutes; turn once and continue baking for 10 minutes or so. Cool and serve with salads. Stores well in containers and will freeze.

## Lemon Bavarian Dip

2 cups sour cream
1-8 ounce container lemon yogurt
1- small box lemon instant pudding
1/2 tsp. lemon extract
juice of 1 lemon
1 tsp. lemon zest

In food processor or mixer add all ingredients and blend for about 1 minute. If too thick add a little more lemon juice or milk. Serve with fresh fruit and especially strawberries.
Makes 3 cups.

*My daughter Kellie found this recipe and sent it to me in 1992. I have made this so many times I don't care if I never make it again, except that it really is a good entrée recipe. Doris my baker and daughter Katie helped one evening late into the night making about 300 of these. Neither one of them were very happy with me at the moment. Katie was only 7 or 8 years old and she got so good at wrapping the chickens, she looked up at me and said, "Mom, I can do this, find something else to do." And I did.*

*The King sauce makes it perfect. Beautiful presentation for individual plates or platter.*

## Chicken Breasts in Phyllo

4-6 large chicken breasts
½ pound Phyllo
1 stick butter, melted

## Filling

1 package frozen spinach, drained well
2 cup sliced mushrooms
8 ounces feta cheese
   Salt and pepper
   Dried dill

Unwrap phyllo and cover with towel. Bring two pieces of pasty to work counter at a time, using a pastry brush cover sides and middle of phyllo with butter. Cut down the middle of pastry making two large pieces. Place chicken breast in center at on end. Season with salt and pepper and dill. Sprinkle spinach, mushrooms and cheese on top. Fold both sides in and begin wrapping towards opposite end until completely folded. Brush ends well with butter and place in a baking dish. Bake in a 350 degree oven for 45 minutes or until golden.

# Ricotta Filling

3 cups chopped fresh spinach
   or 2 packages frozen, squeezed
1 ½ cups shredded Swiss cheese
1 cup ricotta cheese
½ onion, chopped
3 garlic cloves, minced
   Dash of nutmeg
   Salt and cracked pepper

In bowl blend together ricotta, onion, garlic, nutmeg, salt and pepper. Prepare fillo as above, spread ricotta filling on top of chicken; adding spinach and cheese. Wrap and spread with melted butter; bake as above.

Pour king sauce on platter and place chicken breasts over sauce and drizzle sauce on top of chicken.

*This is one of the dishes I have gotten the best reviews on. It is also my friend Vicky's favorite entrée I make and we served this for one of her son's rehearsal dinner. Excellent!*

## Chicken in Madeira Sauce

4 pounds package chicken tenders cooked (poach)
1 stick butter
1 shallot, minced
4 green onion, thinly sliced
16 ounces mushrooms, trimmed and sliced
4 cups chicken broth
2 tbsp. tomato paste
2 bay leaves
2 cups heavy whipping cream
1 cup half-and-half
Salt and ground pepper
½ cup dry Madeira
¼ cup flour
4 tbsp. cognac
2 tbsp. Dijon mustard

In a skillet sauté the green onion and shallots in 2 tbsp. butter adding the mushrooms and salt; cooking for 5 minutes or until almost all the juices have evaporated. Add the Madeira and boil for 1 minute. Set aside.

In a saucepan, melt the remaining butter and add the flour and cook for 2 minutes. Add stock, tomato paste, bay leaf and mushroom mixture and bring to a boil, stirring constantly. Lower heat to low and cook, stirring until thickened and smooth; continue simmering on low while stirring for 15 minutes. Add creams and cook uncovered for 5 minutes to thicken sauce. Add cognac and mustard and season to taste. Fold in chicken and serve. May be chilled for 24 hours after adding creams and before the chicken is added. Serve with rice.

Serves 12-15

# Chicken Tortellini Salad

1 Deli herb roasted chicken, shredded, set aside
1 cup red grapes cut in half
2 packages fresh cheese tortellini, cooked and cooled
½ cup cherry tomatoes cut in half
Homemade croutons
1 cup grated Parmesan cheese
Bottled Caesar dressing
Salt and cracked pepper
1 head romaine lettuce, torn

Toss all ingredients and lightly mix in dressing as needed, season to taste.

*This chicken dish was on the menu for my daughter Kellie's wedding. Displayed in a salad bowl dressed in basil and lime slices is a beautiful presentation.*

## Chicken with Basil and Lime

6-8 chicken breasts cut into strips or packaged chicken strips
Olive oil
5 garlic cloves, minced
2 shallots, minced
½ cup fresh basil leaves
1 tsp. minced jalapeno pepper
1 tsp. dried tarragon
1 ½ cup fresh lime juice
1 tsp. sugar
Salt and ground pepper
2 cups good olive oil

Salt and pepper chicken and sauté in olive oil and 1 tbsp. minced garlic on high heat for 2 minutes. Turn heat to low, cover and simmer for 5 minutes or until tender, but not over done.

Whisk together remaining ingredients and add cooled chicken and refrigerate 24 hours, turning several times.

Line a platter or serving bowl with lots of fresh basil leaves. Drain chicken removing other ingredients and place chicken over basil and garnish with lime slices.

Serves 15

*Another recipe from my friend Suzie with raving reviews!*

# Cilantro Chicken

4 chicken breasts, cubed
3 garlic cubes, minced
½ cup chopped onion
1 cup chopped zucchini
1 cup chopped carrots
2 cans chicken broth
1 15-ounce can diced tomatoes
½ tsp. each, cumin, ginger, cinnamon, coriander, nutmeg
1/8 tsp. paprika
2 tbsp. fresh cilantro
   Salt and pepper

Sauté chicken pieces in olive oil and garlic for about 5 minute. Add vegetables and continue sautéing for another 3 minutes. Add spices, broth, tomatoes and cook for 35 minutes on low heat. Add cilantro and salt and pepper to taste. Serve over rice.

Serves 6-8

# Cranberry Pear and Romaine Salad

10 cups romaine lettuce leaves
1 cup shredded Swiss cheese
1 apple, sliced thin
2 pears, sliced thin
½ cup dried cranberries
   Sugared pecans
12 red onion rings

# Poppy Seed Dressing

½ cup sugar
½ cup red wine vinegar
2 tbsp. lemon juice
2 tbsp. finely chopped onion
½ tsp. salt
2/3 cup oil
2 tsp. poppy seeds

Mix all salad ingredients together, toss with dressing just before serving.

*If you want to really impress your guests, well at least the guys or find a place for the guys to watch football or a television sport so the girls can mingle in their own corner and do girl talk, this is just the dish to make sure the guys will not bother you. Put out the beer and toothpicks and they'll be happy as a clam! Or if you are doing serious elegant entertaining this meatball sauce is sensational.*

# European Meatball Sauce

Pre made packaged meatballs, or your favorite recipe- using nutmeg in the ingredients is good.

# Sauce

3 cans beef broth
2 tbsp. butter
2 tbsp. flour
2 tbsp. dried dill
Salt and pepper
1 cup whipping cream
1 cup half-and-half

In saucepan melt butter and whisk in flour and cook for 2-3 minutes. Whisk in broth, salt and pepper and dill and cook 5 minutes on low heat. Add creams, and simmer for 2 minutes. Heat meatballs in oven or crock-pot. Pour sauce over meatballs and cook in crock-pot for 2-3 hours on low; turn heat to warm until serving, stirring a few times. This recipe will heat and serve 150 meatballs.

Serves 40-50 guests

# Home Made Croutons

Extra sour dough or
Baguette cubes
Butter
Olive oil
2 tbsp. minced garlic
dried oregano, thyme, basil
Pinch of dried sage

    In saucepan mix all ingredients and simmer for 10 minutes on low. Toss butter mixture with bread cubes and lay in a prepared baking sheet. Bake in a 350-degree over for 20-30 minutes, turning once. Turn oven off and leave in for 10 minutes; take out and cool. After completely cool, package or serve on salad. Keeps up to 2 weeks and will freeze for a month or so.

*This is a simple little sauce I made up to go on top of chicken, crepes, beef Wellington and that is why someone named it the King Sauce.*

## King Sauce

2 tbsp. butter
2 tbsp. olive oil
2 tbsp. four
1 cup chicken stock
2 cups cream
½ can cream of mushroom soup
1 tsp. dried dill
   salt and white pepper
1 cup white wine
2 cups sliced mushrooms

In saucepan melt butter and oil; whisk in flour and cook for 2 minutes. Add stock and cook until creamy; add cream, wine, and soup and mix well. Cook for 5 minutes or so and add dill, salt and pepper and sliced mushrooms. Continue cooking for 10 minutes on low, turn off heat and let set a bit. Can be refrigerated; adding a little water and reheating.

*Years ago, the first time I made this was for a baby shower. I thought it would be light and something women would love. Then I made it for a job and OMG everyone raved about it and mostly the men. I make it for nearly every occasion and so many people have asked for this recipe. Here it is, enjoy!*

# Lemon Mousse

2 large boxes or 4 small lemon Jell-O
4 cups boiling water
2 8-ounces cream cheese, softened
1 cup walnuts, chopped fine
1 tsp. lemon extract
2 tbsp. lemon zest
1 container cool whip, or
2 cups whipped, whipping cream

Pour boiling water over jell-o while whisking; let cool a bit. In bowl of electric mixer blend cream cheese, add jell-o, lemon extract and zest. Put bowl in refrigerator and cool until starting to firm. Put bowl back on mixer and blend in the walnuts and topping, mixing well. Pour into a 6-cup mold. Refrigerate overnight. Un mold on platter, dish or glass pedestal. Garnish with a bit of Kale around sides and thinly sliced lemons and a few blueberries. Fill inside of tube with blueberries. Beautiful!

*I made these tarts for one of my first weddings I catered in 1989 - in honor of Bob and Suzanne. Such a hit of the party!*

## Lemon Ricotta Tarts

2 cups fresh Ricotta cheese
1 3- ounce package cream cheese
1 cup sugar
¼ cup fresh lemon juice
1 tsp. lemon extract
1 tbsp. lemon zest
2 eggs
1 egg white
1 tsp. flour

In food processor cream cheeses and sugar, add juice, extract, and zest. With machine running add eggs, eggs white and flour. Pour into tart shells and bake in a 350 degree oven for 35-40 minutes or set in center. Cool completely and refrigerate overnight.

# Tart Pastry

1 cup flour
½ cup butter
1 tsp. baking powder
　Pinch of salt
1 egg
1 tbsp. milk

　　Mix all ingredients, place in refrigerate for 15 minutes.  Cover bottom and sides of tart tins. Makes 36 mini tarts

# Mai Tai Bowl

1/3 cup fresh lime juice
4 tbsp. honey
2 tbsp. light rum
1 tbsp. orange liqueur
1 tsp. lime zest

Mix all ingredients well. Cut a pineapple in half, leaving top in tack; hollow out inside. Mix dressing, tossing gently with assorted fresh cut fruit and marinate for 1 hour. Pour into pineapple shells and serves.

Serves 6-8

*I guess I have a hard time serving anything that looks ordinary and looks like it needs some vim and vigor or call it zest. It would be like just dancing and a snap of the finger take the orchestra to the momba or the rumba. Now that's my kind of enthusiasm!*

## Marinated Olives

2 cans black olives
1 jar Kalama olives
1 jar green garlic stuffed olives
4 tbsp. olive oil
2 tbsp. balsamic vinegar
3 garlic cloves crushed
5 whole garlic cloves
   Dried oregano, basil
   Italian herb blend
   Fresh Rosemary and thyme

Drain olives and rinse. In mixing bowl combine all ingredients and toss well. Marinate for several hours or overnight. Olives keep well for weeks. Serve as part of anti pasta tray or in a serving dish; at room temperature. Be prepared for guests to rave!

*Years ago I had a sit down - served catering event and the guest's main requests was paella. I went right to petrified mode while telling my client that I would be more than happy to accommodate them with this wonderful Spanish dish. I immediately began researching cookbooks and what I found was a wonderful history of a dish that could tell a story. Paella is a famous dish and like Italian Polenta, it's a Spanish poor man's supper. The great thing is every person that has a recipe has a different version of paella, so with the rice add seafood, chicken or chorizo or all three. It's fun, festive, elegant or plain supper in the middle of the week. Enjoy!*

# Paella

¼ cup olive oil
1 frying chicken, pre cut
1 pound Italian sausage, sliced
1 pound jumbo shrimp, deveined
1 pound scallops
1 cup finely chopped onion
3 cloves garlic, minced
1 red and green pepper, seeded and chopped
1 ½ cups chopped fresh tomato
2 cups chicken broth
1 bottle clam juice
1 box frozen peas
1 tsp. oregano
1 small bay leaf
½ tsp. saffron
1 tsp. Spanish paprika
3 cups raw long grain rice
½ cup dry white wine or dry sherry

Sauté chicken and sausage in olive oil and cook on both sides for about 5 minutes; remove from pan.

In same pan sauté onion, garlic, peppers, tomatoes, salt and pepper, bay leaf, oregano, saffron and paprika for 2 minutes. Add broth, wine, clam juice and bring to a boil, add rice and chicken, cover and simmer for 10 minutes.

Place shrimp and scallops on top of rice. Cover and cook on low heat for 15-20 minutes. Sprinkle peas over paella and cover for a few minutes while dish sets.

Serves 6-8

*This recipe is from my daughter Korrie and is one of the best dressings I have ever tasted. When it's time to plan for a family dinner, Korrie is expected to make her dressing. We mix it with romaine and that is all it needs. Many a dinner, I have been stuffed and Korrie and I sip wine and indulge in the remaining salad, it could have been the meal. Now I use it for a dressing in catering and it's always a hit.*

## Parmesan Lemon Dressing

Juice of 2 lemons
5 garlic cloves, minced
½ -1 cup extra virgin olive oil
Salt and pepper
¼ cup grated Parmesan cheese
1 tbsp. Spike Seasoning
1 head fresh romaine lettuce
Good loaf of crusty French bread

Whisk all ingredients and add oil last. Let set for several hours before mixing into the lettuce.

# Pork Tenderloins with Blackberry Sauce and Blackberry Chutney

2 ½ pound pork tenderloins
1 tsp. minced thyme
1 tbsp. fresh rosemary
½ tsp. cinnamon and allspice
4 garlic cloves, minced
4 tbsp. balsamic vinegar
2 tbsp. water
  Fresh ground pepper
  Salt

Trim fat from tenderloins. Mix together next 8 ingredients and rub well over pork and place in zip lock bags. Refrigerate 24 hours, turn occasionally for even marinating.

Grill meat on medium to high heat, turning until cooked through about 30 minutes. Let rest 5 minutes before slicing. Serve with sauce and chutney.

## Blackberry Sauce:

¼ cup water
1 tbsp. cornstarch
¼ cup blackberry jam
3 tbsp. balsamic vinegar
1 tbsp. brown sugar
2 tbsp. honey
¼ cup blackberry liqueur
½ cup blackberries

In saucepan on low heat, combine the jam, vinegar, brown sugar, honey, and liqueur, cooking for about 2 minutes or until jam is melted. Dissolve cornstarch in water and stir into liquid, cook until thick, about 2 minutes. Toss in berries.

# Blackberry Chutney

1 tbsp. garlic, minced
1 orange, peeled and cut into chunks
1 tsp. orange zest
1 fresh pear, diced
1 cup blackberries
3 cups blueberries
¼ cup brown sugar
½ cup balsamic vinegar
1 tbsp. dried tarragon
   Salt

In saucepan over medium heat sauté the garlic for 1 minute. Add the remaining ingredients and cook over low heat for 45 minutes, stirring occasionally, until thickened. Refrigerate up to 1 month.

*By accident or in a hurry; along came Pumpkin Spice Butter to decorate the pumpkin bread. Talk of the wedding!*

# Pumpkin Spice Butter

1 cup butter, softened
½ cup brown sugar
1 tsp. cinnamon
1 tsp. nutmeg
2 tbsp. pumpkin pie spice
½ cup powdered sugar

In food processor combine all ingredients and pulse. Scrap sides and continue mixing. Pour into crock or serving bowl. Butter lasts up to 2 weeks in refrigerator.

*Here it is, the number one asked for recipe in my entire life. First let me give you a little history about it. My friend Diana gave me this recipe in the 80's as it was given to her by her dear friend Cathy. A few years went by and I hadn't tried it and Diana was still urging me to make this great dip. She tried to explain to me that it was one of Cathy's recipes and anything that Cathy makes is excellent. Finally I decided to try it for a catering event and made it with shrimp as that is what the original recipe calls for. In just this one event, I must have had a dozen guests ask me for the recipe or tell me that was the greatest thing they had ever tasted. Little do I need to say why I have continued to make it, only I have gone from shrimp to crab to mock crab and that is why I call it Sea Food Dip. The original name was Shrimp Dip. From family to friends to strangers, this is the first food item dipped into at every occasion. Enjoy!*

*When Diana gives you a recipe she looks at you and says, "Trust me;" meaning that it's the best thing in heaven. I came across the original paper she wrote the recipe down on and at the top of the page it reads: "It's been waiting and it will happen." After the ingredients she wrote: "Appetizer Heaven!" She knew!*

# Sea Food Dip

1-2 lbs. fresh baby shrimp or 1 pound mock crab
2-3 cups grated cheddar cheese
1 cup mayonnaise
1 cup sour cream
5 green onions, sliced
5-6 drops (or more) Tabasco sauce

If using crab or mock crab, put it in food processor and pulse until crumbly. Pour into mixing bowl and blend with remaining ingredients. Chill well. Serve in a bowl that sets in a bowl of ice. Keeps well for several days; serve with crackers or baguettes.

Serves 25

## Seafood Crêpes

# Crêpes:

8 eggs
1 tsp. salt
4 cups whole milk
2-2 ½ cups flour
¼ cup melted butter

In mixer bowl whip eggs and salt for 3 minutes. With mixer running add milk and flour alternately, starting and ending with flour. Add melted butter, blend. Pour into container and chill for 2 hours.  Using a crêpe pan, tilt and move pan in a circular motion while adding crêpe batter; making sure sides and center is lightly coated.  Cook for 1-2 minutes each side.  Let cool several hours, covered lightly.  Makes about 25-30 crêpes.

# Filling:

1 pound small cleaned salad shrimp
1 pound cleaned, flaked fresh crab
2 cups thinly sliced mushrooms
Salt and pepper
3-4 cups grated Swiss cheese
1 cup grated Parmesan cheese
2 cups grated jack cheese

# Sauce:

2 tbsp. butter
1 tbsp. olive oil
3 garlic cloves, minced
2 tbsp. flour
½ cup chicken broth
2 cups cream
½ cup dry white wine
1/2 tsp. nutmeg
1 tsp. seafood seasoning
Sea salt and cracked pepper

Melt butter and oil and sauté garlic for 1 minute.  Add flour and cook on low heat for 2 minutes.  Add chicken broth and wine, blend and simmer for 5 minutes.  Add cream and seasonings; cook on low, stirring for 5 minutes or until thickened.

Mix cheeses together, set aside.  Mix shrimp, crab and mushroom and season well with salt and pepper.  Sprinkle a small amount of seafood in each crêpe and add cheese.  Roll up and lay in casserole dish that has about 1 ½ cups sauce in bottom.  Continue until all crêpes are finished.  Pour sauce over top and sprinkle remaining cheese over sauce.  Bake in a 300 degree oven, covered for about 25 minutes.  Remove cover and bake in a 350-400 degree oven for 5-8 minutes.  Let rest for 5 minutes before serving.

*This is the recipe that won 1st place in the Paradise Butte Community Bank cooking contest in 1996 by Peggy Berry. After weeks of cooking classes I ended it with an appetizer contest and I was thrilled with the dishes these gals arrived with. Now these are bankers, bookkeepers, intelligent people who usually don't work out of the box and whom I drove crazy by demonstrating without measurements. So they all came out of the box, arrived with beautiful platters and blew me away! Well it doesn't end there. Of course I am not going to throw a good recipe out the door, so I started making and serving them and after 11 years, these little guys are the most asked for appetizer of all. Peggy, you did well!*

## Smoked Turkey with Pesto Cream Sauce

1-2 sour dough baguette
1 cup mayonnaise
½ cup prepared pesto sauce
Deli smoked turkey, sliced thin

Slice baguettes. Mix mayonnaise and pesto and spread on bread and top with turkey. Simple, elegant and a winner! Enjoy.

*Here is another Diana recipe. It's a fabulous salad. This is what Diana would say about it. "It's over the top, rock star!"*

*When I looked over this faded, smudged piece of paper, I noticed she wrote smished instead of smashed. My spell check alerted me that this word is not in the dictionary (no kidding). This woman has a brain and language of her own! Then I turn the paper over and this is what she wrote next to the name of the eye drop she jotted down for me. "For when you've been up half the night making 75 other entrees to make someone's special event incredible!" Smiley face. I get teary eyed when I read that part. Now it's no longer the recipe, it's the knowing that a friend gets who you are!*

## Spinach Cauliflower Toss

½ cup pine nuts and almonds each
½ pound spinach, stems removed and torn into bite size pieces
2 cups cauliflower florets, bite size pieces
1 large or 2 small avocadoes
Lemon juice
6 tbsp. olive oil
3 tbsp. balsamic vinegar
2 cloves garlic, smished up
½ tsp. salt, dry mustard, basil
Salt and pepper
Dash of nutmeg

Sauté nuts in butter and set aside. Smash avocado and add some lemon juice. Combine oil, vinegar, garlic, salt, mustard, spices. Add avocado and mix until well blended. Pour dressing over salad, add nuts and toss lightly until well coated.

Serves 6

# Tri-Tip Garlic Ginger Sauce

16 ounces teriyaki sauce
16 ounces teriyaki glaze sauce
¼ cup fresh ginger, minced
6 garlic cloves, minced
¼ cup red wine
1/8 cup Worcestershire sauce

Whisk all ingredients and use to marinade tri-tip over night. Roast meat uncovered in a 400 degree oven for 1 hour 30 minutes. I usually keep about a cup or so separate and use it to drizzle over meat after cooked.

*This is another recipe from the Paradise Butte Community Bank cooking contest. I have used it ever since and my guests love it.*

## Valerie's Dip

2 8-ounce packages cream cheese
1 package buttermilk ranch dressing
1 envelope Knox gelatin
4 tbsp. cold water
1 jar marinated artichokes, drained and diced
1 jar roasted red peppers, drained and diced
½ cup chopped fresh parsley

    Prepare 3 cup mold with cooking spray. In food processor mix cream cheese and package dressing mix and add parsley. Mix gelatin with water and dissolve. Heat on low for a minute; stirring. Add gelatin to cheese mixture. Pour part of mixture into mold, veggies and end with cheese mixture. Refrigerate overnight. Un mold onto serving dish and serve with crackers. I use sun dried tomatoes with the veggies if I have them on hand.

Serves 15-20 guests

## Chapter 24

# Simply Sandarella's Formulas

*Every now and then I run into one of my old restaurant customers and they always tell me how much they miss the food served there. I feel my eyes sting and try not to tear up for I miss them as much as they miss the food and magic of Sandarella's.*

*Coming to Sandarella's, was a nice change from fast food and rushed boxed lunches. On a cold day a bowl of soup felt like a warm hug and even a cup of coffee tasted different. I don't know that I will ever understand the collective ingredients that made up such a sunshiny happy lunch. Somehow I think my heart was one of the ingredients.*

*The following recipes are the favorites of so many people and for every recipe is a fond memory that goes with it.*

# Banana Oat Bread

1 cup sugar
½ cup butter
2 eggs
2 medium bananas, mashed
½ cup sour cream
1 tsp vanilla
2 cups flour
1 tsp. baking soda
1 tsp. baking powder
½ tsp. salt
1/3 cup rolled oats

    Beat together eggs, butter, sugar, bananas, vanilla and sour cream. Mix all dry ingredients together and slowly add to wet mixture. Pour into a buttered loaf pan. Bake 50-60 minutes. Cool and remove from pan. Cool completely and wrap tightly and store in refrigerator.

Makes one loaf

# Basil – Tomato Quiche

1 pkg. refrigerated unbaked piecrust
4 eggs beaten
2 tbsp. mayonnaise
1/2 tsp. nutmeg
1 cup half and half
1 ½ cups grated mozzarella cheese
½ cup grated Parmesan cheese
6 Roma tomatoes, sliced
1 cup fresh basil leaves, stems removed
4 garlic cloves, minced
Salt and freshly ground pepper

Prepare pie crust in pie dish. Mix both cheeses together and add half in pie shell. Place basil leaves on top following with the tomato slices and garlic and remaining cheese. Add cream, mayonnaise, nutmeg and salt and pepper to beaten eggs and pour over cheese mixture. Bake for 50-60 minutes in a 350 degree oven.

# Cheese and Vegetable Strata

8 cups cubed white bread
½ cup onion, chopped fine
2 cups chopped broccoli
1 zucchini sliced thin
2 cups grated cheddar cheese
1 jar sliced pimento, drained
6 eggs
3 cups milk
1 tbsp. Dijon mustard
Salt and pepper

    Butter a 13x9 inch baking dish and layer bread, cheese and vegetables in dish. Beat eggs, add milk, mustard, salt and pepper and pour over vegetable mixture. Refrigerate 4-6 hours or overnight.
    Bake uncovered in a 325 degree oven for 55-70 minutes or until knife inserted comes out clean. Let stand a few minutes before serving.

12-15 servings

*This recipe is from an old friend Renee, a friend of mine and Diana's. I made this cheesecake once a week and took orders for it. Never have tasted a better chocolate cheesecake; hard to beat.*

# Chocolate cheesecake

## Crust:

In food processor mix ¾ cup butter, ¼ cup flour, ¼ cup sugar and 1 egg yolk. Shape into a ball and chill at least 1 hour or overnight.

## Filling:

2 ½ lbs. block Gina Marie
  cream cheese
2 ½ cups sugar
2/3 cup and 2 tbsp.
  cocoa powder
2 tsp. vanilla
5 eggs

## Topping:

1 large carton sour cream
2-3 tbsp. sugar

Press 1/3 of dough into bottom of a springform pan. Bake in a 400 degree oven for 8 minutes; remove, cool slightly. Flour hands and press dough to sides of pan.

In food processor blend cream cheese, sugar, cocoa, vanilla. Add eggs one at a time and blend well after each. Pour into pan and bake in a 350 degree oven for 45-50 minutes. Jiggle and if not moving cool 10 minutes. Spread sour cream mixture over top of cheesecake. Bake in a 400-degree oven for 10 minutes. Turn oven off and leave in oven for 1 hour.

Cool on wire rack for several hours, cover and refrigerate overnight.

*This applesauce was one of the side dishes I made each week and served with a sandwich or slice of quiche. This one was frequently ask for and some would comment that it was like having dessert with lunch.*

# Country French Applesauce

2 lbs. tart apples
¼ cup apple juice
½ cup sugar
1 tsp. lemon juice
½ tsp. cinnamon
½ tsp. nutmeg
½ cup sour cream
1 ½ tbsp. flour
   Slivered toasted almonds
   Crushed macaroons
   Butter

Peel and core apples into quarters. Cook apples with apple juice in covered pot for about 20 minutes on low heat. Cool, put in food processor and pulse until smooth. Add sugar, lemon juice, cinnamon, nutmeg, sour cream and flour and pulse just to mix.

Place in a buttered baking dish. Melt a little butter and mix in almonds and macaroons and sprinkle over applesauce. Bake in a 400 degree oven for 15 minutes. Serve warm.

*I was surprised how many customers ask for this soup and loved it. I served it with a little grated apple and slivered almonds and it became a regular menu item.*

# Cream of Carrot Soup

2 lbs. carrots, cleaned and sliced
4 cups canned vegetable stock
2 tsp. salt
2 tbsp. olive oil
1 small onion, chopped
2 garlic cloves, minced
½ tsp. thyme
Salt and pepper
1 cup milk
1 cup buttermilk
3 tbsp. sour cream
½ tsp. nutmeg
Pinch of ground ginger

In soup pot bring stock, carrots and salt to a boil, cover and simmer for 20 minutes, remove from heat and cool. Sauté onion, garlic, thyme, salt and pepper in olive oil for about 2 minutes while stirring.

Puree carrots and onions in blender or food processor until smooth; return to soup pot. Warm soup and whisk in milk, buttermilk, sour cream, and spices. Serve with grated apple and slivered almonds on top.

Serves 6

# Cream of Zucchini Soup

2 tbsp. butter
½ onion, minced
2 garlic cloves, minced
1 tbsp. flour
½ tsp. each chopped fresh thyme, basil, tarragon
   Salt and pepper
6 cups zucchini, cut into bite size pieces, steamed
4 cups milk, warmed
1 cup cream

    Sauté onion, garlic and salt and pepper and herbs in butter for 2 minutes; stir in flour and cook for 1 minute. Add milk gradually to onion mixture and cook while stirring for about 5 minutes on low heat, remove from heat.
    Puree all ingredients in blender and return soup to pot and add cream, heating on low for a few minutes. Do not boil. Serve with a dollop of sour cream and chives.

Serves 4-6

    *I served this soup every Friday because it was so requested that I decided to just pick a day and let everyone know it. There was never a drop left. It started with just plain potato soup and one day I decided to add some cheese, but didn't want it to taste like a sauce so I added the chilies for a kick and that put the boot in it!*

# Potato Chili Cheese Soup

3 potatoes, cubed small, with peel left on
3-4 cups water
2 tbsp. butter
½ cup onion, chopped fine
1 tsp. salt
2 tbsp. flour
1-2 cups milk
½ cup sour cream
1 tsp. cumin
   Salt and ground pepper
1 can diced green chilies
2 cups grated cheddar cheese

Simmer potatoes and salt covered for about 20 minutes or until tender. Drain potatoes and save 1 cup of water. In soup pot sauté onion in butter for 2 minutes and add flour and cook on low for another minute. Whisk in the milk, sour cream, spices, chilies, potatoes, potato water and cheese. Season with salt and pepper and simmer while stirring until the cheese has melted and soup has thickened.

Serves 6

*I made this soup once a week because it was the only homemade soup my daughter Katie would eat. What kid would ask for lentil soup? Every day after school Katie would come to the restaurant and ask if I made the soup or was there any left over from the day before. If she would have known how good it was for her she probably would never have eaten it. The secret to this soup is the fennel seeds.*

# Lentil Soup

2 cups raw lentils
2 cups water
2 cans vegetable broth
1 large can (15 oz.) crushed tomatoes
2 tbsp. olive oil
2 garlic cloves, minced
½ onion, diced
1 cup celery, chopped
1 cup carrots, diced
1 tsp. dried thyme
1 bay leaf
1 tsp. fennel seeds

In soup pot combine lentils, water, broth and bay leaf and bring to a boil, reduce heat and simmer 1 hour or until lentils are tender. Sauté vegetables in oil and garlic until slightly tender, add herbs toss and add to lentils. Stir in tomatoes and fennel seeds and continue to cook for another 20 minutes. Turn off heat and let set for about 30 minutes before serving.

*This is one of those old fashioned soups you just can't go wrong with. It always tastes better the next day and can be frozen.*

## Minestrone Soup

2 cups each chick-peas and kidney beans
5 cups water
2 bay leaves
¼ cup olive oil
2 onions, diced
4 garlic cloves, minced
1 green pepper, diced
1 tsp. fresh oregano, finely chopped
2 tsp. dried basil
1 tsp. dried marjoram
1 tsp. fresh thyme
1 tsp salt
  Freshly ground pepper
1 potato, diced
2 celery stalks, sliced
2 carrots, diced
2 cups broccoli, diced
2 cups cabbage, chopped
2 large cans diced tomatoes
½ cup red wine
½ cup Italian parsley, chopped
1 small bag fresh spinach

In a large soup pot sauté onion and garlic in oil and add green pepper. Gradually add the carrots, celery, broccoli, cabbage, herbs and sauté for 3 minutes. Add remaining ingredients except for parsley and spinach. Simmer for 30 minutes, stir well and add spinach and parsley and season to taste.

Serves 12-15

# Mushroom Barley Soup

6 cups vegetable or beef broth
½ cup uncooked pearled barley
1 bay leaf
¼ cup finely chopped onion
3 cloves garlic, minced
1 tbsp. olive oil
1 carrot, thinly sliced
1 tsp. fresh thyme
   Salt and pepper
3 cups sliced mushrooms
¼ cup chopped green onions
¼ cup cooking sherry
2 tbsp. tamari

In soup pot add broth, barley and bay leaf; simmer for 1 hour. Sauté carrot, onion, thyme and garlic in oil and add to barley. Add mushrooms, sherry, tamari, green onions and season with salt and pepper and simmer for 20 minutes. Let set a bit before serving.

Serves 6

*Doris the baker made these scones every morning and by the end of the day they were gone. It calls for cream of tarter and for some reason she would loose the tarter and it was constantly on the shopping list. I think she was actually tired of making them but our customers wouldn't let her stop. Poor Doris thought it would probably go on forever.*

# Orange Poppy Seed Scones

2 ½ cups all-purpose flour
½ cup granulated sugar
¼ cup poppy seeds
1 tsp. cream of tartar
¾ tsp. baking soda
½ tsp. salt
½ cup butter, chilled
2 eggs
¼ cup orange juice
1 tsp. orange zest
1 egg white for glaze

    Mix dry ingredients and set aside. Cube the butter and with a pastry blender cut in the butter until the mixture resembles crumbs.
    Mix together the eggs, orange juice, and zest. Add egg mixture to flour mixture and stir to combine. Dough will be sticky.
    Flour hands and pat dough into an 8-9 inch-circle. Brush egg white over circle. Cut dough into 8 wedges and place on a prepared baking sheet. Bake in a 375 degree oven for 25 minutes or until top is golden. Cool on a rack for about 5 minutes. Store in container.

Makes 8 scones

# Pear Bread

2 cups peeled, chopped fresh pears
1 cup sugar
½ cup brown sugar
½ cup butter
1 tsp. fresh grated gingerroot
2 eggs
2 cups flour
2 tsp. baking powder
1 tsp. salt
½ tsp. nutmeg

In electric mixer whip butter and add eggs, sugars, gingerroot and pears. Slowly mix flour, baking powder, salt and nutmeg. Add dry ingredients to pear mixture.

Pour into a loaf pan and bake for 50 minutes in a 350 degree oven. Insert a toothpick in center of bread to make sure it comes out clean. Cool on wire rack. Tightly wrap and store in refrigerator.

Makes 1 loaf

*Enjoy a thick slice of this bread covered in Pumpkin-Spice Butter and you'll know you are experiencing a harvest treat!*

# Pumpkin Bread

2 cups flour
1 cup firmly packed brown sugar
¾ cup sugar
½ tsp. cinnamon
4 tsp. pumpkin pie spice
2 tsp baking powder
¼ tsp. salt
½ cup butter softened
3 eggs
1 cup canned pumpkin
1 tbsp. mayonnaise
3 tbsp. orange-flavored liqueur
1 tbsp. orange zest

Gently mix flour with soda, salt and spices, set aside. With mixer blend butter, mayonnaise, eggs sugars, pumpkin, liqueur and zest. Gradually add flour to pumpkin mixture. Pour into a buttered loaf pan and bake 1 hour in a 350 degree oven. Cool completely and tightly wrap and store in refrigerator.

Makes 1 loaf

*Pumpkin-Spice Butter can be found in the Cateers Pride Gets It's Due Chapter.*

# Roasted Turkey and Cucumber Sandwich

Sour dough sliced bread
Packaged or deli roasted turkey, sliced thin
Whipped cream cheese
Dijon mustard
Thinly sliced cucumbers
Lettuce leaves
Sliced tomatoes
Grated carrots
Salt and pepper
Sliced Munster or Provolone cheese

Mix about 1 tbsp. Dijon mustard into some whipped cream cheese and spread on one side of sliced bread. Spread mayonnaise on the other slice. Layer turkey, cucumber, tomato, carrots and salt and pepper; cheese and lettuce leaf, cut in half.

# Scalloped Pineapple

4 cups fresh French bread crumbs
1 20 oz. can pineapple chunks, drained
1/3 cup melted butter
3 eggs, beaten
1 tbsp. flour
2 cups sugar
1 tsp. nutmeg
½ cup grated cheddar cheese

Toss bread crumbs, melted butter and pineapple chunks and pour into a buttered baking dish. Combine remaining ingredients and pour over pineapple. Bake in a 350 degree oven for 40 minutes.

Serves 8

## Side of Beans

1 can black beans, rinsed and drained
½ cup red onion, sliced thin and chopped
   Juice of 1 lime
3-4 garlic cloves minced
3 tbsp. extra virgin olive oil
   Sea salt and ground pepper

Whisk garlic, lime and drizzle in olive oil.  Add salt and pepper and onion.  Pour over beans and toss well.

Wonderful on a bed of butter lettuce, red onion, slice Roma tomatoes and cracked pepper.

# Skillet Frittata

4 tbsp. butter
2 cups diced turkey ham
½ cup sliced green onion
1 green pepper chopped
2 Roma tomatoes, chopped
8 eggs, beaten well
1 cup whipping cream
1 tsp. fresh thyme
1 tsp. dried oregano
1 cup grated Swiss cheese

In large cast iron skillet melt butter. Add ham, onion, green pepper and herbs and sauté for 5-10 minutes on low heat. Add tomatoes and blend. Add cream to eggs and pour over skillet ingredients. Cook over low heat for about 6-8 minutes. Run a spatula around edges to loosen. Cover and cook 5 minutes. Sprinkle cheese over top, cover and cook an additional 5 minutes. Cut into slices and serve with cheese sauce on top.

Serves 6-8

# Cheese Sauce:

3 tbsp. butter
2 tbsp. flour
2 cups whole milk
2 cups cheddar cheese, grated
Dash Tabasco sauce
Dash of tamari sauce
Salt and pepper

Melt butter in sauce pan and add flour, stirring constantly for 2 minutes. Add milk and cook until thickened. Add cheese, salt and pepper and Tabasco and tamari sauces. Cook until cheese is melted.

# Smoked Turkey and Swiss Quiche

4 eggs
1 cup cream
1 tsp. freshly grated nutmeg
  Salt and pepper
2 tbsp. butter
  Dash of olive oil
½ cup chopped onion
½ cup chopped red pepper
2 cups chopped smoked turkey
2 cups grated Swiss cheese
½ cup grated Parmesan cheese
½ tsp. dried tarragon
1/8 tsp. ground coriander and cinnamon
1 prepared pie shell

Sauté onion and pepper in oil and butter for 2 minutes. Add turkey, tarragon, coriander, cinnamon and toss, remove from heat.

Pour turkey vegetable mixture into pie plate and add cheeses and toss lightly. Beat eggs well add cream, nutmeg and salt and pepper. Pour egg mixture into quiche and top with more Swiss cheese. Bake for 50-60 minutes in a 350 degree oven. Let cool 10-15 minutes before serving.

# Split Pea Soup

3 cups dry green peas
4 cups water
2 cups vegetable broth
1 bay leaf
1 tsp. salt
1 small onion, minced
2 garlic cloves, minced
2 carrots, chopped
3 tbsp. olive oil
¼ tsp. thyme
　Salt and pepper

　　Cook peas, salt and bay leaf in water and broth for 1 hour or so. Sauté onion, carrot, garlic and thyme in oil; season with salt and pepper.
　　Remove bay leaf and puree split peas in blender or food processor and return to soup pot. Add vegetable mixture to soup and simmer for 15 minutes on low heat.

Serves 6-8

*The Tabouli salad was the number one requested salad and so I made it every week. It would only last for two days and some of the guests would call ahead of time to see what days I would be serving it as a side dish. The combination of lots of garlic blended with fresh lime juice is irresistible. I bought fresh bulghar from the health food store and started by soaking it. Now I have noticed Tabouli box mixes on the store shelves. As long as you add the mint, lime and cucumber, it would probably be very good.*

# Tabouli Salad

1 cup dry bulghar wheat
1 ½ cups boiling water
2 tsp. salt
½ cup fresh lime juice
1 tsp. lime zest
2-3 tbsp. fresh garlic, minced
2 tbsp. fresh mint
½ cup extra virgin olive oil
½ cup chopped green onion
3 Roma tomatoes diced
1 ½ cups chopped cucumber
¾ cup grated carrots
   Sea Salt and freshly ground pepper

Mix the bulghar, water and salt in a bowl. Cover and let soak for 20-25 minutes. Add lime juice, zest, garlic, oil and mint. Mix and refrigerate for 3-4 hours. Add vegetables and salt and pepper and toss well.

*Arleen worked at Sandarella's for about 2 years. I asked her to make a salad for lunch and she came up with this egg noodle recipe. At first I thought it was not going to go over big with the customers, but after that day it was requested over and over so we made it a part of the menu. Later I asked her where she got the recipe from and she told me it was from my kitchen....it was what she could find at the moment!*

## Turkey Noodle Salad

1  8-ounce bag egg noodles
2  cups chopped turkey
1  cup frozen peas
1  cup sliced celery
½ cup sliced green onion
4  hard boiled eggs, chopped
1 ½ cups mayonnaise
1  tsp. poppy seeds
   Salt and pepper

Boil noodles and drain. Mix remaining ingredients with cooled noodles. Adjust mayonnaise, salt and pepper.

Serves 10

# Waldorf Coleslaw

12 cups white cabbage, chopped
5 Granny Smith apples, peeled, cut into thin strips
2 cups celery, sliced thin
2 cups toasted walnut pieces
1 cup red and green grapes, sliced in half
1 cup plain yogurt
½ cup mayonnaise
1 ½ tbsp. Dijon mustard
4 tbsp. sugar
¼ cup olive oil
¼ cup red wine vinegar
1 tbsp. orange zest
   Salt and pepper to taste

   Mix first 4 ingredients together. Whisk together the remaining ingredients until smooth. Pour dressing over cabbage and mix well. Chill for 3 hours before serving.

# Waldorf Croissant Sandwich

1 can pre cooked chicken, drained and shredded
1 cup thinly sliced celery
1 cup grapes, halved orange zest
½ cup thinly sliced green onion
 mayonnaise
 Salt and pepper
 Chopped walnuts or pecans

Mix all ingredients and spread on one side of croissant and top with lettuce leaf or sprouts.

## Chapter 25

# Take a Gander at Our Thanksgiving Feast

*A little bit country... a little bit refined...a little bit urban...*
*A little bit country...*

# Menu

### Preview Nibbles

Relish Tray ~ Vegetable Crudités
Cheese and Crackers ~ Dill Deviled Eggs
Spinach Soufflé Stuffed Mushrooms

### Dinner

Roasted Turkey ~ Brandied Gravy
Lemon Parsley Stuffing ~ Garlic Mashed Potatoes
Broccoli Casserole ~ Green bean Mushroom Bake
Sweet Potato Soufflé ~ Carrots Le Crème ~ Scalloped Corn and Tomatoes
Chunky Old Fashioned Applesauce ~ Spirited Cranberry Sauce
Cranberry Salad ~ Spinach Salad with Orange-Poppy seed Dressing
Parsley Dinner Rolls ~ Maple Muffins

### Desserts

Pumpkin Chiffon Pie ~ Chocolate Bavarian Pie
Sour Cream Lemon Pie
Gingersnap-Pumpkin Cheese Cake

*I have been making this casserole for about 25 years and it is still my children's favorite dish I make at holidays. I have been asked and pleaded with for this recipe and I am happy to finally share it with you.. This recipe serves about 6-8 guests, just double for a larger crowd.*

# Broccoli Casserole

2-10 ounce boxes chopped frozen broccoli drained
1- can cream of celery soup
½ onion chopped
2- tablespoons mayonnaise
   Salt and pepper
2-3 packs of Ritz Crackers crushed
1/3 cup melted butter

Put crackers in food processor or use rolling pin to crush. Melt butter and mix with crackers, set aside. Squeeze all water from broccoli and mix in soup, onion, mayonnaise and salt and pepper. Dust the bottom of casserole dish with cracker crumbs and add broccoli mixture and top with remaining crumbs. Bake at 350 oven for about 50 minutes. Let stand 15 minutes before serving.

*Simply elegant entrée; forgetting you're eating carrots.*

## Carrots Le Crème

1 to 2 carrots, sliced thin
3 tablespoons butter, divided
4 tablespoons shredded onion
4 cups shredded carrots
1 tablespoon flour
¼ cup chopped fresh parsley
1 egg, beaten
¼ cups half and half or light cream
¼ teaspoon salt
Dash ground white pepper
1 cup Italian bread crumbs

    Preheat oven to 350 degrees.  In medium saucepan cook sliced carrots in small amount of boiling water 3 to 4 minutes or until crisp-tender; drain and set aside.  Melt 2 tablespoons butter in large skillet.  Add onion and shredded carrots; cook and stir over medium heat until carrots wilt.  Sprinkle flour and parsley over shredded carrots; stir to mix in. Place carrot mixture in buttered 9-inch round glass baking dish.  Combine half and half or light cream, egg, salt and pepper.  Pour over shredded carrots. Place sliced carrots on top of mixture.  Melt remaining 2 tablespoons butter; brush sliced carrots with butter and mix remaining in the bread crumbs.  Sprinkle buttered bread crumbs top of carrots.  Bake in oven 30 minutes or until set.

Makes 8 servings.

*This has always been my family's favorite chocolate pie*

## Chocolate Bavarian Pie

9- inch baked pie shell
2 tsp unflavored gelatin
½ cup milk
2 egg yolks
¼ cup sugar
   Dash of salt
1 tsp vanilla
¼ cup chopped sweet chocolate
2 cups heavy cream
   Chocolate curls

    Bake pie shell and let cool. Sprinkle gelatin over ¼ cup cold water. In top of double boiler heat milk until film forms over surface. Beat egg yolks, sugar, salt, and ½ tsp of vanilla until thick and creamy. Beat a small amount of hot milk into egg mixture. Add all of egg mixture to the hot milk mixture and cook for about 5 minutes. Stir in gelatin and chopped chocolate. Continue cooking over simmering water for 3 minutes or until chocolate is melted. Remove from heat, cover and refrigerate until chilled.

    Whip cream with remaining vanilla. Fold half of whipped cream into chocolate mixture. Pour into baked pie shell. Top with remaining whipped cream and garnish with chocolate curls. Chill well before serving.

*A bit like having a little bit of apple pie with dinner*

# Chunky Old Fashioned Apple Sauce

10 Granny Smith apples peeled and cubed
¼ cup apple juice
2-cups sugar
½ cups brown sugar
1 tablespoon cinnamon
½ teaspoon nutmeg
  Pinch of salt


Cook apples and remaining ingredients in covered sauce pan on low heat for about 30 minutes. Pour into bowl and set aside for about 5 minutes. Mash apples just a bit and then finishing cooling and place in refrigerator.

# Cranberry Salad

¾ cup chopped nuts
1 cup heavy cream
1 cup crushed pineapple
2 tbsp mayonnaise
2 tbsp sugar
2 3 oz. package of cream cheese
1 can whole cranberry sauce
¾ cup water
1 package 3 oz. raspberry gelatin
1 cup cottage cheese
1 tbsp lemon juice

Heat water to boiling and pour over gelatin and stir until dissolved and set aside. Puree cottage cheese with lemon juice on high speed in blender until smooth. Add raspberry gelatin and blend again. Pour into bowl and add cranberry sauce, walnuts, pineapple and chill until mixture begins to thicken. Turn into 1 quart mold and chill until firm. Un- mold onto a plate of lettuce or kale.

*This is the green bean recipe you see in the magazines every holiday since about the 1960's. It's got a little twist that takes it back to the old days.*

# Green Bean Bake

4 cans green beans drained
1 small onion sliced in rings
3- 4 strips of bacon
2 cans cream of mushroom soup
2- 4 oz. cans sliced mushrooms
1- 8 oz. can onion rings or
1- 8 oz. can gourmet onion pieces

Fry bacon until half done and drain. Sauté onion slices in bacon for 2 minutes. Mix green beans, soup, sautéed onions, canned mushrooms and half of the canned onion rings. Spread half of mixture in casserole dish and top with bacon and finish spreading green bean mixture, top with onion rings. Bake at 350 for 30 minutes.

*The trick to these potatoes is the seasoning and cream cheese that replaces the milk. I have found that making these early or at least an hour before serving them allows them to firm up with a covered lid and may need a little reheating. My girls are just crazy about these potatoes and can tell if I have done something wrong and they let me know if I did. This year Katie invited her friends for Thanksgiving and asked me not to mess up the potatoes; "I'm counting on you Mom." No pressure!*

## Garlic Mashed Potatoes

7-10 Russet potatoes peeled and cubed
Salted cold water
1-8 ounce cream cheese
1 cube butter
Natures Seasoning
3 cloves garlic chopped or 1 head roasted garlic

Cook potatoes on medium heat in salted water. Check potatoes with a fork and when they are soft and fork goes nearly through potato they are done, don't over cook potatoes. Drain potatoes well and put them in a mixer with the butter and cream cheese. Mix on medium speed, scraping sides. Mix until all lumps are gone and then add the garlic and enough seasoning to taste. Salt and pepper can be used in place of Natures Seasoning. Do no over mix potatoes in mixer. Put potatoes back in pot with lid on and leave for a bit before serving.

If using roasted garlic, rub olive oil over a head of garlic and cut off the top. Wrap garlic in foil and bake for about 45 minutes and then squeeze into potatoes while mixing.

Makes about 8-10 servings.

# Maple Muffins

1  8 oz. carton sour cream
1  egg, beaten
1  cup sugar
1  tbsp maple flavoring
½ tsp ground allspice
¼ tsp nutmeg
¼ tsp baking soda
   Pinch of salt

   Mix sugar and maple flavoring together.  Combine egg, sour cream, sugar, allspice and nutmeg.  In another bowl combine flour, baking soda, and salt and stir.  Add the flour mixture to the sour cream mixture.  Stir just to blend.
   Turn dough onto a well-floured surface.  Knead about 12 strokes.  Lightly roll dough into a ½ inch thickness.  Cut dough with a floured round cutter.  Place muffins on a greased cookie sheet.  Bake in a 375 degree oven for 12 to 15 minutes r until the bottoms of muffins are brown.  Cool slightly and serve warm.

Makes 12-14 muffins

# Pine Nut-Parsley Rolls

1 16 oz package hot roll mix
1 cup warm water
2 tbsp butter
1 egg
½ cup finely chopped pine nuts
1/3 cup grated Parmesan cheese
¼ cup snipped parsley
2 tbsp butter melted
1 beaten egg
1 tbsp water

    Prepare roll mix according to package directions using the warm water, 2 tbsp butter and egg. Knead dough and let rest as directed on the package. Combine pine nuts, cheese and parsley. Roll dough on a lightly floured surface into an 18-inch square. Brush with 2 tbsp melted butter and sprinkle with cheese mixture. Roll up dough. Cut into twelve 1 ½ inch-thick slices. Place slices on a greased baking sheet. Let stand for about 5 minutes. Press down in middle of each slice to make a deep crease. Stir together beaten egg and water and brush on the dough. Let rise in warm place until nearly double, about 30 minutes.
    Bake in a 375 degree oven about 15 minutes or until golden. Serve Warm.

Makes 12 rolls

*But see, in our open clearings,*
   *How golden the melons lie;*
*Enrich them with sweets and spice,*
   *And give us the pumpkin – pie!*
   *~ Margaret Junkin Preston ~*

## Pumpkin Chiffon Pie

1  9- inch pie shell baked
2  envelope unflavored gelatin
½ cup cold water
1 ½ cups sugar
3  tsp corn starch
½ tsp ginger
½ tsp nutmeg
1  tsp cinnamon
¼ tsp ground cloves
1  cup canned pumpkin
1  cup heavy cream
2  tbsp butter
4  eggs whites
½ cup ground pecans

Sprinkle the gelatin in cold water. In a sauce pan combine ½ of the sugar, corn starch, ginger, nutmeg, cinnamon and cloves. Add the pumpkin and cream and mix well over medium heat until thickened. Add the gelatin mixture and the butter stirring until gelatin is dissolved. Cool to partially set.

Beat the egg whites until soft peaks form and gradually add the remaining sugar. Beat until stiff and then fold carefully into the pumpkin mixture. Place in the baked shell and add the ground pecans. Chill well before serving.

Serves 8

*This Iowa farm dish brings the summer to a Thanksgiving table.*

## Scalloped Corn and Tomatoes

2  14 ½ cans diced tomatoes, drained
1  15 ½ can whole kernel corn, drained
1  14 oz can creamed corn
2  eggs beaten
¼ cup flour
3  tsp sugar
1  tsp pepper
1½ cup onion, finely chopped
½ tsp garlic powder
½ cup butter
2  cups bread crumbs
1  cup grated Parmesan cheese

Mix together tomatoes, one half cup of onion, corn, cream-style corn, eggs, flour, sugar, and pepper and put in buttered casserole dish. Cook onion and garlic in a saucepan with butter until tender. Remove from heat and stir in crumbs and Parmesan. Sprinkle on top of corn mixture. Bake, uncovered in a 350 degree oven for about 1 hour or until brown and set.

Makes 12 servings

# Sour Cream-Lemon Pie

1 baked 9- inch pie shell
1 cup sugar
3 ½ tbsp corn starch
2 tbsp lemon zest
½ cup fresh lemon juice
3 egg yolks, slightly beaten
1 cup milk
1/3 cup butter
1 cup sour cream
1 cup heavy whipping cream, whipped

Mix sugar, lemon zest, corn starch, lemon juice, egg yolks and milk in sauce pan. Cook over medium heat until thick. Add butter and cool mixture to room temperature. Stir in sour cream and pour filling into pie shell. Spread whipped cream on top. Chill well.

# Spinach Soufflé Stuffed Mushrooms

1  12 oz pkg. frozen spinach soufflé
12 to 18 mushrooms
½  cup butter
1 ½ tbsp minced onion
3  tbsp dry Italian bread crumbs
½ tsp lemon-pepper seasoning
½ tsp garlic salt
   Salt and pepper
   Grated Parmesan cheese

   Bake soufflé according to pkg. directions and let cool. Remove stems from mushrooms and finely chop. Melt half of butter in a skillet over medium heat and sauté the chopped mushrooms, bread crumbs and onion until soft. Add the spinach and blend. Clean mushrooms with dry cloth, do not allow mushrooms to be wet. Dip each mushroom in the other half of butter and fill with spinach mixture. Sprinkle with parmesan cheese. Bake 12 to 15 minutes or until cheese is golden in a 350 degree oven. Let set for 5 minutes, serve.

# Spirited Cranberry Relish

1 bag fresh cranberries
2- cups sugar
　zest of one orange
　juice of half fresh orange
½ teaspoon pumpkin pie spice
2 tablespoons cognac

　Add all ingredients in medium sauce pan and heat on low for about 20-30 minutes or until all berries have popped and stir now and then.  Remove from heat and pour in bowl and let cool.  Store in refrigerator.

# Katie's Sweet Potato Soufflé

1 large can yams, mashed
½ cup sugar
2 eggs
¼ cup butter
1 cup canned milk
½ tsp. cinnamon, nutmeg

## Topping:

¾ cup crushed corn flakes
½ cup chopped pecans
½ cup brown sugar
¼ cup melted butter

Mix ingredients and bake for 30 minutes or until almost done in a 375-400 degree oven. Sprinkle topping over soufflé and bake for another 10-15 minutes.

*Chapter 26*

# Christmas Spice

*As I look through these holiday recipes each one recalls in me a different memory; blending of smells, sweet homecomings, a reminder of the season's joyful abundance and the groundwork of family traditions. For many years I designed new menus for our Christmas dinner and through the years that followed I only prepared those dishes around the Christmas season. Now I am looking forward to making every one of these recipes again... only at Christmas. Each of the following recipes became our favorites, our family's Christmas tradition.*

# Apricot Cheesecake

2 ½ cups crushed butter cookies
½ cup butter, melted
1 tbsp. orange zest
1 15-ounce can apricots
3 8-ounce packages cream cheese
1 cup sugar
1 tbsp. apricot liqueur
1 tsp. vanilla
2 tbsp. orange zest
3 eggs
1 10-ounce jar apricot jam
1 tbsp. honey
2 tbsp. reserved syrup
1 tsp. apricot liqueur or orange juice

In food processor grind cookies, add butter and mix. Scrape sides of bowl and add zest. Press mixture evenly onto bottom and 1 ½ inch of sides of a 9-inch spring form pan. Bake in a 325 degree oven for 8-10 minutes. Set aside.

Drain apricots and reserve 4 tbsp. of syrup. Place apricots in food processor and pulse until chopped. Add sugar, 2 tbsp. syrup, zest, liqueur and vanilla. Add cream cheese and pulse until creamy. Add eggs, 1 at a time; scrapping bowl and continue to blend.

Pour mixture into pan and place on a baking sheet; bake for 50-60 minutes. Turn oven off and let set for 15 minutes before removing to a wire rack to completely cool. Carefully remove sides of pan, glaze and refrigerate overnight.

# Glaze:

In saucepan melt apricot jam over low heat. Remove from heat; stir in honey, syrup and liqueur. Spread over cheesecake. Cover and chill.

Makes 16 servings.

# Baked Ham with Gingered Relish

1 whole baked and sliced, honey-baked ham
½ cup dried cranberries
½ cup dried apricots
½ cup dried golden raisins
½ cup dried sour cherries
½ cup dried figs
½ cup sugar
3 tbsp. finely chopped crystallized ginger
½ cup apricot brandy

In a saucepan bring the brandy, sugar and 1/3 cup water to a boil, reduce and cook over low heat about 10-15 minutes. Add the fruit and cook until the sauce thickens, about 5 minutes. Remove from heat and cool. Refrigerate up to one week.

Serve at room temperature with ham.

# Bavarian Torte

1/ cup butter
½ cup sugar
½ tsp. vanilla
1 cup flour
1 8-ounce package cream cheese
¼ cup sugar
1 egg
½ tsp. vanilla
4 cups thinly sliced and peeled apples
1/3 cup sugar
½ tsp. cinnamon
¼ tsp. pumpkin spice
½ cup sliced almonds

Cream butter and sugar until fluffy; blend in vanilla. Add flour, mix well. Spread dough onto bottom and 1 inch high around sides of 9-inch spring form pan.

Combine softened cream cheese and sugar, mixing until well blended. Blend in egg and vanilla; pour into pastry-lined pan.

Toss apples with combined sugar, cinnamon and pumpkin spice. Spoon apple mixture over cream cheese layer; sprinkle with nuts. Bake in a 400 degree oven for 10 minutes. Reduce oven to 350 degrees; continue baking 25 minutes. Loosen cake from rim of pan. Cool; remove rim. Chill cake before serving.

*This has to be one of the best desserts I have ever made. The combination of raspberries and chocolate are divine and almost saintly! Enjoy.*

## Chocolate Raspberry Tart

1 pre made pie crust
10-ounce package frozen raspberries, thawed
1 tbsp. cornstarch
2 tbsp. sugar
1 ½ cups fresh raspberries
½ cup sugar
¼ cup butter
4-ounces white chocolate, melted
2 eggs
3-ounces semi-sweet chocolate, broken into pieces
2 tbsp. butter

Using a 10-inch tart pan or 10-inch springform pan. Press pie crust onto bottom and 1-inch of sides of pan, prick crusts; Bake in a 450-degree oven for 10 minutes or until lightly browned. Cool completely.

Puree raspberries in food processor; strain. Combine cornstarch and 2 tbsp. sugar; blend well in a saucepan. Gradually add raspberry puree. Cook over low heat until thickened, stirring constantly. Cool and spread over crust. Refrigerate.

In a small bowl, beat ½ cup butter and sugar until light and fluffy. Add melted white chocolate, beating constantly. Add eggs on at a time, beat for 3-4 minutes. Pour over raspberries; refrigerate until set.

In small saucepan melt chocolate pieces, 2 tbsp. butter; carefully spread over white mixture. Refrigerate 3 hours. Let stand at room temperature about 30 minutes before serving.

Makes 10 servings

# Cranberry Raspberry Relish

1 pound fresh cranberries, finely chopped
2 tart green apples, peeled and diced
1 cup sugar
½ cup marmalade
1 10-ounce package frozen
  raspberries, thawed and drained
1 tsp. lemon juice

Chop cranberries in food processor and mix all ingredients in medium bowl. May be refrigerated, covered for 1 month.

Makes 6 cups

# Cranberry Relish Ring

## Cranberry Layer

2 envelopes unflavored gelatin
¾ cup sugar divided
1 ½ cups boiling water
1 ½ cups cranberry juice
3 tsp. orange zest
2 cups chopped fresh cranberries

## Cream Layer

1 envelope unflavored gelatin
1/3 cup sugar
2/3 cup orange juice
1 egg, beaten
1 cup sour cream
1 cup half-and-half
½ cup chopped walnuts
Frosted Cranberries for garnish

In medium bowl combine gelatin with ¼ cup sugar. Add boiling water and stir until gelatin is completely dissolved. Add cranberry juice and orange zest. Refrigerate, stirring occasionally until mixture is the consistency of unbeaten egg whites, about 1 hour. Fold in chopped cranberries, spoon into a greased 1-cup ring mold. Refrigerate until almost firm.

Meanwhile in a small saucepan combine gelatin with sugar. Add orange juice with beaten egg. Let stand 1 minute; stir over low heat until gelatin is completely dissolved, about 5 minutes; remove from heat. Whisk in sour cream and half-and-half, refrigerate, stirring occasionally until mixture mounds slightly when dropped from a spoon, about 1-hour. Fold in nuts and spoon gently into almost set cranberry layer, cover and refrigerate overnight. Un-mold on platter and garnish with frosted cranberries.

Frosted Cranberries: Roll ½ cup cranberries, a few at a time in 2 beaten egg whites and then in sugar. Set on wire rack to dry.

Makes 12 servings

# Cranberry Surprise

1 cup graham cracker crumbs
¼ cup butter
2 cups fresh cranberries, chopped
1 cup sugar
½ cup water
½ cup chopped walnuts
3 tbsp. orange marmalade
1 8-ounce package cream cheese
1/3 cup confectioner's sugar
1 tbsp. milk
1 tsp. vanilla
1 cup whipping cream, whipped

    Combine crumbs and butter; press onto a bottom of 8-inch square baking dish.
    Combine cranberries, sugar and water in a saucepan. Bring to a boil; simmer for 15-20 minutes. Stir in nuts and marmalade; chill.
    Combine softened cream cheese, confectioner's sugar, milk and vanilla; mixing well until well blended. Fold in whipped cream. Spoon over crust; top with cranberry mixture. Chill several hours or overnight.

Makes 8 servings

# Holiday Ham with Apple Pear Glaze

1 6-lb. cooked ham
2 cups apple juice
1 cup brown sugar
¼ cup Dijon mustard
1 tsp. pumpkin pie spice
2 tbsp. honey
1/3 cup dried cranberries
2 pears, cored and chopped
2 green apples, peeled, cored and chopped
1 tbsp. finely chopped
  fresh rosemary

    In a saucepan combine apple juice, sugar, honey, mustard, rosemary, pie spice and simmer for 15 minutes. Add fruit and simmer on low for 5 minutes. Cool, serve with ham at room temperature. Can be made ahead of time and warmed in microwave.

# Holiday London Broil

1 2-pound London broil steak
1 cup bourbon
½ tsp. salt and ground pepper
4 garlic cloves, minced
1 tsp. dried oregano
2 cups fresh button mushrooms, sliced
¼ cup chopped shallots
¼ cup brandy
½ cup beef broth
¼ cup heavy cream
¼ cup crumbled blue cheese
¼ cup crumbled gorgonzola cheese

Rub meat with half of the garlic, oregano salt and pepper. In a hot skillet sear the steak 1 minute on both sides. Pour whisky into a shallow dish and add meat. Marinate for 2 hours; turning.

In same skillet sauté the mushrooms and remaining garlic until liquid has evaporated. In a different skillet sauté the shallots for 1 minute, add the brandy and cook until liquid is nearly evaporated. Over medium-high heat add the broth and boil for 5 minutes; add cream and cook for 4 minutes. Add the mushrooms and salt and pepper.

Remove steak from dish discard marinate. Bake in a pre heated oven at 400 degrees for 5 minutes on each side or medium rare. (Slightly less done than desired). Sprinkle the cheeses on top and return to oven or broil for 1 minute or until cheese has melted. Let set about 5 minutes before slicing. Slice meat diagonally across the grain into ¼-1/2 inch slices. Top with mushroom sauce.

Serves 4-6

# Marinated Lamb Chops

2 tbsp. fresh, finely chopped rosemary leaves
1 tbsp. dried thyme
4 garlic cloves, minced
1 tsp. freshly ground pepper
1 cup finely chopped onion
½ cup orange juice
¼ cup dry white wine
4 tbsp. olive oil
6-8 lamb chops

 Combine together spices, onion, salt and pepper, orange juice, wine and half of the olive oil. Reserve ¼ cup of the marinade. Refrigerate for 3 hours.
 Heat oil in large skillet on medium- high heat. Cook chops 3 minutes on each side. Add remaining marinade and simmer 3 minutes.

# Orange Chocolate Cheesecake

¼ cup graham cracker crumbs
¼ cup butter cookies, ground
½ cup pecans, ground
3 tbsp. melted butter
4 8-ounce packages cream cheese, softened
1 ½ cups sugar
2 tbsp. brown sugar
2 tbsp. orange liqueur
1 tbsp. brandy
2 tbsp. orange zest
3 squares semi-sweet chocolate pieces, melted

Mix first 4 ingredients together and press bottom and sides of a greased 9-inch spring-form pan.

In food processor blend together cream cheese until creamy, add sugars, zest; scrap bowl. Add eggs one at a time; scrapping bowl. Add liqueur, brandy and blend.

Pour into pan and add melted chocolate by drops; with a knife swirl into cake.

Bake in a 325 degree oven for 60 minutes or until set. Turn oven off and let set for 15 minutes. Take out of oven and cool on wire rack for several hours. Cover and refrigerate overnight.

Makes 16 servings.

# Pecan Cake

3 cups broken pecans, toasted
1 cup all-purpose flour
1 ½ tbsp. baking powder
6 eggs
1 ½ cup sugar
½ cup butter
1 8-ounce package cream cheese, softened
1 cup brown sugar
1 tbsp. tangerine zest
1 tsp. vanilla
2 tbsp. fresh tangerine juice

# Whipped Frosting

2 cups whipping cream
2 tbsp. sugar
1 tbsp. tangerine zest

Chop pecans in food processor. Combine dry ingredients with pecans in a mixing bowl; set aside.

In food processor place eggs and blend. Add flour mixture and blend until smooth. Mix in tangerine juice and blend. Grease 2 8-inch round cake pans and line with waxed paper; dust with four. Pour cake batter in pans and tap on counter to release air bubbles. Bake in a 350 degree oven for 25-30 minutes; top should be brown. Cool in pans on wire rack. Remove from pans and finish cooling on rack.

For the filling beat the cream cheese and butter in mixing bowl on high speed until fluffy. Gradually add brown sugar and continue mixing for 3 minutes. Mix in 1 of the tbsp. tangerine zest and the vanilla.

Slice cakes in half horizontally. Pace the first layer on the cake plate and spread with a layer of the filling. Place the second layer down on top of filling and frost as the first. Repeat the next 2 layers.

In a chilled mixing bowl whip the whipping cream, sugar, and last tbsp. tangerine zest. Beat until soft peaks form. Frost top and sides of cake.

# Pumpkin Pound Cake with Walnut Sauce

2 ½ cups sugar
1 ¼ cups butter, softened
1 tsp. vanilla
5 eggs
2 ½ cups flour
1 tsp. baking powder
½ tsp. salt
1 tsp. cinnamon
½ tsp. ginger
½ tsp cloves
1 cup canned pumpkin

Cream together sugar and butter until light and fluffy. Add vanilla, eggs, one at a time. Carefully combine flour, baking powder, salt and spices.

Add dry ingredients and pumpkin to butter mixture, mixing well. Pour batter into a greased and floured 12-cup fluted tube or bunt pan. Bake in a 350 degree oven for 60 minutes.

# Walnut Sauce:

1 cup brown sugar
½ cup dark corn syrup
½ cup whipping cream
2 tbsp. butter
½ tsp. salt
1 tsp. vanilla
1 cup chopped or halved walnuts

In saucepan combine brown sugar, corn syrup, cream, butter and salt. Cook over medium heat, stirring constantly, until mixture boils. Reduce heat to low and simmer 5 minutes. Mix in vanilla and walnuts. Serve cake with walnut sauce.

Makes 16 servings.

# Rice Ring

1 ½ cups brown rice
1 ½ cups water
1 cup chicken broth
1/3 cup dry champagne
½ tsp. pepper
2 cup sliced fresh mushrooms
½ cup finely minced onion
1 ½ tsp. curry powder
1 tbsp. olive oil
1/2 cup slivered almonds, toasted
1/2 cup finely chopped pecans
2 tbsp. honey

    In saucepan combine rice, broth, champagne and pepper and bring to a boil. Turn heat to a simmer and cook for about 50 minutes or till rice is tender.
    In a sauce saucepan sauté onions and mushrooms in hot oil until all liquid from mushrooms has evaporated. Add remaining ingredients and blend.
    Spoon mushroom ingredients into a well greased mold. Spoon rice over mushroom mixture and press with spoon or hands to make sure it is firm in mold. Let set for a while or refrigerate. Place mold in a large roasting pan with water and bake in a 350 degree oven for 30 minutes. Remove and cool on a wire rack. Let set for 10 minutes and invert into a serving dish. Serve with hot steamed vegetables in center of rice mold.

Serves 12

*This recipe is from one of my senior clients Iris who is from England*

# Prime-Rib Roast Beef and Yorkshire Pudding

3-4 lb. roast prime-rib
5 garlic cloves minced
  Salt and cracked pepper
  Lemon juice
1 cup flour
pinch of salt
2 eggs
1 cup milk

Rub roast with garlic; squeeze lemon over and sprinkle lots of salt and pepper. Bake roast beef starting at a 475 degree oven for 15 minutes. Reduce heat to 375 and continue cooking 18 minutes per pound of meat. Turn oven off and let set for 15 minutes.

Sift flour and salt into a bowl and make a whole in middle. Brake eggs into and mix; adding milk and beat to a smooth batter. Ladle some of the hot drippings from roast in the bottom of baking tins making sure the bottoms and sides are well covered. Pour in batter and bake for 40 minutes.

# Horseradish Sauce:

2 tbsp. fresh horseradish grated
1 tbsp. vinegar
1 tbs. sugar
  Dash of mustard
½ cup cream
  Salt and pepper

Combine all ingredients and mix well. Add sour cream to lighten taste if desired.

Serves 4-6

# Roasted Duck with Orange Sauce and Orange Stuffing

5 pound duckling
½ onion, quartered
3 whole garlic cloves
½ fresh orange, quartered
3 whole, peeled garlic cloves
½ cup burgundy wine
   Salt
   Orange marmalade

    Remove neck and giblets, rinse and pat dry. Place peeled onion half, garlic and orange quarters inside of duck; follow with orange stuffing. Bring skin of neck over the back and fasten with poultry pins. Poke holes in skin all over duck to make sure fat will be released. Place duck breast up on a rack in shallow baking pan; pour burgundy in bottom of pan. Bake in a 250 degree oven for 2 hours. Increase temperature to 375-400 degrees for 30-50 minutes. Baste with marmalade. Place duck on platter and serve with orange sauce.

### Orange Stuffing:
1 cup finely sliced celery
½ onion, finely chopped
2 garlic cloves, minced
3 cups sour dough bread cubes, tossed in butter and toasted
1/3 cup butter
2 tsp. orange zest
½ cup diced orange pieces
1 egg, beaten
Salt and fresh cracked pepper

Sauté in butter the celery, onion and garlic for 1 minute. In a bowl mix all ingredients and stuff duck.

### Orange Sauce:
3 tbsp. butter
2 tbsp. flour
1 ½ cups giblet broth
½ cup fresh squeezed orange juice
1 tbsp. orange zest
1 tbsp. tomato paste
½ cup orange marmalade
1 tsp. soy sauce
2 tbsp. Grand Marnier

Simmer giblets in 2 cups water for 35 minutes. Melt butter in a skillet and add flour and cook for 3 minutes. Add broth and some of the duck drippings and blend. Add remaining ingredients and simmer, stirring for 15 minutes, season with salt and freshly ground pepper.

# Roasted Rock Cornish Hens with Wild Rice and Mushroom Stuffing

4-6 Hens
1/3 cup blackberry jelly
2 tbsp. balsamic vinegar
3 tbsp. honey

    Remove neck and giblets, rinse and pat dry. Sprinkle with salt and pepper. Stuff each hen; tie legs together at the ankles. Place hens on a rack in a shallow roasting pan, breast side up. Roast in a 375 degree oven for 25 minutes.
    Mix together the jelly, honey and vinegar in a saucepan and simmer for 1 minute, let set a bit. Brush hens with glaze and return to oven for 25 minutes. Place birds on a platter and let stand for 10 minutes.

# Wild Rice and Mushroom Stuffing

2-ounces each dried porcini and shitake mushrooms
1 cup chicken broth, warmed
2 cups sliced button mushrooms
2 tbsp. unsalted butter
2 garlic cloves, minced
¼ cup dry white wine
1/3 cup minced shallots
1 cup cooked wild rice
¼ cup fine bread crumbs
1 cup chopped Italian parsley
½ cup chopped fresh cranberries
   Salt and fresh cracked pepper

Pour hot chicken broth over porcini and shitake mushrooms and let set for 25 minutes. Drain and chop.

Sauté the garlic, shallots in the butter for 1 minute; add all mushrooms and white wine and cook for 12 minutes. Combine remaining ingredients and blend. Stuff hens with stuffing or bake in a buttered baking dish and bake in a 350 degree oven for 50 minutes.

*This is one of my most special recipes because it reminds me of my dear friend Helen. She served these wonderful little half-moon cream cheese cookies when Diana and I visited her. Rugelach is served at Hanukkah time and a Jewish custom. I have been making them ever since Helen introduced them to me and this is her recipe she gave to me.*

# Rugelach

½ pound butter, softened
8-ounces cream cheese, softened
2 cups flour

In food processor, cream the butter and cream cheese together. Beat in the flour, little by little. Knead the dough lightly until all the flour is incorporated. Refrigerate at least 1 hour. Divide the dough into 3 or 4 portions, depending on the size you want the rugelach to be.

Prepare fillings and save ¼ cup sugar for the topping. Roll out one of the portions of dough in a circle about 1/16 inches thick. With a biscuit cutter, cut the pastry into 16 pie-shaped wedges. If the dough is sticky, dust it with a little flour. Dot each round with a little filling. Beginning at the edge, roll the dough up toward the point.

Place on an ungreased baking sheet and carefully sprinkle with a tiny bit of the reserved sugar. Repeat with the rest of the dough and filling. Bake in a 350-degree oven for 20-25 minutes, or until golden, brushing with melted butter after 15 minutes if desired.

## Strawberry Filling:

1 cup ground almonds
1 cup strawberry jam
¼ cup sugar (topping)

## Raisin Nut Filling:

½ cup sugar
½ cup seedless raisins
1 tsp. cinnamon
1 cup finely chopped walnuts
¼ cup sugar (topping)

## Apricot Filling:

½ cup sugar
½ cup chopped figs
1 tsp. cinnamon
½ cup pecans, chopped fine
¼ cup sugar (topping)

# Savory Holiday Stuffing

1- recipe homemade corn bread using buttermilk in place of the milk
1 cup coarsely chopped chestnuts, toasted,
1 cup coarsely chopped pecans, toasted
1 ½ cups chopped dried apricots
½ cup melted butter
½-1 cup chicken broth
1 tbsp. cognac
2 tsp. dried sage
½ tsp. thyme
½ cup chopped fresh parsley
2 beaten eggs
½ cup chopped onion
½ cup sliced celery with leaves
½ tsp. salt and pepper

Sauté the onion and celery in the butter for about 3 minutes. Mix crumbled cornbread and remaining ingredients in large bowl. Stuff bird with stuffing and bake the remaining in a buttered casserole dish.

# Sour Cream Pumpkin Cake

3 cups flour
2 tsp. baking soda
1 tbsp. cinnamon
1 tsp. nutmeg
1 tsp. pumpkin spice
1 tsp. salt
1 cup butter
2 cups sugar
4 eggs
1 cup canned pumpkin
1 cup sour cream
2 tsp. vanilla

    Mix together flour, baking powder, cinnamon, nutmeg, pumpkin spice, and salt. Beat butter and sugar in mixer until creamy. Add eggs, two at a time, beating well after each addition. Beat in pumpkin, sour cream and vanilla. Gradually beat in flour mixture on low speed until blended.
    Spread half of the batter in pan. Sprinkle streusel over batter, making sure streusel does not touch sides of pan. Top with remaining batter making sure batter layer touches sides of pan.
    Bake in a 350 degree oven for 60 minutes. Cool in pan on were rack 30 minutes. Invert onto wire rack; cool completely. Sprinkle with powdered sugar.

# Streusel Mixture:

½ cup brown sugar
1 tsp. cinnamon
½ tsp. allspice
3 tbsp. Butter

    Mix brown sugar, cinnamon and allspice in a bowl. Cut in butter using 2 knives until mixture is crumbly.

*If you have never tried making an old fashioned steam pudding than now is the time of season to try it. It's the perfect addition to a holiday dinner.*

# Steamed Pudding

2 cups flour
2 ½ cups cranberries
2 tbsp. flour
½ cup brown sugar
½ cup sugar
1 tsp. baking soda
1 tsp. cinnamon
½ tsp. nutmeg
¼ tsp. allspice
1 cup milk
1 egg
2 tbsp. butter, melted

In a bowl toss together the cranberries and 2 tbsp. flour; set aside.

In mixing bowl stir together 2 cups flour, sugars, baking soda and spices. Add milk, egg and butter; stir until well combined. Stir in cranberry mixture. Transfer to a well greased 6 cup metal mold. Cover tightly with foil. Place mold on a rack in a Dutch oven or roasting pan. Add boiling water to just below rack; cover.

Bring to a simmer and steam for 1-1 ½ hours or until a wooden toothpick inserted in center comes out clean. Add water to pot as needed.

Remove pudding and let stand 2-4 minutes. Remove foil and un-mold onto serving dish. Garnish with a little powdered sugar, sugared cranberries and Hard Sauce.

Makes 12 servings.

# Hard Sauce:

In a mixing bowl beat together 1 cup sifted powdered sugar and ¼ cup butter on medium speed for 4 minutes. Mix in ½ tsp. vanilla. Chill to a hard stage.

*Chapter 27*

# Simply Handmade Giving

*The heart of Christmas is giving. What is more fun than sharing a family treasure? Tis the season for crowd pleasing treats that get your family and friends into the holiday spirit and make you're giving a surefire success. It is my hope that one of my grandchildren will use these same recipes and keep the giving going.*

# Assorted Toasted Nuts and Rosemary

3 cups walnuts pieces, hazelnuts and whole almonds
2 tbsp. fresh snipped rosemary
½ tsp. black pepper
½ tsp. salt
½ tsp. garlic powder

Line a baking pan with foil. In a bowl whisk the egg white until slightly fluffy. Add the rosemary and spices. Mix in thoroughly the nuts and spread over baking pan. Bake for 20 minutes or till golden; stirring once. Cool on wire rack. Break up large pieces.
Store in airtight container or freezer for a month.

Makes 3 cups

*This is a candy recipe I have used in my gift baskets for 30 years. It comes from my friend Eileen. We made this together with many other baked goodies for years. The rich, buttery candy is laced with chocolate and almonds and I recommend doubling the recipe because you'll want to keep a batch for your family.*

# Butter Crunch

1 1/3 cup sugar
1 lb. real butter
1 tbsp. corn syrup
3 tbsp. water
1 cup ground almonds
2 cups slivered almonds, ground
4-5 ounce package chocolate chips, melted

    Boil first 4 ingredients for 5 minutes; covered. Remove lid and continue to cool candy, using a thermometer until 300 degrees.
    Remove from heat and add 1 cup ground almonds. Pour onto a cookie sheet and let set for 5 minutes. Spread chocolate on top and follow with chopped slivered almonds. Let set for a bit and then mash down with potato masher. After completely cool put in refrigerator.
    When ready to use, break up into bite size pieces.

# Candy Cane Butter Nuts

1 cup butter
2 cups flour
½ cup sugar
½ cup crushed candy canes
1 cup finely chopped walnuts

Heat oven to 350 degrees. Mix thoroughly all ingredients. Roll dough ¼-inch thick on lightly floured covered board. Cut into 1-inch circles. Sprinkle with crushed candy cane. Place on ungreased baking sheet. Bake 10-12 minutes.

# Chocolate Bundles

1 package (8squares), semi-sweet chocolate
1 cup sifted confectioners sugar
1 egg, well beaten
1 tbsp. milk

  Assorted decorations:
Coconut, sugar crystals, finely chopped almonds or pecans

  Melt chocolate in saucepan over low heat, stirring constantly. Remove from heat. Add sugar, egg and milk; beat until smooth. Chill until firm enough to handle, about 30 minutes. Shape into ½-inch balls. Roll in decorations.

Makes about 5 dozen

*There is nothing easier than making and passing on a mini loaf of bread. Easy to wrap and add a bottle of homemade vinegar, olives, or wine and what a nice excuse to stop by with a Christmas wish. This is one of the most amazing Christmas breads I have ever made….don't miss giving it!*

# Chocolate Gingerbread Loaf

½ cup butter
½ cup sugar
1 egg
1 cup molasses
¾ cup buttermilk
2 ¼ cup flour
1 tbsp. ginger
1 ½ tsp. cinnamon
1  tsp. baking soda
¼ tsp. salt
½ cup dark raisins
½ cup semisweet chocolate chips, chopped in food processor

# Topping:

½ cup semisweet chocolate chips
1 tbsp. vegetable shortening
½ cup orange marmalade
½ cup diced crystallized ginger

In bowl of mixer beat butter and sugar until light and fluffy. Beat in egg to blend well; beat in molasses and buttermilk. In small bowl combine flour, ginger, cinnamon, baking soda and salt; with mixer at low speed, beat spice mixture into butter mixture until blended and smooth. Stir in raisins and chocolate chips. Spoon batter into 4 mini buttered and sprayed loaf pans halfway. Bake in a 325 degree oven for 45-50 minutes until tops spring back when lightly touched. Cool on wire rack for 5-10 minutes and remove from pans; continue cooling.

In a saucepan over low heat, melt chocolate and shortening, stirring until melted and smooth. Remove from heat; set aside. In second small saucepan over very low heat stir marmalade just to warm. Brush loaves with marmalade evenly. Using a small spoon drizzle melted chocolate over loaves. Sprinkle loaves with crystallized ginger. Let stand 1 hour or more.

Makes 4 mini loaves.

# Cinnamon and Orange Spiced Nuts

2 cups whole almonds
2 cups pecan halves
1 cup walnut halves
1 ½ cups sugar
½ tsp cinnamon
¼ tsp. nutmeg
¼ tsp. pumpkin spice
   Pinch of salt
2 egg whites
1 tbsp. orange liqueur
2 tbs. orange zest

Heat oven to 325 degrees. In mixer beat egg whites until soft peaks form. Combine sugar, spices and salt in a bowl. Continue beating egg whites while gradually adding spice mixture until stiff peaks form. Fold in nuts, zest and liqueur and toss gently. Spread over a prepared baking sheet. Drizzle melted butter over nuts. Bake for 30-45 minutes, stirring every 10 minutes. Cool completely, store in air tight container.

# Cranberry Banana Bread

2 cups sifted flour
1 tsp. salt
1 egg, beaten
1 tsp. grated orange zest
¼ cup salad oil
1 ¼ cup fresh cranberries, halved
1 tsp. baking soda
1 ¼ cups sugar
1/3 cup orange juice
2 tbsp. white vinegar
2/3 cup mashed ripe bananas
1 cup chopped pecans

In mixing bowl, sift together dry ingredients. Combine egg, orange juice, zest, vinegar and oil. Add all at once to flour mixture, stirring just until all flour is moistened. Fold in mashed bananas, cranberries, and nuts. Pour into greased loaf pans. Bake in a 350 degree oven for 60-70 minutes.

# Fig and Pecan Cookies

1 box pie crust
1 tbsp. sour cream
1 egg white
9- ounces dried figs, stems removed
½ cup golden raisins
¾ cup honey
½ cup fresh squeezed orange juice
1 tbsp. cinnamon
2 tbsp. orange zest
1 cup chopped pecans
½ cup chocolate chips, chopped
1 egg, beaten

    Mix boxed pie dough with sour cream and egg white until a ball forms. Refrigerate for 30 minutes.
    Chop figs in food processor, add raisins, honey, orange juice, cinnamon and zest. Transfer to a box and blend in the pecans and chocolate chips.
    Roll out dough on a floured surface to ¼ inch thickness. Using a biscuit cutter, cut out dough rounds. Spoon a little filling on each round. Fold over one side and press edges together to seal. Crimp edges with fork. Brush with egg wash and bake in a 350 degree oven for 15-20 minutes or until golden.

# Cranberry Lemon Squares

2 cups dried cranberries
1 ½ cups water
½ cup fresh lemon juice
2 lemons – cut in half
1 cup flour
¼ cup confectioner's sugar
6 tbsp. cold butter, cut into small pieces
2 eggs
¾ cup sugar
1 tbsp. lemon zest
¼ cup fresh lemon juice

    In saucepan combine dried cranberries, water, ½ cup lemon juice and whole lemon halves. Bring to a boil; reduce heat and cook, stirring until water is absorbed, about 30 minutes. Place cranberries in food processor and chop coarsely. Set aside in a bowl.
    In mixer combine confectioner's sugar and flour. Add butter, beating on low speed until mixture forms small pieces. Press batter into an 8x8-inch buttered baking dish. Bake in a 325 degree oven until golden, about 20 minutes.
    Beat eggs and sugar in mixer until smooth. Add lemon juice and zest and mix until smooth. Add ¼ cup flour and finish beating, set aside.
    Reduce oven to 300 degrees. Spread cranberry mixture over cooked crust and pour lemon mixture over cranberries. Bake until set, about 40 minutes.
    Let cool on wire rack for about 1 hour. Refrigerate for at least 4 hours. To serve, cut into squares and dust with confectioner's sugar and lemon zest.

    Makes 16 bars

# Gift Popcorn

12 cups popped popcorn
1/2 cup melted butter

## Savory Popcorn:

Mix with melted butter 2 tsp. Worcestershire sauce and drizzle over popcorn; toss. In bowl combine 1tsp. paprika, ½ tsp. Seasoned salt, ¼ tsp. basil leaves, ¼ tsp. thyme leaves, ¼ tsp. garlic powder. Sprinkle over popcorn; toss.

## Pecan Popcorn:

Increase butter 1 cup. Mix 1 cup brown sugar and 1 ½ tsp. cinnamon into melted butter. Cook over medium heat, stirring occasionally until mixture comes to a full boil. Boil, stirring 7 minutes. Remove from heat and stir in 1 ½ cups chopped pecans. Slowly pour over popcorn; break apart.

# Gingerbread Men

½ cup butter
1 cup dark brown sugar
2 eggs
¼ cup molasses
3 ¼ cups flour
3 tsp. ginger
1 ½ tsp. baking soda
½ tsp. cinnamon, nutmeg, allspice
½ tsp. salt

    In mixer beat sugar and butter until fluffy. Add eggs and molasses and blend. Mix together the flour, soda, spices and salt. Gradually add to sugar mixture until well blended. Refrigerate dough for a few hours.
    On floured surface, roll out half of dough at a time to 1/8-inch thickness. Cut into desired shapes and place on greased cookie sheet. Bake in a 350 degree oven for 8-10 minutes. Let cool and decorated gingerbread men with colored icing.

Makes 2 dozen cookies

# Sugar Icing:

Combine confectioner's sugar, milk and food coloring.

# Glistening Fruitcake

## Fruit Mixture:

½ cup dark raisins
1 cup golden raisins
1/3 cup chopped dried apricots
1/3 cup chopped candied pineapple
2 cup dried cherries
½ cup each diced candied lemon and orange peel
1/3 cup diced candied citron
1/3 cup chopped crystallized ginger
1 ½ cups chopped pecans
1 cup blanched almonds
¼ cup brandy
¼ cup cognac
½ cup flour

## Batter:

1 ½ cups flour
2 tsp. baking powder
½ tsp. baking soda
½ tsp. mace
1 tsp. cinnamon
½ tsp. ground cloves
½ tsp. salt
½ cup unsalted butter
1 cup dark brown sugar
½ cup sugar
3 eggs
½ cup cream
¼ cup milk

    In a bowl combine raisins, cherries, brandy and cognac; mix well. Cover and let set overnight. In a bowl combine all candied fruit and nuts. Sprinkle with ½ cup flour and toss. Add raisin mixture and mix well; set aside. Sift together the 1 ½ cup flour, baking soda, baking powder, mace, cinnamon and cloves; set aside.
    Beat eggs, cream, and milk; set aside.
    In mixer bowl beat butter at medium speed until creamy. Beat in sugars until blended. Pour in egg mixture, beating until smooth. Gradually add flour mixture on low speed until blended. Slowly add fruit mixture, mix thoroughly.

Spoon batter into 3 medium loaf pans or 7 mini loaf pans. Make sure pans are buttered and lined with buttered wax paper.

Bake medium loaves in a 285-degree oven for 1-2 hours and small loaves 1 ¼ -1 ½ hours. Check fruitcakes with toothpick in center to make sure they are done.

Cool on rack for 30 minutes. Remove from pans and peel off wax paper. Continue cooling completely.

Wrap cooled cakes in cheesecloth soaked in brandy. Wrap in foil; refrigerate for 2-3 weeks, brushing with more brandy.

Makes 3 medium or 7 small loaves.

*This recipe comes from my friend Cathy who is the source of so many of the best finds in this book. Cathy's grandmother would make this cookie and put into an 8 x8 pan and top with chocolate. Cathy's mother took over making them when Grandma Austin passed away. Now Cathy and her sister continue the tradition by making the families cookie recipe every Christmas season as part of the gift plates they share.*

## Grandma Austin's Chocolate Balls

2 cups Graham Cracker crumbs
1 lb. powdered sugar
½ cup peanut butter (smooth)
1 cup chopped nuts (walnuts or pecans)
1 cup coconut
1 tsp. pure vanilla

Mix all of above ingredients together. Roll into balls the size of walnuts. Set aside.

## Coating:

2 cups chocolate chips
½ bar paraffin

Melt over hot water. Dip each ball into chocolate and place on wax paper until set.

# Miniature Pecan Tarts

## Dough:

½ cup butter
3-ounce package cream cheese
1 cup flour

## Filling:

1 egg, beaten lightly
¾ cup brown sugar
2 tbsp. butter
1 tsp. vanilla
1 cup chopped pecans

    Mix dough and shape into a ball and chill for 2 hours. Shape into 20 balls and put each into a greased miniature muffin tin or tart pan. Press into bottom and sides to make the crusts. Pour filling ¾ full. Bake in a 350 degree oven for 15-18 minutes. Remove from pan, cool on wire rack.

*My mother's homemade fudge reminds me of old movies and Dodger and Giants baseball on the old black and white television. A wonderful memory surrounding a dish of fudge.*

## Mother's Fudge

2 cups sugar
½ cup heavy cream
½ cup half and half
½ cup light corn syrup
　Dash of salt
6-ounces bittersweet chocolate,
　finely chopped
2 tbsp. unsalted butter, softened
1 tsp. vanilla
1 cup chopped walnuts
1 cup chopped pecans

　　In a heavy bottomed saucepan combine first 5 ingredients. Over low heat, cook for about 5 minutes, stirring. Bring to a boil for 1 minute. Remove from heat and stir in chocolate until melted.
　　Over medium heat use a warm candy thermometer in the pan and cook the candy without stirring until thermometer reaches 236-238 degrees. Remove from heat.
　　Without stirring add the butter and vanilla. Place pan in cool water to stop the cooking until thermometer reaches 110 degrees. Use a wooden spoon to beat the candy until it begins to thicken and lose its shine, about 5-10 minutes. Make sure candy does not become too thick.
　　Stir in chopped nuts. Pour candy in a buttered pan. Cut candy into squares and refrigerate overnight. Store in refrigerator up to 1 month.

　　To make serving candy easier line pan with buttered wax paper before pouring candy in pan.

*This is a great bread recipe and makes a wonderful gift because it's not the norm for bread giving; therefore your gift is unique. This is superb!*

## Pistachio Date Nut Bread

1 cup chopped dates
1 cup boiling water
1 ¼ cup flour
1 cup chopped, good pistachios
1 tsp. baking powder
1 tsp. baking soda
½ cup sugar
¼ tsp. salt
2 eggs, beaten
2 tbsp. butter, melted
1 tsp. orange zest

Soak dates in boiling water; cool. Combine flour, pistachios, sugar, baking powder, baking soda, and salt. Combine date mixture, eggs, butter, vanilla and orange zest; Mix only until moistened. Spoon into greased and sprayed loaf pan. Bake in a 350-degree oven for 45-50 minutes or until wooden pick inserted in center comes out clean.

Makes 1 loaf.

# Pumpkin Chocolate Cheesecake Bars

## Crust:

1 ½ cups graham cracker crumbs
1/3 cups sugar
½ cups butter, melted

## Filling:

2 8-ounce packages cream cheese,
 softened
1 ¾ cups sugar
3 eggs
1 cup canned pumpkin
½ tsp. pumpkin pie spice
½ tsp. brandy
¼ tsp. salt
8-ounces semisweet chocolate,
 cut up
3 tbsp. butter
1 ¼ cup sour cream
¼ cup sugar
 Fresh nutmeg

Mix crumbs and sugar and add melted butter; mix thoroughly. Press into a greased 13x9-inch baking dish; set aside.

In mixing bowl or food processor blend cream cheese and sugar. Add eggs one at a time, beating after each. Stir in pumpkin, spice, brandy and salt. Pour 1 ¼ cups of filling into a separate bowl; set aside.

In saucepan over low heat melt the chocolate and butter, stirring until smooth. Stir melted chocolate into the 1 ¼ cups of filling. Carefully spread chocolate mixture evenly over crust. Bake 15 minutes in a 325 degree oven. Remove from oven. Carefully pour remaining pumpkin over chocolate baked layer, spreading evenly.

Bake 40-45 minutes. Make sure cake is set in center; cool for 30 minutes. Combine sour cream and sugar; cover and let stand at room temperature.

Carefully spread sour cream mixture over bars. Cool. Refrigerate overnight. Sprinkle lightly with grated nutmeg just before serving.

Makes 24 servings

*Toast your friends with cakes of spirit. Wrap up rum-soaked cakes in a keepsake tin and share!*

# Rum Cakes

3 eggs
1 ½ cups butter
1 ½ cups eggnog
2 ¼ cups flour
2 tsp. baking powder
¾ tsp. nutmeg
1 cup mixed candied fruits
1 tsp. orange and lemon zest
½ cup golden raisins
½ cup chopped pecans
2 tbsp. flour
1 cup sugar
1 cup dark rum
1 tsp. rum extract
2 tbsp. orange juice concentrate
   Glaze

Grease and flour 12 1-cup fluted tube pans. Make sure eggs, eggnog and butter are at room tempter.

Stir together flour, baking powder and nutmeg. In a separate small bowl mix the fruits, raisins, nuts, zest and 2 tablespoons of the flour; set aside.

In mixing bowl beat butter on medium speed for 1 minute. Slowly add sugar; beat until fluffy; about 10 minutes. Add eggs, one at a time, beating 1 minute after each. Add flour mixture and eggnog alternately to egg mixture, beating after each addition on low speed until combined. Stir in ¼ cup of the rum, orange concentrate and rum extract. Pour batter into prepared pans. Bake in a 350-degree oven for 30 minutes for small pans and 60 minutes for larger pans.

Cool on wire rack for 15 minutes. Remove from pan and set on wire rack. Poke holes in top on cakes and drizzle with rum. Make glaze and drizzle glaze over top and sides of cake. Let dry out before serving or wrapping.

# Glaze:

In small bowl mix together 1 cup sifted powdered sugar, 1 tbsp. eggnog, 1 tbsp. light corn syrup, and ½ tsp. rum or rum extract. Add more eggnog till icing is of glazing consistency.

*A well-loved steamed pudding is quintessentially a British delight and dear to their hearts. Different than American-style puddings using milk, butterscotch or rice; steam puddings are denser, cake-like potions made in tin molds or a bowl and steamed to perfection. Unmolding of the pudding from the different shaped tins hold their shape with grand perfection, while others wobble yet remain charming. This old-fashioned dessert will crown your Christmas table with a Victorian tradition. Anyone special enough to receive a gifted pudding will never forget it. My dear friend Rubby who grew up in England and was a war bride, gave me this recipe. When she was a child she helped her grandmother stir the pudding every Christmas eve.*

## Steamed Figgy Pudding

½ cup unsalted butter, softened
½ cup cream
½ cup brandy
2 8-ounce packages Calimyrna figs
1 tsp. vanilla
1 cup finely chopped apple
½ cup coarsely chopped walnuts
1 ½ fresh bread crumbs
3 eggs
1 cup dark brown sugar
4-ounces candied lemon and orange peel
1 ½ cups flour
1 tsp. baking soda
1 tsp. baking powder
½ tsp. salt
2 tsp. cinnamon and nutmeg
1 tsp. ground cloves

Snip ends of figs and cut figs into small pieces. In a sauce pan simmer on low heat the figs, cream and brandy for 15 minutes, stirring and do not boil.

In a large mixing bowl cream butter and sugar on medium speed; beat in eggs and vanilla. Add apples, figs, walnuts, lemon and orange peel and blend well.

In separate bowl combine flour, baking soda, baking powder, salt and spices; add to fig mixture. Add bread crumbs and blend. Pack mixture into a greased 1 ½ quart mold or bowl; leaving 1 inch of space at top of mold. Cover mold tightly with a greased piece of foil and place on a rack in a large kettle.

Pour boiling water into kettle to a depth halfway up the outside of the mold. Cover kettle; simmer pudding for 2-3 hours. Remove mold from kettle and let stand 10-15 minutes. Unmold pudding on serving plate and serve with Brandied Hard Sauce. If not serving immediately cool completely and wrap tightly in foil; refrigerate several days to blend flavors. To serve, warm pudding in oven or re-steam.

Makes 12-16 servings

# Brandied Hard Sauce:

In mixing bowl blend 1 ½ cups confectioner's sugar, ½ cup softened butter, 2 tbsp. brandy and ½ tsp. vanilla on medium speed until creamy. Refrigerate if not using right away.

Makes 1 cup

# Steamed Ginger-Pumpkin Pudding

1 ½ cups flour
2 tsp. baking soda
2 tsp. cinnamon
1 tsp. ground cloves
1 cup canned pumpkin
¼ cup heavy cream
1 tbsp. lemon juice
1 stick unsalted butter
1 cup dark brown sugar
3 eggs, beaten
½ cup crystallized ginger, chopped

Sift flour with baking soda, cinnamon, cloves and salt. Set aside. Mix together the pumpkin, cream and lemon juice. Set aside. Combine butter in mixing bowl and add sugar. Beat until fluffy and add the beaten eggs; continue beating for 3 minutes.

Fold in flour mixture alternating with the pumpkin mixture. Mix in ginger and carefully spoon batter into a 2 quart mold, cover and place on a rack in large kettle, filled with boiling water 2/3 of the way up the sides of the mold. Simmer for 1 1/2 -2 hours. Remove and let rest for 5 minutes. Un-mold onto a serving plate and serve with whipped cream.

# Whipped Cream:

1 pint heavy cream
3 tbsp. sour cream
3 tbsp. confectioner's sugar
1 tbsp. fresh lemon juice
2 tsp. lemon zest

Combine cream and sour cream and beat until it thickens. Add sugar, lemon juice and zest. Continue beating until soft peaks form. Refrigerate for 1 hour before serving.

# Sugar and Spice Nuts

## Walnuts or Pecans

4 egg whites
1/3 cup champagne
2 cups sugar
½ tsp. salt
1 tsp. cinnamon, nutmeg,
¼ tsp. ground cloves
½ tsp. pumpkin pie spice

Or

## Cinnamon Almonds

3 tsp. cinnamon

Or

## Gingered Pecans

3 tsp. cinnamon
1 ½ tsp. ground ginger

Whisk egg whites until lightly stiff; add champagne, sugar, and salt. Add spices and nuts. Spread on baking sheet and bake in a 350 degree oven for 12 minutes and turn oven down to 250 degrees for 50 minutes; stirring occasionally. Cool and separate nuts.

Makes 12 cups

# White Chocolate Cranberry Bread

1 box white cake mix
¾ cup flour
1 tsp. orange zest
1 cup fresh cranberries
1 large egg
2 large egg whites
¾ cup water
½ cup orange juice
2 tbsp. unsweetened applesauce
1 cup white chocolate chips
½ cup white mini chocolate chips

    Preheat oven to 350 degrees. Mix cake mix, flour and orange zest. Add egg, egg whites, water, orange juice and applesauce. Fold in cranberries and white chocolate chips. Spread batter evenly between the two sprayed loaf pans and bake for 45 minutes or until a toothpick inserted in the middle comes out clean.

Makes 2 loaves or 20 servings.

# White Chocolate-Apricot Sweet Treat

¼ cup coarsely chopped macadamia nuts
1 pound white baking chocolate
1/3 cup finely diced apricots
2 tbsp. finely diced apricots

Spread nuts on baking sheet and toast in a 350 degree oven for 5-8 minutes; stirring occasionally; cool.

Line baking sheet with foil; set aside.

In saucepan heat chocolate over low heat, stirring constantly till melted and smooth. Remove from heat and stir in nuts and the 1/3 cup dried apricots.

Pour mixture onto the prepared baking sheet, spreading into a 10-inch circle. Sprinkle with the 2 tbsp. apricots, lightly pressing them into the mixture. Chill about 35 minutes.

Use foil to lift candy from baking sheet and break into pieces. Store candy tightly covered in refrigerator.

Makes 30-40 servings

*Other than my mother's extraordinary fudge, this is the next best thing; especially at Christmas. It screams holiday celebrating, beautifully presented and is not short on taste!*

# White Christmas Fudge

2 ½ cups confectioners sugar
¼ cup butter
2/3 cup milk
12- ounces white chocolate, finely chopped
1 tsp. almond extract
1 cup mixture of dried cherries, cranberries, apricots, finely chopped
1 cup toasted sliced almonds

    Mix sugar and milk in saucepan over medium heat, add butter and stir constantly, bring to a boil. Boil over low heat, without stirring for 5 minutes.
    Add chocolate and almond extract; whisking until chocolate melts and mixture is smooth. Mix in dried fruit and almonds. Pour mixture into an 8-inch square dish lined with foil. Refrigerate several hours. Invert fudge and peel off foil; cut into 1-inch squares. Garnish with cherries on top.

*Chapter 28*

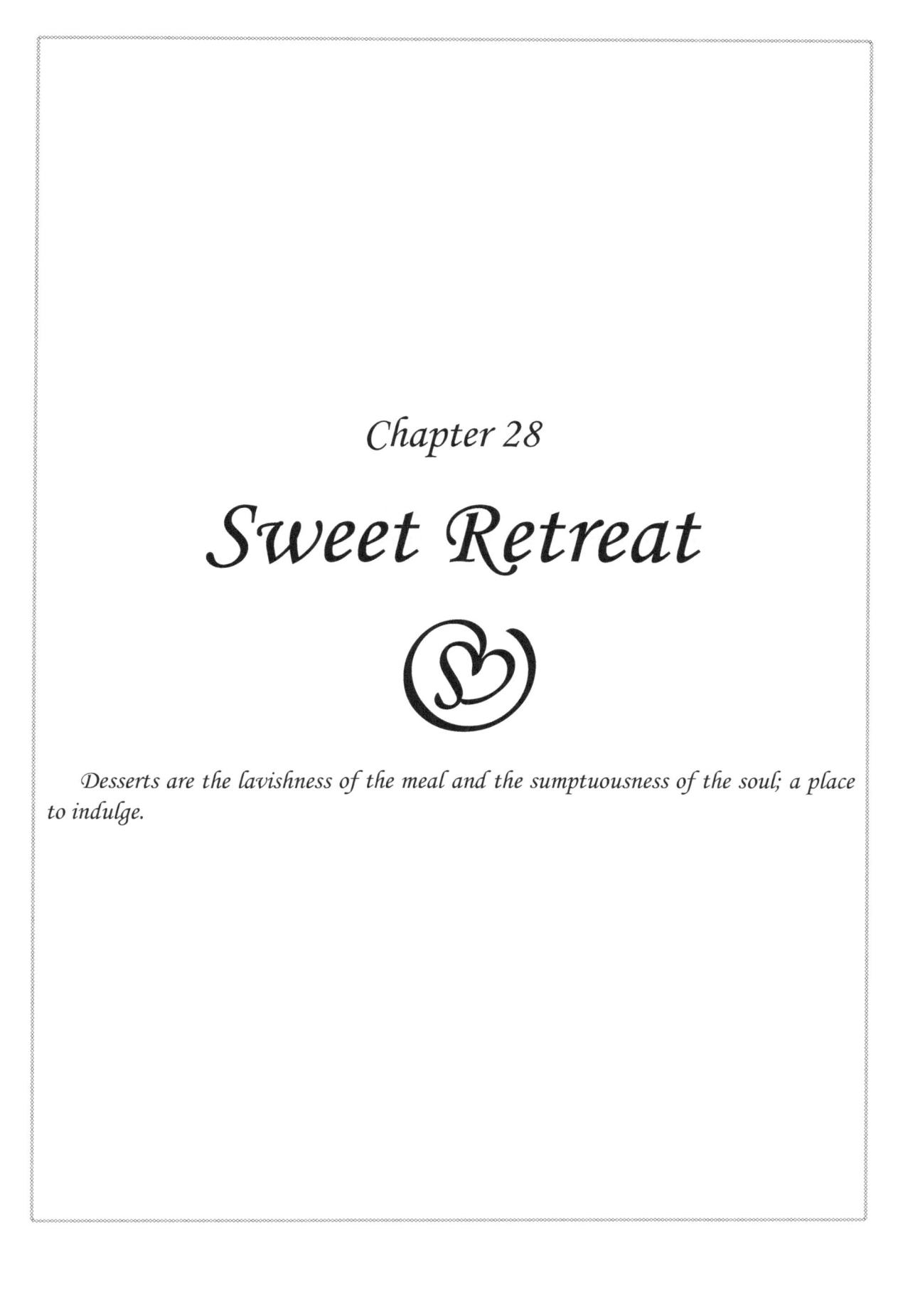

# Sweet Retreat

*Desserts are the lavishness of the meal and the sumptuousness of the soul; a place to indulge.*

## Apple-Butter Cake

1 ½ cup butter, softened
1 cup sugar
2 cups powdered sugar
1 ½ cups flour
1 tsp. baking powder
3 eggs
5 egg whites, whipped
1 tbsp. each lemon and orange zest
1 tsp. almond extract
2 cups peeled and finely chopped Golden Delicious apples
1 ½ cups coarsely chopped ground almonds

 In sauté pan brown almonds, cool and set aside. In mixing bowl on medium speed blend butter and add eggs and blend until fluffy. Add sugars, zest, almond extract and blend. Add apples and almonds and mix well; fold in egg whites.
 Butter and flour a spring-form pan and pour batter into pan. Bake in a 325 degree oven for about 45-50 minutes or until golden and firm in center.

 Makes 10 servings

# Apricot-Pineapple Cobbler

6 cups halved fresh or canned apricots
1 can pineapple junks, drained
1 cup sugar
2 cups apricot jam
¼ cup quick-cooking tapioca
2 tbsp. flour
1 tbsp. almond extract
1 tsp. apricot brandy
1 tsp. cinnamon
¼ cup melted butter

In a large mixing bowl, mix all ingredients well, except butter and pour into a buttered baking dish. Pour melted butter over cobbler.

# Crust:

1 ½ cups flour
1 ½ tsp. baking powder
½ cup sugar
½ cup melted butter
3 eggs, beaten
½ cup sour cream
¼ tsp. cinnamon

Mix all ingredients until a soft dough forms. Drop spoonfuls of batter over cobbler, spread over top. Place cobbler on a baking sheet and bake in a 400-degree oven for 30 minutes or until a toothpick inserted in center comes out clean. Cool 30 minutes before serving.

Serves 12

# Black Walnut Cake

½ cup butter, softened
½ cup shortening
2 cups sugar
5 eggs, separated
1 cup buttermilk
1 tsp. soda
2 cups flour
1 tsp. Vanilla
1 ½ cups chopped
  black walnuts
3 ounces coconut
½ tsp. cream of tartar
  Cream cheese frosting

Cream butter and shortening in mixer until light and fluffy. Add sugar and beat until dissolved. Add egg yolks, beating well.

Combine buttermilk and soda; stir until soda dissolves.

Add flour to creamed mixture alternately with buttermilk, beginning and ending with flour. Stir in vanilla; add walnuts and coconut, stirring well.

Fold egg whites into batter. Pour batter into 3 greased and floured 9-inch pans. Bake 30 minutes in a 350-degree oven. Cool 10 minutes in pans on wire rack; remove from pans and frost when cake is cool.

# Cream Cheese Frosting:

3 cups powdered sugar
1 8-ounce package cream cheese, softened
½ cup butter, softened
1 tsp. vanilla
2 tsp. milk or more

In mixing bowl blend butter and cream cheese; add sugar and blend well. Add milk and vanilla until the frosting is spreadable.

# Brownie Torte

## Brownie Mix:

1 1-pound packaged brownie mix
½ cup softened butter
3 tbsp. amaretto liqueur
2 eggs
1 cup miniature semi-sweet chocolate chips

## Filling:

1 ½ cup toasted almonds, ground
2 tbsp. flour
½ cup sweetened condensed milk
½ tsp. almond extract
1 egg

## Vanilla Glaze:

1/3 cup canned vanilla frosting
1 tbsp. amaretto liqueur

## Chocolate Glaze:

½ cup semi-sweet chocolate chips
2 tbsp. whipping cream
2 tbsp. butter

Combine all brownie ingredients mixing in chocolate chips last.

Combine all filling ingredients; blend well. Pour brownie mixture into a greased 10-inch springform pan; spread evenly. Drop filling mixture over brownie and carefully mix into brownie mixture, making sure both mixtures are the same level. Bake in a 350 degree oven for 50-60 minutes or until center is set. Cool on wire rack 20 minutes. Remove sides of pan and refrigerate.

Combine vanilla glaze and drizzle over brownie. In saucepan, combine ingredients for chocolate glaze. Simmer over low heat for 3 minutes, stirring. Drizzle over vanilla glaze. Sprinkle sliced almonds on top.

Serves 12

*This has to be one of the best desserts I have ever made. It plates beautifully and is pure indulgence.*

# Chocolate Terrine with Raspberry Sauce

## Semisweet chocolate layer:

8-ounces semisweet chocolate
2 ½ tbsp. unsalted butter
5 tbsp. heavy whipping cream
1 tbsp. cognac
1 egg white stiffly beaten
1 egg yolk

## Milk Chocolate layer:

8-ounces milk chocolate
2 ½ tbsp. unsalted butter
5 tbsp. heavy whipping cream
1 tbsp. cognac
1 egg white, stiffly beaten
1 egg yolk

## White Chocolate layer:

8-ounces white chocolate
5 tbsp. unsalted butter
2 tbsp. heavy whipping cream
1 tbsp. cognac
1 egg white, stiffly beaten
1 egg yolk

In a double boiler add the chocolate, butter, cream and cognac and simmer until the chocolate and butter are melted, stirring well. Cool slightly and add the egg yolk. Carefully fold in egg white.

Pour into a loaf pan lined with wax paper and then cooking spray. Cool in refrigerator until set.

Repeat same procedure with the milk chocolate and then the white chocolate. Refrigerate overnight.

Put 1 pint fresh raspberries in food processor and purée. In sauce pan add fresh raspberries with 2 tbsp. raspberry jam, 1 tbsp. sugar and 1 tbsp. raspberry liqueur. Simmer for 3 minutes, cool.

Spread sauce over a dessert plate. Place chocolate slice over sauce; drizzle a little sauce over top of chocolate. Top with toasted sliced almonds.

*Yet another wonderful recipe from my friend Susie; making this my favorite desert she made, absolutely wonderful!*

# Chocolate Mousse Pie

## Crust:

3 cups chocolate thin wafer crumbs
½ cup unsalted butter, melted

## Filling:

1 lb, semi sweet chocolate
2 eggs
4 egg whites
2 cups whipping cream
6 tbsp. powdered sugar
4 egg whites, room temperature

For crust; combine wafers and butter and press on bottom and completely up sides of a 10-inch springform pan. Refrigerate 30 minutes.

For filling; Melt chocolate in top of double boiler over simmering heat; let cool to lukewarm. Add whole eggs and mix well. Add egg yolks and mix until thoroughly blended.

Whip cream with sugar until soft peaks form. Beat egg whites until stiff (not dry). Stir a little of the cream and whites into the chocolate mixture to lighten. Fold into large bowl with cream and whites until completely incorporated.

Turn into crust and chill at least six hours or overnight.

Whip 2 cups of whipping cream for topping.

*Countless special dinners gave this easy, light dessert a home. Always served in a glass flute gave it importance.*

# Chocolate Mousse

2 tbsp. boiling water
2 tbsp. cold water
1 ½ envelopes unflavored gelatin

Sprinkle gelatin over cold water in a bowl; wait 5 minutes and stir in boiling water, mix well and let set.

2/3 cup powdered baking chocolate
½ cup sugar
1 cup heavy whipping cream
1 tsp. brandy

In mixer blend chocolate and sugar. On medium speed whip cream until stiff, add gelatin mixture and brandy; mixing well.
Scoop into individual serving glasses, top with whip cream, raspberry sauce and chocolate curls. Chill several hours or overnight before serving.

# Raspberry Sauce:

3/4 cup raspberry jam
1 tbsp. raspberry liqueur

In saucepan melt jam over low heat; stir in liqueur; set aside to cool.

# Cream Cheese Cookies

¼ cup butter, softened
1 8-ounce package cream cheese, softened
1 egg yolk
¼ tsp. vanilla
1 package yellow or devils food cake mix

Cream butter and cheese; blend in egg yolk and vanilla. Add cake mix 1/3 at a time, mixing well. Cover and chill 30 minutes.

Drop tsp. of dough onto an un-greased baking sheet. Bake 8-10 minutes. Cool slightly before removing from baking sheet.

Makes 6-8 dozen cookies

*This is a moist cake and should not be over baked. Was given to me in 1991 from Joyce, one of my best restaurant customers; a delightful soul.*

# Easy Party Cake

1 package Swiss chocolate cake mix
1 large box chocolate instant pudding
8-ounces sour cream
12- ounces chocolate chips
4 eggs
½ cup oil
½ cup water

Mix all ingredients in mixing bowl on medium speed for 3-4 minutes. Pour in a greased and floured bunt pan.

Bake in a 350-degree oven for 1 hour or less (no more). Serve on pedestal cake plate with paper doily and dust with powdered sugar.

# Fruit Trifle

1 prepared pound cake, sliced
1 container lemon curd
¼ cup Grand Marnier liqueur
1 cup Lemon Bavarian Dip
1 pint blackberries or boysenberries
1 pint strawberries
1 pint blueberries
2 peaches, sliced thin
2 tbsp. sugar

    Put fruit in a bowl and toss with sugar. Line a glass trifle bowl with slices of pound cake and brush with liqueur. Spoon a layer of lemon dip over cake followed by a layer of fruit. Dollop lemon curd over fruit. Repeat layers ending with fruit and sprinkle a little sugar over fruit. Chill for several hours.

Serves 10

    Lemon Bavarian Dip recipe can be found in the Caterer's Pride Gets It's Due Chapter.

*This is the cake my grandmother Stella made for me and one that yields to memories of love, affection and connection.*

# Ginger Pound Cake

2/3 cup butter, softened
1 cup sugar
3 eggs
2 ¼ cups flour
1 tsp. baking powder
1 tsp. salt
½ cup buttermilk
2 tbsp. minced fresh ginger
½ tsp. Grand Marnier liqueur
½ tsp. vanilla

Beat butter in mixer at medium speed for 2 minutes. Add sugar and beat 5 minutes. Add eggs, 1 at a time, beating after each.

Combine flour, baking powder, and salt; add to butter mixture alternately with milk, ending with flour. Beat mixture at low speed just until blended. Stir in ginger, vanilla and liqueur.

Pour batter into a buttered and floured loaf pan and bake in a 325 degree oven for 1 hour and 20 minutes or until wooden pick comes out clean when inserted in center of cake. Cool on wire rack for 5-10 minutes; remove from pan and continue to cool on rack.

Makes 1 loaf

*This is one of the best lemon cakes and is so moist; another great recipe from my friend Terry. I made this for a baby shower and the last name of the new baby is Lemons. I incorporated lemon into almost everything on the brunch table. This was one of the desserts.*

# Lemonade Cake

1 1/3 cups sugar
6 tbsp. butter, softened
1 tbsp. lemon zest
3 tbsp. thawed lemonade concentrate
2 tbsp. vanilla extract
2 large eggs
2 large egg whites
2 cups flour
1 tsp. baking powder
½ tsp. salt
½ tsp. baking soda
1 ¼ cups buttermilk

Place first 5 ingredients in a large mixing bowl and mix on medium speed until well blended, about 5 minutes. Add eggs and egg whites, 1 at a time, beating well after each addition. Lightly spoon flour into dry measuring cups; level with a knife. Combine flour, baking powder, salt, and baking soda; stir well with a whisk. Add flour mixture and buttermilk alternately to sugar mixture, beginning and ending with flour; beat well after each addition.
Pour batter into 2 9-inch round cake pans coated with cooking spray. Tap pans to remove air bubbles. Bake in a 350 degree oven for 20 minutes or until wooden picks inserted in center comes out clean. Cool in pans 10 minutes on wire rack; remove from pans. Cool completely on wire rack.
Place 1 layer cake on cake plate and spread with ½ of frosting. Top with second layer and frost. Store cake covered in refrigerator.

# Frosting:

2 tbsp. butter, softened
2 tsp. lemon zest
2 tsp. lemonade concentrate
½ tsp. vanilla extract
8-ounces cream cheese
1 ½ cups powdered sugar

Place butter and the next 4 ingredients in mixer and beat on high speed until fluffy. Add powered sugar and beat at low speed just until blended. Chill 1 hour.

Makes 16 slices

*I adore a light mousse for dessert and I have several very good recipes in my collection; this being my favorite!*

## Lime Mousse

1 envelope unflavored gelatin
¼ cup cold water
3 eggs, separated
¾ cup light corn syrup
1 tsp. lime zest
½ cup fresh lime juice
2 drops green food coloring, (optional)
¼ cup sugar
1 cup heavy whipping cream, whipped

    In a saucepan sprinkle gelatin over water. Stir in egg yolks, corn syrup, lime zest, and juice. Stirring constantly; cook over low heat until gelatin is completely dissolved, about 5 minutes. Stir in food coloring. Pour into a large bowl and chill, stirring occasionally, about 1 hour or until mixture mounds slightly when dropped from a spoon.
    In small bowl with mixer at high speed beat egg whites until soft peaks form. Gradually beat in sugar until stiff peaks form. Fold into lime mixture. Fold in whipped cream. Turn into a 2-quart serving dish. Chill 4 hours or overnight. Garnish with whip cream and lime slices.

Makes 8 servings.

*Here is Madge's Peach Cobbler recipe I wrote about. Madge's family thought it was a taste of heaven; a place where stories and families will always share. There are many blessed stories that go with this signature cobbler.*

## Madge's Peach Cobbler

7-8 ripe peaches
2 cups sugar
½ cup brown sugar
2-3 tbsp. flour
1 tsp. cinnamon
¼ tsp. allspice
¼ tsp. cloves, nutmeg, ginger
2 tsp. vanilla
2 tbsp. melted butter
   Pie crust dough

   Peel and slice peaches. Mix sugars, flour and spices together; mix with peaches. Add melted butter and vanilla and put in a buttered 13x10 baking dish.
   Roll out pie crust dough and cover dish. Make slits on top; add dots of butter and sprinkle with sugar and cinnamon on top. Bake about 20-30 minutes or until brown on top and bubbly.

Serves 10-12

# Mango-Orange Cheesecake

3 ripe mangoes
¼ cup fresh squeezed orange juice
1 tbsp. orange zest
2 tbsp. lime zest
¼ tsp. ground ginger
4 tbsp. brown sugar
3 8-ounces cream cheese
1 cup sour cream
4 eggs
1 cup sugar
1 tbsp. flour
1 tbsp. rum
1 cup crushed gingersnap cookies
2 tbsp. melted butter

    Preheat oven to 350 degrees. Mix together the crushed cookies and butter. Grease or spray an 8-inch cheesecake pan. Wrap sides and bottom of pan with foil. Press crumbs on bottom and sides of pan and bake for 7 minutes; cool.
    Peel 2 mangos and chop. Place chopped mango, orange juice and ginger in a saucepan and simmer for about 5 minutes. Remove from heat and mix in brown sugar; pour into food processor and purée until smooth. Scrap into a small bowl; set aside.
    In food processor cream the cream cheese and sugar. Add the sour cream, zest, rum, flour and blend. With machine running add eggs, one at a time.
    Pour half of mixture in the pan and half of mango mixture over cream cheese. Add remaining cheese mixture and top with mango. Use a knife to swirl the mixture.
    Place pan in a large shallow baking pan with 2-inches of hot water. Bake for 60 minutes. Turn oven off and let cake set for 1 hour. Remove to a rack and cool for 1-2 hours. Chill, covered overnight.
    Peel remaining mango and slice. Lay in a circle pattern to garnish cheesecake.

Serves 12

*Mother's Cake is made with layers of memories. An ordinary cake has made many a birthday seem special; it is truly the perfect chocolate cake.*

# Mother's Birthday Cake

2 ¾ cup sifted flour
2 tsp. baking soda
½ tsp baking powder
½ tsp. salt
1 cup unsweetened cocoa
2 cups boiling water
1 cup butter, softened
2 ½ cups sugar
4 eggs
2 tsp. vanilla

# Frosting:

1 6-ounce package semisweet
  chocolate chips
½ cup cream
1 cup butter, softened
2 1/3 cups powdered sugar

# Filling:

1 ½ cup heavy cream, chilled
½ cup powdered sugar
1 tsp. vanilla


Whisk boiling water into cocoa until smooth. Cool completely. Sift flour with soda, baking powder and salt.

In mixing bowl of mixer, on high speed beat butter, sugar, eggs and vanilla, scrapping bowl. Beat about 4-5 minutes until fluffy. On low speed add flour, alternately with cocoa mixture, beginning and ending with flour. Do not over-beat.

Pour batter into 3 greased and floured cake pans. Bake in a 350 degree oven for 25-30 minutes. Center will spring back when pressed. Cool pans on wire rack for about 12 minutes. Loosen sides and carefully remove cakes from pans. Cool on racks.

In a saucepan combine chocolate pieces, cream, butter and stir over medium heat until smooth.

Pour chocolate in a small glass bowl and place bowl in a larger bowl filled with ice. With hand mixer add powdered sugar and beat frosting until stiff. Set aside.

Whip cream with sugar and vanilla in chilled mixing bowl; chill.

On cake plate place first layer; top side down. Spread with half of filling mixture. Place second layer, top side down; spread with remaining cream. Place third layer; top side up. Frost sides, covering the whip cream; frost top. Chill for 2 hours before serving.

Serves 12-15

*If you like baking the old fashioned way and don't mind the time it takes to beat a good, stiff egg white, then you will taste the lightest cake ever!*

# Orange Cake

1 ¾ cup flour
6 egg whites
½ tsp. salt
1 ½ cups sugar
6 egg yolks
¼ cup fresh squeezed orange juice
2 tbsp. orange peel
  Powdered sugar

    Bring egg whites to room temperature. Measure flour and sift it 3 times, now lightly spoon sifted flour into measuring cup, add salt.
    On medium speed beat egg whites until foamy. Gradually beat in ½ cup of the sugar. Continue beating until stiff peaks form; set aside.
    In a small bowl of mixer, beat egg yolks at high speed until thick, about 4 minutes. Gradually beat in remaining 1 cup granulated sugar until mixture is smooth.
    On low speed, add flour mixture and alternate with orange juice into egg yolk mixture ending with flour, scraping sides while mixer is running. Add orange peel. With rubber spatula carefully fold yolk mixture into egg whites.
    Pour batter into a greased 9x10x4-inch baking mold or tube pan. Bake in a 350 degree oven for 50-60 minutes or 40 minutes in a tube pan. Cake will spring back when pressed with finger. Cool on wire rack for 20 minutes. Run knife or spatula around edge of cake and remove from pan. Sift powdered sugar over cake.

Makes 12 servings

# Peach-White Chocolate Tart

## Filling:

1 8-ounce package cream cheese
4 tbsp. sugar
1 tbsp. cognac
2 tbsp. vanilla
5 medium peaches, pitted, peeled, sliced
1 cup whipping cream
8-ounces white chocolate

In a saucepan warm milk and add chocolate; simmer until chocolate is melted, remove from heat.

In mixing bowl beat cream cheese. Add sugar, vanilla, cognac; mixing well. Fold in chocolate mixture.

Toss peaches in some sugar and place in the bottom of baked tart. Pour chocolate mixture over peaches. Refrigerate for 4 hours or overnight.

## Crust:

1 ½ cups ground, toasted almonds
2 cups ground almond biscotti
1 ½ cups melted butter
½ tsp. Nutmeg

Preheat oven to 350 degrees. Mix all ingredients and press mixture onto bottoms and sides of an 11-inch tart pan. Bake 15 minutes or until crust is golden. Cool completely on wire rack.

# Pineapple Sherbet

1 16-ounce can cream of coconut
1 16-ounce can crushed pineapple
1 cup fresh orange juice
¼ cup light rum

    In food processor combine coconut, un-drained pineapple, orange juice and rum. Blend till nearly smooth. Pour into a loaf pan; cover and freeze until firm.
    Place half of mixture at a time in a blender and blend till fluffy. Return mixture to pan and continue to freeze for 4-5 hours.

Makes 6 cups

## Pistachio Cookies

1 box white cake mix
1 box pistachio pudding
½ cup oil
3 tbsp. seven-up
2 eggs
½ cup chopped pistachio nuts
½ cup coconut

Mix thoroughly all ingredients. Drop by teaspoonful 2-inches apart on a greased cookie sheet. Bake 10-12 minutes at 350 degrees. (green food coloring may be added).

*This recipe is from my friend Sandy. I am honored to share this old recipe and its history with you. Sandy tells me that her mother, Joy made up this recipe when she was a young girl. She started baking very early in life. She was raised by her grandmother who didn't really like to bake. She'd make a deal with Joy; if she would make a dessert for dinner, her grandma would clean up the mess. Joy made this cake for over 60 years. It won several baking contests and is a family favorite.*

# Prune Cake

Cream together: 1 cup sugar, 1 cup Crisco
Add together: 3 unbeaten eggs, ½ cup sour cream
Sift together: 1 ¾ cup flour, 3 tsp. cinnamon, 1 tsp. allspice
                1 tsp. soda, ½ tsp. salt
Beat in: 1 cup seeded prunes

    Bake at 350 degrees for 25 minutes in 2 round cake pans

    Cook Prune Filling until thick and spread between and on top and sides of cake:
2 eggs, ½ cup sour cream, 1 cup sugar, ¼ tsp salt, 1 cup seeded prunes
Beat with electric mixer while cooking.
Use caution not to scorch!

# Sour Cream Pound Cake

4 tbsp. breadcrumbs
3 ¼ cups flour
½ tsp. baking soda
¼ tsp. salt
¾ cup butter, softened
2 ½ cups sugar
3 tsp. lemon extract
2 tbsp. lemon zest
3 large eggs
¼ cup fresh lemon juice
1 8-ounce container sour cream
1 cup powdered sugar

Coat a 10-inch tube pan with cooking spray and dust with bread crumbs.

Carefully spoon flour into measuring cup and level. Combine flour, soda, and salt in a bowl; mix well.

Beat butter in mixer at medium speed until light and fluffy. Add sugar and lemon extract, beating until blended. Add eggs, 1 at a time, beating after each. Add lemon zest and juice; beat 1 minute. Add flour mixture and sour cream, beating at low speed ending with flour.

Spoon batter into pan and bake in a 350 degree oven for 1 hour and 10 minutes. Cool in pan about 10 minutes. Cool completely on wire rack.

Combine 2 tablespoons lemon juice and powdered sugar. Drizzle glaze over cake.

Makes 20 servings.

*This is the wonderful cake Susan and Heather made for my Birthday Potluck Theme.*

# Susan and Heather's Baked Alaska Cake

Start by making your own devils food cake or a boxed devils food cake mix.

Make two rounds either 8 or 9 inches; bake until done.

You will need:
4 egg whites
½ tsp. cream of tartar
½ cup brown sugar
2-1/2 quarts ice cream

After baking cakes, completely cool and remove from pan. Line pans with plastic wrap; fill round pans with ice cream until just within ¼ of the rim. Invert one cake on to the top of ice cream and wrap tightly with saran wrap and re-freeze. For at least 2 hours.

Preheat oven to 500 degrees. Meanwhile, prepare egg whites. Beat whites and cream of tartar until foamy; begin adding in brown sugar one tablespoon at a time. Continue beating until peaks are stiff and glossy.

Cover a baking sheet in aluminum foil. Remove cake from freezer (only work with one cake at a time) and invert onto baking sheet. Completely cover with meringue. Bake for 305 minutes on lowest rack in oven. Remove from oven and trim foil and transfer to serving platter.

We used a vanilla ice cream with chunks of cherry and chocolate for our cakes. They were incredibly delicious and don't worry about them melting they will be eaten before you know it. They can be frozen or kept cool until serving.

# Tropical Mousse

2 envelopes unflavored gelatin
¼ cup cold water
½ cup boiling water
1 ½ cups chopped, peeled papaya
1 cup chopped, peeled mango
4 eggs
½ cup sugar
1 tsp. lemon juice
1 ½ cups ice cubes

    In a blender sprinkle gelatin over cold water; let stand 3-4 minutes. Add boiling water, cover and blend at low speed until gelatin is completely dissolved, about 2 minutes. Add remaining ingredients. Blend at high speed for 1 minute. Pour ½ cup into 8 dessert dishes or glasses. Chill until set, about 30 minutes.
    Garnish with strawberries, raspberries and fresh mint.

Serves 8

*Chapter 29*

# Treasure Trove of Menus

# *Bridal Luncheon*

*Korrie Norris-Hood*
*April-2000*

## *Appetizers*

Stuffed Soufflé Mushrooms
Choux Puffs ~ Waldorf Filling
Spinach Rolls
Smoked Salmon Mousse on Cucumber Rounds
Walnut Bread ~ with Apricot Walnut Spread
Smoked Turkey on Orange Raspberry Muffins
Crêpe's with sweetened Strawberries
Croustades ~ with French Cheese, Artichokes & Capers

## *Buffet*

Red Pepper ~ Zucchini Quiche
Steamed Asparagus ~ with Lemon Dill Sauce
Pasta Salad
Assorted Fresh Fruit
Assorted Muffins
Savory Cheese Spread
Brie

## *Dessert*

Fruit Tarts
Chocolate Dipped Strawberries
Bridal Cake

# Wedding Menu

✺

*Kellie and Jim Ritter*
*August 23, 1997*

## Appetizers

Beef Pin Wheels ~ Phyllo Triangles
Cucumber Rounds with Smoked Salmon
Fresh Crab in Sourdough Round
Antipasto Platter ~ Stuffed Mushrooms
Domestic and Imported Cheese Display
Lime-Chili Chicken Wings
Roasted Red Peppers with Mozzarella

## Buffet

Baked Salmon with Boston Glaze ~ Smoked Turkey
Lime and Fresh Basil Chicken Salad
Prawns with Lime-Coriander Sauce
Roasted Garlic Rosemary Potatoes
Caesar Salad ~ Pasta Salad
New Potato and Green Bean Salad with Walnut Dressing
Strawberry Mousse ~ Lemon Mousse
Fresh Fruit Cascade ~ Lemon Bavarian Dip
Cream Cheese Stuffed Strawberries ~ Minted Melon Balls

## Wedding Cake

## Dinner for Oprah

### Menu

✺

Apple-Acorn Squash Soup
*
Roasted Herb Chicken with Pecan Stuffing
*
Scalloped Potatoes ~ Grilled Asparagus
*
Wild Rice Artichoke Salad
*
Brussels Sprouts with Orange Five Spice Sauce
*
Spinach Cauliflower, Pine Nut Salad
*
Lemon Mousse
*
Assorted Artesian Breads

# *International Vegetarian Luncheon*

## *Menu*

✸

Soufflé Roll with Artichokes and Mushrooms

Cheese Strudel ~ Ricotta Herb Tarts

Swiss Chard Tart with Pine Nuts

Cucumber Rounds with Salmon Mousse

California Sushi

Vegetables Stuffed with Blue Cheese and Cashews

Egg Rolls ~ Pissalader`e

Swan Cream Puffs

Cucumber Mold ~Artichoke Mousse

Cream cheese, Pest and Munster – Tea Sandwiches

Wedding Cake

# *Baby Lemons Luncheon*

## *Menu*

✹

Chicken Crêpes ~ Quiche Lorraine
Pasta Salad ~ Tossed Greens with Mango Dressing
Marinated Mushrooms ~ Strawberry Cascade ~ Lemon Mousse
Gourmet Cheese Array ~ Chicken Salad Tarts
Baguettes with Smoked Turkey and Pesto Cream Sauce
Figs in Merlot Reduction with Prosciutto and Goat Cheese Spread
Seafood Dip with Cracker and Baguettes
Cranberry-Orange Muffins ~ Lemon Poppy Seed Bread
Zucchini Chocolate Chip Bread ~ Croissants
Pumpkin Spice Butter
Lemon Bavarian Fruit Dip

## *Desserts*

Lemon Cake
Lemon Cheese Cake with Lemon Curd Topping
Fruit Tarts ~ Chocolate Tarts
Lemon Fruit Trifle

# Christmas Senior Dinner

## Menu

✺

Bourbon London Broil
*
Duck a la Orange
*
Garlic Mashed Potatoes
*
Broccoli Soufflé
*
Ambrosia
*
English Pop Over

## Dessert

English Steamed Pudding

# Birthday Dinner

*Candy Hadley*
*1999*

## Menu

Ginger Salmon
*
Potatoes Anna
*
Stuffed Zucchini
*
Spinach Salad with Papaya Raspberry Dressing
*
Dill-Cheese Bread

## Dessert

Pina Colada Sherbet
Chocolate Terrine with Raspberry Sauce

## Hawaiian Menu
*Financial Title*

Skewered Shrimp with apricot Mango Sauce
Luau Pork with orange glaze & Mango Chutney
Orange Chicken ~ Rice
Rice Mingle ~ Island Macaroni Salad
Avocado Bread ~ Fresh Fruit & Coconut Dip
Seafood Dip ~ Smoked Salmon Mold
Won Tons with Sweet & Sour Sauce
Assorted Dried Fruit ~ Macadamia Nuts

❈

## Tracy's Summer Event
*Financial Title*

## Menu
*Table One*

Sautéed Shrimp with Coconut Rice
Skewered Chicken ~ Scallop Wraps
Fresh Shrimp with Apricot Sauce
European Meatballs ~ Anchovies and Blue Cheese
Figs in Merlot Reduction ~ Anti Pasto Tray
Tri-Tip with Roasted Red Peppers and Goat Cheese
Assorted Cheese Tray ~ Celebration Brie
Stuffed Cherry Tomato ~ Brie Phyllo Triangles
Smoked Turkey on Baguettes with Pesto Cream Sauce
Gouda Cheese Cake
Tortellini Chicken Salad ~ Herb Polenta

### Table Two

Black Bean Wraps ~ Bean Dip with Cinnamon Chips
Grape Salsa ~ Roasted Mango Salsa
Chicken Empanadas

# Wedding Menu

✸

*Amy Swell*
*November 19, 2005*

## *Appetizers ~ Family Style*

Homemade Minestrone Soup
Anti Pasto Platter
Fuchsia Bread

## *Buffet*

Assorted Roasted Vegetables
Pasta Salad
Fresh Fruit Cascade
Assorted Domestic and Imported Cheese Display
Assorted Rustic Breads
Assorted Sweet Breads with Pumpkin Spice Butter

## *Dessert*

*Homemade Apple Pie*

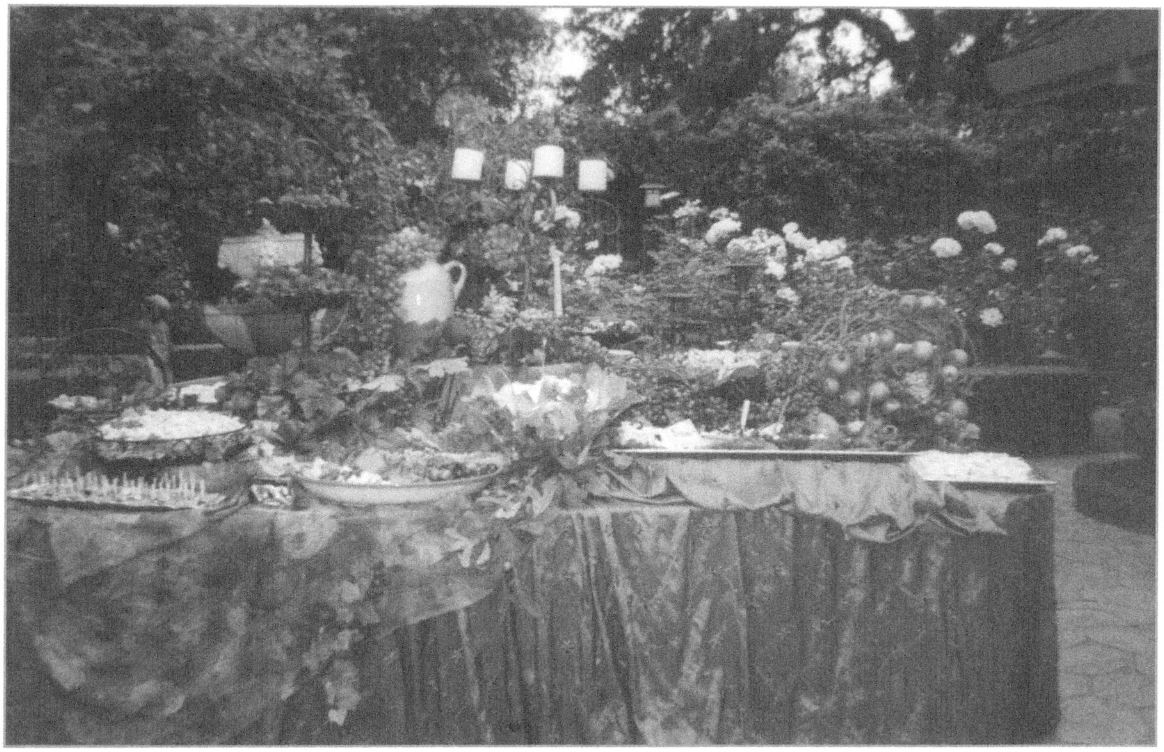

CPSIA information can be obtained at www.ICGtesting.com
Printed in the USA
LVOW01s1551240914

405680LV00005B/568/P

9 781434 347039